BARRON'S
BUSINESS
REVIEW
SERIES

Accounting

Peter J. Eisen

Assistant Principal,
Department of Accounting and Marketing
Murray Bergtraum High School for Business Careers
New York, New York

Lecturer in Accounting
College of Staten Island
Staten Island, New York

BARRON'S
New York • London • Toronto • Sydney

In this book the names of individuals and companies,
and their type of business, are fictitious. Any similarity
with the name and type of business of a real person
or company is purely coincidental.

All inquiries should be addressed to:
Barron's Educational Series, Inc.
250 Wireless Boulevard
Hauppauge, New York 11788

Library of Congress Catalog Card No. 85-20065

International Standard Book No. 0-8120-3574-7

Library of Congress Cataloging-in-Publication Data

Eisen, Peter J.
  Accounting

  (Business review series)
  Includes index.
  1. Accounting. I. Title. II. Series.
HF5635.E33 1985   657   85-20065
ISBN 0-8120-3574-7

PRINTED IN THE UNITED STATES OF AMERICA

8 9   800   9 8 7 6 5 4

CONTENTS

PREFACE

Barron's Business Review Series: Accounting is designed for individuals who have some knowledge of accounting as well as for individuals who have none at all. The subject matter is presented in a traditional sequence that follows closely that found in standard college accounting textbooks. Each chapter begins with a listing and definition of **Key Terms.** At appropriate areas within the chapter a brief review section entitled **You Should Remember** is presented. Throughout the chapter the reader is asked to complete **Computational Problems,** Parts A and B, referred to by page location at the end of the chapter. For each Part A problem there is a *detailed solution* at the end of the chapter. A *checklist of key figures* is also provided for the Part B problems. These problems, if completed when requested, allow the reader to apply knowledge just learned and then check his or her work against the solutions at the end of the chapter. Clear, apt examples illustrate accounting principles throughout the book. Finally, a *comprehensive glossary* includes definitions of important accounting terms, and a detailed *cross-referenced index* is provided to assist the student in locating specific topics.

Since no prior knowledge of accounting is needed to master the subject matter in *Barron's Business Review Series: Accounting,* the student will find this book an excellent self-study guide and an invaluable companion to any textbook used in a principles of accounting I college level course. Unlike traditional college textbooks that present accounting principles for various forms of business organizations all at the same time, *Barron's Business Review Series: Accounting* concentrates on accounting for a sole proprietorship and thus gives a simpler, more direct, less confusing presentation of the subject. The partnership and corporate forms of business organizations are discussed briefly in the last chapter.

I would like to take this opportunity to thank my wife, Amy, for her continuing support and encouragement in writing this book. Special thanks are due to my son, Howard, for his invaluable assistance in instructing me in the use of word processing hardware and software and for modifying the word processing software used in the preparation of this book.

October 1985   Peter J. Eisen

1
THE ACCOUNTING EQUATION

KEY TERMS

asset Anything that is owned and has money value.

capital The ownership of the assets of a business by the proprietor(s).

expenses The costs of doing business, that is, the costs that must be incurred in order for an organization to generate revenue. A retail store must incur the expense of renting the store in order to operate the business.

liabilities Amounts due creditors and other interested parties; also, the ownership of certain assets of an organization by creditors. The ownership extends to the creditors' right to collect what is due them before any distribution to the owners of the business.

revenue The receipt, from sales of a product or service, of assets such as cash or accounts receivable that will eventually have an effect on the owner's equity.

SOME BASICS

• WHAT IS ACCOUNTING?

Accounting is the art of organizing, maintaining, recording, and analyzing financial activities. Accounting is generally known as the "language of business." The accountant translates this accounting information into meaningful terms that are used by interested parties. Every organization—profit, nonprofit, charitable, religious, or governmental—requires the services of accountants in providing accounting information.

• WHO USES ACCOUNTING INFORMATION?

Accounting information is used by everyone. The manager of an organization, who is charged with the responsibility of seeing that the enterprise is properly directed, relies upon the accounting information provided to make appropriate decisions. Investors in an enterprise need information about the financial status and future prospects of an organization. Bankers and suppliers grant loans and extend credit to organizations based on their financial soundness as evidenced by accounting information. Even customers and employees concerned about the condition of an organization make use of accounting information.

• *WHAT INFORMATION DOES AN ACCOUNTANT GATHER?*

The accountant keeps track of all **business transactions.** A business transaction is any business activity that affects what a business owns or owes, as well as the ownership of that business.

YOU SHOULD REMEMBER

Accounting is the art of organizing, maintaining, recording, and analyzing financial activities.

Accounting information is used by managers of all business organizations and in some cases by others who have an indirect financial interest in the business.

Business transactions represent economic events that affect the financial condition of the business.

WHAT ARE ASSETS?

The things that are owned by any business organization are known as **assets.** In order for an item to be considered an asset, it must meet two requirements: (1) it must be owned by the organization, and (2) it must have money value. **Ownership** is the exclusive right to possess, use, enjoy, and dispose of property. **Money value** exists if a buyer is willing to pay a sum of money to a seller for the property. **Complete "Do You Know The Basics?", Exercises 1, 2, and 3** (p. 10).

• *KEEPING TRACK OF ASSETS*

Since there apparently are many different kinds of assets, how does the accountant keep track of all of the assets? The accountant does not keep track of all of them individually, but rather combines assets of a similar nature into common groups. For example, an individual or business organization may have such assets as coins, bills, money orders, and checks. These assets would be placed in a category or grouping known as **cash.** Thus, any money, regardless of its actual form, would be known and categorized as cash. Cash also includes money in bank accounts of the individual that is available for payment of bills. It is the responsibility of the accountant to follow generally accepted accounting principles in placing individual assets in a specific and appropriate category. **Complete "Do You Know The Basics?", Exercise 4 (p. 10).**

• *TYPES OF ASSETS*

Assets may take many forms. While they may be grouped together into categories, as stated above, they may be considered to be tangible and intangible assets as well. A *tangible* asset is one that can be readily seen, and possibly touched, such as those previously illustrated and those in the first three categories listed below. They are physical assets. An *intangible* asset is without physical qualities, but has a value based on rights or privileges belonging to the owner. Two examples of intangible assets are patents and franchises.

The assets of an organization are usually divided into four categories: (1) current assets, (2) investments, (3) property, plant, and equipment, and (4) intangible assets.

Current assets are defined as cash and other assets that can reasonably be expected to be converted to cash, used up, or sold within 1 year or less. Examples of current assets include cash, accounts receivable (obligations due from customers), and supplies.

Investments are generally of a long-term nature, are not used in the normal operations of the organization, and are not expected to be converted to cash within the year. Examples of investments are stocks and bonds of other organizations.

Property, plant, and equipment are long-term or long-life assets that are used in the continuing operations of the organization and are expected to be used by the organization for more than a year. These kinds of assets are also known as *plant assets* or *fixed assets*. Examples of these assets are land, buildings, machinery, and equipment.

Intangible assets are usually of a long-term nature and have no physical substance but are of value to the owners of the organization. Examples of these assets are copyrights, goodwill, and trademarks. **Complete "Do You Know the Basics?", Exercise 5 (p. 11).**

YOU SHOULD REMEMBER

Assets represent anything that is owned and has money value.
Assets are organized into four groups: current assets; investments; property, plant, and equipment; and intangible assets.

• *A COMMON WAY TO EXPRESS ASSETS*

We have indicated that the accountant keeps track of all business transactions. So far, the only business transactions we have discussed are things that the organization owns, namely, assets. In order to keep track of these assets, there must be a common way of expressing them.

The common way of expressing the values of items in a business is known as the **monetary principle.** All business transactions are recorded in terms of money. Money is the only factor that is common to all assets, as well as to other items we will shortly be discussing. If we were to say that we have the asset "office supplies," the accountant would express the ownership of this asset in terms of a money value assigned to it. The money value assigned would be based on what the office supplies cost when they were purchased. If we acquired office supplies that cost us $50, we would then say that the value of the asset office supplies is $50. All things owned by and owed to an organization, as well as the ownership of the organization, are expressed in terms of money value. Money or cash becomes the common denominator in presenting accounting information.

DETERMINING THE MONEY VALUES OF ASSETS

In the case of the office supplies illustrated, the value assigned was based on the cost of the item. This is known as the **cost principle.** The cost assigned to the asset includes not only the purchase price, but also transportation charges, installation charges, and any other costs associated with placing the asset into use by the organization.

Although every form of organization previously mentioned uses accounting information, we will assume from this point on that we are dealing with a profit-making business. We will further assume that the business is that of a single owner (sole proprietorship). A sole proprietorship is a business that is formed by one individual. This individual is considered the owner of the business and receives any profits that the business earns and sustains any losses that the business incurs. The assets that the business owns are separate and apart from the assets that the owner may personally own. This is known as the **business entity concept. Complete Computational Problems 1 and 2, Part B** (pp. 15–16).

YOU SHOULD REMEMBER

The assignment of values to items in a business is based on the monetary principle.

The assignment of costs to all noncurrent assets is based on the cost principle. The cost assigned to the asset includes all costs necessary to make the asset operational for the business.

According to the business entity concept, the personal assets of the owner are separate and apart from the assets of the business.

MONITORING THE PROPRIETOR'S OWNERSHIP

The proprietor in beginning a business contributes assets to the business. These assets contributed may consist of cash, supplies, or equipment. Each asset is assigned a money value based on the cost of the asset to the proprietor. Since the proprietor is also the owner of the business, the assets contributed represent the proprietor's ownership or equity in the business. A record is set up by the accountant to represent the proprietor's ownership in the business. This record is called **capital**.

Capital is the ownership of the assets of the business by the proprietor. For every asset that the proprietor contributes to the business a corresponding value is assigned to the record of proprietor's capital. **Complete Computational Problem 3, Part B** (p. 16).

YOU SHOULD REMEMBER

Capital is the ownership of the assets of the business by the proprietor.

ASSETS = CAPITAL

From the relationship described above we can develop a simple equation that relates assets to capital. This equation will be expressed as follows: Assets = Capital.

Thus, if Ms. Taylor contributed to the business assets valued at $6,075, the equation would be expressed as:

Assets = Capital
$6,075 = $6,075

If at some future date the proprietor contributes additional assets to the business, both the value of the total assets and the value of the capital will increase by the same amount; thus the equation will remain in balance. Should the proprietor decide to take an asset out of the business for personal use, this will cause a corresponding decrease in the value of the total assets and in the value of the total capital.

If a business uses an existing asset to acquire another asset, only the assets, not the proprietor's capital, are affected. A transaction of this type represents an **exchange of assets. Complete Computational Problems 1 and 2, Part A** (pp. 12–14).

EXPRESSING BORROWED ASSETS

The owner of a sole proprietorship will use the assets that he or she contributed to the business to acquire other assets that the business needs to function. In some circumstances the assets available may be inadequate to meet the needs of the business. When this situation occurs, it may be necessary for the business to obtain the needed assets from other sources.

The most obvious way in which additional assets can be obtained for the business is by borrowing. When cash or any other asset is borrowed, the firm is said to have incurred a debt or liability. Regardless of what is borrowed, it is customary to repay the obligation in cash. When the obligation is initially incurred, the business obtains the asset borrowed. At the same time, a liability is incurred which has to be recognized as an obligation of the business. Until the debt is paid, the creditor (the person to whom the money is owed) is said to have a claim upon the assets originally loaned. **Liabilities** are defined as amounts due creditors and other interested parties. A liability is also said to be the ownership of the assets of a business by its *creditors*. Notice that this definition of a liability is identical to the definition of capital, except for the last word. (Capital is the ownership of the assets of a business by the *proprietor*.) Since a liability is, by definition, not an asset or ownership (that is, capital), it becomes necessary to establish a third classification of items, namely, that of liabilities.

Since a liability is closely associated with the ownership of the business assets, it is shown on the equation on the same side as capital. The final form of the equation that is generally known as the **accounting equation** is:

$$\text{Assets} = \text{Liabilities} + \text{Capital}$$

Liabilities may take many forms. If the owner of a business has to borrow money and promises orally to pay back the obligation, this obligation is known to the borrower as an **account payable** and to the lender as an **account receivable.** If the promise made takes the form of a written document, such as an IOU or a promissory note, then the obligation is known as a **note payable** to the borrower and a **note receivable** to the lender. Regardless of the form that the actual obligation takes, its placement in the accounting equation remains the same. Let's assume the following information:

$$
\begin{aligned}
\text{Assets} &= \text{Liabilities} + \text{Capital} \\
\$14{,}000 &= \qquad 0 \qquad + \$14{,}000
\end{aligned}
$$

The business borrows $6,000 from a local bank. What will happen to the various classifications within the accounting equation? Show the new totals (balances) as a result of recording the transaction.

$$\begin{array}{rcll}
\text{Assets} & = & \text{Liabilities} + & \text{Capital} \\
\$14{,}000 & = & 0 + & \$14{,}000 \\
+\$\ 6{,}000 & = & +\$6{,}000 + & 0 \\
\hline
\$20{,}000 & = & \$6{,}000 + & \$14{,}000
\end{array}$$

If at a later date the loan is repaid, determine the effects of the repayment on the total values of the assets, liabilities, and capital. **Complete "Do You Know the Basics?", Exercise 6** (p. 12), and **Computational Problems 3 and 4, Part A** (p. 14).

YOU SHOULD REMEMBER

Liabilities are claims on the assets of the business by its creditors and may be either short-term or long-term obligations.

Accounts payable are expected to be paid within 1 year or less. Notes payable, if not payable within a year, are considered to be long-term liabilities.

The accounting equation is as follows:

$$\text{Assets} = \text{Liabilities} + \text{Capital}$$

WHAT ARE REVENUE, EXPENSES, AND PROFIT?

Every business exists primarily to earn a profit. This profit is realized through **revenue** earned by an organization as a result of the sale of a service or product by that business. Our primary concern here will be with a business that provides a service. Examples of persons in service-oriented occupations are accountants, lawyers, doctors, beauticians, real estate and insurance brokers, and travel agents. The resulting profits of a service business belong to the owner (sole proprietor) of the enterprise. The revenue generated through the services provided is recognized as an increase in the capital of the owner. This is justified because the profits that the business earns belong to the owner of the business, and the revenue earned should be reflected in the record of ownership.

Profit and revenue are not the same. **Profit** represents the income that a business has earned after certain deductions have been made from revenues. Revenue is one component that permits the recognition of profit.

• *RECORDING REVENUE*

If revenue of $500 cash is received by the business, this revenue should be recorded as an increase in cash of $500 and a resulting increase in proprietor's capital of $500. Revenue may be received in forms other than cash. An organization may receive payment for services rendered in the form of other assets such as supplies, equipment, and even someone's promise to pay at a future time (accounts receivable). The effects on the accounting equation will still be an increase in the specific asset received and a corresponding increase in capital.

An increase in the proprietor's capital will result not only from an investment by the owner, but also as a result of revenue earned for services provided

• *RECORDING EXPENSES*

Every business, regardless of its nature, must incur certain costs in order to operate. These costs are known as **expenses.** Expenses are generally referred to as the "costs of doing business." Examples of business expenses are rent expense, insurance expense, salary expense, and supplies expense. Expenses are also known as "necessary evils," because they must be incurred in order to obtain revenue which ultimately will be translated into profits for the business. We learned that revenue causes an increase in capital; an expense has the opposite effect and results in a decrease in capital.

If rent expense for the month amounting to $300 is paid, the results will be a decrease in the asset cash and a corresponding decrease in the proprietor's capital.

A decrease in the proprietor's capital will result from a permanent reduction in the owner's investment in the business, from the proprietor taking assets out of the business, and now as a result of the payment of an expense.

Transaction	Effect on Proprietor's Capital
Owner's investment	Increase
Owner's withdrawals	Decrease
Revenues	Increase
Expenses	Decrease

YOU SHOULD REMEMBER

All businesses exist for the purpose of earning a profit.
An excess of revenue over expenses represents a profit.
If expenses exceed revenue, the result is known as a loss.
Resulting profit or loss will cause a change in the proprietor's capital.

• *HOW REVENUE AND EXPENSES AFFECT CAPITAL*

When the proprietor makes the initial investment or subsequent investments in the business, such investment is said to be **permanent** in nature. An assumption is made that the assets contributed through the investment will be used on an ongoing basis to maintain the business and contribute to future growth.

The revenue and expenses that affect capital are also used to determine whether the business has earned a profit. Since profit is determined periodically, these records (revenue and expenses) are considered to be **temporary** in nature. Also, when the proprietor borrows assets from the business, this withdrawal is considered to be temporary.

Permanent capital = Proprietor's capital (Investment)
Temporary capital = Revenue, Expenses, Withdrawals

To distinguish temporary capital from permanent capital, the accountant maintains separate records for each specific kind of temporary capital account. An **account** is a separate record maintained for each category of asset, liability, and permanent and temporary capital record. The proprietor's capital account is affected only by changes that are considered to be permanent in nature. Business transactions that result in the receipt of revenue or the payment of expenses are recorded in separate specific accounts. These accounts will increase and decrease in the same way as if the changes were made directly to the proprietor's capital account. Just as revenue would be considered as an increase in the proprietor's capital, it is expressed as an increase in the specific revenue account. An expense, as a cost of doing business, has a decreasing effect on the proprietor's capital. Business transactions, directly affecting these expenses, while increasing the value of the individual expense, also have a decreasing effect on the proprietor's capital. **Complete Computational Problem 5, Part A** (p. 10), and **Computational Problems 4 and 5, Part B** (pp. 16–18).

YOU SHOULD REMEMBER

Capital may be divided into two categories: permanent and temporary.

Permanent capital represents the investment that the owner makes in the business.

Temporary capital represents revenue, expenses, and withdrawals (Commonly referred to as "drawing").

An account is an individual record of each item that a business owns and owes and of permanent and temporary capital.

KNOW THE CONCEPTS

DO YOU KNOW THE BASICS?

1. Indicate by checking the appropriate column whether each of the following items is or is not an asset. Remember: an asset must be owned and have money value.

Item	Yes	No
Automobile		
Jewelry		
Apartment (rented)		
Clothing		
Money		
Typewriter		
Checks		
Library Book (on loan)		
Shopping List		
IOU from a Friend		

2. Prepare a list of ten assets that you personally own. You may include the assets listed in Exercise 1, but attempt to list as many other personal assets as you can. Remember that an asset must be owned and have money value.

3. Prepare a list of ten assets that a business organization would own. Although personal and business assets may be the same, attempt to list business assets that an individual might not have.

4. Test your ability to assign specific assets to various categories. Here are 20 specific assets: traveler's checks, tables, truck, typewriter, adding machine, lamp, pencils, typing paper, chairs, stationery, wrapping paper, automobiles, coins, money in bank, desk blotters, light bulbs, desk, pens, currency, and showcases.

Place each of these assets under the appropriate specific asset category heading in the following form:

Cash	Furniture and Fixtures	Delivery Equipment	Office Supplies	Office Equipment

(a) What is the difference between office supplies and office equipment?
(b) Why is a typewriter ribbon considered an office supply, even though it is an integral part of the typewriter?
(c) Will we replace a typewriter as frequently as a typewriter ribbon? Why or why not?
(d) What type of asset (short-life or long-life) is a supply?
(e) What type of asset (short-life or long-life) is a typewriter?

5. Place each of these 16 assets in the appropriate column of the form following them: cash in bank, office equipment, First National City bonds, patents, accounts receivable, office supplies, notes receivable (due in 90 days), building, office machines, furniture and fixtures, mortgage notes receivable (due in 6 years), store equipment, petty cash, goodwill, factory supplies, and merchandise.

Current Asset	Investment	Plant Asset	Intangible Asset

6. Using the following columnar headings: Transaction, Asset, Liabilities, and Capital, show a + (plus) for an increase or a − (minus) for a decrease resulting from each of the business transactions listed below. Remember that each transaction must involve at least two changes. The changes must cause the accounting equation to remain in balance. The proprietor:

(a) Purchased equipment, paying cash.
(b) Paid the monthly rent expense.
(c) Bought supplies on credit.
(d) Made an additional investment in the company.
(e) Charged customers for services provided on account.
(f) Paid creditor on account.
(g) Received payment from customers on account.
(h) Received cash for services provided this day.
(i) Permanently reduced his investment in the business by taking out cash.
(j) Paid salaries for the week.
(k) Purchased equipment, paying half cash with the balance due in 30 days.

TERMS FOR STUDY

account	investments
accounting	monetary principle
accounting equation	money value
account payable	note payable
account receivable	note receivable
business entity concept	ownership
business transaction	permanent capital
cash	permanent investment
cost principle	profit
current asset	property, plant, and equipment
exchange of assets	temporary capital
footing	temporary investment
intangible asset	

PRACTICAL APPLICATION

PART A. COMPUTATIONAL PROBLEMS WITH COMPLETE SOLUTIONS

1. Using the chart presented below, show the effects on the ASSETS = CAPITAL equation caused by the following business transactions. After you have recorded the transactions on the chart, add the individual columns and verify that the equation is still in balance. (Remember that assets are set up in various categories depending on the nature of the asset. Transactions (d) and (e) should not affect capital; they represent an exchange of assets.)

(a) The proprietor invested $5,000 cash in the business.
(b) The proprietor invested in a typewriter valued at $250.
(c) The proprietor took $200 out of the business as a permanent reduction in investment.
(d) The proprietor purchased supplies for the business, paying for the supplies with $75 in cash from the business.
(e) The proprietor purchased an adding machine for $50, paying cash from the business.

	Assets			=	Capital
Trans-action	Cash +	Supplies +	Equipment	=	Capital
(a)					
(b)					
(c)					
(d)					
(e)					

2. List the following headings on a sheet of paper: Cash + Accounts Receivable + Store Supplies + Office Supplies + Furniture and Fixtures + Equipment = Capital.

Record each of the following business transactions in the appropriate column. Identify each by number, and after each transaction is recorded, verify that the equation is in balance by **footing** (adding) the columns. The proprietor of the business:
(a) Invested $20,000 in the business.
(b) Purchased furniture and fixtures for use in the business, paying $1,200 in cash.
(c) Purchased store supplies, paying $170 in cash.
(d) Purchased equipment for use in the business, paying $1,500 in cash.
(e) Lent a business associate $750 in cash, which the associate promised to repay in 10 days.
(f) Contributed to the business office supplies that had a value of $60.

(g) Received a check for $300 in partial payment of the amount that his associate owed him.

(h) Permanently reduced his investment in the business by taking out a desk worth $100 and $900 in cash.

(i) Returned equipment previously purchased and received a cash refund of $175.

(j) Bought office supplies paying $65 in cash.

3. Calculate the value of the missing element of the accounting equation in each of situations (a)-(e):

    Assets = Liabilities + Capital
(a) $6,000   = $2,000   +   ?
(b) $5,500   =   ?   + $2,300
(c)   ?   = $4,500   + $3,650
(d) $10,550 = $485   +   ?
(e) $8,400   =   ?   + $8,400

4. A. L. Brandon is the owner of the Brandon Small Appliance Repair Shop. On January 1, 198–, the assets, liabilities, and proprietor's capital in the business were: Cash, $2,000; Accounts Receivable, $400; Supplies, $500; Equipment, $6,000; Accounts Payable, $900; A. L. Brandon, Capital, $8,000. The business transactions for the month of January were as follows:

(a) Paid $300 of the outstanding accounts payable.
(b) Received $100 on account (part payment) from customers.
(c) Purchased $250 worth of supplies on account (on credit).
(d) Returned a defective piece of equipment that was purchased last month and received a cash refund of $1,200.
(e) Borrowed $1,000 from a supplier, giving word to repay the loan in 30 days.
(f) Paid creditor $200 on account (part payment).
(g) Purchased equipment for $800, giving $200 cash and promising to pay the balance in 60 days.
(h) Bought supplies, paying $65 cash.
(i) Received a $250 check from customer on account.

Set up a chart using a form similar to that in Computational Problem 2. (Include a column for liabilities that follow the accounting equation form.) Record the January 1 balances immediately under the various assets, liability, and capital item headings. Record the business transactions listed above. Be certain to label each transaction with the corresponding number assigned, and foot the columns after each transaction has been recorded to verify the balance of the equation. Notice that every business transaction involves a minimum of two changes. Transaction 7 has three changes, but notice that the dollar changes are equal; thus the equation in this case, as with all the business transactions, remains in balance.

5. Upon finishing law school, Caroline M. Jones set up a law practice. During the first month, she completed the following business transactions:

   (a) Invested $3,000 cash in the business.
   (b) Purchased a law library for $1,200 cash.
   (c) Received $500 for services rendered.
   (d) Purchased office supplies on credit for $150.
   (e) Paid rent for the month amounting to $300.
   (f) Sent a bill for $1,100 for services rendered.
   (g) Sent a check for $50 in part payment of accounts payable.
   (h) Received $200 from customers as a result of services previously rendered and recognized.
   (i) Sent a check for $60 to the local utility company for costs incurred in beginning service.
   (j) Borrowed $200 from the business (show the effect of this loan in the Caroline M. Jones drawing account).

   Set up a chart using a form similar to that in Computational Problem 4. The following account headings are to be used: Assets—Cash, Accounts Receivable, Office Supplies, Law Library; Liabilities—Accounts Payable; Capital—Caroline M. Jones, Capital; Caroline M. Jones, Drawing; Income from Services; Rent Expense; Utilities Expense. Record the business transactions listed above, making certain to verify the balance in the accounting equation as a result of each business transaction. Remember that revenue increases capital; expenses decrease capital; drawing decreases capital.

PART B. COMPUTATIONAL PROBLEMS WITH PARTIAL SOLUTIONS OR KEY ANSWERS

1. Mr. Jones, the owner of a limousine business, purchases an automobile from the Friendly New Car Dealership. The purchase price of the automobile is $7,850. There are make-ready charges of $225, delivery charges of $78, and applicable state sales taxes amounting to $471.

   (a) Determine the cost at which the new automobile should be recorded on the books of Mr. Jones's business.
   (b) If, upon leaving the dealership, Mr. Jones was offered $9,000 for the automobile, at what price should the new automobile be recorded on his records? Why?
   (c) Does Mr. Jones own the asset "automobile"? Why or why not?

2. Mr. Glenn is negotiating to buy a parcel of property for his business. The seller is asking $170,000 for the property. The assessed value of the property for property tax purposes is $125,000. The property is presently insured by the owner for $135,000. Mr. Glenn originally offered the seller $130,000 for the property. Later, Mr. Glenn and the seller agreed on a purchase price of $150,000.

Shortly after the purchase is made by Mr. Glenn, he is offered $175,000 for the same property. At which price would Mr. Glenn record the property on the books of his business?

3. Ms. Taylor began a business on April 1, 198–, contributing to the business the following assets: Cash, $3,000; Office Supplies, $275; Office Equipment, $700; Furniture and Fixtures, $2,100.

   (a) What is the total value of the assets that Ms. Taylor contributed to the business?

   (b) What is the value of Ms. Taylor's ownership (capital) in the business?

4. On November 1 of the current year Albert Wave opened a hair styling center under the name of Unisex Styles. Set up the following columnar headings: Date; Assets—Cash, Accounts Receivable, Styling Supplies, Office Supplies, Equipment; Liabilities—Accounts Payable; Capital—Arthur Wave, Capital; Explanation. Record the following daily business transactions. Where capital is affected, use the explanation column to indicate the nature of the capital item change. Be certain to verify that the accounting equation is in balance after recording each business transaction. Mr. Wave:

198–

Nov. 1 Opened a business checking account by making a deposit of $3,000.

2 Purchased styling supplies, paying $210 cash.

3 Paid the November rent on the store amounting to $300.

5 Purchased 3 hair dryers and styling equipment for $1500 cash. Paid $500 cash with the balance due in 30 days.

6 Purchased needed office supplies for $35 cash.

7 Deposited cash revenue from sales for the week amounting to $275.

10 Paid salary for week ending 11/7 amounting to $85.

14 Sent a check for $150 on account to creditor.

198–

Nov. 16 Made an additional investment in the business of $2,000.

18 Deposited cash revenue from sales for the week ending 11/14, amounting to $385.

19 Earned revenue from sales for the week ending 11/14 that amounted to $150 on credit. Customers to be billed monthly.

23 Bought styling supplies for $200 on credit.

27 Sent a check in payment for amount owed creditor for 11/5 purchase of equipment. (Refer to transactions of Nov. 5 and Nov. 14.)

29 Received $70 cash from customers on account.

30 Paid amount owed creditor for purchase of Nov. 23.

5. Sylvia Meyers is the owner and operator of a sole proprietorship known as Meyers Cleaners. The business provides both laundering and dry cleaning services to its customers. Actual dry cleaning is not done on the premises. The assets and liabilities of the business on March 1 of the current year are as follows: Cash, $2,600; Accounts Receivable, $450; Supplies, $80; Cleaning Equipment, $5,900; Delivery Equipment, $4,500; Accounts Payable, $970.

   (a) Set up columnar headings similar in form to those for Problem 1-2, using the specific headings given above.
   (b) Record the beginning balances, assigning a March 1 date, on the first line under the headings.
   (c) Determine the value of Sylvia Meyers' capital and show her balance on the first line.
   (d) Record the following business transactions for the month of March on the columnar form prepared. Be certain to indicate the date of the transaction and to show an explanation to the right of the capital column when appropriate.

198–

Mar. 3 Paid rent for the month of March of $180.

6 Purchased supplies on account, $50.

7 Received cash from customers for dry cleaning sales, $1,800, and laundry sales, $700.

10 Paid creditors on account, $810.

11 Billed customers for dry cleaning sales on account, $590.

13 Received monthly invoice for dry cleaning expense for February (to be paid on Apr. 10), $1,080.

15 Paid the following: wages expense, $250; delivery equipment expense, $70; utilities expense, $55; miscellaneous expense, $85.

16 Purchased cleaning equipment on account for $265.

18 Received cash from dry cleaning customers on account, $520.

21 Paid creditor for purchase made on Mar. 6.

26 Paid a customer $60 for a garment lost by the cleaning company, which agreed to deduct the amount from the invoice received on Mar. 13.

28 Purchased cleaning equipment for $2,000, paying half cash with the balance due in 30 days.

30 Determined by taking an inventory the cost of supplies used during the month of March, $33. (The value of the asset used is to be converted to an expense.)

31 Borrowed $1,500 from the bank, and signed a note indicating repayment in full in 90 days.

ANSWERS

KNOW THE CONCEPTS

1.

Item	Yes	No
Automobile	X	
Jewelry	X	
Apartment (rented)		X
Clothing	X	
Money	X	
Typewriter	X	
Checks	X	
Library Book (on loan)		Y
Shopping List		X
IOU from a Friend	X	

Apartment (rented) and library book are not assets because the requirement of ownership is lacking. The shopping list is not an asset because the requirement of money value is lacking.

2. Personal assets may include: cash, coins, currency, checks, money orders, clothing, jewelry, real estate (land and/or building), obligations owed to you (accounts and notes receivable), supplies (office, store), equipment, automobile, and tools.

3. Business assets may include: cash, coins, currency, checks, money orders, accounts receivable, investments, marketable securities, notes receivable, land, building, patents, goodwill (intangibles), equipment, office supplies, delivery equipment, store supplies, machinery, furniture and fixtures, and leased property.

4.

Cash	Furniture and Fixtures	Delivery Equipment	Office Supplies	Office Equipment
traveler's checks	tables	truck	pencils	typewriter
coins	lamp	automobiles	typing paper	adding machine
money in bank	chairs		stationery	
currency	desk		wrapping paper	
	showcases		desk blotters	
			light bulbs	
			pens	

(a) Supplies represent assets that are expected to be used up within a relatively short period of time (less than 1 year). Equipment usually has a useful life in excess of 1 year.

(b) As a supply, a typewriter ribbon is expected to be used up in less than 1 year.

(c) No; a typewriter ribbon is a supply and as such it has a relatively short useful life. The extent of its use determines how quickly it will be replaced. A typewriter is classified as equipment, and its useful life far exceeds that of the typewriter ribbon.

(d) A supply is a short-life asset that is expected to be used up or converted to cash in less than a year.

(e) A typewriter is a long-life asset with an expected useful life in excess of 1 year.

5.

Current Assets	Investments	Plant Assets	Intangible Assets
cash in bank	First National	office equipment	patents
accounts receivable	City bonds	building	goodwill
office supplies	mortgage notes	office machines	
notes receivable	receivable	furniture & fixtures	
petty cash		store equipment	
factory supplies			
merchandise			

6.

Transaction	Asset	Liabilities	Capital
(a)	+ −		
(b)	−		−
(c)	+	+	
(d)	+		+
(e)	+		+
(f)	−	−	
(g)	+ −		
(h)	+		+
(i)	−		−
(j)	−		−
(k)	+ −	+	

PRACTICAL APPLICATION
PART A

1.

Trans-action	Cash	+	Supplies	+	Equipment	=	Capital
(a)	+$5,000						+$5,000
(b)					+$250		+ 250
(c)	− 200						− 200
(d)	− 75		+75				
(e)	− 50				+ 50		
	$4,675	+	$75	+	$300	=	$5,050

Header spanning: Assets = Capital

2.

Trans-action	Cash	+ Accounts Receivable	+ Store Supplies	+ Office Supplies	+ Furniture & Fixtures	+ Equipment	= Capital
(a)	+$20,000						+$20,000
(b)	− 1,200				+$1,200		
(c)	− 170		+$170				
(d)	− 1,500					+$1,500	
(e)	− 750	+$750					
(f)				+$60			+ 60
(g)	+ 300	− 300					
(h)	− 900				− 100		− 1,000
(i)	+ 175					− 175	
(j)	− 65			+ 65			
	$15,890 +	$450 +	$170 +	$125 +	$1,100+	$1,325 =	$19,060

3.

Situation	Assets	=	Liabilities	+	Capital
(a)					$ 4,000
(b)			$3,200		
(c)	$8,150				
(d)					$10,065
(e)			0		

4.

	Cash	+ Accounts Receivable	+ Supplies	+ Equipment	= Accounts Payable	+ A. L. Brandon, Capital
Jan. 1 Balance	$2,000 +	$400 +	$500 +	$6,000 =	$ 900 +	$8,000
(a)	− 300				− 300	
	1,700 +	400 +	500 +	6,000 =	600 +	8,000
(b)	+ 100	− 100				
	1,800 +	300 +	500 +	6,000 =	600 +	8,000
(c)			+ 250		+ 250	
	1,800 +	300 +	750 +	6,000 =	850 +	8,000
(d)	+ 1,200			− 1,200		
	3,000 +	300 +	750 +	4,800 =	850 +	8,000
(e)	+ 1,000				+ 1,000	
	4,000 +	300 +	750 +	4,800 =	1,850 +	8,000
(f)	− 200				− 200	
	3,800 +	300 +	750 +	4,800 =	1,650 +	8,000
(g)	− 200			+ 800	+ 600	
	3,600 +	300 +	750 +	5,600 =	2,250 +	8,000
(h)	− 65		+ 65			
	3,535 +	300 +	815 +	5,600 =	2,250 +	8,000
(i)	+ 250	− 250				
	$3,785 +	$ 50 +	$815 +	$5,600 =	$2,250 +	$8,000

5.

Trans-action	Cash +	Acc. Rec. +	Office Supplies +	Law Library =	Acc. Pay. +	C. M. Jones, Capital −	C. M. Jones, Drawing +	Income from Services −	Rent Expense −	Utilities Expense
(a)	+$3,000					+$3,000				
(b)	−1,200			+$1,200						
	1,800			1,200 =		3,000				
(c)	+ 500							+$ 500		
	2,300			1,200 =		3,000		500		
(d)			+$150		+$150					
	2,300		150	1,200 =	150	3,000		500		
(e)	− 300								−$300	
	2,000		150	1,200 =	150	3,000		500	− 300	
(f)		+$1,100						+ 1,100		
	2,000	1,100	150	1,200 =	150	3,000		1,600	− 300	
(g)	− 50				− 50					
	1,950	1,100	150	1,200 =	100	3,000		1,600	− 300	
(h)	+ 200	− 200								
	2,150	900	150	1,200 =	100	3,000		1,600	− 300	
(i)	− 60									−$60
	2,090	900	150	1,200 =	100	3,000		1,600	− 300	− 60
(j)	− 200						−$200			
	$1,890 +	$ 900	$150 +	$1,200 =	$100 +	$3,000	−$200 +	$1,600	−$300	−$60

PART B

1. (a) The cost assigned to the asset is $8,624. This cost is determined based on the cost principle. The cost assigned to an asset includes the purchase price, transportation costs, and installation costs, as well as any other costs necessary to place the asset in use.

(b) The new automobile is recorded at the cost of $8,624 regardless of the offer made for it.

(c) Although the business is owned by the proprietor, his rights to the assets extend only to the dollar value of his investment. The asset automobile belongs to the business; it is not the proprietor's personal asset.

2. The cost principle still applies. The asset is recorded on the books of Mr. Glenn's business at $150,000.

3. (a) The value of the assets contributed by Ms. Taylor is equal to the capital, that is, $6075.

(b) Her ownership value is $6075.

4. Total assets, $5,425; total liabilities, 0; total capital, $5,425

5. Beginning capital balance, $12,560; total assets, $17,842; total liabilities, $3,945; total capital, 13,897

2
FINANCIAL STATEMENTS

KEY TERMS

balance sheet A financial statement that shows the financial position of a business at a particular moment in time—a detailed presentation of the assets, liabilities, and owner's equity. Actually, it is a detailed accounting equation, in which the total value of the assets is equal to the total liabilities plus proprietor's capital.

income statement A financial statement that presents revenue and expenses and the net income or loss for a specific period of time.

statement of capital A financial statement that shows the change in the value of the ownership in a business over a period of time. The change in capital is due to income or loss and withdrawals by the owner over a period of time.

WHAT ARE FINANCIAL STATEMENTS?

In Chapter 1 we learned that one of the functions of the accountant is to keep track of accounting information. The accountant is also called upon to prepare various reports from the accounting information. There are three basic reports that the business organization uses on a regular basis:

- Income statement
- Statement of capital
- Balance sheet

These financial statements present the accounting information in formal reports that tell interested groups, such as managers, creditors, prospective investors, and governmental agencies, how the business is doing. These reports are prepared from information obtained from the various business transactions that the business recorded. Thus, transactions involving assets, liabilities, and permanent and temporary capital become the data used in the preparation of the financial statements.

Financial statements are prepared at least once a year. This is known as the **accounting period.** An accounting period may follow the calendar, in which case it begins on January 1 and ends on December 31 of the same year. The business is then said to have a calendar-year accounting period. Any business that has an accounting period consisting of 12 months other than a calendar year is generally known as a fiscal-year accounting period.

Organizations may prepare financial statements for periods of time that are less than the accounting period; such statements are generally known as **interim statements.** An interim statement is prepared for a period of time other than a fiscal year or calendar year. Examples of interim statements are statements prepared for 6-month, 3-month, or even monthly periods. Regardless of the periods of time covered by the individual financial statements, the kinds of information presented by the various statements do not change.

YOU SHOULD REMEMBER

All businesses are organized and maintain records based on an accounting period of 12 months that follows either the calendar year or any other complete 12-month period known as a fiscal year.

Whether the business is on a calendar or a fiscal year, it must prepare various statements to satisfy the needs of government (federal, state, and local), as well as other interested parties.

In addition, the accountant may be called upon to prepare financial statements, known as interim reports, for a period of time less than a complete accounting period.

Basically three financial reports are prepared: the income statement, the capital statement, and the balance sheet.

THE INCOME STATEMENT

The income statement is a report that presents the revenue, expenses, and net income or net loss for a business for a period of time. The income statement is divided into two parts. The first part is known as the ''heading,'' and the second part as the "body" of the report. The heading of the income statement asks three questions:

Whose business is it?
What statement is being prepared?
When is it being prepared?

The body of the income statement lists the revenue and expenses. A comparison of these two items will show either net income or net loss. When total revenue exceeds total expenses, the excess represents the net income. When the total expenses exceed the total revenue, the difference represents a net loss.

Example: The Income Statement

<table>
<tr><td colspan="4" align="center">**Jones Limousine Service**
Income Statement
For the Year Ended December 31, 198–</td></tr>
<tr><td>Revenue:</td><td></td><td></td><td></td></tr>
<tr><td>Limousine Rental</td><td></td><td></td><td>$24,000</td></tr>
<tr><td>Expenses:</td><td></td><td></td><td></td></tr>
<tr><td>Repairs Expense</td><td></td><td>$ 2,350</td><td></td></tr>
<tr><td>Salaries Expense</td><td></td><td>14,500</td><td></td></tr>
<tr><td>Gas and Oil Expense</td><td></td><td>3,000</td><td></td></tr>
<tr><td>Total Expenses</td><td></td><td></td><td>19,850</td></tr>
<tr><td>Net Income</td><td></td><td></td><td>$ 4,150</td></tr>
</table>

Notice that the date assigned to the income statement covers a period of time. This is true of all income statements regardless of whether they are prepared for an accounting period or on an interim basis. **Complete Computational Problem 1, Part A** (p. 34).

YOU SHOULD REMEMBER

The income statement compares the revenue earned for a period of time with the expenses incurred for the same period.

If the revenue exceeds the expenses, the excess is known as net income.

If total expenses are greater than revenue, the resulting difference is known as a net loss.

THE STATEMENT OF CAPITAL

We learned in Chapter 1 that the proprietor's capital account represents his or her ownership in the assets of the business. Part of the earlier discussion centered around the fact that whatever net income the business earns also belongs to the owner. The owner has the right either to withdraw the profits that the business earns or to reinvest the income in the business. If the latter approach is chosen, the profits are added to the proprietor's capital record. If the proprietor withdraws from the business more than the business earns, the result is a decrease in proprietor's capital. Whichever approach is taken, it must be reflected in the record of the proprietor's ownership. The statement of capital shows the changes that take place in the proprietor's capital over a period of time (usually an accounting period).

Because some information used in the statement of capital comes from the income statement, the statement of capital is prepared after the income statement. The statement of capital, like the income statement, consists of two parts: the heading and the body of the statement. The heading answers the same three questions as does the income statement heading: Whose statement? What statement? When is it prepared?

Example: The Statement of Capital

Jones Limousine Service		
Statement of Capital		
For the Year Ended December 31, 198–		
Randolph Jones, (Beginning) Capital, January 1, 198–		$23,200
Plus: Net Income for the Year	$4,150	
Less: Randolph Jones, Drawing	3,200	
Net increase in Capital		950
Randolph Jones, (Ending) Capital, December 31, 198–		$24,150

The body of the statement of capital shows what happened to the proprietor's record of ownership in the business during the year. If the proprietor had made an additional investment in the business, this would have appeared as an additional increase, in a fashion similar to showing the income for the year. Changes in the proprietor's capital from the beginning of an accounting period to the end of that period, or a period as indicated by an interim statement, will occur as a result of the following situations:

1 A permanent increase in the proprietor's investment in the business. (Addition to Capital)

2. A permanent decrease in the proprietor's investment in the business. (Subtraction from Capital)

3. The proprietor's withdrawal of assets from the business, usually in anticipation of profits. (Subtraction from Capital)

4. The recognition of net income for the period. (Addition to Capital)

5. The recognition of a net loss for the period. (Subtraction from Capital)

In the Jones Limousine Services statement of capital, if the subtraction from capital had exceeded the addition to capital, the result would have been a *net decrease in capital,* which would have been subtracted from the original capital to arrive at the new capital balance. **Complete Computational Problems 2 and 3, Part A (pp. 34–35).**

YOU SHOULD REMEMBER

The capital statement reflects the change that takes place in the proprietor's capital account as a result of business activities of the firm.

A change in the investment, the resulting net income or loss, the proprietor's drawing in anticipation of profit—each has an effect on the proprietor's capital account at the end of the specific accounting period.

THE BALANCE SHEET

The balance sheet shows the financial position of a business on a specific date. It represents a detailed presentation of the accounting equation. In Chapter 1 the final form of this equation was given as:

$$\text{Assets} = \text{Liabilities} + \text{Capital}$$

The balance sheet provides a detailed listing of the various assets that a business owns, the liabilities that are owed to creditors and other parties, and the proprietor's equity interest. It is known as the balance sheet because, upon its completion, it must be in balance. In other words, the total value of the business's assets must be in agreement with the total value of the liabilities and capital (total equity) of the business. The balance sheet is cumulative in nature in that it reports the results of all the financial activities of the business since its formation.

As pointed out previously, the statement of capital is prepared after the income statement. The balance sheet may be prepared at any moment in time. However, it is usually prepared after the preparation of the income statement and the statement of capital. This is due to the fact that information obtained from the statement of capital is essential for proper and complete preparation of the balance sheet. The capital balance found on the balance sheet is obtained from the new capital found on the last line of the statement of capital.

Although the heading of the balance sheet is basically the same as that of the other two financial statements, it does differ in one important respect: the date assigned to the balance sheet does not cover a period of time, but rather represents a moment in time. It is in essence a snapshot of the entity's financial position at period-end. If we were to prepare a balance sheet on January 31, 198–, it would reflect the financial position of the business at that time. This balance sheet would be different from one prepared on the previous or the following day.

YOU SHOULD REMEMBER

The balance sheet, which consists of a detailed listing of the various assets, liabilities, and proprietor's capital on a specific date, shows the financial position and condition of the organization at that moment in time.

The balance sheet relies on the preparation of the statement of capital for the determination of the new proprietor's capital balance.

The statement of capital in turn relies on the income statement preparation for the determination of the change in capital for the particular period.

Because of these relationships, the order of preparation of the financial statements never changes.

• *THE REPORT AND ACCOUNT FORMS*

There are two forms that the balance sheet takes: (1) the report form and (2) the account form. Although both forms provide identical information, their appearance differs according to the use to be made of the forms by the accountant.

Example: Report Form of Balance Sheet

Jones Limousine Service
Balance Sheet
December 31, 198–

Assets

Cash	$16,000	
Accounts Receivable	2,500	
Automobile Supplies	1,200	
Limousines	38,000	
Total Assets		$57,700

Liabilities and Capital

Accounts Payable	$ 3,200	
Notes Payable	30,350	
Total Liabilities		$33,550
Randolph Jones, Capital		24,150
Total Liabilities and Capital		$57,700

Example: Account Form of Balance Sheet

Jones Limousine Service
Balance Sheet
December 31, 198–

Assets		Liabilities and Capital	
Cash	$16,000	Accounts Payable	$ 3,200
Accounts Receivable	2,500	Notes Payable	30,350
Automobile Supplies	1,200	Total Liabilities	33,550
Limousines	38,000	Randolph Jones, Capital	24,150
Total Assets	$57,700	Total Liabilities & Capital	$57,700

Complete Computational Problems 4 and 5, Part A (p. 35).

• *THE CLASSIFIED BALANCE SHEET*

On every balance sheet we have prepared so far, regardless of its form, items have been classified according to categories. Assets, liabilities, and proprietorship were grouped separately.

CLASSIFYING ASSETS

Assets, we have learned, may be further grouped according to the degree of liquidity or the expected conversion to cash or the time it takes to use up the asset. For analytical purposes, assets are classified as follows:

Current assets are cash and other assets that can reasonably be expected to be converted to cash, used up, or sold within 1 year or less. Thus, on the classified balance sheet, current assets are listed first, based on their relative degrees of liquidity (ready conversion to cash). Examples of current assets include supplies, insurance, and accounts receivable.

Investments may be either short- or long-term assets depending on the nature of the investments. Generally, bonds are considered long-term investments, whereas stocks may be either long- or short-term investments. Investments generally appear immediately following current assets on the *classified balance sheet*.

Property, plant, and equipment are tangible, long-term assets; they are used in the continuing operations of the business and are expected to have useful lives of more than 1 year. They are also known as *plant assets* or *fixed assets*.

Intangible assets are usually long-term in nature and are traditionally shown on the classified balance sheet after plant assets. They lack physical substance and in some cases represent a right granted by a government (patent) or another company (franchise).

CLASSIFYING LIABILITIES

Liabilities are classified in a similar manner.

Liabilities are considered to be **current liabilities** if the obligation is to be settled within 1 year or within the current accounting period. These debts are usually settled with the payment of current assets. Examples of current liabilities are accounts payable, taxes payable, salaries payable, and notes payable (if the obligation is due within 1 year).

Following current liabilities on the balance sheet are **long-term liabilities,** which are usually payable in more than a year. Examples of long-term liabilities include bonds payable and mortgages payable. In the year in which a long-term liability becomes payable, it is usually converted to a current liability (appearing under the Current Liability heading of the balance sheet).

Example: Classified Balance Sheet—Report Form

Jones Limousine Service
Balance Sheet
December 31, 198–

Assets

CURRENT ASSETS		
Cash	$16,000	
Accounts Receivable	2,500	
Automobile Supplies	1,200	
Total Current Assets		19,700
FIXED ASSETS		
Limousines		38,000
Total Assets		$57,700

Liabilities and Capital

CURRENT LIABILITIES		
Accounts Payable	$ 3,200	
Notes Payable (current)	3,035	
Total Current Liabilities		$ 6,235
LONG-TERM LIABILITIES		
Notes Payable		27,315
Total Liabilities		33,550
Randolph Jones, Capital		24,150
Total Liabilities and Capital		57,700

Complete Computational Problem 6, Part A (p. 35).

YOU SHOULD REMEMBER

The primary benefit of the classified balance sheet is that it classifies assets and liabilities into significant groups according to the useful lives of the items.

In general, assets that can be expected to be used up or converted to cash within 1 year, and liabilities that will be paid within 1 year, are classified as current items.

Assets and liabilities that are expected to exist for more than 1 year are generally grouped as long-term items.

* * * * *

Up to this point we have been dealing exclusively with a sole-proprietorship form of business. The form and the content of financial statements vary according to the nature of a particular business organization. At this point, however, it would be counterproductive to illustrate corporate or partnership financial statements. They will be presented in Chapter 12, which deals specifically with those forms of business organizations.

For more practice in mastering the material in this chapter, **complete Computational Problems 7, 8, and 9, Part A** (p. 36), and **Computational Problems 1 and 2, Part B** (pp. 36–37).

KNOW THE CONCEPTS

DO YOU KNOW THE BASICS?

1. Referring to the Jones Limousine Service income statement on page 26, answer the following questions:
   (a) What is the period of time covered by the income statement?
   (b) What is the source of the revenue?
   (c) What is the total revenue?
   (d) What are the total expenses?
   (e) Why is there a resulting net income?
   (f) Is this statement an interim statement? Why or why not?
   (g) Who does the net income belong to?

2. Referring to either form of the balance sheet illustrated on page 30, answer the following questions:
   (a) When was the balance sheet prepared?
   (b) How does the date on this balance sheet differ from the date on the statement of capital or the income statement?
   (c) Can Randolph Jones purchase another limousine for the business paying cash of $19,900? Why or why not?
   (d) What is the total equity of the Jones Limousine Service?
   (e) What is the total amount of Randolph Jones's claim against the total assets of the business?
   (f) What is the amount of the creditors' claims against the assets of the business?
   (g) What is the net income for the period?
   (h) What was the value of Randolph Jones's ownership in this business on January 1, 198– (beginning of the accounting period)?
   (i) In order to prepare this financial statement, which business reports had to precede it and why?
   (j) What is the difference between the account form and the report form of the balance sheet?

3. Test your knowledge of this chapter by answering each of the following questions:

   (a) What specific names have been given to the three accounting reports that were discussed?

   (b) What is the order of preparation of the accounting reports? Why?

   (c) What is the name of the accounting report that may show either a net profit or a net loss for an accounting period?

   (d) What are the two main parts of the body of the income statement known as?

   (e) If total revenue exceeds total expenses for an accounting period, what is the difference called?

   (f) What accounting report shows the change that may take place in proprietorship during the accounting period?

   (g) What are the two primary items that bring about a change in proprietorship during the accounting period?

   (h) What business record shows the results of the proprietor's borrowing assets from the business, usually in anticipation of profits?

   (i) What temporary capital records are found in the income statement?

   (j) What temporary capital record appears on the statement of capital?

   (k) In the body of a balance sheet, what are the three sections called?

   (l) Of the two forms of the balance sheet, which form more closely approximates the accounting equation in form?

TERMS FOR STUDY

accounting period	interim statement
current asset	investments
current liability	long-term liability
intangible asset	property, plant, and equipment

PRACTICAL APPLICATION

PART A. COMPUTATIONAL PROBLEMS WITH COMPLETE SOLUTIONS

1. Bambi Sobel owns the New Wave Beauty Parlor. From the information listed below, prepare an income statement for the month ending January 31, 198–.

Revenue from Sales	$1,350	Rent Expense	$175
Salaries Expense	500	Supplies Expense	300
Service Revenue	4,580	Advertising Expense	850

2. Prepare a statement of capital for the New Wave Beauty Parlor for the month ending January 31, 198–. The proprietor, Bambi Sobel, had a beginning capital

balance of $14,500. During the month she withdrew $1,600 in anticipation of profits. The net income earned for the month amounted to $4,105.

3. Albert Bradley owns the Bradley Cleaning Service. On January 1, 198–, Mr. Bradley's capital balance was $20,500. During the year the following activities affected his ownership (equity) in the business: net income for the year was $18,300; on March 23, 198–, the proprietor made an additional permanent investment in the business of $5,000; during the year the proprietor withdrew assets worth $15,600 from the business. Prepare a statement of capital for the year ended December 31, 198–.

4. The New Wave Beauty Parlor had the following assets, liabilities, and proprietor's capital as of January 31, 198–. Cash, $2,380; Accounts Receivable, $1,400; Beauty Equipment, $15,000; Bambi Sobel, Capital, ?; Notes Payable, $2,275; Beauty Supplies, $800; Accounts Payable, $300. Prepare an account-form balance sheet for the New Wave Beauty Parlor. Note that the proprietor's capital account balance is not provided. Using the accounting equation will enable you to determine the capital balance.

5. Betty Smith is the owner of the Accurate Tax Service. For the year ended April 30, 198–, the following information is available for this service business: Cash, $12,500; Accounts Receivable, $3,700; Office Furniture and Fixtures, $11,300; Office Machines and Computers, $15,000; Automobile, $9,500; Accounts Payable, $1,700; Betty Smith, Capital, $32,000; Betty Smith, Drawing, $18,600; Revenue from Income Tax Preparation, $21,300; Revenue from Monthly Clients, $43,800; Salaries Expense, $12,500; Advertising Expense, $900; Rent Expense, $6,000; Automobile Expense, $1,300; General Office Expenses, $7,500.

Prepare the Accurate Tax Service's income statement, statement of capital, and balance sheet for the year ended April 30, 198–.

6. Prepare a classified balance sheet for the North Stars Realty Co. As of December 31, 198–, the assets, liabilities, and proprietor's capital for the business were as follows:

Cash	$2,960
Office Equipment	2,005
Insurance	30
Office Salaries Payable	60
Samuel Fields, Capital	6,900
Office Supplies	75
Accounts Payable	65
Automobile	2,030
Accounts Receivable	125
Mortgage Payable	200

7. Robert Granville is the owner of the Altuna Cinema. During the month of December of the current year, the following revenue was received and expenses incurred:

Advertising Expense	$ 750	Rent Expense	$1,100
Revenue from Ticket Sales	13,450	Film Rental Expense	6,725
Maintenance Expense	520	Concession Revenue	1,500
Salaries Expense	2,340	Utilities Expense	355

Prepare an income statement for the Altuna Cinema for the month of December of the current year.

8. Robert Granville (refer to Computational Problem 7) had a capital balance on December 1 of the current year of $25,000. During the month of December he borrowed $1,200, in cash, in anticipation of profits from the Altuna Cinema. Using the information obtained from Exercise 7 and the above information, prepare a statement of capital for the month ending December of the current year.

9. The assets and liabilities of the Altuna Cinema on December 31 of the current year were as follows:

Cash	$ 5,320	Projection Supplies	$ 450
Projection Equipment	12,400	Cleaning Supplies	150
Display Fixtures	7,250	Accounts Payable	2,200
Ticket Supplies	1,300	Prepaid Advertising	2,290

Prepare a balance sheet, dated December 31 of the current year, using the information provided above as well as the information used in completing Exercises 7 and 8.

PART B. COMPUTATIONAL PROBLEMS WITH PARTIAL SOLUTIONS OR KEY ANSWERS

1. Dr. Candy Berman began the practice of dentistry on January 1 of the current year. On December 31 of the same year the records of her practice showed the following items:

Cash	$ 900	Accounts Receivable	$ 2,300
Office Equipment	15,350	Office Supplies	400
Office Supplies Expense	700	Candy Berman, Capital	12,150
Candy Berman, Drawing	10,400	Professional Fees Earned	25,500
Accounts Payable	250	Rent Expense	2,400
Salaries Expense	5,100	Utilities Expense	350

For the end of the current year prepare, based on the above information, (a) an income statement, (b) a statement of capital, (c) a balance sheet.

2. Donna Elder is the owner of the Ellison Insurance Brokerage Group. The books of account showed the following balances as of the end of the company's fiscal year, June 30, 198–.

Cash	$11,500	D. Elder, Capital	$32,520
Accounts Receivable	2,200	D. Elder, Drawing	15,600
Office Furniture	3,250	Revenue from Commissions	61,600
Automobile	8,900	Telephone Expense	2,150
Building	26,000	Salaries Expense	23,600
Accounts Payable	1,800	Utilities Expense	1,120
Maintenance Expense	1,600		

On the basis of the above information, prepare the following financial statements for the end of the current fiscal year: (a) an income statement, (b) a statement of capital, (c) a balance sheet.

ANSWERS

KNOW THE CONCEPTS

1. (a) The income statement covers the year ended Dec. 31, 198–. This means the statement reflects Jan. 1–Dec. 31 of that year.
   (b) The source of the revenue is limousine rentals.
   (c) The total revenue is $24,000.
   (d) The total expenses are $19,850 consisting of:

Repairs expense	$ 2,350
Salaries expense	$14,500
Gas and oil expense	$ 3,000

   (e) A net income results when total revenue ($24,000) is greater than total expenses ($19,850). The excess of revenue over expenses ($4,150) is the net income.
   (f) This statement is *not* an interim statement because it covers an entire accounting period. If it were for a period of less than 1 year, it would then be considered an interim statement.
   (g) The net income belongs to Jones. We have been assuming a sole proprietorship form of business. Thus, the income of the business belongs to the owner.

2. (a) December 31, 198–.
   (b) The balance sheet date represents the moment in time when the statement was prepared. The other financial statements (income statement, statement of capital) represent the period of time during which the changes indicated

on the statement took place. A balance sheet prepared on another date would probably not have the same values as the one illustrated. The differences would be due to changes in values as a result of business transactions.

(c) No. The business has only $16,000 cash available.

(d) The total equity consists of total liabilities and proprietor's capital. The combined amount equals $57,700.

(e) $24,150. This represents the extent of Jones's ownership as shown by proprietor's capital.

(f) $33,550. These claims consist of accounts payable of $3,200 and notes payable of $30,350.

(g) This information cannot be obtained from the balance sheet. Refer to page 26, where the income statement appears. The income statement indicates net income of $4,150.

(h) This information cannot be obtained from the balance sheet. Refer to the statement of capital on page 27 for the answer to this question. The January 1, 198– capital balance was $23,200.

(i) The income statement and statement of capital had to be prepared prior to preparing the balance sheet. This is necessary in order to determine the new capital balance, which reflects changes enumerated on pages 27–28.

(j) The difference is only in the manner in which the information is listed on the reports. The appearance of an equality is more clearly evident using the account form, which follows more closely the accounting equation form.

3. (a) Income statement, statement of capital, and balance sheet.

(b) Income statement, statement of capital, and balance sheet. The statement of capital relies on the results of the preparation of the income statement to determine the change in capital. The balance sheet relies on the statement of capital for its new capital balance.

(c) The income statement.

(d) Revenue (income) and expenses.

(e) Net income.

(f) The statement of capital.

(g) Net income and drawing.

(h) Proprietor's withdrawals.

(i) Revenue and expenses.

(j) Proprietor's withdrawals.

(k) Assets, liabilities, and capital.

(l) The account form.

PRACTICAL APPLICATION
PART A

1.
New Wave Beauty Parlor
Income Statement
For the Month Ended January 31, 198–

Revenue:		
Revenue from Sales	$1,350	
Service Revenue	4,580	
Total Revenue		$5,930
Expenses:		
Rent Expense	$ 175	
Salaries Expense	500	
Supplies Expense	300	
Advertising Expense	850	
Total Expenses		$1,825
Net Income		$4,105

2.
New Wave Beauty Parlor
Statement of Capital
For the Month Ended January 31, 198–

Bambi Sobel, (Beginning) Capital, January 1, 198–		$14,500
Plus: Net Income for the Month	$4,105	
Less: Bambi Sobel, Drawing	1,600	
Net Increase in Capital		2,505
Bambi Sobel, (Ending) Capital, January 31, 198–		$17,005

3.
Bradley Cleaning Service
Statement of Capital
For the Year Ended December 31, 198–

Albert Bradley, (Beginning) Capital, January 1, 198–		$20,500
Add: Additional Investment, March 23, 198–	$ 5,000	
Net Income for the Year	18,300	
	23,300	
Less: Albert Bradley, Drawing	15,600	
Net Increase in Capital		7,700
Albert Bradley, (Ending) Capital, December 31, 198–		$28,200

New Wave Beauty Parlor
Balance Sheet
January 31, 198–

Assets		Liabilities and Capital	
Cash	$ 2,380	Accounts Payable	$ 300
Accounts Receivable	1,400	Notes Payable	2,275
Beauty Supplies	800	Total Liabilities	2,575
Beauty Equipment	15,000	Bambi Sobel, Capital	17,005
Total Assets	$19,580	Total Liabilities & Capital	$19,580

Accounting Equation:

$$\frac{ASSETS}{\$19,580} = \frac{LIABILITIES}{\$2,575} + \frac{CAPITAL}{?}$$

Oʀ

$$\frac{ASSETS}{\$19,580} - \frac{LIABILITIES}{\$2,575} = \frac{CAPITAL}{?}$$

5.

Accurate Tax Service
Income Statement
For the Year Ended April 30, 198–

Revenue:		
Revenue from Income Tax Preparation		$21,300
Revenue from Monthly Clients		43,800
Total Revenue		$65,100
Expenses:		
Salaries Expense	$12,500	
Advertising Expense	900	
Rent Expense	6,000	
Automobile Expense	1,300	
General Office Expenses	7,500	
Total Expenses		$28,200
Net Income		$36,900

Accurate Tax Service
Statement of Capital
For the Year Ended April 30, 198–

Betty Smith, (Beginning) Capital, May 1, 198–		$32,000
Plus: Net Income for the Year	$36,900	
Less: Betty Smith, Drawing	18,600	
Net Increase in Capital		18,300
Betty Smith, (Ending) Capital, April 30, 198–		$50,300

Accurate Tax Service
Balance Sheet
April 30, 198–

Assets

Cash	$12,500
Accounts Receivable	3,700
Office Furniture & Fixtures	11,300
Office Machines & Computers	15,000
Automobile	9,500
Total Assets	$52,000

Liabilities and Capital

Accounts Payable	$ 1,700
Betty Smith, Capital	50,300
Total Liabilities & Capital	$52,000

6.

North Stars Realty Co.
Balance Sheet
December 31, 198–

Assets

CURRENT ASSETS		
Cash	$2,960	
Accounts Receivable	125	
Insurance	30	
Office Supplies	75	
Total Current Assets		$3,190
PLANT ASSETS		
Office Equipment	2,005	
Automobile	2,030	
Total Plant Assets		4,035
Total Assets		$7,225

Liabilities and Capital

CURRENT LIABILITIES		
Accounts Payable	$ 65	
Office Salaries Payable	60	
Total Current Liabilities		125
LONG-TERM LIABILITIES		
Mortgage Payable		200
Total Liabilities		325
Samuel Fields, Capital		6,900
Total Liabilities and Capital		$7,225

7.

Robert Granville
Income Statement
For the Month Ended December 31, 198–

Revenue:		
Revenue from Ticket Sales	$13,450	
Concession Revenue	1,500	
Total Revenue		$14,950
Expenses:		
Advertising Expense	$750	
Rent Expense	1,100	
Maintenance Expense	520	
Salaries Expense	2,340	
Film Rental Expense	6,725	
Utilities Expense	355	
Total Expenses		11,790
Net Income		$3,160

8.

Robert Granville
Statement of Capital
For the Month Ended December 31, 198–

Robert Granville, (Beginning) Capital, December 1 198–		$25,000
Add: Net Income for the Month	$3,160	
Less: Robert Granville, Drawing	1,200	
Net Increase in Capital		1,960
Robert Granville, (Ending) Capital, December 31, 198–		$26,960

9.

Robert Granville
Balance Sheet
December 31, 198–

Assets

Cash	$5,320
Ticket Supplies	1,300
Projection Supplies	450
Cleaning Supplies	150
Prepaid Advertising	2,290
Display Fixtures	7,250
Projection Equipment	12,400
Total Assets	$29,160

Liabilities and Capital

Accounts Payable	$2,200
Robert Granville, Capital	26,960
Total Liabilities and Capital	$29,160

PART B

1. Net income, $16,950; Candy Berman, capital, December 31, 198–, $18,700; total assets, $18,950; total liabilities, $250

2. Net income, $33,130; Donna Elder, capital, June 30, 198–, $50,050; total assets, $51,850; total liabilities, $1,800

3

RECORDING BUSINESS TRANSACTIONS

KEY TERMS

account An individual record of specific items that a business owns (assets) and owes (liabilities), as well as a recognition of ownership (capital).

double-entry accounting A method of accounting in which, for every debit entry, there must be a corresponding credit entry of the same amount. Every business transaction *must* be represented by at least two changes.

journal A book of original or first entry. The basic two-column journal provides for entering business transactions in dated order. All parts of every transaction are recorded, and provision is made for adequate explanation.

ledger A book of secondary or final entry, containing individual accounts. The term "ledger account" refers to an individual account in the ledger. A ledger may be a bound book, a looseleaf-type book, or a computer printout.

trial balance A record prepared at any moment in time to prove the accuracy of the ledger. If the totals of the debit and credit balances in the individual ledger accounts agree, the ledger is said to be in balance.

WHAT ARE BUSINESS TRANSACTIONS?

A **business transaction** is any business activity that affects what a business owns and owes, as well as the ownership of the business. We learned in Chapter 1 to keep track of business transactions by using an expanded form of the accounting equation. Most businesses, however, are involved in daily business transactions so numerous as to make this method unwieldy. Since we cannot expect an accountant to remember everything that has happened to the value of a specific asset or to keep mental notes of all the numerous records of an organization, another method must be devised to record business transactions.

• *INFORMATION TO KEEP TRACK OF*

When we added a business transaction to the accounting equation, we showed the change that took place in the specific record. This *increase* or *decrease* is an important part of our record, but we also want to keep track of the *date* that a particular transaction takes place. Some form of *explanation* is also helpful, especially if the specific item acquired may not be apparent from the title of the record we maintain for it. Thus, every business transaction should contain three kinds of information:

1. The date of the transaction.

2. An explanation of the transaction (where necessary).

3. The amount of the transaction and its result—whether it represents an increase or a decrease.

• *CHANGES RESULTING FROM A BUSINESS TRANSACTION*

Every business transaction involves at least two changes. A review of the business transactions affecting the accounting equation will vividly illustrate this statement. If we were to acquire the asset equipment and give in payment the asset cash, we can see that both records would be affected. This is known as "double entry." If we were to acquire the asset supplies and at the same time also acquire the asset equipment as a result of paying cash, this would also be considered double entry because the total value of the two assets obtained would be equal to the value of the asset cash given up. If two or more accounts are debited or credited in an entry, we refer to it as a **compound entry.**

• *WHERE TO RECORD BUSINESS TRANSACTIONS*

Business transactions are recorded in a record known as an **account.** Each asset, liability, and capital record that is maintained is kept on a separate account page. The purpose of the account is to facilitate the recording of the essential information generated by the business transaction. These individual account pages are kept in a bound or looseleaf-type binder known as a **ledger.** If we were to record the purchase of equipment and a resulting payment of cash, it would be necessary to set up two accounts in the ledger. The first ledger account would be headed "Cash." The second ledger account would have the heading "Equipment." Changes made to these respective assets would then be recorded on the specific account pages.

YOU SHOULD REMEMBER

The accountant is called upon to keep track of changes that occur as a result of business transactions. Every business transaction involves at least two changes.

Business transactions are recorded in accounts. Individual account pages are kept in a ledger.

THE ACCOUNT

• *THE STANDARD FORM OF THE LEDGER ACCOUNT*

The standard form of the ledger account is very similar to the basic account form of the balance sheet. The account form of the balance sheet consists of two sides. In its simplest form the ledger account is known as the "T"-account because it looks like the capital letter "T," just as the account form of the balance sheet does. The standard form of the account is shown below. This is the most widely used form.

Account   Account No.

Date	Item	PR	Debit	Date	Item	PR	Credit

The three major parts of the account form are (1) the account title, (2) the **debit** side, and (3) the **credit** side. The account is divided into two equal parts. The left, or debit, side has provisions for the date, item (explanation), and amount. The right, or credit, side also has provisions for the date, item (explanation), and amount.

• *MAKING ENTRIES IN LEDGER ACCOUNTS*

Each part of a business transaction will have an effect on a specific ledger account. The effect will be either an increase or a decrease in the existing account. In order for an account to exist it must have a balance. This **balance** represents the value or worth of the specific account at a moment in time. When a balance sheet is prepared, it represents the balances from the accounting equation at a specific moment in time. The value of each asset, liability, and proprietor's capital as shown on the balance sheet can then become the basis for establishing the individual accounts in the ledger.

Using the account form of the balance sheet provides an outline of how the balances in the individual ledger accounts should be shown. The following simple balance sheet will serve to illustrate how beginning balances are recorded in the ledger accounts:

Jones Limousine Service
Balance Sheet
December 31, 198–

Assets		**Liabilities and Capital**	
Cash	$16,000	Accounts Payable	$ 3,200
		R. Jones, Capital	12,800
Total Assets	$16,000	Total Liabilities & Capital	$16,000

Since the assets are shown on the left side of the balance sheet, we will show this balance on the left side of the ledger account for the asset cash and *all* assets. The beginning balances of all asset accounts are shown on the left side (debit side) of the account.

Cash

$16,000 |

The liability and proprietor's capital account balances are shown on the right side of the balance sheet. The beginning balances of *all* liability and proprietor's permanent capital accounts will be shown on the same side as they appear on the balance sheet. Thus, the beginning balances of *all* liabilities and proprietor's permanent capital account will be shown on the right side (credit side) of the ledger account.

Accounts Payable	R. Jones, Capital
$3,200	$12,800

YOU SHOULD REMEMBER

An account must have a balance, which represents its value at a particular time. (This balance may be zero.)

The beginning balances of asset accounts are shown on the left (debit) side of the ledger account.

The beginning balances of liability and the proprietor's capital account are shown on the right (credit) side of the ledger account.

• *RECORDING ASSET CHANGES*

As we have just learned, the beginning balances for all assets are recorded on the debit, or left, side of the account. This balance on the ledger account will appear in the same position as it appears on the balance sheet. The asset account cash is said to have a debit balance.

When we wish to record an increase in any asset account, the increase is shown on the same side as the beginning balance of the account. If we were to show an increase in the asset cash, this increase would appear on the same side of the ledger account as did the original balance.

Since the balance and any subsequent increase are shown on the debit, or left, side of the ledger account, any decrease in an asset account is shown on the opposite side of the account. Thus a decrease in any asset account is shown on the right, or credit, side of the account. The following illustrative account applies to all assets:

Asset Accounts	
Beginning Balance Increases	Decreases

If we wished to know the new balance in the account after changes had taken place in it, we would add both sides of the account and determine the difference between the totals. The excess of debits over credits would give us a resulting balance known as a **debit balance.** This is a normal balance for an asset account. If the resulting balance was zero, this would indicate that total debits equaled total credits and that the asset had no value at that point in time.

It is possible for an asset account to have a **credit balance,** that is, an excess of credits over debits. This, however, is quite unusual, so we will defer discussion of it to Chapter 4.

YOU SHOULD REMEMBER

If ledger accounts are established based on an existing balance sheet, the beginning balances in the individual accounts are shown on the same side of the accounts as increases in these specific accounts will be recorded.

Thus, the usual beginning balance for an asset is recorded on the debit side of the account. Increases to that asset are recorded on the same (debit) side.

Decreases in the values of assets are recorded on the credit side of the account.

• *RECORDING CHANGES IN LIABILITY AND PERMANENT CAPITAL ACCOUNTS*

The beginning balances of the proprietor's permanent capital account and all liability accounts are shown on the same side of the account as they appear on in the balance sheet. To record an increase in a capital or a liability account we would credit the account. An increase in a capital or liability account is shown on the same side as the beginning balance in that account.

If we were to record an additional obligation in the form of an accounts payable, this would be credited to the liability account entitled "Accounts Payable." Any time a liability account is credited, the result is an increase in the value of that account. Should the proprietor make an additional investment in the company, this would result in an increase in the ownership as reflected in the proprietor's capital account. To record this increase, the proprietor's capital account would be credited. The beginning balance and any increase in a liability or permanent capital account are recorded as credits to the account. When an account is being credited, we record the entry to the right side of the account.

When a liability or permanent capital is to be decreased, this reduction is shown as an entry on the left, or debit, side of the particular account. In other words, any time there is to be a decrease in the value of a liability or permanent capital, it is recorded as a debit. The following account illustrates what changes take place and where they take place in the ledger account:

All Liability and Permanent Capital Accounts

Decrease	Beginning Balance Increase

If we are interested in finding the new balance for any liability or permanent capital account, we will total both the debit and credit columns of each account. If we then subtract the total debits from the total credits, the resulting difference will represent either a credit balance or a zero balance. When total credits exceed total debits, the resulting difference is called a credit balance. When total credits are equal to total debits, a zero balance results. **Complete Computational Problems 1 and 2, Part A** (pp. 64–65).

YOU SHOULD REMEMBER

Increases in all liabilities and in proprietor's capital are recorded as *credits*.

Decreases are recorded as *debits*.

• *ANALYZING BUSINESS TRANSACTIONS*

The process of recording business transactions as in Computational Problem 2 should include analysis of the individual transactions. To merely debit cash and credit furniture and fixtures for $5,000 on January 4, 198– is not sufficient. Although the entry is correct, there is no indication of what has taken place.

The analysis for the January 4 entry should be as follows:

1. The asset cash increased; therefore, we debit the account.

2. The asset furniture and fixtures decreased; therefore, we credit the account.

Analysis will always entail classifying the account as either an asset, a liability, or a form of capital. Then it is necessary to indicate the change and its nature, that is, whether the change is a debit or a credit.

The analysis of the transaction on January 26 would be as follows:

1. The asset service supplies increased; therefore, we debit the account.

2. The liability account, accounts payable, increased; therefore, we credit the account.

The analysis of the transaction of January 14 would be as follows:

1. The asset furniture and fixtures increased; therefore, we debit the account.

2. The capital account, Jill Baxter, Capital, increased; therefore, we credit the account.

It is obvious that the accountant must be thoroughly familiar with how to record an increase and a decrease in the various accounts.

• RECORDING TRANSACTIONS
IN TEMPORARY CAPITAL ACCOUNTS

Ledger accounts, in addition to being established for all assets, liabilities, and proprietor's capital, must also be set up for temporary capital accounts. The temporary capital accounts for a sole proprietorship consist of revenue, expenses, and the proprietor's drawing account. Since these accounts are directly related to permanent capital, and will affect proprietorship as shown by the statement of capital, changes in these accounts will mirror the changes in permanent capital.

An *increase* in permanent *capital* is recorded as a *credit* to the account. Since revenue represents an increase in capital, all *revenue* entries in the ledger account are recorded as *credits*.

R. Jones, Capital	Income from Services
$10,000	$200

The preparation of the income statement compares revenue with expenses. If the resulting difference is net income, it is the net income that is shown as an increase in capital. If there were no expenses, then total revenue would cause a direct increase in capital.

Since the accountant must keep track of expenses as well as revenue, specific expense accounts are established. Since expenses have a decreasing effect on net income, they also cause an indirect reduction in permanent capital. Just as a *decrease* in proprietor's *capital* is recorded as a *debit,* recognition of an *expense* on the ledger account is recorded as a *debit.* In other words, all expenses are recorded in their respective accounts as debits. As the amount of the same expense is recorded numerous times during the month (e.g., salaries expense), each entry is recorded as a debit. As the total value of the expense increases, the proprietor's capital decreases.

The proprietor's drawing or personal account will also decrease the proprietor's permanent capital, as shown by the statement of capital. The proprietor uses the **drawing account** to take cash and other assets out of the business, for personal use, in anticipation of profits. If the business were neither to recognize a profit nor to sustain a loss, the drawing account would cause a reduction in permanent capital. Entries to the Drawing account are recorded as debits.

The following T-accounts illustrate the entries as they would appear in the drawing and expense accounts. Notice their relationship to the normal balance in the proprietor's permanent capital account, which is also shown here.

R. Jones, Capital	R. Jones, Drawing		Salaries Expense
$10,000	$100		$50
			50

Finding the balances in the ledger accounts would be simply a matter of adding (footing) the column in which the amounts appear. The balance in income from services (page 51) is a credit balance of $200. The balance in R. Jones, drawing is a debit balance of $100. The balance in the salaries expense account is a debit balance of $100.

YOU SHOULD REMEMBER

Changes in temporary capital accounts are recorded so as to reflect the changes in permanent capital.

Revenue causing an increase in permanent capital is credited, while expenses and withdrawals are debited, causing a decrease in permanent capital.

• THE RULE OF DOUBLE-ENTRY ACCOUNTING

We have learned that every business transaction involves at least two changes. These two changes must agree as to amount. In other words, the changes must cause the accounting equation to maintain its equality. Now that we are recording transactions directly in the ledger accounts, the concept of **double-entry accounting** must be applied completely.

For every debit entry, there must be a corresponding credit entry of the same amount. For a simple business transaction, such as an investment of $1,000 in the business by the proprietor, the following entries in the ledger accounts would be recorded: debit the asset cash for $1,000; credit the permanent proprietor's capital account for $1,000.

If a compound business transaction such as the purchase of supplies for $100, the purchase of equipment for $300, and the payment of $400 cash takes place, the following entries to the ledger accounts would be recorded: debit the asset supplies for $100; debit the asset equipment for $300; credit the asset cash for $400. The requirements of double-entry accounting have been met because the total debits are equal in amount to the total credits. A compound entry may represent any number of accounts being debited and credited at the same time. The important concept is that *total debits must equal total credits* for every business transaction.
Complete Computational Problem 3, Part A (p. 66).

YOU SHOULD REMEMBER

Every business transaction must meet the requirements of double-entry accounting—that is, for every debit entry, there must be a corresponding credit entry of the same amount.

A compound entry may involve numerous debits and/or credits to various ledger accounts.

The total amount of the debits must equal the total amount of the credits for each transaction in order to meet the requirements of double-entry accounting.

• STANDARD FORM FOR THE LEDGER ACCOUNT

Checking your work on Computational Problem 3 with the solution provided, notice the manner in which the information is placed in the account. The current year does not take up a line, but rather is inserted at the very top of the date column. The month (abbreviated) is followed by the day of the month. If another entry debiting cash were to follow, the year and month would not be repeated on the next line. Only the day of the month would appear. If the next entry were in a new year, then the year would appear followed by the month and the day of the month.

Since the information used to set up the ledger accounts came from the balance sheet, the explanation indicates "balance." This entry was *not* the result of a daily business transaction, but rather was an existing balance from the December 31, 198–, balance sheet. Subsequent business transactions recorded in these accounts would contain information in the explanation area of the account. In practice, when an entry in the ledger account is not unusual, the accountant may choose to omit any explanation.

The amount areas of the ledger account do not include dollar signs. Since the T-account form does not provide specially ruled columns, it is appropriate to use a comma to separate thousands from hundreds of dollars and a decimal point to distinguish dollars from cents.

The following standard form of the ledger account does not use dollar signs, commas, or decimal points. The specific columnar format differentiates these areas. **Complete Computational Problem 4, Part A** (p. 66).

Example: Standard Form of Ledger Account

Cash

Date		Explanation	PR	Debit Amount	Date		Explanation	PR	Credit Amount
198– Jan	1	Balance	✔	5000 00	198- Jan	3			200 00
	4			600 00		9			125 00
									325 00
	7	6975.50		900 00					
	12	− 325.00 6,650.50		475 50					
				6975 50					

• OTHER FORMS OF THE LEDGER ACCOUNT

There are basically two other forms that the ledger account may take: the three-column, or Boston, ledger and the four-column ledger account.

Example: Three-Column Ledger Account

Cash

Date		Explanation	PR	Debit	Credit	Balance
19- Jan	1	Balance	✔			5000 00
	3				200 00	4800 00
	4			600 00		5400 00
	7			900 00		6300 00
	9				125 00	6175 00
	12			475 50		6650 50

Example: Four-Column Ledger Account

Cash

Date		Explanation	PR	Debit	Credit	Balance Debit	Credit
19- Jan	1	Balance	✔			5000 00	
	3				200 00	4800 00	
	4			600 00		5400 00	
	7			900 00		6300 00	
	9				125 00	6175 00	
	12			475 50		6650 50	

To determine the balance in the account form of the ledger, it is necessary to *foot* both the debit column and the credit column and then find the difference between the amounts. Using the three-column or four-column form of the ledger makes it possible to maintain a running balance in each account. If we want to know the balance in any account at a particular moment, we simply refer to the account and the last figure found in the balance column, which represents the balance in the account. When the three-column account is used, it is assumed that the amount shown in the balance column represents the normal balance in the account. Should an unusual balance appear, it will be shown either in brackets or encircled. When the four-column ledger account is used, the balance will be shown either in the debit-balance column or the credit-balance column. Unusual balances, such as a credit balance in an asset account, will be shown in the credit-balance column of the account. The four-column ledger account, while used as part of a manual accounting system, was more appropriately used with accounting posting machines. **Complete Computational Problem 5, Part A** (pp. 66–67).

• *PROVING THE ACCURACY OF RECORDED TRANSACTIONS*

At regular intervals, such as once a month, the accountant will want to prove that the requirements of double-entry accounting have been met. In order to do so, a form is prepared that will prove the accuracy of the ledger. This form is known as a **trial balance.** A trial balance represents a listing of the ledger account balances as of a particular moment in time. After the listing of the account balances, the footing of the debit column and that of the credit column of the trial balance should agree. If the two columns agree, the trial balance is said to be in balance, which means that the ledger is in balance. This does not mean that the individual business transactions were recorded to the appropriate ledger accounts; it merely means that for every debit there was a corresponding credit of the same amount. Thus an error may still have occurred.

Example: Trial Balance

	DEBIT	CREDIT
John Graves		
Trial Balance		
October 30, 198–		
Cash	$14,950	
Delivery Equipment	10,500	
John Graves, Capital		$23,000
Delivery Service Income		4,200
Warehouse Supplies	500	
Rent Expense	500	
Repairs and Gasoline Expense	250	
Utilities Expense	50	
Salaries Expense	450	
	$27,200	$27,200

After completing the trial balance and totaling the debit column and the credit column to prove that they agree, the final procedure is to *double underscore* the debit column and the credit column. Double underlining the two totals indicates that the ledger is in balance and the work has been appropriately recorded for the month. Keep in mind that this trial balance does not indicate that the entries were recorded in the proper accounts; it merely indicates that double-entry accounting has been followed correctly.

YOU SHOULD REMEMBER

Most accountants verify the accuracy of the ledger once a month by preparing a trial balance, that is, a listing of the ledger account balances as of a specific date.

If the totals of the debit and credit columns agree, the ledger is said to be in balance.

THE JOURNAL

Each business transaction has at least two parts: an entry that is recorded as a debit to a ledger account, and a corresponding credit to another account. Although a date and possibly an explanation are assigned to the transaction, there are still aspects of the transaction that are not readily apparent from this entry system. If you were to refer to a transaction that took place last month involving the receipt of cash, the debit portion of the entry would be obvious. The problem might center around the reason for the receipt of cash. Was the receipt of cash the result of the recognition of revenue, the result of an additional investment, the result of a customer paying off an obligation, or the result of a loan obtained from a local bank? In the last case did an oral or a written promise serve as evidence of the loan? It should be obvious that the receipt of cash could have resulted from many activities on one given day.

A deficiency inherent in merely using the ledger account is that the entire transaction is not recorded together. Also, the ledger account lacks a chronological order of transactions such as would be found in a diary or some other record of dated events. Although an explanation can be written into the ledger, it is often not practicable to do so because of insufficient room. To correct the inadequacies of the ledger account system, a record known as the journal, or businessperson's diary, can be used.

• THE PURPOSE AND FORM OF THE JOURNAL

The **journal** is known as the book of original or first entry. All business transactions are first recorded in the journal. The journal has three basic advantages
over the ledger:

1. It shows the complete business transaction in one place. Regardless of the
   number of debits or credits to a particular business transaction, all parts of
   the transaction are shown together.

2. All business transactions are recorded in the journal in chronological order.
   This is the reason that it is known as the businessperson's diary. Like a diary
   that records events in dated order, the journal records business transactions
   in dated order.

3. The journal provides for an adequate explanation of what took place. Regardless of the nature of the transaction being recorded, provision is made
   for as detailed an explanation as the accountant considers necessary.

The following represents the typical form of the journal. It is sometimes referred
to as the "general journal" because *all* business transactions are first recorded
in it.

General Journal

Date	Account and Explanation	PR	Debit	Credit

• RECORDING BUSINESS TRANSACTIONS IN THE JOURNAL

Since the information to be recorded in the journal is basically the same as that
which we have been recording in the individual ledger accounts, we must start by
briefly reviewing what we are already doing:

1. Recording the date of the entry.

2. Debiting the ledger account for the amount of the debit.

3. Crediting the ledger account for the amount of the credit.

4. Recording a brief explanation where necessary and appropriate.

We will continue doing these four steps, but now they will be done directly in
the general journal, rather than through the individual ledger accounts.

If on January 3, 198–, the proprietor was to send a check for $500 in payment of the January rent to the Able Realty Co., the general journal entry would be as follows:

General Journal

Date		Account and Explanation	PR	Debit	Credit
19	8–				
Jan.	3	Rent Expense		500 00	
		Cash			500 00
		Paid Able Realty Co.			
		for month of January			

Note that a separate line was used for each debit and credit entry. The debit entry began at the margin, followed by the credit entry, which was indented. The explanation followed the business transaction and provided the necessary information that the actual accounts being debited and credited could not provide. It was not necessary to indicate in the explanation that this transaction was in payment of rent, for this was understood. The month that the payment represented and the company being paid were not part of the transaction itself; hence, this information was included as part of the explanation.

Regardless of the kind of business transaction to be recorded, it must first be recorded in the book of original entry, that is, the journal. Each transaction begins with the date of the entry, followed by the debit entry or entries and then the credit entry or entries, which are indented. This is all followed by an explanation on the next available line.

Record the following compound journal entry using the proper accounting form: On June 22, 198–, the business acquired office furniture at a cost of $1,200 and related office supplies costing $75. The entire amount was paid by issuing check No. 345 to the Green Office Equipment and Supply Co. of Andover, Mass.

General Journal

Date		Account and Explanation	PR	Debit	Credit
19	8–				
June	22	Furniture and Fixtures		1200 00	
		Office Supplies		75 00	
		Cash			1275 00
		Sent check No. 345 to			
		Green Office Equipment			
		and Supply Co. of			
		Andover, Mass.			

Although the preceding illustrations show the explanation starting at the margin immediately following the credit entry, some accountants will indent the explanation and still others will indent the explanation and enclose it in brackets. The form of the explanation is not as important as its use. It serves as an important part of the recording process and should not be omitted. **Complete Computational Problem 6, Part A** (pp. 67–68).

RECORDING TRANSACTIONS IN BOTH JOURNAL AND LEDGER

Although it may appear that recording transactions in both the journal and the ledger duplicates work, there are important reasons for doing so. Let us briefly review the purpose of each record.

The journal is the book of original entry; all business transactions are first recorded in it. All transactions are recorded in chronological order. All parts of the transaction are recorded together, and an adequate explanation is provided.

The ledger is a bound or looseleaf-type book that contains various records called accounts. Each account represents individual asset, liability, or form of capital. Changes in the various accounts are recorded as debit and credit entries. At any moment in time, the accountant can easily determine the balance of the account. From the accounts found in the ledger, the accountant can prepare a trial balance. This trial balance will verify that double-entry accounting has been adhered to. From the trial balance, the accountant can prepare various financial statements as needed by the organization and other interested parties.

It should be obvious from this discussion that both the journal and the ledger represent important documents that a business organization must maintain.

YOU SHOULD REMEMBER

Business transactions are recorded in two sets of books.
Each business transaction is first recorded in the journal (book of original entry), and then transferred to the individual accounts found in the ledger (book of final entry).

• *TRANSFERRING TRANSACTIONS FROM THE JOURNAL TO THE LEDGER*

The journal was defined as the book of original or first entry. This designation indicates that business transactions are first recorded in the general journal. The ledger may then be defined as the book of secondary or final entry. The daily business transactions are transferred from the journal to the ledger. The process of accomplishing this transfer is known as **posting** and is similar to mailing a letter. The writer of a letter places the addressed letter in a mailbox, where it is then transferred by the postal service to the person named on the face of the envelope. When a business transaction is posted, the information recorded in the journal is transferred to the specific ledger accounts involved. The process of analyzing the business transaction does not change, but the record of the transaction can now be found in two places.

If the accountant, after posting a business transaction from the journal to the ledger, wishes to know the effect of the transaction on a specific account, there is an easy way to do this. It is accomplished by using the **post reference** or **reference** columns found in both the ledger account and the journal. Each journal page is assigned a number, usually in consecutive or numerical order. A designation such as J-1 indicates page 1 of the journal. Each page in the ledger is given a number as well. The ledger account page number usually represents a specific kind of account. The account entitled "Cash" might be assigned the number 1, the account headed "Supplies" might be assigned the number 2, and so forth. The *reference columns* in the journal and ledger account would then be used to indicate, respectively, where the information had been transferred to and where it had been obtained from.

The following business transaction will illustrate the process of posting the information:

198–
Jan. 10   Paid $50 for supplies acquired today.

General Journal						Page 1
Date	Account and Explanation	PR	Debit		Credit	
19 8– Jan 10	Supplies	2	50 00			
	Cash	1			50 00	
	Acquired today					

Cash								Account No. 1
Date	Explanation	PR		Debit	Date	Explanation	PR	Credit
19 8– Jan. 1	Balance	✔		300 00	19 8– Jan. 10		J-1	50 00

Supplies								Account No. 2			
Date	*Explanation*	*PR*			*Debit*	*Date*	*Explanation*	*PR*			*Credit*
19 8- Jan. 10		J-1		50 00							

The check mark indicates that the balance remaining in the cash account on January 1 is a result of previous business transactions. **Complete Computational Problem 7, Part A** (pp. 68–69).

YOU SHOULD REMEMBER

Each journal page is assigned a number. Transactions are recorded in chronological order, using each page in numerical order.

Each ledger account is also assigned a specific page number that is unique to that account.

Business transactions are first recorded in chronological order in the journal and then posted daily to the specific numbered ledger account.

The reference column in the account indicates the source of the posting; thus, "J-12" in the reference column of the cash account indicates that the entry came from page 12 of the journal. The number 1 placed in the reference column of the journal (on page 12) indicates that the amount was posted to the cash account.

When a transaction has been recorded in the journal but the reference column is blank, posting has not yet taken place.

A posting reference in the journal indicates that posting has been done and also indicates to which account the individual entry has been posted.

VERIFYING LEDGER BALANCES

As discussed in a preceding section, the balances in the ledger are verified by preparing a trial balance. A trial balance may be prepared at any time, such as at the end of a month, 3 months, 6 months, or a year. A trial balance must be prepared at least once a year; however, it is more practical for the accountant to prepare the trial balance more frequently. This enables the accountant to verify that the requirements of double-entry accounting have been met. It also reduces the amount of checking that may be necessary in the event that the trial balance does not balance.

Before we discuss what to do when the trial balance is not in balance, let's review the accounting process from the business document to the preparation of the trial balance. An accountant takes the following steps in recording a business transaction:

1. Record the transaction from the business document into the journal.

2. Post the journal entry to the specific ledger account, and note the posting in the journal and ledger reference columns.

3. Find the balance in the standard T-account, or verify the balances in the three- or four-column ledger accounts.

4. Prepare the trial balance.

In Computational Problem 7, Part A, you had an opportunity to follow through the steps enumerated above. Hopefully, you were able to get the trial balance to balance. If you were not, be aware that this situation is not unusual and can occur even with the experienced accountant. If your trial balance did not balance, you should follow specific steps to locate the error, correct it, and get the trial balance to balance. These steps are basically the same ones that are followed in recording the transactions initially, but now they are done in reverse order.

The accountant proceeds as follows:

1. Re-add the debit and credit columns of the trial balance to check the totals obtained.

2. Verify that the amounts carried to the trial balance from the accounts are the same amounts and have been recorded in the appropriate columns of the trial balance. It is not uncommon for a *transposition* (reversing numbers—e.g., 45 becomes 54) or a *slide* (mistakenly adding or deleting zeros—e.g., $3,000 becomes $30,000 or $300) to occur.

3. Verify that the balances in the individual ledger accounts were correctly determined.

4. Verify the posting process by first checking to see whether all post references are indicated in the journal.

5. Verify that each journal entry has been properly posted to the appropriate ledger account and the correct side of the account (e.g., a debit posting may have inadvertently been recorded on the credit side of the account), and that all journal entries have actually been posted to accounts.

6. Verify that each business transaction recorded in the journal has met the requirements of double-entry accounting. When you originally journalize and you reach the bottom of the journal page, it is customary to foot the debit and credit columns. Both columns should have the same totals. This is a way of verifying double-entry accounting even before posting. Remember that errors made in journalizing will be compounded if not corrected before posting.

The six steps listed above may not all be necessary. Once you have located an error, you then correct it and indicate the correction on the trial balance. By re-adding the trial balance you may find it to be in balance, unless there are other errors that you have not yet located.

YOU SHOULD REMEMBER

If a trial balance is not in balance, the accountant must redo the steps of preparation in reverse order until the error or errors have been located and corrected.

For more practice in mastering the material in this chapter, **complete Computational Problems 8 and 9, Part A** (pp. 69–70), and **Computational Problems 1, 2, 3, 4, 5, and 6, Part B** (pp. 71–74).

KNOW THE CONCEPTS

DO YOU KNOW THE BASICS?

1. Answer the following questions to test your understanding of the materials presented on pp. 44–63:

   (a) Where does the accountant keep track of changes in the values of specific assets, liabilities, and proprietor's capital?

   (b) What is the bound or looseleaf-type book in which individual records of assets, liabilities, and proprietor's capital are kept?

   (c) What are the three kinds of information that appear on each side of the T-account?

   (d) What is the left side of the ledger account known as?

   (e) What is the right side of the ledger account called?

   (f) On which side of the account are the beginning balances for assets shown?

   (g) On which side of the account do we show increases in assets?

   (h) On which side of the account do we show the beginning balances for the proprietor's permanent capital and all liabilities?

   (i) On which side of the account do we show increases in the value of the various liabilities and the proprietor's permanent capital?

(j) Where are decreases in the values of assets, liabilities, and proprietor's permanent capital recorded in the account?

(k) What does the term "balance" refer to?

(l) What does the term "double entry" mean?

(m) What document may assist us in remembering where to record the beginning balance for an item?

(n) How may we determine the balance in a ledger account after transactions have been recorded in it?

2. Test your knowledge of pages 44–63 by classifying each of the following statements as *True* or *False:*

(a) An increase in permanent capital is recorded as a credit to the account.

(b) The basic concept of double-entry accounting is that total debits must equal total credits for every business transaction.

(c) In the standard form of the ledger account, the year and the month are repeated for each entry, even if the year is the same.

(d) Dollar signs are used in the amount areas of the ledger accounts.

(e) A trial balance represents a listing of the ledger accounts and balances at a particular moment in time.

(f) If the trial balance shows that the ledger is in balance, this means that the individual business transactions were recorded to the appropriate ledger accounts.

(g) The ledger account provides a chronological order of transactions.

(h) Every business transaction is first recorded in the journal.

(i) Post reference columns are found only in the journal, not in the ledger.

(j) If a trial balance does not balance, there are six basic steps to take to locate the error(s).

TERMS FOR STUDY

balance	debit balance
business transaction	drawing account
compound entry	posting
credit	post reference column
credit balance	

PRACTICAL APPLICATION

PART A. COMPUTATIONAL PROBLEMS WITH COMPLETE SOLUTIONS

1. From the following balance sheet, set up the ledger accounts in T-form and record the beginning balances. Be certain to head the account properly and also date each entry in the individual accounts to correspond with the date of the balance sheet.

Jill Baxter
Balance Sheet
January 1, 198–

Assets

Cash	$ 4,000
Service Supplies	2,000
Furniture and Fixtures	7,000
Total Assets	$13,000

Liabilities and Capital

Accounts Payable	$ 2,000
Jill Baxter, Capital	11,000
Total Liabilities and Capital	$13,000

---

2. Using the ledger accounts completed in Computational Problem 1, record the following business transactions for the month of January 198–. Jill Baxter, the proprietor:

Jan. 4 Received cash amounting to $5,000 as a result of returning furniture and fixtures that had recently been purchased.

  8 Sent out a check for $600 in partial payment of the accounts payable.

 14 Made an additional investment in the business by contributing furniture and fixtures valued at $1,500.

 26 Purchased additional service supplies for $200. Agreed to pay the obligation in 30 days.

 31 Purchased service supplies paying cash of $50.

After you have recorded the transactions in the appropriate ledger accounts, find the balances in the respective accounts. Then, after finding the balances, prepare a balance sheet for Jill Baxter, dated January 31, 198–. Remember to use the balances that you have just determined from the individual ledger accounts.

3. Refer to the Jones Limousine Service balance sheet presented on page 47. Set up a T-account for each item on the balance sheet. Be sure to include the date, an explanation, and the amount of the entry in the individual ledger accounts. Also verify double-entry accounting based on the beginning balances in the ledger accounts.

4. In Computational Problem 5, Part A, in Chapter 1 you recorded Caroline M. Jones's business transactions for her first month in business in the expanded accounting equation. Assume that Ms. Jones established her law practice on July 1, 198–. Further assume that the numbered business transactions represented days in the month of July. Set up T-accounts as needed. Record the ten business transactions in the appropriate ledger accounts. Working with the narrative to the exercise and the accounting equation solution will assist you in successfully completing this exercise.

As you work, keep in mind the following:

The beginning balance and increases in all assets are recorded on the debit side of the account. All decreases in assets are recorded as credits to the account.

The beginning balance and all increases in liability and permanent capital accounts are recorded on the credit side of the account. Decreases are recorded on the debit side of the account.

The recognition of a revenue transaction is recorded on the credit side of the account.

The recognition of an expense or proprietor's drawing is recorded on the debit side of the account.

5. Using either a three-column or a four-column ledger account, record the following business transactions for the month of October, 198–. The proprietor, John Graves:

Oct. **1** Began the Graves Delivery Service by investing the following: Cash, $12,000; Delivery Equipment, $8,000; J. Graves, Capital, $20,000.

3 Received $3,000 in revenue as a result of delivery service income.

5 Made an additional investment in the business consisting of delivery equipment valued at $2,500 and warehouse supplies worth $500.

8 Paid $500 in rent for the warehouse for the month of October.

15 Paid $250 for repairs and gasoline expenses for the first half of the month of October.

Oct. 19 Received a check for $1,200 from a customer for delivery services rendered.

25 Sent a check for $50 to pay for deposits required by the local utilities company for electricity. Designated this payment as a utilities expense.

30 Paid employees' salaries for the month amounting to $450.

After recording the business transactions in the various ledger accounts, prepare a listing of the accounts and their various balances. If the total debit balances equal the total credit balances, this should indicate that the transactions were recorded correctly in the various ledger accounts.

6. Record the following business transactions in the general journal of the Albert Kranz Trucking Service. The proprietor:

198–

Aug. 1 Purchased a used delivery truck, paying A-1 Used Truck Co. $2,300 cash.

4 Received a check from the Stevens Department Store in payment of trucking charges as shown by a bill sent today for $900.

6 Withdrew $200 from the business for personal use.

9 Paid radio station XYZZ $300 for advertising services for the week.

10 Sent a check for $230 in payment of an outstanding obligation to the Ready Repair Shop. The form of the obligation was an oral promise (accounts payable).

16 Paid salaries for the 2 weeks ending today, amounting to $370.

19 Sent a bill to Jim's department store for $340 for goods transported.

198–

Aug. 23 Paid $120 for gasoline and oil used in trucks for the 3-week period ending this date.

27 Took $150 home for personal use.

29 Paid salaries for the 2 weeks ending today, amounting to $385.

31 Received payment from Jim's department store for obligation of Aug. 19.

7. Set up the following ledger accounts for the Speedy Car Wash Co., including the account numbers and balances and using a June 1, 198–, date: Cash (#101), $2,000; Accounts Receivable (#102), $1,500; Supplies (#110), $300; Car Wash Equipment (#115), $5,000; Accounts Payable (#201), $500; Ralph Speedy, Capital (#301), $8,300; Ralph Speedy, Drawing (#302); Car Wash Revenue (#310); Salaries Expense (#320); Rent Expense (#321); Laundry Expense (#322); Utilities Expense (#323).

Prepare a trial balance dated June 1, 198–. Having verified that the ledger is in balance, journalize and post to the ledger accounts the following business transactions for the month of June, 198–. The proprietor:

198–

June 3 Paid monthly rent of $200 to Ajax Realty Co. in cash.

5 Received a check for $500 from Adams Bros. in part payment of their obligation to us. (Cr. A/R)

8 Received $1,000 for car wash revenue for the week ending today.

9 Paid salaries for the 2 weeks ending today, amounting to $480.

14 Sent a check for $300 in payment of our obligation to Randolph Supply Co. due today. (Dr. A/P)

15 Took $500 out of the business for personal use.

198–

June 22 Sent a bill today for $200 to the Granger Trucking Co. for services provided on credit. (Dr. A/R)

26 Paid monthly water bill amounting to $85.

27 Sent the Clean Towel Co. a check for $60 for the monthly laundry expense.

29 Purchased a new wind machine for $1,200 and agreed to pay Car Wash Equipment Co. in 30 days. (Cr. A/P)

30 Bought car wash supplies consisting of soap powder and liquid wax, paying $120 cash.

After you have journalized and posted the transactions, find the balances in the ledger accounts and prepare a trial balance dated June 30, 198–.

8. Esther Rodriquez is an architect who operates her own business. During the month of April of the current year the following business transactions occurred. Ms. Rodriquez:

Apr. 1 Invested $8,500 in cash in the business.

3 Paid $450 for rent for the month of April.

5 Purchased office furniture for $1,500 cash.

7 Bought office supplies for $200 cash.

9 Received $970 cash for services rendered.

11 Purchased a typewriter and calculator for a total cost of $500. Paid $150 cash with the balance due in 30 days.

14 Provided services on credit amounting to $300.

Apr. 16 Paid $130 for office cleaning services.

17 Sent a check for $100 to creditors on account.

19 Received $150 from customers on account.

21 Paid the telephone bill for the month, amounting to $93.

22 Received $560 in cash for services rendered.

24 Purchased an office chair for $230 cash.

25 Provided services on credit amounting to $875.

27 Paid the electric bill for the month, amounting to $75.

28 Received $400 on account from customers.

30 Paid $65 for miscellaneous expenses incurred during the month.

Record the above business transactions in ledger accounts that you establish as needed. After recording all the business transactions, find the balances in the individual accounts, list them according to debit and credit balances, and then summarize the two columns. The total of the debit balance should agree with the total of the credit balance.

9. Sheila Tone, the accountant for the Riverdale Insurance Agency, found the following balances in the ledger accounts as of February 28 of the current year:

Land	$ 25,200	Building	$52,020
Accounts Payable	26,100	Notes Payable	4,140
Alan Bates, Capital	105,120	Office Equipment	7,740
Automobiles	8,820	Cash	14,040
Accounts Receivable	23,540	Office Supplies	4,000

Prepare a trial balance dated February 28 of the current year. List the above accounts on the trial balance in the order that they would normally be found in the ledger.

PART B. COMPUTATIONAL PROBLEMS
WITH PARTIAL SOLUTIONS OR KEY ANSWERS

1. D. Roth started a washing machine repair business with $1,000 cash, a truck worth $5,000, and tools worth $1500 on May 1 of the current year. On the basis of this information and the information that follows, establish the necessary ledger accounts and record these business transactions to the accounts. Mr. Roth:

May 2 Bought a desk and chair paying $185 cash.

3 Paid $142 for washing machine parts.

4 Paid $125 for special tools.

5 Received $510 for washing machine repairs.

8 Sent a bill to a customer for $290 for washing machine repairs. Payment to be received in 30 days.

11 Made an additional cash investment in the business of $500.

14 Received a check for $90 in part payment from a customer.

16 Purchased washing machine parts for $560 on account.

20 Sent a check for $160 to a creditor on account.

25 Received a check for $245 for washing machine repairs.

2. Janet Smith started a truck rental business with $5,000 cash and a fleet of trucks worth $38,000. Set up the necessary ledger accounts, and record the preceding entry, as of August 1 of the current year, as well as the business transactions that follow.

Aug. 3 Received $225 for truck rentals for the day.

5 Bought office furniture for $560, paying half cash with the balance due in 10 days.

Aug. 6 Received $545 for truck rentals for the day.

  7 Purchased a typewriter for the office, paying $200.

  9 Paid month's rent amounting to $300.

  12 Purchased truck supplies for $235.

  14 Paid balance owed creditor for office furniture purchased on Aug. 5.

  15 Income from truck rental for the week ending today amounted to $2,300. Of that amount $1,300 was in cash with the balance on credit.

  18 Received a check for $400 from a customer on account.

  23 Income from truck rentals for the week amounted to $1,275 in cash.

3. Refer to Computational Problem 8, Part A, and find the balances in the individual ledger accounts. Prepare a trial balance dated April 30.

4. Refer to Computational Problem 1, Part B, and find the balances in the individual ledger accounts. Prepare a trial balance dated May 25.

5. Lester D. Zimmerman organized his own real estate brokerage company on July 1 with an investment of $60,000 in cash. The following business transactions occurred during the first month of operation:

July 5 Purchased land and a small office building at a total price of $86,400, with a cash payment of $38,400 and the issuance of a note for the balance. The land was valued at 25% of the total purchase price.

  7 Sold land at a price of $14,400. Terms of the sale called for cash of $4,800 payable in 10 days with the balance within 30 days.

  11 Purchased office equipment for $5,040. Payment to be made in 30 days.

July 16 Received cash amounting to $4,800 from sale of land on July 7.

   19 Sent a check for $2,040 in part payment to creditor.

(a) Record general journal entries for the month of July.
(b) Post the journal entries to either three- or four-column ledger accounts. Use the following page designations: "100" for assets, "200" for liabilities, and "300" for capital accounts.
(c) Pencil-foot and prove the balances in the individual ledger accounts. Prepare a trial balance dated July 19.

6. Sheldon Rosenberg began the Staten Landscaping Service on June 1 of the current year. Transactions for the first month of operation were as follows. The proprietor:

June 1 Invested $6,000 in the business.

   2 Purchased a used truck for $3,000. Paid $2,000 cash with the balance due in 60 days.

   4 Purchased gardening equipment for $500 cash.

   5 Paid 2-year liability insurance premium of $240.

   7 Purchased gardening supplies for $200 on account.

  10 Sent a bill for $680 to customers for services, on account.

  14 Paid salaries to part-time workers amounting to $290.

  17 Received $1,400 for landscaping services provided.

  21 Sent a check for $250 in part payment for outstanding obligation to a creditor.

June 23   Received a part payment of $200 from a customer.

28   Provided landscaping services on credit amounting to $900.

30   Purchased gardening supplies for $125 cash.

(a)   Journalize the transactions for the month of June.
(b)   Set up ledger accounts as needed and post the journal entries.
(c)   Prepare a trial balance dated June 30.

ANSWERS

KNOW THE CONCEPTS

1. (a) In the account.
   (b) The ledger.
   (c) Date, explanation, and amount.
   (d) Debit.
   (e) Credit.
   (f) Debit (left side).
   (g) Debit. Increases in assets are shown on the same side as the beginning balance.
   (h) Credit (right side).
   (i) Increases in liability and/or permanent capital are added on the same side as the beginning balances.
   (j) Decreases are shown on the side opposite the beginning balances. Thus, a decrease in an asset is credited. To show a decrease in a liability or permanent capital, the account is debited.
   (k) A balance in an account represents the dollar value of that particular account at a specific moment in time.
   (l) Every business transaction involves a minimum of two changes. The system used to reflect this is known as double-entry accounting.
   (m) The account form of the balance sheet indicates the positioning of the various accounts' beginning balances.
   (n) Total the debit and credit money columns. If the totals are the same, the account is said to be in balance. If the totals are not the same, then the balance is the excess of the two totals. The normal account balances follow their location on the balance sheet.

2. (a) True   (d) False   (g) False   (i) False
   (b) True   (e) True   (h) True   (j) True
   (c) False   (f) False

PRACTICAL APPLICATION
PART A

1.

Cash			Accounts Payable		
198–				198–	
Jan. 1	4,000			Jan. 1	2,000

Service Supplies			Jill Baxter, Capital		
198–				198–	
Jan. 1	2,000			Jan. 1	11,000

Furniture and Fixtures		
198–		
Jan. 1	7,000	

2.

Cash						Accounts Payable				
198–			198–			198–		198–		
Jan. 1	9,000	4,000	Jan. 8	600		Jan. 8	600	Jan. 1	2,200	2,000
4	−650	5,000	31	50				26	−600	200
	8,350	9,000		650					1,600	2,200

Service Supplies			Jill Baxter, Capital		
198–				198–	
Jan. 1		2,000		Jan. 1	11,000
26		200		14	1,500
31		50			12,500
		2,250			

Furniture and Fixtures				
198–			198–	
Jan. 1	8,500	7,000	Jan. 4 5,000	
14	−5,000	1,500		
	3,500	8,500		

Jill Baxter
Balance Sheet
January 31, 198–

Assets

Cash	$ 8,350
Service Supplies	2,250
Furniture and Fixtures	3,500
Total Assets	$14,100

Liabilities and Capital

Accounts Payable	$ 1,600
Jill Baxter, Capital	12,500
Total Liabilities and Capital	$14,100

---

3. Setting up the ledger account, even though you have used the T-account form, still requires the inclusion of specific information. Note how this specific information is presented.

Cash

198–		
Dec. 31 Balance	16,000	

Accounts Payable

	198–	
	Dec. 31 Balance	3,200

R. Jones, Capital

	198–	
	Dec. 31 Balance	12,800

4.

Cash

198–		198–	
July 1	3,000	July 2	1,200
3	500	5	300
8	200	7	50
		9	60
		10	200

C. Jones, Capital

		198–	
		July 1	3,000

	Law Library		
198– July 2	1,200		

	Income from Services		
		198– July 3	500
		6	1,100

	Office Supplies		
198– July 4	150		

	Accounts Payable		
198– July 7	50	198– July 4	150

	Rent Expense		
198– July 5	300		

	Accounts Receivable		
198– July 6	1,100	198– July 8	200

	Utilities Expense		
198– July 9	60		

	C. Jones, Drawing		
198– July 10	200		

5.

Cash

Date		Explanation	Debit	Credit	Balance
19	8–				
Oct.	1		12,000 00		12,000 00
	3		3,000 00		15,000 00
	8			500 00	14,500 00
	15			250 00	14,250 00
	19		1,200 00		15,450 00
	25			50 00	15,400 00
	30			450 00	14,950 00

Delivery Equipment

Date		Explanation	Debit	Credit	Balance
19	8–				
Oct.	1		8,000 00		8,000 00
	5		2,500 00		10,500 00

John Graves, Capital

Date		Explanation	Debit	Credit	Balance
19	8–				
Oct.	1			20,000 00	20,000 00
	5			3,000 00	23,000 00

Delivery Service Income

Date		Explanation	Debit	Credit	Balance
19	8-				
Oct.	3			3000 00	3000 00
	19			1200 00	4200 00

Warehouse Supplies

Date		Explanation	Debit	Credit	Balance
19	8-				
Oct.	5		500 00		500 00

Rent Expense

Date		Explanation	Debit	Credit	Balance
19	8-				
Oct.	8		500 00		500 00

Repairs & Gasoline Expense

Date		Explanation	Debit	Credit	Balance
19	8-				
Oct.	15		250 00		250 00

Utilities Expense

Date		Explanation	Debit	Credit	Balance
19	8-				
Oct.	25		50 00		50 00

Salaries Expense

Date		Explanation	Debit	Credit	Balance
19	8-				
Oct.	30		450 00		450 00

ACCOUNT LISTING

	BALANCES	
	DEBIT	CREDIT
Cash	$14,950	
Delivery Equipment	10,500	
John Graves, Capital		$23,000
Delivery Service Income		4,200
Warehouse Supplies	500	
Rent Expense	500	
Repairs & Gasoline Expense	250	
Utilities Expense	50	
Salaries Expense	450	
	$27,200	$27,200

6.

Albert Kranz
General Journal   Page 1

Date		Account and Explanation	PR	Debit	Credit
19	8–				
Aug.	1	Delivery Equipment		2300 00	
		Cash			2300 00
		From A-1 Used Truck Co.			
	4	Cash		900 00	
		Income from Services			900 00
		From Stevens Department Store			
	6	Albert Kranz, Drawing		200 00	
		Cash			200 00
		For personal use			
	9	Advertising Expenses		300 00	
		Cash			300 00
		Paid Radio Station XYZZ for the week			
	10	Accounts Payable		230 00	
		Cash			230 00
		Paid Ready Repair Shop			
	16	Salaries Expense		370 00	
		Cash			370 00
		For 2 weeks ending today			
	19	Accounts Receivable		340 00	
		Income from Services			340 00
		Sent bill to Jim's Department Store			
	23	Gasoline & Oil Expense		120 00	
		Cash			120 00
		For 3 weeks ending this date			
	27	Albert Kranz, Drawing		150 00	
		Cash			150 00
		For personal use			
	29	Salaries Expense		385 00	
		Cash			385 00
		For 2 weeks ending today			
	31	Cash		340 00	
		Accounts Receivable			340 00
		Payment from Jim's Department Store			

7.

Ralph Speedy
General Journal

Page 1

Date		Account & Explanation	PR	DR	CR
19	8–				
June	3	Rent Expense	321	2 0 0 00	
		Cash	101		2 0 0 00
		To Ajax Realty Co. for June			
	5	Cash	101	5 0 0 00	
		Accounts Receivable	102		5 0 0 00
		From Adams Bros. part payment			
	8	Cash	101	1 0 0 0 00	
		Car Wash Revenue	310		1 0 0 0 00
		For week ending tóday			
	9	Salaries Expense	320	4 8 0 00	
		Cash	101		4 8 0 00
		For 2 weeks ending today			
	14	Accounts Payable	201	3 0 0 00	
		Cash	101		3 0 0 00
		To Randolph Supply Co. due today			
	15	Ralph Speedy, Drawing	302	5 0 0 00	
		Cash	101		5 0 0 00
		For personal use			
	22	Accounts Receivable	102	2 0 0 00	
		Car Wash Revenue	310		2 0 0 00
		To Granger Trucking Co.			
	26	Utilities Expense	323	8 5 00	
		Cash	101		8 5 00
		Paid monthly water bill			

Page 2

Date		Account & Explanation	PR	DR	CR
19	8–				
June	27	Laundry Expense	322	6 0 00	
		Cash	101		6 0 00
		To Clean Towel Co.			
	29	Car Wash Equipment	115	1 2 0 0 00	
		Accounts Payable	201		1 2 0 0 00
		From Car Wash Equipment Co.,			
		payable in 30 days			
	30	Supplies	110	1 2 0 00	
		Cash	101		1 2 0 00
		For soap powder and liquid wax			(Cont' d)

General Ledger   Page 101

Cash

Date			#101	PR	DR	CR	Balance
19	8–						
June	1	Balance		✔			2000 00
	3			J-1		200 00	1800 00
	5			J-1	500 00		2300 00
	8			J-1	1000 00		3300 00
	9			J-1		480 00	2820 00
	14			J-1		300 00	2520 00
	15			J-1		500 00	2020 00
	26			J-1		85 00	1935 00
	27			J-1		60 00	1875 00
	30			J-2		120 00	1755 00

Page 102

Accounts Receivable

19	8–						
June	1	Balance		✔			1500 00
	5	From Adams Bros.		J-1		500 00	1000 00
	22	To Granger Trucking Co.		J-1	200 00		1200 00

Page 110

Supplies

19	8–						
June	1	Balance		✔			300 00
	30			J-2	120 00		420 00

Page 115

Car Wash Equipment

19	8–						
June	1	Balance		✔			5000 00
	29			J-2	1200 00		6200 00

Page 201

Accounts Payable

19	8–						
June	1	Balance		✔			500 00
	14	Randolph Supply Co.		J-1	300 00		200 00
	29	Car Wash Equipment Co.		J-2		1200 00	1400 00

Page 301

Ralph Speedy, Capital

19	8–						
June	1	Balance		✔			8300 00

Ralph Speedy, Drawing

19	8–						
June	15			J-1	500 00		500 00

Page 310

Car Wash Revenue

June	8			J-1		1000 00	1000 00
	22			J-1		200 00	200 00

Page 320

Salaries Expense

19	8–						
June	9			J-1	480 00		480 00

Page 321

Rent Expense

19	8–						
June	3			J-1	200 00		200 00

Page 322

Laundry Expense

19	8–						
June	27			J-1	60 00		60 00

General Ledger   Page 323

Utilities Expense								
19	8–							
June	26		J-1		8 5 00			8 5 00

Ralph Speedy
Trial Balance
June 30, 198–

	DEBIT	CREDIT
Cash	1755	
Accounts Receivable	1200	
Supplies	420	
Car Wash Equipment	6200	
Accounts Payable		1400
Ralph Speedy, Capital		8300
Ralph Speedy, Drawing	500	
Car Wash Revenue		1200
Salaries Expense	480	
Rent Expense	200	
Laundry Expense	60	
Utilities Expense	85	
	10,900	10,900

8.

	DEBIT	CREDIT
Cash	$7,587	
Esther Rodriquez, Capital		$8,500
Rent Expense	450	
Office Furniture	1,730	
Office Supplies	200	
Office Equipment	500	
Office Cleaning Expense	130	
Accounts Payable		250
Income from Services		2,705
Accounts Receivable	625	
Utilities Expense	168	
Miscellaneous Expense	65	
	$11,455	$11,455

9.

	Sheila Tone Trial Balance February 28, 198–		
		DEBIT	CREDIT
Cash		$14,040	
Accounts Receivable		23,540	
Office Supplies		4,000	
Office Equipment		7,740	
Automobiles		8,820	
Land		25,200	
Building		52,020	
Accounts Payable			$26,100
Notes Payable			4,140
Alan Bates, Capital			105,120
		$135,360	$135,360

PART B

1. Total ledger account debit balances, $9,445; total ledger account credit balances, $9,445

2. Total ledger account debit balances, $47,345; total ledger account credit balances, $47,345

3. April 30, 198–, trial balance total, $11,455

4. May 25, 198–, trial balance total, $9,445

5. July 19, 198 , trial balance total, $111,000

6. June 30, 198–, trial balance total, $9,930

4

RECORDING ADJUSTING, CLOSING AND REVERSING ENTRIES

KEY TERMS

adjusting entries Journal entries recorded in order to reflect properly the appropriate balances in the various ledger accounts for a specific accounting period. The entries are usually prepared at the end of the accounting period but may be prepared at any time that the accountant considers appropriate.

closing entries Journal entries usually prepared at the end of the accounting period to eliminate the balances in the temporary capital accounts and to transfer these balances to the income summary account and eventually to the permanent capital account.

reversing entries Entries recorded at the very beginning of the new accounting period, each representing the exact opposite of the adjusting entry recorded at the end of the previous accounting period. A reversing entry is necessary any time an adjusting entry sets up an account that will not be closed at the end of the accounting period and that does not normally carry a balance on the books during the year.

ADJUSTING ENTRIES

The business transactions recorded thus far represent activities that affect the accounting period in which they are recorded. There may be transactions, however, that will affect not only the current period, but possibly also a prior or future period.

For the ledger accounts to properly reflect the activities for the current accounting period, it may be necessary for the accountant to prepare adjusting entries. **Adjusting entries** are journal entries that are recorded in order to properly reflect the appropriate balances in the various ledger accounts for a specific accounting period. Although these entries are usually prepared at the end of the accounting period, they can be prepared at any time that the accountant considers appropriate. Let us assume here that we will prepare adjusting entries only at the end of the accounting period.

• *TYPES OF ADJUSTING ENTRIES*

There are basically two categories of adjusting entries that must be considered: accruals and deferrals. To understand how these adjustments are used it is first necessary to be familiar with the nature of a particular business.

Most businesses are on what is called the **accrual basis.** This system assumes that revenue is recognized when earned, regardless of when the revenue is actually received in the form of cash, and that expenses are recognized when incurred (e.g., rent for December is an expense for December, even if it isn't paid until January), regardless of when payment in the form of cash is actually made. This concept is known as the **principle of matching costs and revenue.**

Individuals, unlike businesses, are on the **cash basis.** This means that revenue is recognized when received and expenses are recognized when paid. Although there are situations where a business may be on the cash basis, we will assume here that all businesses are on the accrual basis.

YOU SHOULD REMEMBER

Adjusting entries are usually recorded at the end of the accounting period.

The purpose of these entries is to ensure that the principle of matching costs and revenue is followed.

Adjusting entries may represent accruals or deferrals.

ACCRUALS

The word "accrue" means to accumulate. In accounting it is necessary to recognize that, although certain items may have accumulated, they may not have been recognized as yet. Such an accumulation of items is known as an **accrual.**

ACCRUED EXPENSES

Frequently, expense items have been incurred but have not necessarily been recorded, because the business either is not obligated to pay the expense yet or for any number of reasons has failed to do so. When this situation occurs, it is necessary to record an adjusting entry.

Example: Adjusting Entry for Accrued Expenses

Let's say that the December, 198–, rent is due to be paid at the beginning of December. The amount of the payment should be $500. The business fails to pay the rent by December 31, which is the end of the accounting period. The following journal entry represents the adjusting entry that the accountant would prepare on December 31, 198–:

198–
Dec. 31   Rent Expense   500
                 Rent Payable   500
            To recognize the expense for Dec.

By recording this adjusting entry, the business is able to recognize an expense incurred during the accounting period that includes the month of December, even though the actual expense will not be paid until the following accounting period. The principle of matching costs and revenue has been met. When an income statement for the year ending December 31, 198–, is prepared, it will properly include rent expense for the year, including the expense for December. In this situation when the rent is actually paid in the new year, the following entry will be recorded in the journal:

198–
Jan. 4   Rent Payable   500
                Cash   500
           To pay Dec. rent past due.

In our earlier discussion of current assets, it was stated that a current asset is one that will be used up or converted to cash within a year or less. The asset supplies, for instance, is generally classified as a current asset. It is anticipated that part if not all of the asset supplies will be used up within the course of an accounting period. The ledger account for supplies records the beginning balance in the account as well as increases due to purchases and decreases as a result of supplies being returned. If the accountant takes a physical count of the supplies at the end of the accounting period, this count will probably represent a dollar cost assigned to the supplies that is less than the value as stated in the ledger account. The reason for this is that the supplies were probably used up in part during the period. A supply that is used up is considered to have become an expense. It becomes necessary to recognize this expense on the books—thus the need for an adjusting entry.

Example: Adjusting Entry to Recognize Expense

The balance in the supplies ledger account on December 31, 198–, indicates a debit balance of $1,200. An actual physical count of the supplies on hand indicates that the value of these supplies is actually $750. The difference between the value of the supplies on hand and the balance in the account indicates that $450 worth of supplies has been used up. It becomes necessary for the accountant to record the following adjusting entry to recognize the expense and at the same time to adjust the supplies account so that it shows the true value of the supplies on hand:

198–
Dec. 31   Supplies Expense   450
                     Supplies   450
              To recognize the supplies used up.

Let us examine the ledger account affected as a result of the posting of this adjusting entry.

Supplies				Supplies Expense		
198–		198–		198–		
Dec. 31	1,200	Dec. 31	450	Dec. 31	450	

As a result of the adjusting entry, the supplies used up ($450) have been recognized as an expense, and at the same time the value of the asset supplies has been reduced by the amount of the supplies no longer in existence.

These two examples illustrate **unrecorded expenses** that have been adjusted at the end of the accounting period. Any current asset that is subject to use and thus becomes an expense is treated in the same manner as in the supplies illustration. When an expense has been incurred but not yet paid, as in the case of the rent expense, it is treated in a similar fashion. Note that the rent expense was *not* paid in December, so it became necessary to set up a liability when recognizing the rent expense. **Complete Computational Problem 1, Part A** (p. 109).

ACCRUED REVENUE

In Computational Problem 1, Part A, adjusting entries resulting in the recognition of expenses were highlighted. In each adjusting entry an accrual was made to recognize the expense. In some cases the expense had not been paid; thus, to recognize it a liability had to be set up. In other situations a current asset that was used up was converted to an expense through the adjusting process.

The principle of accrued expenses can also apply to **accrued revenue.** When income has been earned as a result of a service provided but payment is not yet due from the customer, we record the transaction as a credit sale of services. In doing so we are accruing revenue. This kind of transaction is not normally considered an adjusting entry because of the nature of credit transactions. When we provide a service on credit, it is important for us to record the revenue and the resulting accounts or notes receivable, so that we have a record of who owes us money as a result of the credit sale.

There are situations where revenue earned has not been recognized because it has not been received. Accrued revenue represents revenue that has been accumulating during the accounting period and that will probably be received during a future accounting period. Thus, it has not been recognized in the current accounting period. It is the accountant's responsibility to recognize this **unrecorded revenue** and to see that an appropriate adjusting entry is made.

Example: Adjusting Entry for Unrecorded Revenue

A customer borrowed $1,000, giving you a 90-day promissory note that called for interest at the annual rate of 8%.

The note began to earn interest on December 1, 198–, which was the date the note was given to you. The agreement calls for the interest on the note to be paid to you on the date that the note becomes due. Since the interest income will not be received until the note is due, an adjusting entry is necessary to recognize the unrecorded revenue. Assuming that the accounting period ends on December 31, 198–, it will be necessary to recognize accrued revenue from December 1 through December 31 of the current year. The income earned but not received and not recognized would be calculated as $1,000 (amount owed) × 8% (interest rate) × 1/12 (30 days as compared to a banking year, which consists of 360 days) = $6.67 (accrued interest). The appropriate journal entry is:

198–
Dec. 31   Interest Receivable   6.67
               Interest Income   6.67
               For interest earned but not yet received on
               90-day note.

Note that this entry is very similar to the first example of an unrecorded expense. In that situation a liability was established in order to recognize the expense. In this case an asset interest receivable is set up. It would not be appropriate to debit the notes receivable account because the face value of the note has not changed.

When the note becomes due on March 1 of the new accounting period, the following entry will be made:

198–
Mar. 1   Cash   1,020.00
               Interest Receivable   6.67
               Interest Income   13.33
               Notes Receivable   1,000.00
               Customer paid maturity value of promissory note
               due today.

If the interest-bearing promissory note had come due in the same accounting period as when it was issued, there would have been no need for an adjusting entry. The above entry would have combined the interest receivable and the interest income entries with the $20 being credited to interest income.

YOU SHOULD REMEMBER

An accrual adjusting entry recognizes expenses that have been accrued but not yet paid.

It may also represent the recognition of income earned but not yet received.

Accrual adjusting entries are made at the end of the accounting period so as to properly match costs and revenue for that period.

DEFERRALS

We have seen that adjusting entries can result from unrecorded expenses and unrecorded revenue. The accumulation of these items and their subsequent adjusting entries are known as "accruals." The required adjusting entries affect liabilities and/or assets.

It is also possible to encounter situations in which expenses recorded during an accounting period have not actually been used up to the extent indicated in the account. Revenue recognized during an accounting period may not have been entirely earned, even though recorded as such. When the accountant becomes aware of these facts, he or she must record an adjusting entry known as a **deferral.** A deferral represents the postponement of the recognition of either an expense or a revenue item.

Certain business transactions may be interpreted differently depending on the accountant or the philosophy of the business, as well as the nature of the transaction. A simple business transaction, such as the payment of the monthly rent, can be handled in two different ways:

1. Since the rent payment represents a right to use property that will be used up at the end of each month, the rent should initially be recorded as an expense.

2. Since the rent payment represents a right to use property and that property has a money value, the rent can be considered a form of asset. Since rent is usually payable at the beginning of the month and the right to use the property extends to the end of the month, the rent is an asset.

Both approaches are reasonable and appropriate, given the proper circumstances. If the first approach is used and the rent is recognized as an expense, no adjusting entry is necessary except in the following situation:

Example: Adjusting Entry for Deferral

The terms of the 1-year lease on the premises that was signed and became effective on November 1, 198–, were:

The annual rent is $6,000. It is to be paid in two installments of 50% each. The first installment is due November 1, 198–. The entry made to reflect this transaction is as follows:

```
198–
Nov. 1   Rent Expense                            3,000
             Cash                                        3,000
         For 6-month prepayment.
```

Notice that the rent expense recognized is for 6 months. The number of months remaining in this accounting period is 2: If we do not prepare an adjusting entry, the rent expense for the year will be overstated. Ask yourself three questions:

1. For what period of time did we prepay the rent? (Six months)
2. How many months and what amount should actually be recognized as an expense through the end of the accounting period? (Two months, $1,000)
3. What adjusting entry should be made, and what will the deferral of the expense create? It should be obvious that the existing expense is overstated to the extent of 4 months and $2,000. To correct this situation the following entry is made:

```
198–
Dec. 31   Prepaid Rent                           2,000
              Rent Expense                             2,000
          To defer 4 months' rent
```

The credit to rent expense reduces the expense to be recognized for the accounting period (a postponement). The debit entry converts the expense to an account generally known as a **prepaid expense.** This term is somewhat confusing because of its literal meaning: it represents an expense that was paid in advance. Since the expense was paid in advance and at this point is not used up, it is actually classified as an *asset*.

If the accountant had used the second approach, considering the rent payment to represent an asset or initially a prepaid expense, then the entry for the payment would have been the following:

```
198–
Nov. 1   Prepaid Rent (or Rent)                  3,000
             Cash                                        3,000
         For 6-month prepayment.
```

This approach assumes that the item initially is an asset and that by the end of the accounting period the portion of prepaid rent that has been used up will be converted to an expense in a similar fashion to the conversion of supplies to an expense. In this case the adjusting entry would be:

198–
Dec. 31   Rent Expense   1,000
          Prepaid Rent   1,000
          To recognize the expense for the 2 months.

Note that the adjustment permits the recognition of the proper expense for the period and at the same time corrects the asset prepaid rent to show a proper balance of $2,000 for the remaining 4 months. This approach is an accrual.

When an expense previously paid has not been fully used up, it is necessary to defer the portion not used and convert it to an asset. The usual title of such an asset has the term "prepaid" placed before it. Accounts such as prepaid insurance, prepaid supplies, prepaid rent, and prepaid commissions were all created as a result of an adjusting entry when it became necessary to postpone the recognition of an expense already paid for.

DEFERRED REVENUE

When revenue has been received but not earned entirely within the accounting period, recognition of the revenue must be deferred. **Unearned revenue** represents revenue received but not earned within the accounting period, and the accountant must record an adjusting entry to defer this income. The principle of matching costs and revenue requires that revenue be recognized when earned, regardless of when received. Here the situation is that the revenue has been received, and yet it may not be earned until some future period.

Example: Adjusting Entry for Unearned Revenue

You receive a rent check from your tenant on November 1, 198–. The check is for $800 and is payment of 4 months' rent beginning with November. The entry recorded upon receipt of the check is as follows:

198–
Nov. 1   Cash   800
         Income from Rental   800
         Four months' rent beginning this date.

At the end of the accounting period, what adjusting entry would the accountant have to make? Obviously, if the income received represents 4 months' rental income, then part of the income should be recognized; however, the balance would have to be deferred. The following adjusting entry would be recorded:

198–
Dec. 31   Income from Rental   400
         Unearned Rental Income (*Liability*)   400
         To defer unearned rent.

The deferral of the income permits the income for the period to be properly stated. The adjustment also results in the recognition of a *liability* for the income received, but at this point not earned. The tenant has the right to use the premises for the months of January and February. The landlord has an obligation to supply the premises; thus, a liability exists as a result of the adjusting entry.

During the next accounting period, when the income actually becomes earned, the following entry would be made. This entry could be made at the very beginning of the new year (as will be discussed shortly) or at the time the income actually becomes fully earned.

198–
Jan. 1   Unearned Rental Income   400
            Income from Rental   400
            To recognize income earned in the new year.

Complete Computational Problem 2, Part A (pp. 109–110).

YOU SHOULD REMEMBER

A deferral represents a postponement.

Expenses paid but not fully used up must be deferred. An adjusting entry will bring about reduction of the expense and establishment of an asset in an account preceded by the term "prepaid."

Revenue received in advance but not entirely earned by the end of the accounting period must be deferred. An adjusting entry reduces the revenue recognized and establishes a liability in an account usually preceded by the term "unearned."

ADJUSTING NONCURRENT ASSETS

Noncurrent, or plant, assets are subject to a loss in value due to the item being used. A current asset such as supplies obviously loses value because the item is used up. The loss in value of plant assets is not obvious because the asset still exists in its complete form at the end of the accounting period. It is necessary, however, to recognize a loss in value due to use.

This loss is known as **depreciation,** which is the recognition of a loss in value of a plant asset due to wear and tear over its useful life. When depreciation is recognized as an adjusting entry at the end of the accounting period, an expense is charged. Since the expense does not represent an actual outlay of cash, and the cost principle prevents us from reducing the value of the asset directly, it becomes necessary to credit a new account entitled "Accumulated Depreciation." The following entry illustrates the recognition of depreciation of office equipment at the end of the accounting period:

198–
Dec. 31   Depreciation Expense—Office Equip.   300
                    Accumulated Depreciation   300
              To record annual depreciation.

This adjusting entry recognizes the expense and records a credit entry to the accumulated depreciation account. This account is classified as a **contra-asset.** The purpose of the account is merely to offset the plant asset account. The net or book value of the plant asset is determined by subtracting the accumulated depreciation account from the value of the plant asset. The most commonly used form of depreciation is known as the **straight-line method.** Under this method, the value of the asset is divided by its useful life in years to determine the amount of depreciation to be recognized annually:

$$\frac{\text{Cost of asset}}{\text{Useful life}} = \text{Annual depreciation}$$

Example: Adjusting Entry for Depreciation

The original cost of a truck is $20,000. The truck is expected to have a useful life of 10 years and at the end of 10 years to have no value. The annual depreciation on the truck would be determined as follows:

$$\frac{\text{Cost of asset}}{\text{Useful life}} = \frac{\$20,000}{10 \text{ Years}} = \frac{\$2,000 \text{ Annual}}{\text{Depreciation}}$$

The method used to determine depreciation may change, but the adjusting entry to recognize depreciation is the same. We indicated that adjusting entries can be made as frequently as once a month or whenever necessary. We are still assuming that these accruals and deferrals are being made annually. To find depreciation for 1 month, we would first find it for 1 year and divide the result by 12.

When a plant asset is expected to have a **residual value** or scrap value at the end of its useful life, this value is not subject to depreciation. If the asset in the preceding example had a scrap value of $1,000, then the annual depreciation recognized would amount to $1,900. After the asset had been fully depreciated, the book value and the residual value would be the same. The following calculation would be made, assuming a scrap value of $1,000:

$$\frac{\text{Cost of asset} - \text{Scrap value}}{\text{Useful life}} = \frac{\$20,000 - \$1,000}{10 \text{ Years}} = \frac{\$1,900 \text{ Annual}}{\text{Depreciation}}$$

Complete Computational Problem 3, Part A (p. 110).

YOU SHOULD REMEMBER

A loss in value of a plant or fixed asset is recognized through an adjusting entry for depreciation.

Depreciation is the recognition of a loss in value of a fixed asset over its useful life.

• *RECORDING ADJUSTING ENTRIES*
PREPARING THE WORKSHEET

Adjusting entries recorded at the end of the accounting period permit revenue to be recognized when earned and expenses to be recognized when incurred. Since the adjustment process can take place monthly as well as annually, the accountant may be called upon to prepare financial statements following the adjusting process. To expedite the preparation of financial statements and the preparation of adjustments prior to statement preparation, the **worksheet** is prepared.

In Chapter 3 we discussed and illustrated the preparation of the trial balance, which was used to verify that the ledger was in balance. The trial balance is prepared before adjusting entries are recorded and becomes the backbone of the worksheet. Some accountants define a worksheet as an expanded trial balance, which it literally is. Unlike financial statements, the worksheet is used and viewed by the accountant only, so it is usually prepared in pencil. The form consists of a column to list the accounts from the ledger followed by eight money columns.

The preparation of the worksheet precedes the recording of adjusting entries. At the end of the accounting period or a month, a trial balance is prepared on the worksheet. Necessary adjusting entries are recorded directly on the worksheet using the adjustments columns. The information in the adjustments column is then extended, along with the trial balance information, to the remaining two sets of the worksheet columns, that is, the income statement and balance sheet columns.

Assets, liabilities, permanent capital, and the proprietor's drawing account are extended from the trial balance columns through the adjustments columns and recorded in the appropriate balance sheet column. Similarly, revenue and expenses are extended from the trial balance columns through the adjustments columns to the appropriate income statement column. (See page 98.) The function of the adjustments columns is to adjust the balances in the ledger accounts to match costs and revenue for the specific accounting period covered by the worksheet. No journal entries or related postings are made at this time. If the accountant is preparing interim statements from the worksheet, no adjusting journal entries will be made.

The illustration on page 95 shows the worksheet before adjusting entries have been recorded on it. The accountant gathers information relevant to the adjusting process. The adjusting entries are then recorded directly on the worksheet. **Complete Computational Problem 4, Part A** (p. 110), **which is based on the illustrative worksheet on page 98.**

Example: Worksheet Without Adjusting Entries

Avery Rental Services
Worksheet
For the Year Ended December 31, 198—

Account Title	Trial Balance		Adjustments		Income Statement		Balance Sheet	
	Debit	Credit	Debit	Credit	Debit	Credit	Debit	Credit
Cash	5600 00							
Accounts Receivable	1000 00							
Equipment	4500 00							
Accumulated Depreciation		1000 00						
Accounts Payable		500 00						
Avery, Capital		5000 00						
Avery, Drawing	900 00							
Rental Income		32000 00						
Salaries Expense	9000 00							
Supplies Expense	6500 00							
Rent Expense	11000 00							
	38500 00	38500 00						

HOW TO RECORD ADJUSTING ENTRIES ON THE WORKSHEET

The trial balance contains only accounts that have balances as of December 31, 198–. When adjustments must be recorded to the worksheet for missing accounts, such as adjustment (a) noted below, the needed account is added below the trial balance. Notice that letters are used to relate debit adjustments to corresponding credits. Once the adjustments have been recorded in the adjustments column, the accountant will foot the debit and credit adjustments columns. If the totals are in agreement, they are then double underscored.

Accounts not having adjustments are simply extended to the appropriate set of columns. Thus, assets and the proprietor's drawing account are extended to the debit side of the balance sheet column. Liabilities and the proprietor's capital are extended to the credit side of the balance sheet column. Revenue and expense accounts are extended to the credit and debit sides of the income statement, respectively. The extensions of the accounts that were affected by the adjustments are treated according to the specific adjustment.

Adjustment (a) causes a change in the accumulated depreciation account that began with a credit balance on the trial balance. There was a credit adjustment to it that caused it to increase to $1,500. This new *adjusted* balance is carried to the credit side of the balance sheet column. (Remember that this account is a contra-asset.) The debit entry to adjustment (a) recognizes a depreciation expense and extends the amount to the debit, or expense, side of the income statement column.

Adjustment (b) causes an increase in salaries expense that is extended to the debit side of the income statement column. The corresponding credit to salaries payable establishes this liability, which was not previously on the books, and extends the amount to the credit side of the balance sheet column.

Adjustment (c) reduces rental income as a result of its not having been earned, causing the balance in the account to be reduced and extended to the credit, or income, side of the income statement column. The corresponding credit establishes the liability unearned rental income, which is extended to the credit side of the balance sheet column.

Adjustment (d) recognizes that what had been considered to be entirely an expense apparently is still in inventory. This causes a reduction in the supplies expense, the new balance of which is extended to the debit side of the income statement column and creates the prepaid supplies account (an asset) with the extension to the debit side of the balance sheet column.

Following the extensions of the trial balance and adjustments to entry amounts, the four remaining columns are footed. Note that the results of the footing are four different totals. Comparison reveals, however, that the differences between the two income statement column totals and the two balance sheet column totals are the same. The reason that the same difference appears is that this difference represents either a net income or a net loss.

In the illustrative worksheet, note that there is an excess of credits on the income statement column as compared with debits. This excess represents net income, which is shown on the debit side of the income statement to allow the two columns to be balanced. Note that the debit total exceeds the credit total on the balance sheet columns. This is the case because the income earned by the business has not yet been transferred to the owner of the business (it is not reflected in Avery's capital account). Remember that temporary capital accounts are eventually transferred to the proprietor's capital account.

If the balances in the income statement and the balance sheet columns had been reversed, this would mean that the business had sustained a loss. A credit entry to get the income statement columns to balance would indicate that the total expenses (debits) exceeded the total revenues (credits). This loss would be reflected in a debit entry to get the balance sheet columns to agree. The debit entry would represent the net loss that would have to be taken out of the proprietor's capital account.

The extension of the drawing account is made to the debit side of the balance sheet column. This is done because the drawing account has a reducing effect on proprietor's permanent capital.

USING THE COMPLETED WORKSHEET

If the accountant had been requested to prepare interim financial statements, the information needed could be taken directly from the worksheet. There would be no need to journalize and post adjusting entries. This is especially important if a company normally adjusts its books only at the end of the accounting period. If the worksheet is prepared at the end of the accounting period, the accountant can record and post the adjusting entries properly after preparing the worksheet.

Financial statement preparation is greatly expedited by the preparation of the worksheet. The actual adjustment to the books can take place at any future time without holding up the preparation of these statements. In preparing the statements from the worksheet, the income statement is taken directly from the income statement columns of the worksheet. The preparation of the statement of capital requires the accountant to obtain the beginning capital balance from the balance sheet, as well as the drawing and net income figures. In the preparation of the balance sheet all the information in the balance sheet columns is used, except for the drawing, net income or loss, and proprietor's capital balance. The statement of capital will provide the new capital balance for the proprietor. **Complete Computational Problem 5, Part A** (pp. 110–111).

Example: Worksheet with Adjusting Entries

Avery Rental Services
Worksheet
For the Year Ended December 31, 198–

Account Title	Trial Balance		Adjustments		Income Statement		Balance Sheet	
	Debit	Credit	Debit	Credit	Debit	Credit	Debit	Credit
Cash	5600 00						5600 00	
Accounts Receivable	1000 00						1000 00	
Equipment	4500 00						4500 00	
Accumulated Depreciation		1000 00		(a) 500 00				1500 00
Accounts Payable		500 00						500 00
Avery, Capital		5000 00						5000 00
Avery, Drawing	900 00						900 00	
Rental Income		32000 00	(c) 1200 00			30800 00		
Salaries Expense	9000 00		(b) 120 00		9120 00			
Supplies Expense	6500 00			(d) 600 00	5900 00			
Rent Expense	11000 00				11000 00			
	38500 00	38500 00						
Depreciation Expense			(a) 500 00		500 00			
Salaries Payable				(b) 120 00				120 00
Unearned Rental Income				(c) 1200 00				1200 00
Prepaid Supplies			(d) 600 00				600 00	
			2420 00	2420 00	26520 00	30800 00	12600 00	8320 00
Net Income					4280 00			4280 00
					30800 00	30800 00	12600 00	12600 00

YOU SHOULD REMEMBER

A worksheet is an invaluable tool in preparing financial statements.

When the worksheet is prepared in the interim, adjusting journalization and posting is not necessary.

A year-end worksheet expedites the preparation of the financial statements, as well as the journalizing and posting of adjusting and closing entries.

CHART OF ACCOUNTS

If you wanted to find where a particular topic is covered in this book, you would use the table of contents at the beginning of the book. In organizing the ledger the accountant will establish a **chart of accounts,** which is comparable to a table of contents. The purpose of the chart of accounts is to provide the user of the ledger with a means of determining the accounts included in the ledger and their locations within the ledger. The organization of the chart of accounts follows the accounting equation format very closely, in that the chart lists asset accounts first, followed by liability accounts and then proprietor's capital, drawing, revenue, and expense accounts. In every ledger and trial balance form previously presented this format has been followed. Note that the numbering of the account pages also follows this format. The asset accounts are assigned the numbering series beginning with 100. Liabilities are assigned the 200 series, and capital accounts use the 300 series.

Example: Typical Chart of Accounts Found on the First Page of a Ledger

Chart of Accounts

	Assets		
	Cash	101	
	Accounts Receivable	102	
	Supplies	105	
	Equipment	120	
	Liabilities		
	Accounts Payable	201	
	Notes Payable	205	
	Capital		
J. Jones, Capital	300	Salaries Expense	355
J. Jones, Drawing	301	Supplies Expense	356
Service Revenue	310	Insurance Expense	357
Rental Revenue	320	Utilities Expense	358
Commission Revenue	330	Miscellaneous Expenses	370
Rent Expense	350	Income Summary	400

Notice that, even though the accounts are listed in numerical order, not all numbers have been used. This is to allow for future expansion when additional accounts will need to be inserted in the correct areas of the ledger.

YOU SHOULD REMEMBER

A chart of accounts, because of its logical organization, enables the user to locate a specific account quickly in the ledger.

CLOSING ENTRIES

In Chapter 1 we distinguished between permanent and temporary capital accounts. Temporary capital accounts consist of the proprietor's drawing account and all of the revenue and expense accounts. The word "temporary" means NOT permanent or subject to change. Temporary accounts are eventually eliminated, and their contents transferred to permanent capital. We accomplish this through the preparation of the statement of capital. The *statement of capital* compares the drawing account with the net income or loss shown by the income statement. The resulting balance causes either an increase or a decrease in the proprietor's capital. While this process is necessary in order to prepare financial statements, it must also be reflected in the various ledger accounts. This is accomplished through the recording of **closing entries.**

The closing entry involves transferring the balances of the temporary capital accounts to the proprietor's permanent capital account. To accomplish this, each temporary capital account must be either debited or credited to eliminate its balance, while a corresponding debit or credit is summarized in another temporary account designed exclusively for that purpose. This new temporary account is known as the **income summary** or **net earnings summary.** The name of the account may vary from business to business, but the closing process remains basically the same.

The procedure for closing the ledger accounts is as follows:

1. All revenue accounts are closed to the income summary account.

2. All expense accounts are closed to the income summary account.

3. The proprietor's drawing account is closed to the income summary account.

4. The income summary account is closed to the proprietor's permanent capital account.

Example: Closing Entries

The following partial trial balance is illustrated for Mary Lang Co. (after adjusting entries have been recorded and posted to the ledger):

<table>
<tr><td colspan="3" align="center">**Mary Lang Co.**
Trial Balance
December 31, 198–</td></tr>
<tr><td></td><td>DEBIT</td><td>CREDIT</td></tr>
<tr><td>Mary Lang, Capital</td><td></td><td>5,000</td></tr>
<tr><td>Mary Lang, Drawing</td><td>645</td><td></td></tr>
<tr><td>Service Revenue</td><td></td><td>2,000</td></tr>
<tr><td>Rental Revenue</td><td></td><td>1,200</td></tr>
<tr><td>Salaries Expense</td><td>800</td><td></td></tr>
<tr><td>Rent Expense</td><td>450</td><td></td></tr>
<tr><td>Miscellaneous Expenses</td><td>1,250</td><td></td></tr>
</table>

The following closing entries would be recorded in the ledger of the Mary Lang Co.:

198–

Dec. 31	Service Revenue	2,000	
	Rental Revenue	1,200	
	Income Summary		3,200
	To close revenue to income summary.		
31	Income Summary	2,500	
	Salaries Expense		800
	Rent Expense		450
	Miscellaneous Expenses		1,250
	To close expense to income summary.		
31	Income Summary	645	
	Mary Lang, Drawing		645
	To close expense to income summary.		
31	Income Summary	55	
	Mary Lang, Capital		55
	To close income summary to capital.		

Notice the effects on the individual ledger accounts as a result of these closing entries being posted.

Mary Lang, Capital		
	198–	
	Balance	5,000
	Dec. 31	55

Mary Lang, Drawing			
198–		198–	
Balance	645	Dec. 31	645

Services Revenue			
198–		198–	
Dec. 31	2,000	Balance	2,000

Rental Revenue			
198–		198–	
Dec. 31	1,200	Balance	1,200

Salaries Expense			
198–		198–	
Balance	800	Dec. 31	800

Rent Expense			
198–		198–	
Balance	450	Dec. 31	450

Miscellaneous Expenses			
198–		198–	
Balance	1,250	Dec. 31	1,250

Income Summary			
198–		198–	
Dec. 31	2,500	Dec. 31	3,200
31	645		
31	55		

After the closing entries have been journalized and posted, the only accounts that will have balances in the ledger will be the permanent accounts—namely, assets, liabilities, and proprietor's permanent capital. The temporary accounts will still be found in the ledger; however, these accounts will now have no balances.

The process of closing the ledger takes place at the end of the accounting period, so that at the start of the next accounting period the accountant can begin to accumulate information in the temporary accounts again. Remember that the income statement covers a period of time. The closing process permits the elimination of one accounting period's temporary accounts, and thus the accumulation of revenue, expenses, and proprietor's drawings begins again in the following period. **Complete Computational Problem 6, Part A (p. 111).**

YOU SHOULD REMEMBER

Closing entries are recorded at the end of the accounting period. These entries close the temporary capital accounts, and the resulting balances either increase or decrease the proprietor's permanent capital.

POST-CLOSING TRIAL BALANCE

End-of-the-year activities involve the preparation of the worksheet, making any necessary adjusting entries. The next step is to journalize and post these adjusting entries. Closing entries are then journalized and posted. The adjusting and closing process has a dramatic effect on the ledger, in that the trial balance prepared to verify that the ledger was in balance is no longer valid. It then becomes necessary to prove that the ledger is still in balance.

To do this, the accountant prepares another trial balance, called a **post-closing trial balance.** Prepared at the end of the accounting period, the post-closing trial balance differs significantly from the previous trial balance in that its accounts reflect adjusting entries that have been made and its temporary accounts no longer have balances. Successful completion of the post-closing trial balance proves that the ledger is in balance at the end of the accounting period. Before recording any business transactions for the new accounting period, this post-closing trial balance must be prepared. **Complete Computational Problem 7, Part A** (p. 112).

YOU SHOULD REMEMBER

The preparation of a trial balance and a post-closing trial balance enables the accountant to check that the ledger is in balance.

STEPS IN THE ACCOUNTING CYCLE

We will assume that the accountant is called upon to prepare financial statements once a year at the end of the accounting period. Given this fact, the following steps would be followed in maintaining accounting records for the accounting cycle:

1. Journalize daily business transactions.

2. Post to the various ledger accounts.

3. Prepare a trial balance monthly.

4. Prepare a worksheet with necessary adjusting entries at the end of the accounting period.

5. Prepare financial statements from the year-end worksheet.

6. Journalize and post adjusting entries to the ledger.

7. Journalize and post closing entries to the ledger.

8. Prepare a post-closing trial balance.

When the accountant is requested to prepare **interim financial statements,** the procedures just presented are slightly modified. Since in most business organizations adjusting entries are journalized and posted at the end of the accounting period, to do so during the year would entail additional unnecessary work. An interim statement is prepared at any time other than the end of the accounting period. The accountant may prepare these statements monthly, quarterly, semi-annually, or for any period of time of less than 1 year. Generally accepted accounting principles require that adjustments take place to reflect revenue and expenses properly; however, for interim purposes these adjustments need not be reflected in the journal or ledger.

In preparing an interim statement the accountant prepares the worksheet with adjusting entries reflecting the specific period of time covered by the statement, but does not journalize or post the adjusting entries or prepare closing entries. Journalizing and posting adjusting and closing entries takes place only at the end of the accounting period.

REVERSING ENTRIES

The process of recording adjusting entries creates certain ledger accounts that are not normally recorded to in the accounting period. For example, in the process of recognizing accrued salaries, the salaries payable account is established. Note the following adjusting entry:

198–
Dec. 31   Salaries Expense   1,800
           Salaries Payable   1,800
           To recognize accrued salaries

Although the salaries payable account will be listed on the chart of accounts and an actual page for it will be found in the ledger, no entries are normally made in this account during the year, with the exception of the adjusting entry just illustrated. The payroll clerk or bookkeeper in charge of preparing the payroll at the end of the week is familiar with the basic procedure of recording the salaries expense and reducing the amount of cash.

Example: Need for a Reversing Entry

Salaries are paid on Friday for the week ending that day. December 31 ends on Tuesday, and salaries are not to be paid until Friday of that week. Accrued salaries for those 2 days amount to $1,800. The following adjusting entry is recorded by the accountant as part of the adjusting process:

198–
Dec. 31   Salaries Expense   1,800
           Salaries Payable   1,800
           To recognize accrued salaries

As a result of closing the ledger at the end of the accounting period, the salaries expense account will have a zero balance going into the new accounting period. We recognize that salaries payable, being a liability, will appear on the post-closing trial balance and will have a balance at the beginning of the new accounting period. When the payroll entry is made on January 3 of the new year, the amount of the payroll is $4,500. The payroll clerk is used to recording the following entry and would normally do so on January 3:

```
198–
Jan. 3    Salaries Expense                        4,500
              Cash                                            4,500
          For the week ending today
```

How much of this expense should be recognized in the new year? (Only $2,700 representing three days' earnings in the new year.)

How much of this expense has already been recognized in the preceding year? ($1,800 as a result of the December 31 adjusting entry.)

How much of the expense was recognized by the bookkeeper on January 3? ($4,500)

Since the bookkeeper or payroll clerk are not expected to be involved with the adjusting entry process, the above problem can be solved by recording a reversing entry on the first day of the new accounting period. The ledger accounts following the preparation of the post-closing trial balance appear as follows:

Salaries Expense		Salaries Payable	
		198–	
		Dec. 31	1,800

Since the salaries payable account is not one of the accounts found to have a balance during the year, the accountant will record the following reversal entry:

```
198–
Jan. 1    Salaries Payable                         1,800
              Salaries Expense                             1,800
          To reverse adjusting entry
```

Note that the reversal entry is the exact opposite of the adjusting entry recorded on December 31. Notice the effect this entry has when posted to the ledger accounts.

Salaries Expense		Salaries Payable			
198–		198–		198–	
Jan. 1 (New		Jan. 1 (New		Dec. 31	1,800
Year)	1,800	Year)	1,800		

The balance in the salaries payable account has been eliminated, and the balance transferred to the salaries expense account as a **credit balance,** which, in effect, says that this expense account is temporarily being classified as a liability. When the bookkeeper makes the entry paying the payroll on January 3 (as shown above), the effect of the posting on the salaries expense account will be as follows:

Salaries Expense

198–	198–
Jan. 3 Payment 4,500	Jan 3 (reversal) 1,800

What is the balance in the salaries expense account on January 3? ($2,700)

What is the total salaries expense that should be paid for the week ending January 3? ($4,500)

What was the salaries expense recognized for the old year as a result of the adjusting entry? ($1,800)

What is the salaries expense that is being recognized for the new year as of January 3? ($2,700)

• *WHEN TO USE REVERSING ENTRIES*

A **reversing entry** is required whenever an adjusting entry results in the establishment on the books of an account that normally does not carry a balance during the year. The reversing entry will take place on the first day of the new accounting period, and the entry will be the exact reverse of the previous adjusting entry recorded.

Example: Use of a Reversing Entry

At the end of the accounting period, the balance in the supplies expense account is $900. After a physical inventory, it is determined that $125 in supplies has not been used up and has to be adjusted.

1. Record the necessary adjusting entry.

2. Record the closing entry necessary based on the information provided.

3. Record the reversal entry.

(Old Year)

Dec. 31	Prepaid Supplies (Asset)	125
	Supplies Expense		125
	To recognize the expense not used up during the accounting period.	
31	Income Summary	775
	Supplies Expense		775
	To close the expense account.	

(New Year)

Jan. 1   Supplies Expense   125
              Prepaid Supplies   125
          To record the reversal entry.

Note the effects on the accounts after these entries have been posted.

Supplies Expense				Prepaid Supplies			
198–		198–		198–		198–	
Balance	900	Dec. 31	125	Dec. 31	125	Jan. 1	125
Jan. 1	125	31	775				

What was the supplies expense recognized in the old year? ($775)

What account did the adjusting entry establish, and how is it classified? (Prepaid supplies are classified as an asset.)

What did the reversing entry convert the asset prepaid supplies into? (Supplies expense.)

What benefit does the reversing entry provide in this instance? (The supplies expense has been reestablished with a balance of $125, which represents a probable expense in the new year.)

The question of whether to record reversing entries is left to the discretion of the accountant. We have previously discussed situations where adjusting entries created balances in accounts that are not normally used during the accounting period. Although it is advisable to utilize reversing entries, it is not mandatory to do so. In a situation where the bookkeeper is not familiar with reversible accounts, it is advisable to record reversing entries. On the other hand, when the bookkeeper or accounting clerk is familiar with the accounts established as a result of adjusting entries and can properly record future period transactions involving them, reversing entries may not be needed. **Complete Computational Problems 8 and 9, Part A (p. 112).**

YOU SHOULD REMEMBER

Reversing entries are recorded at the beginning of the new accounting period.

Completion of these entries makes it easier for the accountant to monitor the recording of the daily business transactions by the bookkeepers and accounting clerks.

> For more practice in mastering the material in this chapter, **complete Computational Problems 1, 2, 3, and 4, Part B** (pp. 113–114).

KNOW THE CONCEPTS

DO YOU KNOW THE BASICS?

Below are listed, in random order, ten procedures necessary for the maintenance of adequate, appropriate accounting records. Test your knowledge of this chapter by placing the items in correct chronological order, that is, by listing the ten numbers in the order in which the procedures should be done.

1. At the beginning of the new accounting period, reversal entries are recorded to eliminate accounts established as a result of the adjusting process.

2. Financial statements are prepared from the year-end worksheet.

3. Business transactions are journalized on a daily basis.

4. Business transactions are posted to appropriate ledger accounts.

5. The balance in the ledger is verified by the preparation of the post-closing trial balance.

6. A trial balance proving that the ledger is in balance is usually prepared monthly.

7. At the end of the accounting period, a worksheet is prepared with the necessary adjusting entries for the year.

8. A worksheet is prepared whenever interim financial statements are needed by the organization.

9. Closing entries are journalized and posted, causing the temporary capital accounts to be closed to income summary, and the resulting balance closed to proprietor's permanent capital.

10. Adjusting entries on the year-end worksheet are journalized and posted to the ledger.

TERMS FOR STUDY

accrual	net earnings summary
accrual basis	post-closing trial balance
accrual revenue	prepaid expense
cash basis	principle of matching costs and revenue
chart of accounts	residual value
contra-asset account	straight-line method
credit balance	unearned revenue
deferral	unrecorded expenses
depreciation	unrecorded revenue
interim financial statement	worksheet

PRACTICAL APPLICATION

PART A. COMPUTATIONAL PROBLEMS WITH COMPLETE SOLUTIONS

1. Record the appropriate adjusting journal entries for the following situations. Assume that the accounting period ends on December 31, 198–, and that all adjusting entries are made as of that date.

   (a) A physical count of office supplies indicates that $250 worth of office supplies were used up during the accounting period.

   (b) Rent totaling $800 for the months of November and December has not been paid by December 31, 198–.

   (c) You received a bill from the *Daily Standard News* for advertisements placed in the newspaper during the second week of November. The bill is for $200, not to be paid until January 15, 198–.

   (d) On December 1, 198–, you borrowed $1,000 from the First City Bank. The bank charges you interest at an annual rate of 10% on the obligation, and interest is not to be repaid for 90 days. Record the adjusting entry to recognize the interest expense on the loan from December 1 to December 31, 198–.

   (e) On July 1, 198–, you took out a fire insurance policy on the business premises. At that time you recorded the insurance premium in an asset account entitled "Prepaid Insurance" for the amount of the yearly premium of $600. On December 31, 198–, record the adjusting entry for this asset. Remember: an asset that has been used up becomes an expense.

   (f) Salaries are paid on Fridays for the week ending on the same day. The salaries for the week amount to $5,000. The last day of the accounting period is Wednesday, December 31, 198–. Record the adjusting entry necessary to recognize the salaries expense for the last 3 days of the year. The actual payment of the week's salaries will not take place until January 2 of the following accounting period.

2. Record the following adjusting entries to reflect the accrual and deferral of expenses and revenue for the calendar year.

   (a) Recognized the interest income accumulated on a $5,000 note bearing interest of 9% dated November 2.

   (b) Recorded an adjusting entry to recognize that income from commissions previously received but not yet earned to the extent of 40% of the $800 commission.

   (c) Determined that the balance in the ledger account for office supplies was $990, but that an inventory showed only $260 worth of office supplies remaining.

   (d) Accrued salaries for the last 3 days in the old year amounting to $1,500.

   (e) Showed a balance of $2,270 in the prepaid insurance account. Insurance records indicate that $1,245 of the insurance expired during the year.

(f) Borrowed $6,000 for 90 days, with interest at an annual rate of 12%. The loan was taken out 45 days before the end of the accounting period and is due to be paid in full 45 days into the new year.

3. Office equipment was purchased at a cost of $3,400. It has an expected useful life of 6 years, and after it has been fully depreciated, it will have a scrap value of $400.

(a) How much of the asset is subject to depreciation?
(b) What will be the annual depreciation recognized?
(c) Assuming that the asset was acquired at the beginning of the year, record the adjusting entry to recognize depreciation for the first full year.
(d) Determine the book value of the asset after the first year's adjusting entry.
(e) What is the book value of the asset after it has been depreciated for 6 years?
(f) What happens to the book value of the asset during each year of its useful life? Why?
(g) When recording annual depreciation, why doesn't the accountant credit the asset account directly?

4. Record in journal form the following adjusting entries, using the information provided in the worksheet on page 95 for Avery Rental Services.

(a) Depreciation for the year amounts to $500.
(b) Salaries are paid on Friday for the week including the payday. December 31, 198–, falls on Thursday this year. The daily payroll amounts to $30. An adjusting entry is needed to recognize the accrual of salaries for 4 days.
(c) Included in the rental income account is income received but not yet earned amounting to $1,200.
(d) Supplies recognized as an expense amounting to $600 have not been used up during the current accounting period.

Verify the correctness of your journal entries by comparing them with the adjustments appearing on the completed worksheet on page 98.

5. The following trial balance was prepared for the Beldon Service Co. as of December 31, 198–.

Beldon Service Co.
Trial Balance
December 31, 198–

	DEBIT	CREDIT
Cash	16,900	
Accounts Receivable	2,000	
Prepaid Insurance	600	
Supplies	300	
Furniture	13,500	
Accumulated Depreciation		500
Accounts Payable		1,500
Notes Payable		8,000
L. Beldon, Capital		12,000
L. Beldon, Drawing	4,000	
Service Revenue		21,000
Rental Revenue		1,600
Salaries Expense	5,000	
Rent Expense	1,400	
Utilities Expense	900	
	44,600	44,600

The following information is provided for adjustment purposes:

(a) An analysis of the insurance files indicates that there is a balance in the insurance account of $400.
(b) Supplies used during the year amounted to $175.
(c) Depreciation expense on the furniture amounted to $500 for the year.
(d) Of the service revenue recorded, $400 was not earned for the current year.
(e) Salaries earned but not paid for the last week in the fiscal year amounted to $300.
(f) Interest expense incurred but not yet paid on a promissory note amounted to $40.

(a) Set up an eight-column worksheet, using the trial balance presented above.
(b) Record the adjusting entries directly on the worksheet, using the letters assigned.
(c) Complete the worksheet.
(d) Using the completed worksheet, prepare an income statement, statement of capital, and balance sheet.

6. Using the worksheet prepared for Computational Problem 5, set up a T-account for each account found in the trial balance. Record the balances in the individual T-accounts. Journalize the adjusting entries from the worksheet, and post to the T-accounts. Take the information as to proprietor's drawing, as well as the information in the income statement, and journalize and post the closing entries.

7. Having completed Computational Problem 6, prepare a post-closing trial balance for the Beldon Service Co.

8. On the basis of the following information, record the necessary adjusting entries. Having done so, record reversing entries where needed.

   (a) Salaries for the week amounted to $3,500. For the week ending January 4 (payday) record the adjusting entry needed for the old year.

   (b) The office supplies account has a balance before adjustments of $530; the office supplies inventory at the end of the year is $160.

   (c) The insurance expense on the trial balances has a balance of $1,350. An analysis of the various policies shows that $450 in unexpired premiums remain at the end of the year.

   (d) You signed a new lease with a tenant that requires the tenant to pay his rent for a 6-month period at $100 per month. The effective date of the lease was November 1. At that time you received a check for $600, which you credited to the rental income account.

9. The trial balance of the Brandeis Co. appears below. The company adjusts its books once a year. Using the information presented immediately following the trial balance, prepare the necessary adjusting entries.

Brandeis Co.
Trial Balance
December 31, 19–

Cash	$15,000	
Accounts Receivable	4,300	
Prepaid Insurance	4,700	
Supplies	6,000	
Office Equipment	20,000	
Accumulated Depreciation—Office Equipment		$ 3,000
Notes Payable		6,000
L. Brandeis, Capital		39,000
L. Brandeis, Drawing	5,000	
Revenue from Services		15,000
Salaries Expense	5,000	
Rent Expense	3,000	
	$63,000	$63,000

   (a) The balance in the prepaid insurance account represents the cost of an insurance policy that was purchased on February 1 of the current year. The original policy covers 2 years.

   (b) A physical inventory taken of the supplies on hand indicates a total of $2,500 of unused supplies as of December 31.

(c) The office equipment was acquired on July 1 (1½ years ago). It has an expected useful life of 10 years and will not have any residual value after the 10 years. Record the depreciation to be recognized for the current year.

(d) The notes payable account represents a note signed on April 1 of the current year. It is an 8%-interest-bearing note that is due in 2 years. Record the adjusting entry to recognize the accrued interest on the note.

(e) Of the revenue from services recorded, it was determined that $950 had been received but not earned as of the date of the trial balance.

(f) Accrued salaries for the last day of the year ending on Wednesday amounted to $70.

PART B. COMPUTATIONAL PROBLEMS WITH PARTIAL SOLUTIONS OR KEY ANSWERS

1. Prepare an eight-column worksheet from the trial balance of Exercise 9, Part A. Record the necessary adjusting entries to the worksheet, and prepare the three financial statements. Record the closing entries.

2. The trial balance of Meyer's Dry Cleaners on June 30, the end of the current fiscal year, appears below. Immediately following the trial balance is the information needed to record the year-end adjusting entries.

Meyer's Dry Cleaners
Trial Balance
June 30, 19–

Cash	$ 3,025	
Dry Cleaning Supplies	2,070	
Prepaid Insurance	820	
Laundry Equipment	53,650	
Accumulated Depreciation—Laundry Equipment		$19,700
Notes Payable		925
Sam Meyer, Capital		24,180
Sam Meyer, Drawing	12,600	
Revenue from Dry Cleaning		54,125
Salaries Expense	15,215	
Rent Expense	6,000	
Utilities Expense	4,550	
	$98,930	$98,930

(a) Year-end inventory of dry cleaning supplies amounted to $700.
(b) The expired insurance premium was $700.
(c) Annual depreciation on equipment was $1,950.
(d) Dry cleaning revenue earned, but not yet received, amounted to $375.
(e) Accrued salaries amounted to $250.
(f) Interest accrued on notes payable amounted to $85.

3. Prepare an eight-column worksheet based on the trial balance for Computational Problem 2. Complete the worksheet, recording the adjusting entries to it. From the completed worksheet prepare the three financial statements. Record the necessary two-column general journal closing entries.

4. The Freeport Marina is owned and operated by Fred Freeman. The primary business of the marina is the rental of dock space to owners of small boats in the area. The trial balance that follows is to be used to set up and record adjusting entries to a worksheet, using the information given below the trial balance. After the preparation of the eight-column worksheet, necessary closing entries are to be recorded, and the three financial statements prepared.

Freeport Marina
Trial Balance
December 31, 19–

Cash	$ 1,360	
Accounts Receivable	2,440	
Supplies	516	
Prepaid Insurance	742	
Dock	30,600	
Accumulated Depreciation—Dock		$ 5,000
Accounts Payable		1,100
Fred Freeman, Capital		31,023
Fred Freeman, Drawing	12,000	
Dock Rental Income		19,400
Boat Rental Income		2,350
Wages Expense	9,750	
Insurance Expense	915	
Utilities Expense	550	
	$58,873	$58,873

(a) Expired insurance amounted to $346.
(b) The inventory of unused supplies still on hand was $76.
(c) The annual depreciation on the dock was 5% of $30,000.
(d) Unrecorded utilities expense owed at the end of the year amounted to $50.
(e) Accrued wages amounted to $85.
(f) Income received but not yet earned on boat rental amounted to $225.

ANSWERS

KNOW THE CONCEPTS
The correct order of procedures is as follows: 3, 4, 6, 8, 7, 2, 10, 9, 5, 1.

PRACTICAL APPLICATION
PART A

1.

	Date		Account and Explanation	PR	Debit	Credit
	19	8-				
a.	Dec.	31	Office Supplies Expense		250 00	
			Office Supplies			250 00
			To adjust for supplies used up			
b.		31	Rent Expense		800 00	
			Rent Payable			800 00
			To recognize Nov. and Dec. rent			
c.		31	Advertising Expense		200 00	
			Advertising Payable			200 00
			For second week of Nov.			
d.		31	Interest Expense		8 33	
			Interest Payable			8 33
			To recognize accrued interest expense			
e.		31	Insurance Expense		300 00	
			Prepaid Insurance			300 00
			To recognize insurance expense from			
			July 1 through Dec. 31			
f.		31	Salaries Expense		3000 00	
			Salaries Payable			3000 00
			To recognize accrued salaries for last			
			3 days of accounting period			

2.

	Date		Account and Explanation	PR	Debit	Credit
	19	8-				
a.	Dec.	31	Interest Receivable		7 5 00	
			Interest Income			7 5 00
			To recognize accrued interest			
			income from Nov. 2 to date			
b.		31	Income from Commissions		3 2 0 00	
			Unearned Comm. Income			3 2 0 00
			To defer income previously received			
			but not earned			
c.		31	Office Supplies Expense		7 3 0 00	
			Office Supplies			7 3 0 00
			To recognize supplies used up			
d.		31	Salaries Expense		1 5 0 0 00	
			Salaries Payable			1 5 0 0 00
			Accrued salaries for last 3 days of			
			accounting period			
e.		31	Insurance Expense		1 2 4 5 00	
			Prepaid Insurance			1 2 4 5 00
			To recognize expired insurance			
f.		31	Interest Expense		9 0 00	
			Interest Payable			9 0 00
			($6000 × .12 × 45/360)			
			To recognize interest expense			
			incurred but not payable at the end of			
			the accounting period			

3. (a) Amount subject to depreciation: $3,000.

Depreciable value = Original cost − Scrap value

$3,400 − $400 = $3,000

(b) $500.

$3,000 ÷ 6 years = Annual depreciation

(c) Dec. 31   Depreciation Expense $500

      Accumulated Depreciation $500

    To record adjustment for annual

    depreciation

(d) $2,900.
  Original cost − Accumulated depreciation = book value
     $3,400   − $500   = $2,900
(e) $400. (Annual depreciation of $500 × 6 years = $3,000 accumulated depreciation. Original cost − accumulated depreciation = book value: 3,400 − 3,000 = 400.)
(f) The book value is reduced by the annual depreciation recognized. The loss in value is recognized in the contra-asset accumulated depreciation.
(g) The cost principle requires that plant assets be shown on the books at their actual costs.

4.

	Date		Account and Explanation	PR	Debit	Credit
	19	8-				
a.	Dec.	31	Depreciation Expense		500 00	
			Accumulated Depreciation			500 00
			For the year			
b.		31	Salaries Expense		120 00	
			Salaries Payable			120 00
			For last 4 days of accounting period			
c.		31	Rental Income		1200 00	
			Unearned Rental Income			1200 00
			To recognize unearned income			
d.		31	Prepaid Supplies		600 00	
			Supplies Expense			600 00
			To recognize unused supplies expense			

5. (a),(b),(c)

Beldon Service Co.
Worksheet
For the Year Ended December 31, 198–

Account Title	A.N.	Trial Balance Debit	Trial Balance Credit	Adjustments Debit	Adjustments Credit	Income Statement Debit	Income Statement Credit	Balance Sheet Debit	Balance Sheet Credit
Cash		16900 00						16900 00	
Accounts Receivable		2000 00						2000 00	
Prepaid Insurance		600 00			(a) 200 00			400 00	
Supplies		300 00			(b) 175 00			125 00	
Furniture		13500 00						13500 00	
Accumulated Depreciation			500 00		(c) 500 00				1000 00
Accounts Payable			1500 00						1500 00
Notes Payable			8000 00						8000 00
L. Beldon, Capital			12000 00						12000 00
L. Beldon, Drawing		4000 00						4000 00	
Service Revenue			21000 00	(d) 400 00			20600 00		
Rental Revenue			1600 00				1600 00		
Salaries Expense		5000 00		(e) 300 00		5300 00			
Rent Expense		1400 00				1400 00			
Utilities Expense		900 00				900 00			
		44600 00	44600 00						
Insurance Expense				(a) 200 00		200 00			
Supplies Expense				(b) 175 00		175 00			
Depreciation Expense				(c) 500 00		500 00			
Unearned Service Revenue					(d) 400 00				400 00
Salaries Payable					(e) 300 00				300 00
Interest Expense				(f) 40 00		40 00			
Interest Payable					(f) 40 00				40 00
				1615 00	1615 00	8515 00	22200 00	36925 00	23240 00
Net Income						13685 00			13685 00
						22200 00	22200 00	36925 00	36925 00

(d)

Beldon Service Co.
Income Statement
For the Year Ended December 31, 198–

Revenue:

Service Revenue	$20,600	
Rental Revenue	1,600	
Total Revenue		$22,200

Expenses:

Salaries Expense	5,300	
Rent Expense	1,400	
Utilities Expense	900	
Insurance Expense	200	
Supplies Expense	175	
Depreciation Expense	500	
Interest Expense	40	
Total Expenses		8,515
Net Income		$13,685

Beldon Service Co.
Statement of Capital
For the Year Ended December 31, 198–

L. Beldon, (Beginning)* Capital, January 1, 198–		$12,000
Plus: Net Income	$13,685	
Less: L. Beldon, Drawing	4,000	
Net Increase in Capital		9,685
L. Beldon, (Ending)* Capital, December 31, 198–		21,685

*In practice the words "beginning" and "ending" are omitted when recording the capital balances. These terms are understood from the date of the proprietor's capital.

Beldon Service Co.
Balance Sheet
December 31, 198–
Assets

Cash		$16,900
Accounts Receivable		2,000
Prepaid Insurance		400
Supplies		125
Furniture	$13,500	
Less: Accumulated Depreciation	1,000	12,500
Total Assets		$31,925

Liabilities and Capital

Accounts Payable	1,500	
Unearned Service Revenue	400	
Interest Payable	40	
Salaries Payable	300	
Notes Payable	8,000	
Total Liabilities		$10,240
L. Beldon, Capital		21,685
Total Liabilities and Capital		$31,925

6.   **Adjusting Journal Entries (explanation omitted):**

	Date		Account and Explanation	PR	Debit	Credit
	19	8–				
a.	Dec.	31	Insurance Expense		200 00	
			Prepaid Insurance			200 00
b.		31	Supplies Expense		175 00	
			Supplies			175 00
c.		31	Depreciation Expense		500 00	
			Accumulated Depreciation			500 00
d.		31	Service Revenue		400 00	
			Unearned Service Revenue			400 00
e.		31	Salaries Expense		300 00	
			Salaries Payable			300 00
f.		31	Interest Expense		40 00	
			Interest Payable			40 00

Closing Journal Entries (explanations omitted):

Date		Account and Explanation	PR	Debit	Credit
19	8-				
Dec.	31	Service Revenue		20600 00	
		Rental Revenue		1600 00	
		Income Summary			22200 00
	31	Income Summary		8515 00	
		Salaries Expense			5300 00
		Rent Expense			1400 00
		Utilities Expense			900 00
		Insurance Expense			200 00
		Supplies Expense			175 00
		Depreciation Expense			500 00
		Interest Expense			40 00
	31	Income Summary		4000 00	
		L. Beldon, Drawing			4000 00
	31	Income Summary		9685 00	
		L. Beldon, Capital			9685 00

7.

Beldon Service Co.
Post-Closing Trial Balance
December 31, 198–

	DEBIT	CREDIT
Cash	$16,900	
Accounts Receivable	2,000	
Prepaid Insurance	400	
Supplies	125	
Furniture	13,500	
Accumulated Depreciation		$ 1,000
Accounts Payable		1,500
Unearned Service Revenue		400
Salaries Payable		300
Interest Payable		40
Notes Payable		8,000
L. Beldon, Capital		$21,685
	$32,925	$32,925

8.

Adjusting Entries:

			Adjusting Entries				
	19	8–					
a.	Dec.	31	Salaries Expense	7 0 0 00			
			Salaries Payable			7 0 0 00	
			To recognize accrued salaries for one day				
b.		31	Office Supplies Expense	3 7 0 00			
			Office Supplies			3 7 0 00	
			To recognize supplies used up				
c.		31	Prepaid Insurance	4 5 0 00			
			Insurance Expense			4 5 0 00	
			To recognize expense not used up				
d.		31	Rental Income	4 0 0 00			
			Unearned Rental Income			4 0 0 00	
			To recognize 4 mo. income received in advance				
			but unearned at the end of the Accounting Period				

Reversing Entries:

			Reversal Entries				
	19	8–					
a.	Jan.	1	Salaries Payable	7 0 0 00			
			Salaries Expense			7 0 0 00	
			To recognize expense for new year				
c.		1	Insurance Expense	4 5 0 00			
			Prepaid Insurance			4 5 0 00	
			To record reversal				
d.		1	Unearned Rental Income	4 0 0 00			
			Rental Income			4 0 0 00	
			To recognize income for new year				

Note that the second adjusting entry does not need a reversing entry since the office supplies expense account, created as a result of the adjusting process, was eliminated as part of the closing process. All other accounts created through the adjusting process required reversing entries.

9. **Adjusting Entries:**

		Adjusting Entries										
	19	8–										
a.	Dec.	31	Insurance Expense	2	1	5	4	17				
			Prepaid Insurance						2	1	5	4	17
			To recognize expired cost.										
b.		31	Supplies Expense	3	5	0	0	00				
			Supplies						3	5	0	0	00
			To recognize supplies used.										
c.		31	Depreciation Expense	2	0	0	0	00				
			Accumulated Depreciation						2	0	0	0	00
			To recognize depreciation on										
			office equipment for the year.										
d.		31	Interest Expense		3	6	0	00				
			Accrued Interest Payable							3	6	0	00
			To recognize 9 months' interest.										
e.		31	Revenue from Services		9	5	0	00				
			Unearned Revenue from Services							9	5	0	00
			To recognize unearned revenue.										
f.		31	Salaries Expense			7	0	00				
			Salaries Payable								7	0	00
			To recognize salaries expense incurred										
			but not paid.										

(a) Adjusted prepaid insurance balance, $2,545.83; (b) supplies expense, $3,500; (c) accumulated depreciation on office equipment balance, $5,000; (d) interest expense, $360; (e) unearned revenue, $950 (revenue from services balance, $14,050); (f) salaries expense, $70

PART B

1. Net loss, $2,033.83; L. Brandeis, capital, December 31, 198–, $31,965.83

2. (a) Dry cleaning supplies expense, $1,370; (b) prepaid insurance balance, $120; (c) accumulated depreciation on laundry equipment balance, $21,650; (d) revenue from dry cleaning balance, $54,500; (e) salaries expense balance, $15,465; (f) interest expense, $85

3. Net income, $24,380

4. (a) Prepaid insurance balance, $396; (b) supplies expense, $440; (c) accumulated depreciation on dock balance, $6,500; (d) utilities expense balance, $600 (utilities payable, $50); (e) wages expense balance, $9,835 (wages payable, $85); (f) boat rental income balance, $2,575; net income $8,339

5
A TRADING
BUSINESS

KEY TERMS

cash discount A reduction in price offered by a seller to a buyer as an incentive to pay the obligation to the seller before the buyer is actually required to do so.

merchandise inventory Goods on hand at the end of an accounting period. The value of the inventory is determined by taking a physical inventory of goods previously purchased but not sold during the current accounting period. The ending inventory becomes the beginning merchandise inventory at the beginning of the new accounting period.

sales discount A reduction of sales price offered by a seller to a buyer. The difference between the amount owed by the customer and the amount of cash received is known as the sales discount.

terms The means or method of payment of an obligation. Terms are established by the seller and are included on the invoice.

HOW SERVICE AND TRADING BUSINESSES DIFFER

There are primarily two functions of businesses: service and trading.

A service business sells knowledge and/or skill, while a trading business sells a particular product or group of products. Obviously, there are businesses that specialize in the manufacture of the product that the trading business sells; however, this type of business organization will be presented in a cost accounting course.

Up to now we have concentrated exclusively on accounting for a service business. The accounting for a trading business is primarily the same as that for a service business, except that in a trading business a product is being sold. Service companies, such as law firms, accounting firms, and advertising agencies, perform services and the compensation received for these services is recorded in various accounts, for example, income from fees, commissions income, and income from services. These revenue totals, when compared with total expenses, enable the accountant to determine whether the service business has earned a profit or sustained a loss. The determination of profit or loss for a trading business is somewhat more involved, however, because of a significant added component: the cost of purchasing the product to be sold. Because of this cost, it is necessary to be familiar with a number of ledger accounts that are used only by organizations that sell products.

• *SPECIAL ACCOUNTS FOR A TRADING BUSINESS*

Since a trading business's primary reason for existence is to sell a product, it is necessary to talk in terms of the product being sold. In order to sell the product, it is first necessary to acquire it. Since the goods that we are purchasing are being bought not for use but rather for resale, we usually maintain records on them separate from records on traditional assets that are bought for use.

The account title used for goods that are bought for resale is usually "Merchandise Purchases." Merchandise purchases are all goods bought exclusively for the purpose of resale. This account is classified as an *expense*. It is expected that, as the goods are sold, the cost will be recognized as an expense known as "Cost of Goods Sold."

From time to time goods that are purchased may not meet the owner's expectations. When this happens, the buyer will request the right to return the goods. The goods being returned are recorded in a separate account entitled "Purchases Returns and Allowances." This account is classified as a contra-expense account because it directly offsets the merchandise purchases account.

In order for goods to be available for sale, it is necessary first to have them transported to the retailer's establishment. By agreement, the cost of transporting the goods can be borne by either the buyer or the seller. If the cost is the responsibility of the buyer, this cost is recorded in an account entitled "Freight on Purchases" or "Freight In." It is appropriate to maintain a separate record for freight charges so that an accurate analysis of the accounting data can be made.

As an incentive to pay their obligations early, buyers of goods may be offered a discount by the seller. This discount, which is recognized only if and when it is taken by the buyer, is recorded in a ledger account called "Purchases Discount" or "Discount on Purchases." Thus, the discount represents a reduction in cost due to early payment and is a form of revenue to the buyer of the goods, recognized only when taken by the buyer.

YOU SHOULD REMEMBER

The distinction between a service business and a trading business is evident in the accounts of the trading business.

Since a trading or merchandising business is concerned with the sale of a product, the following accounts are usually an integral part of this type of business: merchandise purchases, purchases returns and allowances, discount on purchases, and freight on purchases.

• *METHODS OF DETERMINING INCOME*

The primary difference between a service business and a trading business is the product sold by the trading business. The primary expense of a trading business is usually the cost of the item sold. Because of this fact, a trading business's income statement is traditionally broken down into a number of sections. The following represents a skeletal form of an income statement for a trading business:

Net sales
– Cost of goods sold =
Gross profit on sales
– Expenses =
Net income

DETERMINING NET SALES

Merchandise sold by a trading (retail) business is usually recorded in an account entitled "Sales." This revenue account may have other titles, such as "Income from Sales," "Sales Income," "Sales Revenue," or others that provide a better description of the product being sold. Every sale, whether it is made for cash or on credit, is credited to the sales account. The balance in the sales account at the end of the accounting period is usually known as GROSS SALES. Gross sales represents the total sales made by the organization for the particular accounting period.

A customer who receives a defective or otherwise unsatisfactory item from the seller usually has the right, recognized by the seller, to return the product. Since the original intent of the buyer was to retain the goods, an assumption is made that the reason for the return was the fault or negligence of the seller. It is important that a record be maintained for the return of these items. The accountant will set up a separate account called "Sales Returns and Allowances" to show these returns. Since the effect of the return is to offset the original sale, this account can be classified as a contra-revenue account. Entries recorded in the sales returns and allowances account represent debits.

At the end of the accounting period or for interim statement purposes, the calculation of net sales results from subtracting sales returns and allowances from the figure for gross sales.

Example: Net Sales Section of an Income Statement
for a Trading Business

Revenue

Gross Sales	65,000	
Less: Sales Returns and Allowances	2,380	
Net Sales		62,620

RECORDING SALES, AND SALES RETURNS AND ALLOWANCES

Sales both on credit and for cash cause the revenue account (sales) to be credited. The following examples illustrate the journal entries for recording both cash and credit sales:

198–

July 3	Cash	1,357	
	Sales		1,357
	For merchandise sold for cash.		
7	Accounts Receivable	985	
	Sales		985
	For merchandise sold on credit.		

Usually a customer does not automatically have the right to return goods to the seller. The customer will request the right to return the goods.

If the original sale was paid for, then the following entry would reflect the refund issued on the books of the seller of the merchandise:

198–

July 5	Sales Returns and Allowances	78	
	Cash		78

If the original sale was made on credit, the seller's permission to return the goods comes in a form known as a **credit memorandum.** This is the authorization needed by the buyer to return the goods. The *credit memo* becomes the document that is used to record the following entry:

198–

July 12	Sales Returns and Allowances	102	
	Accounts Receivable		102
	Issued credit memo No. 453 for defective merchandise returned.		

RECORDING SALES DISCOUNTS

A **discount** is a reduction in price. A **sales discount** represents a reduction in price related to a sale. The seller of goods has a choice as to how the goods are to be sold. Basically, goods may be sold for cash or on credit. Competition among sellers really determines whether an item is to be offered for sale for cash or on credit. Where credit is extended on sales, the terms given the buyer are stated on the sales invoice. Such **terms** (means and methods of payment allowed) are calculated from the date of the invoice. Terms such as ''n/30'' mean that the entire obligation is due the seller within 30 days of the invoice date. Terms of ''n/60'' or ''n/90'' or ''n/120'' or longer periods of time may be given to the purchaser to pay the obligation. The terms offered usually depend on the custom of the trade. In some trades, it is customary for invoices to become due and payable 10 days after the end of the month in which the sale occurred. Such a term is expressed as ''n/10 EOM.''

When credit periods are long, creditors may offer the buyer a **cash discount,** which is a price reduction offered to the buyer as an incentive to pay the obligation to the seller before the buyer is actually required to do so. A term of ''2/10, n/30'' may be offered. This term states that a 2% discount will be given if the obligation is paid within 10 days of the invoice date, or the entire amount (net) is due within 30 days from invoice. The sales discount is offered by the seller, but it is the buyer who exercises the option of taking or rejecting the cash discount. To the seller the sales discount represents an expense of the business. As such, when it is taken by the buyer, it is recorded on the seller's books as an expense. The account title used to recognize this expense is ''Sales Discount'' or ''Discount on Sales.'' On the buyer's books this cash discount represents a reduction in cost and is generally entitled ''Purchases Discount'' or ''Discount on Purchases.'' When the discount is taken by the buyer, it is recorded as a credit to the purchases discount account.

When a customer sends payment within the discount period offered by the seller, the transaction on the seller's books is recorded as shown in the following example:

Sale made on credit on January 5, 198–. The amount of the sale was $500; the terms: 2/10, n/30. The following entries were made to record the credit sale and the subsequent payment received from the buyer on January 13, 198–:

198–

Jan.	5	Accounts Receivable	500	
		Sales		500
		2/10, n/30		
	13	Cash	490	
		Sales Discount	10	
		Accounts Receivable		500
		Inv. paid within discount period.		

Sales discounts are accumulated in a contra-revenue account that is classified as an expense account. Since these discounts represent a cost of doing business and are directly related to the sale of the product, it is appropriate to show them as a reduction from gross sales on the income statement. The following section of the income statement illustrates the placement of sales discounts:

Revenue
Gross Sales		50,000
Less: Sales Returns and Allowances	1,350	
Sales Discounts	940	2,290
Net Sales		47,710

Complete Computational Problems 1 and 2, Part A (pp. 138–139).

YOU SHOULD REMEMBER

Income determination for a trading business usually takes the following form:

Net sales
− Cost of goods sola =

Gross profit on sales
− Operating expenses =

Net income

The sale of the product is handled in the same manner as the sale of a service, which may be either for cash or on credit.

Since goods sold may be returned by the buyer, the seller must record the goods returned in a sales returns and allowances account. This account (contra-revenue) is subtracted from the sales account, with the resulting amount being called "net sales."

As an incentive to the buyer to pay for credit sales sooner than obligated to do so, the seller offers the buyer a cash discount. If taken by the buyer, this discount is recorded on the seller's books as a sales discount (expense).

DETERMINING THE COST OF GOODS AVAILABLE FOR SALE

The primary cost in a trading business is the cost of the merchandise sold. In order for the sale of merchandise to take place, the goods must first be available for sale. Goods available for sale consist of two components: net purchases and merchandise inventory.

During the current accounting period, goods that are purchased are charged to the merchandise purchases account. Any returns or goods taken out of the business by the proprietor are credited to the purchases returns and allowances account. Delivery charges on purchases are charged to a freight on purchases account. Discounts earned as a result of early payments of credit purchases are credited to the purchases discount account. Net purchases would be determined in the following manner:

Merchandise Purchases		15,000
Less: Purchases Returns & Allowances	400	
Purchases Discount	500	900
		14,100
Add: Freight on Purchases		200
Net Purchases		14,300

Merchandise purchased in a previous accounting period that remains unsold into the current accounting period is known as **merchandise inventory.** The inventory on hand at the beginning of the new accounting period is known as beginning merchandise inventory. During the current accounting period this inventory remains on the books with no changes being recorded to it. At the end of the accounting period the accountant determines the value of the goods sold. Before this can be done, however, the accountant must determine the *cost of merchandise available for sale.*

Example: The-Cost-of-Merchandise-Available-for-Sale Section of an Income Statement for a Trading Business

Merchandise Inventory, January 1, 198–			4,000
Merchandise Purchases		15,000	
Less: Purchases Returns & Allowances	400		
Purchases Discount	500	900	
		14,100	
Add: Freight on Purchases		200	
Net Purchases			14,300
Cost of Merchandise Available for Sale			18,300

• DETERMINING THE MERCHANDISE INVENTORY

The inventory of a trading business consists of goods on hand and available for sale to the customer. The inventory available at the beginning of the accounting period is known as beginning inventory. Merchandise inventory on hand at the end of the accounting period is known as ending inventory. The beginning inventory figure is needed in order to determine the cost of goods available for sale. Because the merchandise inventory represents unsold goods available for sale, there must be a method for determining both the quantity and the cost of the merchandise on hand.

Companies that sell a great quantity and variety of items, such as department stores, keep track of their stock of goods by using the **periodic inventory method,** which entails taking a physical count of the merchandise on hand at a particular moment in time. Usually the physical inventory is taken at the end of the accounting period. The cost value of this inventory is calculated by multiplying the quantity of each item by its appropriate unit cost. A total cost figure for the entire inventory is then determined by adding the total costs of all the kinds of merchandise in the inventory. Since the physical inventory taken represents a combination of goods purchased during the year and merchandise that the firm had on hand at the beginning of the year, this inventory is actually an asset and must be reflected on the books as such at the end of the year. The following adjusting entry is made to establish the ending inventory on the books of the company:

198–

Dec. 31	Merchandise Inventory	3,500	
	Income Summary		3,500
	To establish ending inventory on books.		

The debit entry establishes the asset value on the books. The credit entry acts to offset the value of the net purchases and the beginning inventory, which in combination represent the cost of goods available for sale.

The merchandise inventory taken at the end of the accounting period also represents the beginning inventory for the next accounting period. This beginning inventory is necessary to determine the cost of goods available for sale in the next accounting period.

Another system used to determine the value of the inventory on hand is known as the "perpetual inventory system." This method of taking inventory will be discussed in Chapter 10.

YOU SHOULD REMEMBER

In a trading concern using the periodic inventory system, a merchandise inventory account is used.

The physical inventory that is taken annually becomes the basis for recognizing the asset value of the goods on hand at the end of the period.

This ending inventory for one accounting period becomes the beginning inventory for the following period.

• DETERMINING THE COST OF MERCHANDISE SOLD

The cost of goods sold represents the cost assigned to the actual merchandise that was sold during the accounting period. To determine the cost of goods sold under a periodic inventory system, it is necessary to compare the cost of merchandise available for sale with the cost of the goods that were not sold. Goods not sold are represented by the ending merchandise inventory. The following section of the income statement provides the value of the goods sold during the accounting period:

Cost of Merchandise Available for Sale	18,300
Less: Merchandise Inventory, December 31, 198–	3,500
Cost of Merchandise Sold	14,800

Example: The Actual-Cost-of-Merchandise-Sold Section of an Income Statement for a Trading Business

COST OF MERCHANDISE SOLD

Merchandise Inventory, January 1, 198–			4,000
Merchandise Purchases		15,000	
Less: Purchases Returns & Allowances	400		
Purchases Discount	500	900	
		14,100	
Add: Freight on Purchases		200	
Net Purchases			14,300
Cost of Merchandise Available for Sale			18,300
Less: Merchandise Inventory, December 31, 198–			3,500
Cost of Merchandise Sold			14,800

Complete Computational Problems 3 and 4, Part A (p. 139).

YOU SHOULD REMEMBER

The cost-of-goods-sold section of an income statement for a trading business shows the interaction of the inventory in relation to the goods purchased:

Cost of Goods Sold

Merchandise inventory, January 1, 198–
+ Merchandise purchases (Net) =

Cost of goods available for sale
– Merchandise inventory, December 31, 198– =

Cost of goods sold

RECORDING DAILY BUSINESS TRANSACTIONS

As you read through this section, post the journal entries presented to T accounts. Set up the following T accounts: Cash; Accounts Receivable; Merchandise Inventory; Accounts Payable; Sales; Sales Returns and Allowances; Sales Discounts; Merchandise Purchases; Purchases Returns and Allowances; Purchases Discounts; and Freight on Purchases. Allow four lines for each ledger account.

The following business transactions are presented in narrative form for the Acme Department Store. As you read the narrative, analyze the information and determine the appropriate journal entry called for. Compare your entry with the journal entry immediately following the narrative, and then proceed to post the journal entries to appropriate ledger accounts.

On January 1, 198–, the following selected balances appeared in the ledger account for the Acme Department Store: Merchandise Inventory, January 1, 198–, $12,000.

(Jan. 4—Sales on credit amounted to $3,000. Terms: 2/10, n/30.)

198–

Jan. 4	Accounts Receivable	3,000	
	Sales		3,000
	2/10, n/30		

(Jan. 5—Purchased merchandise on credit for $900. Terms: 1/10, n/30.)

Jan. 5	Merchandise Purchases	900	
	Accounts Payable		900
	Credit terms offered: 1/10, n/30		

198–

(Jan. 7—Sent a credit memo to our customer allowing a return of $200 on goods sold on Jan. 4.)

Jan. 7	Sales Returns and Allowances	200	
	Accounts Receivable		200
	Issued credit memo No. 202		

(Jan. 13—Received a check from our customer in payment of the invoice of Jan. 4, less the return of Jan. 7, and the discount taken by the customer.)

Jan. 13	Cash	2,744	
	Sales Discount	56	
	Accounts Receivable		2,800
	Customer paid inv. of Jan. 4, less 2% discount.		

(Jan. 15—Sent a check for $891 in payment of purchase made on Jan. 5.)

Jan. 15   Accounts Payable   900
    Purchases Discount   9
    Cash   891
   Paid inv. of Jan. 5, less 1% discount.

(Jan. 18—Cash sales amounted to $5,500.)

Jan. 18   Cash   5,500
    Sales   5,500
   Cash sales

(Jan. 25—Purchased merchandise on credit for $1,200. Terms: 1/10, n/30.)

Jan. 25   Merchandise Purchases   1,200
    Accounts Payable   1,200
   Credit terms offered: 1/10, n/30

(Jan. 27—Received authorization to return $200 in goods purchased on Jan. 25.)

Jan. 27   Accounts Payable   200
    Purchases Returns & Allowances   200
   Received credit memo for Jan. 25 inv.

(Jan. 31—Paid for freight charges on purchase of Jan. 5. The amount of the bill was $40.)

Jan. 31   Freight on Purchases   40
    Cash   40
   Paid freight charges on Jan. 5 purchase.

After you have posted the above transactions to the appropriate ledger accounts, foot the accounts and determine their balances as of January 31, 198–. Using the appropriate ledger accounts, prepare an income statement for the Acme Department Store (through the gross-profit-on-sales section).

ADJUSTING AND CLOSING ENTRIES

The adjusting entries previously discussed for service businesses apply as well to trading businesses. Accounts are used in a trading business, however, that are not part of a service business and thus require discussion.

The merchandise inventory account on the chart of accounts is listed as an asset. This account is not recorded to during the accounting period. Any adjustments to the goods available for sale are shown in the merchandise purchases or the purchases returns and allowances account. At the end of the accounting period, the beginning merchandise inventory is considered to have been sold. Because of this concept, it is necessary to convert the asset to an expense. To do so, the following journal entry is recorded:

198–

Dec. 31	Income Summary	10,500	
	Merchandise Inventory		10,500
	To close merchandise inventory.		

This adjusting entry eliminates the balance in the merchandise inventory account and converts the value of the inventory to an expense. The debit side of the income summary account represents all the expenses of the business. At this point it is assumed that all of the goods in the inventory account have been sold.

At the end of the accounting period, the business will take a physical inventory to determine the value of the goods on hand that were not sold. This inventory represents the ending inventory of the period. Since the beginning inventory has been closed to income summary, it is then appropriate to recognize the value of the new ending inventory on the books. The following entry is made to set up the ending inventory:

198–

Dec. 31	Merchandise Inventory	9,300	
	Income Summary		9,300
	To set up ending merchandise inventory.		

This adjusting entry has brought about two changes. First, the new ending inventory (asset) is recognized on the books. Second, the value of goods not sold reduces the cost of goods available for sale to represent the cost of goods sold.

The following example illustrates how the adjusting and closing process determines the cost of goods available for sale and the cost of goods sold.

The following balances appear in the ledger account:

Merchandise Inventory, January 1, 198–, $4,000; Merchandise Purchases, $6,000. The value of the December 31, 198–, inventory is $3,000. The following are entries to adjust and close the accounts:

198–

Dec. 31	Income Summary	6,000	
	Merchandise Purchases		6,000
	To close expenses.		

Dec. 31   Income Summary   4,000
              Merchandise Inventory   4,000
          To close beginning inventory.

Dec. 31   Merchandise Inventory   3,000
              Income Summary   3,000
          To set up ending inventory.

	Income Summary	
198–		
Dec. 31	6,000	
Dec. 31	4,000	

The balance of $10,000 represents the cost of goods available for sale following the posting of the first and second entries.

	Income Summary		
198–		198–	
Dec. 31	6,000	Dec. 31	3,000
Dec. 31	4,000		

The balance of $7,000 represents the cost of goods sold after the posting of the third entry.

• PREPARING A WORKSHEET

A trading concern's worksheet contains the same adjusting entries that characterize a service business's worksheet. The accounts unique to a trading business are merchandise purchases, purchases returns and allowances, purchases discount, freight on purchases, sales, sales returns and allowances, and sales discount. These are adjusted when necessary and closed to income summary, because they are all temporary accounts. The treatment of the inventory accounts is unique to a trading business and thus requires further discussion.

The daily business transactions just illustrated involved the merchandise inventory account in the adjusting and closing process. These entries, as with all adjusting entries, are preceded by their appearance on the worksheet. The trading organization's first adjusting entry on the worksheet will transfer the beginning merchandise inventory account, located on the trial balance, to income summary. This entry causes the balance in the merchandise inventory to become zero. The debit entry to income summary recognizes that the beginning merchandise inventory, carried as an asset during the year, is now considered to be an expense. The second adjusting entry establishes the ending merchandise inventory on the books as an asset by debiting merchandise inventory and crediting income summary. The credit to income summary recognizes that *not all* of the purchases or beginning merchandise inventory sent to income summary really represents an expense.

The following partial worksheet illustrates these procedures:

Example: Partial Worksheet for a Trading Business

Eversharp Trading Co.
Worksheet
For the Year Ended December 31, 198-

Account Title	Trial Balance		Adjustments	
	Dr.	Cr.	Dr.	Cr.
Cash	1 2 0 0 0 00			
Merchandise Inventory	4 0 0 0 00		(b) 3 0 0 0 00	(a) 4 0 0 0 00
(wavy break)				
Income Summary			(a) 4 0 0 0 00	(b) 3 0 0 0 00

Adjusting entry (a) converts the beginning inventory to an expense. Adjusting entry (b) sets up the asset value of the new ending inventory. **Complete Computational Problem 5, Part A** (pp. 139–140).

YOU SHOULD REMEMBER

The adjusting process for a trading organization differs from that for a service business only in respect to the merchandise inventory account.

At the end of the accounting period, the accountant must close the beginning inventory to income summary, thus making it possible to recognize the conversion of the asset to an expense.

Once the physical inventory has been taken at the end of the period, it is necessary to establish the new inventory on the books.

The entry requires a debit to merchandise inventory and a credit to income summary. The debit recognizes the asset value, and the credit recognizes that all the goods available for sale have not been sold.

REVERSING ENTRIES

The reversing entries discussed in Chapter 4 apply to a trading business as well as a service business. The criterion for recording a reversing entry is whether that particular account, having been set up as a result of an adjusting entry, normally carries a balance in the ledger account during the year. If it does, no reversing entry is needed. If the account normally does not have a balance in the ledger during the year, the balance in the account is eliminated at the very beginning of the new accounting period through the recording of a reversing entry. Remember that the reversing entry is the opposite of the original adjusting entry. **Complete Computational Problems 6 and 7, Part A** (p. 140).

> For more practice in mastering the material in this chapter, **complete Computational Problems 1, 2, 3, and 4, Part B** (pp. 141–143).

KNOW THE CONCEPTS
DO YOU KNOW THE BASICS?
The various expenses presented below were incurred by a trading business during the current year. Analyze the numbered items presented, and for each item determine in which of the following expense section of the income statement it should be reported: (a) selling, (b) general, (c) other.

1. Fire insurance premiums expired on inventory.
2. Advertising materials used.
3. Salary of the general manager paid.
4. Heating and lighting expenses incurred.
5. Gasoline and oil used in the delivery equipment.
6. Depreciation expense on office equipment accrued.
7. Salary of the salespersons paid.
8. Interest expense on notes payable incurred.
9. Salespersons' health insurance premiums paid.
10. Store rent for the month paid.

TERMS FOR STUDY
credit memorandum   gross sales
discount   periodic inventory method

PRACTICAL APPLICATION

PART A. COMPUTATIONAL PROBLEMS WITH COMPLETE SOLUTIONS
1. The Spencer Department Store bought $2,400 of merchandise, terms: 2/10, n/30, from the Gigi Company. Assuming that the store paid for the goods within the discount period, make the following entries on the books of the seller:

(a) the recording of the original sale and (b) the entry for the payment of the liability within the discount period by the customer.

2. Merchandise is sold on account to a customer for $12,000, terms: 2/10, 1/15, n/30. The date of the invoice is March 6, 198–. The bill is paid by the customer on March 20, 198–. Determine the amount of cash to be received by the seller, and record the journal entry on the books of the seller to reflect the receipt of the money on March 20.

3. At the end of the accounting period the information relating to a trading business was as follows: Sales, $219,180; Merchandise Inventory, December 31, 198–, $46,200; Purchases Returns and Allowances, $2,500; Merchandise Inventory, January 1, 198–, $52,390; Freight on Purchases, $2,600; Purchases, $97,500. Determine: (a) net purchases; (b) cost of goods available for sale; (c) cost of goods sold; and (d) gross profit on sales.

4. Prepare an income statement for a trading business through the gross-profit-on-sales section. The following account balances were included in the ledger of the Reliable Dry Goods Co. as of December 31, 198–: Merchandise Inventory, January 1, 198–, $28,650; Sales, $172,200; Sales Returns and Allowances, $3,430; Purchases, $138,900; Freight on Purchases, $2,300; Purchases Returns and Allowances, $1,820; Purchases Discount, $1,300; Merchandise Inventory, December 31, 198–, $31,200.

5. The following trial balance for the Xavier Co. is presented:

	DEBITS	CREDITS
Xavier Co.		
Trial Balance		
June 30, 198–		
Cash	$ 6,500	
Merchandise Inventory, July 1, 19–	3,000	
Notes Receivable	1,500	
Accounts Receivable	2,200	
Office Supplies	500	
Equipment	1,850	
Accounts Payable		$ 1,550
Notes Payable		250
Sales		12,640
Sales Returns and Allowances	150	
Merchandise Purchases	8,025	
Purchases Returns and Allowances		150
Discount on Purchases		340
Discount on Sales	110	
Freight on Purchases	45	
Rent Expense	600	
Interest Income		25
A. Xavier, Capital		10,000
A. Xavier, Drawing	475	
	$24,955	$24,955

The following information was available as of June 30, 198–, the end of the fiscal year:

(a) The ending physical inventory was $3,950.
(b) Office supplies used amounted to $60.
(c) Annual depreciation of equipment was $175.
(d) Interest accrued on notes payable amounted to $11 for the year.
(e) Interest income on notes receivable earned but not received amounted to $75.

(a) Prepare a worksheet for the Xavier Co.
(b) Record the adjusting and closing entries to the general journal.
(c) Prepare the necessary financial statements for the Xavier Co.

6. From the following information (a) prepare journal entries to adjust the books at the end of the accounting period, (b) prepare the necessary closing entries, and, where appropriate, (c) prepare the reversing entries needed. Assume that the end of the accounting period coincides with the calendar year.

(1) Merchandise inventory, January 1, $35,700; merchandise inventory, Dec. 31, $36,500.
(2) Sales salaries are paid for a 5-day week ending on Friday. The last payday of the year was Friday, December 26, 198–. If the weekly payroll for a 5-day week is $4,500, prepare the adjusting entry to recognize the accrual for the last 3 days in the year.
(3) The prepaid insurance account before adjustments at the end of the accounting period has a balance of $2,396. An analysis of the policies indicates that the actual balance in the account should be $1,800.
(4) Interest on a promissory note had been paid 1 year in advance. The amount of the income recognized was $45 for a period of 1 year. The income was recognized for the full amount on the day the note was issued, which was July 1, 198–.

7. Prepare an income statement for the Trudy Right Ladies Apparel store through the gross-profit-on-sales section, based on the following information provided at the end of the year:

General Expenses	$ 27,600	Purchases R & A	$ 8,300
Merchandise Inv. (Beg.)	56,000	Rental Income	3,600
Merchandise Inv. (End)	48,300	Sales	320,000
Merchandise Purchases	198,000	Sales Discount	2,500
Prepaid Insurance	2,100	Sales R & A	5,400
Purchases Discount	2,800	Selling Expenses (total)	63,540

PART B. COMPUTATIONAL PROBLEMS WITH FINAL ANSWERS

1. For each of the following invoices determine (a) the amount of the discount, (b) the last date on which the discount can be taken, and (c) the correct amount of the remittance based on the actual payment date:

	Invoice Date	Invoice Price	Credit Terms	Payment Date	Answers		
					(a)	(b)	(c)
(1)	Jan. 10	$2,500	2/10, n/30	Jan. 19			
(2)	Apr. 17	1,800	1/15, n/60	May 1			
(3)	Aug. 6	1,500	1/10, n/30	Aug. 21			
(4)	Nov. 23	900	3/10, n/60	Dec. 3			
(5)	Feb. 12	1,000	8%, EOM	Feb. 28			

2. The trial balance for the Carol Williams Boutique appears below.

Carol Williams Boutique
Trial Balance
December 31, 19–

	DEBIT	CREDIT
Cash	$ 6,790	
Accounts Receivable	23,650	
Merchandise Inventory, January 1, 19–	76,540	
Furniture and Fixtures	30,940	
Accounts Payable		$ 59,340
Carol Williams, Capital		36,000
Carol Williams, Drawing	13,500	
Sales		282,430
Sales Returns and Allowances	3,400	
Merchandise Purchases	183,200	
Freight on Purchases	5,100	
Purchases Returns and Allowances		1,590
Salaries Expense	12,400	
Advertising Expense	4,000	
Store Supplies Expense	3,150	
Rent Expense	7,050	
Utilities Expense	710	
Insurance Expense	1,790	
Discounts on Sales	4,700	
Discounts on Purchases		3,620
	$354,580	$354,580

Merchandise Inventory, December 31, 19– $49,500

(a) Determine: (1) The net sales, (2) the net purchases, (3) the cost of goods available for sale, (4) the cost of goods sold, (5) the gross profit on sales, and (6) the net income for the year.

(b) Prepare a multiple-step income statement.

(c) Record the necessary adjusting entries.

(d) Record the necessary closing entries.

3. Using the trial balance presented in Exercise 2, prepare a worksheet. The following additional information is to be assumed for the preparation of this worksheet:

Merchandise Inventory, December 31, 19–	$49,500
Prepaid Insurance	200
Accrued Salaries	2,300
Unused Store Supplies	430

(*Note:* The net income determined from the worksheet will not agree with the net income of Exercise 2 because of the additional information provided in this problem.)

4.

Jane Kennedy
Trial Balance
December 31, 19–

	DEBIT	CREDIT
Cash	$ 4,700	
Accounts Receivable	11,200	
Merchandise Inventory, July 1, 19–	1,500	
Notes Receivable	1,000	
Delivery Equipment	4,500	
Accumulated Depreciation—Delivery Equipment		$ 500
Accounts Payable		3,300
Notes Payable		1,700
Jane Kennedy, Capital		14,690
Jane Kennedy, Drawing	180	
Sales		16,300
Discount on Sales	130	
Sales Returns and Allowances	440	
Merchandise Purchases	9,460	
Purchases Returns and Allowances		220
Discount on Purchases		280
Rent Expense	1,200	
Freight on Purchases	340	
Freight on Sales	260	
Interest Expense	130	
Interest Income		260
Rental Income		470
Office Supplies Expense	280	
Salaries Expense	2,400	
	$37,720	$37,720

Additional Information

Merchandise Inventory, December 31, 19–	$3,200
Office Supplies on hand, December 31, 19–	80
Rent Expense paid in advance	200
Interest Expense paid in advance	35
Depreciation Expense for the 6-month period	250

On the basis of the trial balance and the additional information presented, do the following:

(a) Prepare an eight-column worksheet.
(b) Record adjusting journal entries.
(c) Record closing journal entries.
(d) Record reversing entries where needed.
(e) Prepare an income statement for the 6 months ending 12/31.
(f) Prepare a capital statement for the 6 months ending 12/31.
(g) Prepare a balance sheet dated December 31, 19–.

ANSWERS

KNOW THE CONCEPTS

Item	Expense Category
1	General
2	Selling
3	Other
4	Selling
5	Selling
6	General
7	Selling
8	Other
9	Selling
10	Selling

Some of the items may be appropriately listed in more than one expense category. The above responses represent placement within the category where the item most commonly is found.

PRACTICAL APPLICATION
PART A

1. (a) Accounts Receivable   2,400
             Sales   2,400
         To Spencer Dept. Store, 2/10, n/30.
   (b) Cash   2,352
        Sales Discount   48
             Accounts Receivable   2,400
         From Spencer Dept. Store, less discount.

On the books of the seller, the discount taken by the buyer represents an expense. On the buyer's books, the $48 represents a purchases discount, which is a form of income. On either books, the amount of the respective accounts receivable and accounts payable is eliminated in full when the obligation is paid.

2. Since 14 days have elapsed between the date of the sale and the date of payment, the discount that the buyer is entitled to take is 1%. Since the total obligation is $12,000, the amount of the purchases discount to which the buyer is entitled is $120. The amount of cash received by the seller on March 20 is $11,880 ($12,000 − $120). The entry to record the receipt of the payment is as follows:

198–
Mar. 20   Cash   11,880
              Sales Discount   120
                  Accounts Receivable   12,000
              From customer, less 1% discount.

3.   Net Purchases
   (a) Purchases $ 97,500
             Add: Freight on Purchases   2,260
                                                                 99,760
             Less: Purchases Returns and Allowances   2,500
        Net Purchases   97,260
   (b) Cost of Goods Available for Sale
             Merchandise Inventory, Jan. 1   52,390
             Add: Net Purchases   97,260
        Cost of Goods Available for Sale   149,650
   (c) Cost of Goods Sold
             Cost of Goods Available for Sale   149,650
             Less: Merchandise Inv. 12/31   46,200
        Cost of Goods Sold   103,450
   (d) Gross Profit on Sales
             Sales   219,180
             Less: Cost of Goods Sold   103,450
        Gross Profit on Sales $115,730

4.

Trading Business
Income Statement
For the Year Ended December 31, 198–

Income:			
Sales			$172,200
Less: Sales Returns and Allowances			3,430
Net Sales			168,770
Cost of Goods Sold:			
Merchandise Inventory, 1/1/19–		$ 28,650	
Purchases	$138,900		
Freight on Purchases	2,300		
Less:	141,200		
Purchases Discount	$1,300		
Purch. Ret. & Allow.	1,820	3,120	
Net Purchases:		138,080	
Cost of Goods Available for Sale		166,730	
Less: Merchandise Inventory, 12/31/8–		31,200	
Cost of Goods Sold			135,530
Gross Profit on Sales			$ 33,240

5. (a)

Xavier Co.
Worksheet
For the Year Ended June 30, 198–

Account Title	A.N.	Trial Balance Debit	Trial Balance Credit	Adjustments Debit	Adjustments Credit	Income Statement Debit	Income Statement Credit	Balance Sheet Debit	Balance Sheet Credit
Cash		6500 00						6500 00	
Merchandise Inventory, 7/1/198–		3000 00		(a)3950 00	(a)3000 00			3950 00	
Notes Receivable		1500 00						1500 00	
Accounts Receivable		2200 00						2200 00	
Office Supplies		500 00			(b) 60 00			440 00	
Equipment		1850 00						1850 00	
Accounts Payable			1550 00						1550 00
Notes Payable			250 00						250 00
Sales			12640 00				12640 00		
Sales Returns and Allowances		150 00				150 00			
Merchandise Purchases		8025 00				8025 00			
Purchases Returns and Allowances			150 00				150 00		
Discount on Purchases			340 00				340 00		
Discount on Sales		110 00				110 00			
Freight on Purchases		45 00				45 00			
Rent Expense		600 00				600 00			
Interest Income			25 00		(e) 75 00		100 00		
A. Xavier, Capital			10000 00						10000 00
F. Xavier, Drawing		475 00						475 00	
		24955 00	24955 00						
Income Summary				(a)3000 00	(a)3950 00	3000 00	3950 00		
Office Supplies Expense				(b) 60 00		60 00			
Depreciation Expense				(c) 175 00		175 00			
Accumulated Depreciation					(c) 175 00				175 00
Interest Expense				(d) 11 00		11 00			
Interest Payable					(d) 11 00				11 00
Interest Receivable				(e) 75 00				75 00	
				7271 00	7271 00	12176 00	17180 00	16990 00	11986 00
Net Income						5004 00			5004 00
						17180 00	17180 00	16990 00	16990 00

(b) **Adjusting Journal Entries:**

198–
June 30
(a)   Income Summary 3,000
         Merchandise Inventory 3,000
      To close old inventory to income summary.

(a1) **30** Merchandise Inventory 3,950
        Income Summary 3,950
    To set up new inventory.

(b) **30** Office Supplies Expense 60
        Office Supplies 60

(c) **30** Depreciation Expense 175
        Accumulated Depreciation 175

(d) **30** Interest Expense 11
        Interest Payable 11

(e) **30** Interest Receivable 75
        Interest Income 75
    To recognize interest income
    accrued but not received.

Closing Journal Entries:

198–
June 30 Sales 12,640
    Interest Income 100
    Purchases Returns and Allowances 150
    Discount on Purchases 340
        Income Summary 13,230
    To close revenue items to Income
    Summary.

    30 Income Summary 9,176
        Sales Returns and Allowances 150
        Merchandise Purchases 8,025
        Discount on Sales 110
        Freight on Purchases 45
        Rent Expense 600
        Office Supplies Expense 60
        Depreciation Expense 175
        Interest Expense 11
    To close expense items to Income
    Summary.

(c)

Xavier Co.
Income Statement
For the Year Ended June 30, 198–

Income:			
Sales			$12,640
Less: Sales Returns and			
Allowances		$ 150	
Discount on Sales		110	260
Net Sales			$12,380
Cost of Goods Sold:			
Merchandise Inventory, 7/1/8–		$ 3,000	
Merchandise Purchases	$8,025		
Add: Freight on Purchases	45		
	8,070		
Less: Discount on Purchases	$340		
Purch. Returns & Allow.	150	490	
Net Purchases		7,580	
Cost of Goods Available for Sale		10,580	
Less: Merchandise Inventory, 6/30/–		3,950	
Cost of Goods Sold			6,630
Gross Profit on Sales:			5,750
Operating Expenses			
Rent Expense		$ 600	
Office Supplies Expense		60	
Depreciation Expense		175	
Interest Expense		11	
Total Operating Expenses			846
Net Income from Operations			4,904
Other Income			
Interest Income			100
Net Income			$ 5,004

Xavier Co.
Statement of Capital
For the Year Ended June 30, 198–

A. Xavier, (Beginning) Capital, July 1, 198–		$10,000
Add Net Income	$5,004	
A. Xavier, Drawing	475	
Net increase in capital		4,529
A. Xavier, (Ending) Capital, June 30, 198–		$14,529

Xavier Co.
Balance Sheet
June 30, 198–

Assets			Liabilities and Capital	
Cash		$ 6,500	Accounts Payable	$ 1,550
Merchandise Inventory		3,950	Interest Payable	11
Accounts Receivable		2,200	Notes Payable	250
Notes Receivable		1,500	Total Liabilities	1,811
Interest Receivable		75	A. Xavier, Capital	14,529
Office Supplies		440		
Equipment	$1,850			
Less: Accumulated				
Depreciation	175	1,675	Total Liabilities &	
Total Assets		$16,340	Capital	$16,340

6. (a) (Explanations omitted) Adjusting entries are as follow:

198–

(1)	**Dec. 31**	Income Summary	35,700.00	
		Merchandise Inventory		35,700.00
(1a.)	**31**	Merchandise Inventory	36,500.00	
		Income Summary		36,500.00
(2)	**31**	Salaries Expense	2,700.00	
		Salaries Payable		2,700.00
(3)	**31**	Insurance Expense	596.00	
		Prepaid Insurance		596.00
(4)	**31**	Interest Income	22.50	
		Unearned Interest Income		22.50

(b) The closing entries are recorded to eliminate all the temporary capital accounts resulting from daily business transactions and from the adjusting entries recorded at the end of the accounting period.

(c) The reversing entry necessary for this exercise would be for the fourth entry only and is as follows:

198–

Jan. 1	Unearned Interest Income	22.50	
	Interest Income		22.50
	To recognize interest income		
	to be earned in new year.		

7.

Trudy Right Ladies Apparel
Income Statement
For the Year Ended December 31, 198–

Revenue:			
Gross Sales			$320,000
Less: Sales Returns and Allowances		$5,400	
Sales Discount		2,500	7,900
Net Sales			312,100
Cost of Merchandise Sold:			
Merchandise Inventory, 1/1/8–		$56,000	
Merchandise Purchases	$198,000		
Less: Purchases R & A	$8,300		
Purchases Discount	2,800	11,100	
Net Purchases		186,900	
Cost of Merchandise Available for Sale		242,900	
Less: Merchandise Inventory, 12/31/8–		48,300	
Cost of Merchandise Sold			194,600
Gross Profit on Sales			117,500

PART B

1. (1)–(c), $2,450; (2)–(c), $1,782; (3)–(c), $1,500; (4)–(c), $873; (5)–(c), $920

2. Net income, $38,100

3. Net income, $36,430

4. Net income, $4,655

6
SPECIAL JOURNALS AND CONTROLS

WHAT ARE SPECIAL JOURNALS?

The accountant is responsible for the design and implementation of the accounting system used by the business organization. Whether the accountant is the controller of the business or comes into the organization as an outside consultant, his or her function entails the recording, classifying, and summarizing of data, accomplished by the use of either manual systems or mechanical, electrical, or electronic equipment. Although the current trend toward high technology focuses on the use of mini- and microcomputers for accounting purposes, it is necessary that the accountant be thoroughly familiar with the manual systems that have been traditionally used. The traditional manual systems are easier to understand and more adaptable to learning through practice. This chapter will focus in part on special journals designed for manual accounting systems. These special journals can also be readily applied to the microcomputer.

All transactions discussed in Chapters 1–5 were illustrated using the two-column general journal. Although the entries were appropriately recorded and would be done in a similar fashion in most business concerns, there are situations where special journals will take the place of the general journal as illustrated. The need for an alternative approach to the exclusive use of the general journal arises out of the volume of business transactions to be recorded by an organization. In a large business there may be hundreds or even thousands of business transactions to be recorded daily.

To handle these transactions rapidly and efficiently, special journals must be developed. Special journals divide the labor that is required with a two-column general journal, so that more than one bookkeeper and/or accountant can work on the books of the organization at the same time. **Special journals** are books of original entry that are specifically designed for the purpose of recording similar kinds of transactions. Because of the similarity in the transactions recorded in the individual special journals, substantial time and labor are saved in the actual recording and posting.

YOU SHOULD REMEMBER

As the size of a business organization increases as measured by the volume of its business transactions, two factors must be recognized: (1) the need for a division of labor so that necessary record-keeping can be done efficiently and accurately, and (2) the need to introduce various special journals and ledgers to permit the division of labor and at the same time to reduce the amount of repetitive work required of those in charge of the financial records.

KINDS OF SPECIAL JOURNALS

There are primarily four special journals that are used by most businesses:

- Sales Journal
- Cash Receipts Journal
- Purchases Journal
- Cash Payments Journal

Regardless of the nature of the business enterprise, one or all of these journals may be used. The criteria for using one or all of the special journals are the volume of business transactions and the need for a division of labor.

The organization of the special journal is tailored to the particular needs of the business. Special columns are used to record repetitive transactions. This procedure permits the posting of transactions or parts to be done in total (summary) at the end of the month, rather than daily. Picture a transaction that may be recorded 300 times per month, such as the receipt of cash. Using a special journal, you can reduce posting to the cash account by 299 entries. This can be accomplished by posting the debit to the cash account once at the end of the month, rather than 300 times during the month.

In addition to special journals, special ledgers will be introduced to show how certain kinds of transactions are posted to separate ledgers, known as **subsidiary ledgers.** A subsidiary ledger is separate and apart from the general ledger and, like the special journals, contains specific accounts not specifically found in the general ledger.

YOU SHOULD REMEMBER

The four special journals used by most businesses are the sales, cash receipts, purchases, and cash payments journals.

The use of special journals requires that subsidiary ledgers be kept in addition to the general ledger.

• *SALES JOURNAL*

RECORDING TRANSACTIONS

Sales of goods and/or services may be made for cash or on credit. When the terms of a sale call for payment in 30, 60, or 90 days, the use of a special journal is appropriate. In fact, any sale of a product or service on credit (regardless of the credit terms) will be recorded in the **sales journal.**

The recording of the following credit sale was made to the general journal:

198–

Jan. 10	Accounts Receivable	400	
	Sales		400
	R. Jones, terms: n/30		

This credit sale requires the journalizing of both the debit and credit parts of the entry and subsequent postings. The use of a sales journal will reduce the work in both journalizing and posting. Another disadvantage, not previously discussed, to using the general journal for this kind of entry is that the oral promise represented by the debit to accounts receivable does not specify the person who owes the money as a result of the credit sale.

Example: Typical Sales Journal Entry

Sales Journal

Date		Account Debited	Inv. #	Terms	PR	Amount
19 8– Jan. 10		R. Jones	101	n/30		4 0 0 00

The same basic information previously recorded to the general journal appears in the sales journal. There are certain obvious advantages to the sales journal form. The transaction is recorded on a single line. The debit entry is to a specific customer's name. The amount appears only once, and the credit portion of the entry is assumed. Every credit sale is recorded in the sales journal, and each credit entry will affect the sales account. It is necessary to present an accounts debited column because of the many customers to whom a business will sell on credit. During the month each sale on credit previously recorded in the general journal had to be posted immediately to the two accounts in the general ledger.

Using the sales journal permits the bookkeeper to put off posting the credit portion of the entry until the end of the month. At that time the total of the amount column will be posted in summary to the credit side of the sales account.

The debit postings must be made daily, and at this point what we previously learned has to be modified. The daily postings of the debit entries are made to a subsidiary ledger known as an **accounts receivable ledger.**

The accounts receivable ledger is a separate ledger that contains individual accounts for each customer who has been sold goods on credit. The form of the customer accounts is the same as that of the previous ledger accounts presented. The customer's name appears on the top of the account. Increases to the account are recorded as debit entries, and decreases are recorded as credit entries. Transactions recorded to the sales journal on a daily basis require daily postings to the various customer accounts found in the accounts receivable ledger.

Many business organizations assign a specific page designation to each customer's account. This page designation is used to indicate that posting has taken place. We will use a page designation that corresponds to the first letter of the last name of the customer. Thus, R. Jones's page designation in the accounts receivable ledger will be the letter "J," to correspond to the first letter of his last name.

Example: Sales Journal Entry and Daily Posting
to Subsidiary Accounts Receivable Ledger

Sales Journal   *Page S-1*

Date	Account Debited	Inv. #	Terms	PR	Amount
19 8– Jan. 10	R. Jones	101	n/30	J	400 00

Accounts Receivable Ledger

R. Jones   *Page J*

Date		PR	Debit	Credit	Balance
19 8– Jan. 10	n/30	S-1	400 00		400 00

All credit sales would be recorded to the sales journal in the same manner as the transaction just illustrated. The posting procedure would be the same for each credit sale except that now they would be posted to a specific customer's account.

The accounts receivable ledger will contain as many accounts as there are customers. Be particularly aware of the designations used in the post-reference (PR) columns of the sales journal, as well as the customer's account. The "J" in the post-reference column of the sales journal indicates that posting to the ledger has taken place and that it was made to the account page "J." The S-1 in the post reference of the customer's account indicates the source of the information. Notice that the terms given the customer are also shown in the customer's ledger account.

Notice how the following additional credit sales are recorded and posted to the respective accounts:

198–
Jan. 12   Sold goods to D. Lane for $3000, terms: n/30
    15   Sold goods to R. Jones for $500, terms: as had

Sales Journal   *Page S-1*

Date	Account Debited	Inv. #	Terms	PR	Amount
19 8– Jan. 10	R. Jones	101	n/30	J	400 00
12	D. Lane	102	n/30	L	3000 00
15	R. Jones	103	n/30	J	500 00

Accounts Receivable Ledger

R. Jones   Page J

Date			PR	Debit	Credit	Balance
19 8– Jan. 10	n/30		S-1	4 0 0 00		4 0 0 00
15	n/30		S-1	5 0 0 00		9 0 0 00

D. Lane   Page L

Date				Debit	Credit	Balance
19 8– Jan. 12	n/30		S-1	3 0 0 00		3 0 0 00

A letter appearing in the post-reference column (also known as the ledger-reference column) in the sales journal indicates two things: (1) that the transaction has been posted, and (2) to what account the posting has been made. The January 10 entry in the sales journal has been posted to account "J," which represents the page in the accounts receivable ledger where the R. Jones account is found. The same fact is true for the entry of January 15. The entry of January 12 indicates that the posting was made to the D. Lane account in the accounts receivable ledger.

Although the format of the general journal is lacking in the sales journal, it is understood that the only part of each entry that must be posted immediately is the debit to the various customer accounts in the subsidiary ledger. This is necessary because of the many different credit customers an organization will be dealing with. Remember: we will no longer debit the accounts receivable account, but will record all credit sales in the sales journal and post the debit part of the entry to the individual customer's account in the accounts receivable ledger. The time- and labor-saving aspects of this journal enable us to post the credit to the sales account, in summary, at the end of the month. No posting to the sales account will take place during the month. The individual customer accounts established for R. Jones and D. Lane reflect the postings made from the sales journal. The source of these postings is shown in the post-reference column (also known as the journal-reference column) by the "S-1" notation. This information came from the first page of the sales journal.

THE SUMMARY ENTRY

During the month, only the debit entries are posted from the sales journal. At the end of the month, the summary entry enables us to complete the posting so that double-entry accounting is maintained. Notice in the sales journal completed below that the total is obtained at the end of the month. This total represents the amount of the credit entry to be posted to the sales journal.

The accounts receivable account found in the general ledger is known as a **control account.** The function of the **accounts receivable control account** is to provide a summary of the activities posted to the subsidiary ledger. This account is necessary in order to prepare a trial balance at the end of the month. Since individual customers' accounts are not found in the general ledger (the source for the preparation of the trial balance), it is necessary to have a "control" figure in the ledger. The individual in charge of the subsidiary ledger prepares a **schedule of accounts receivable** to verify that the control account is in agreement with the subsidiary ledger. The posting to the accounts receivable control account in the general ledger is a direct result of the posting of the debit portion of the summary entry illustrated.

Sales Journal   *Page S-1*

Date		Account Debited	PR	Terms	Inv. #	Amount
19 8– Jan.	10	R. Jones	J	n/30	101	4 00 00
	12	D. Lane	L	n/30	102	3 000 00
	15	R. Jones	J	n/30	103	5 00 00
	31	Dr. Accounts Receivable, Cr. Sales	5/30			3 9 00 00

General Ledger

Accounts Receivable (Control Account)   Page 5

Date			PR	Debit	Credit	Balance	
						Debit	Credit
19 8– Jan.	31		S-1	3 9 00 00		3 9 00 00	

Sales   Page 30

Date			PR	Debit	Credit	Balance	
						Debit	Credit
19 8– Jan.	31		S-1		3 9 00 00		3 9 00 00

The following schedule of accounts receivable would be prepared to verify the control balance:

A Business
Schedule of Accounts Receivable
January 31, 198–

R. Jones	900
D. Lane	3,000
Total	3,900

Once the control account balance has been verified, the trial balance may then be prepared. **Complete Computational Problem 1, Part A** (pp. 170–171).

The accounts receivable ledger contains customer accounts that are organized in a fashion similar to the telephone directory. Some accountants prefer giving individual customer account numbers rather than letters. When this approach is used, the control account is given an account designation such as "5." All customer accounts then use the designation "5.01," "5.02," "5.03," and so on. Either method is acceptable and appropriate.

A mere checkmark in the post-reference column of the sales journal indicate that posting has taken place (and is acceptable), but does not indicate where the posting has been made to. This method is the least desirable, but in many cases it is the one used.

YOU SHOULD REMEMBER

All credit sales of goods or services are recorded in the sales journal.

Debit entries are posted daily to individual customer accounts found in the subsidiary accounts receivable ledger.

At the end of the month a summary entry is made causing a debit entry ("Total") to the control account (accounts receivable) in the general ledger, followed by a corresponding credit to the sales account.

The total of the individual customer balances from the subsidiary accounts receivable ledger (known as the "schedule of accounts receivable") must agree with the balance in the general ledger accounts receivable (control) account before a trial balance is prepared.

• *CASH RECEIPTS JOURNAL*

RECORDING TRANSACTIONS

The accountant justifies the use of the sales journal based on the substantial volume of credit sales recorded during the month. If the terms of the credit sale call for payment by the customer in 30 days, the volume of cash receipts will equal and probably substantially exceed the number of credit sale entries. This then justifies the introduction of the multicolumn **cash receipts journal.** All transactions, regardless of their source, that result in the receipt of cash are recorded in the cash receipts journal. Although it is obvious that obligations due a business as a result of prior credit sales will be recorded in the cash receipts journal, the same organization may have as many, if not considerably more, cash sales. These sales, as well as other transactions causing an inflow of cash, will be recorded in the cash receipts journal.

The following cash receipts journal is a typical form used in business:

Example: Typical Form of Cash Receipts Journal

Cash Receipts Journal

Date 19 8-		Account Credited	PR	General Acct. Cr.	Sales Cr.	Accounts Receivable Cr.	Sales Discount Dr.	Cash Dr.
Feb.	9	R. Jones	J			4 0 0 00		4 0 0 00
	10	D. Lane	L			3 0 0 00		3 0 0 00
	15	R. Jones	J			5 0 0 00	5 00	4 9 5 00
	17	Sales	✔		7 0 0 00			7 0 0 00
	21	Notes Receivable	8	4 5 0 00				4 5 0 00
	28			4 5 0 00	7 0 0 00	3 9 0 0 00	5 00	5 0 4 5 00
				(4 0)	(5)	(5)	(4 4)	(1 1)

The multicolumn cash receipts journal contains special columns representing the accounts most frequently encountered in recording cash receipts. The criterion for using a special column is the volume of monthly transactions to that account. The most obvious column needed is a **cash debit column.** Every transaction in this journal will cause a debit to cash to be recorded. As mentioned earlier, the advantage of this column is that posting to the cash ledger account will take place only once, at the end of the month. During the month, no postings will be made to the cash account in the general ledger. The number in parentheses under the total of the cash debit column represents the post reference for the summary entry posted to the cash account in the general ledger at the end of the month.

Cash receipts result from a number of different kinds of daily business transactions; however, the most common transactions resulting in the debit to cash are cash sales and payment by customers of their outstanding obligations. Thus, two primary special columns are headed "Sales (Cr.)" and "Accounts Receivable (Cr.)."

Any time a cash sale is made to customers, the transaction is recorded in the cash receipts journal. Note the February 17 transaction in the cash receipts journal just illustrated. Since both parts of the transaction are recorded in special columns, there is no need for daily postings to take place. In fact, the accountant uses a checkmark in the post-reference column to indicate that no posting is to be made at this time. From the standpoint of labor and time savings, the accountant has eliminated the posting of daily transactions involving cash sales and simply posts the two column totals at the end of the month.

The transactions of February 9, 10, and 15 represent the payment of obligations by customers. Note that in each case the credit entry is recorded in the accounts receivable credit column. Unlike the sales and the cash columns, this accounts receivable column has to be posted daily because each customer's account must be reduced to the extent of the payments made. Notice that the post-reference column reflects the postings that were made to the various customer accounts found in the accounts receivable ledger. At the end of the month, the summary total of the accounts receivable credit column is posted to the accounts receivable control account in the general ledger.

The entry of February 15 also involved the taking of a discount by the customer. Apparently the customer paid within the discount period and was entitled to a 1% discount. The effect of this discount caused a reduction in the amount of cash received, the recognition by the seller of an expense, and the elimination of the obligation, in full, by crediting the customer's account. The posting of the sales discount takes place at the end of the month, since only entries involving sales discounts are recorded in that specific column.

Whenever an account is credited in the cash receipts journal and there is no specific column set up for that account, the entry must be recorded in the general accounts credited column. These accounts are general ledger accounts; and since they may be various accounts, it is necessary to post them on a daily basis to the general ledger. The entry in the cash receipts journal for February 21 illustrates how the general accounts credited column is used. Notice that at the end of the month there is a checkmark under the general accounts credit column. This checkmark indicates that no posting is to be made. This is due to the fact that the accounts recorded in this column have been posted during the month and a summary posting is not necessary.

THE SUMMARY ENTRY

At the end of the month the columns of the cash receipts journal are pencil-footed. The debit column totals (sales discount and cash) are then compared with the totals of the credit columns (general accounts, sales, and accounts receivable). If the total of the debit column totals agrees with the total of the credit column totals, the journal is said to be in balance. The totals are then recorded in ink, the date (usually the last day of the month) is assigned, the totals are double underscored, and the posting of the totals takes place. The summary entry in the cash receipts journal involves the posting of the totals of all the columns of the journal. The general accounts credited column is not posted at the end of the month, since it was posted daily in the general ledger. The sales, accounts receivable, sales discount, and cash columns are all posted at the end of the month to their respective accounts in the general ledger. The accounts receivable credit column was posted to the individual customer accounts in the subsidiary ledger during the month. The summary entry ensures that the accounts receivable control account in the general ledger reflects what was shown in the customer's accounts during the month. **Complete Computational Problems 2 and 3, Part A** (pp. 171–172).

YOU SHOULD REMEMBER

All receipts of cash, regardless of source, are recorded in the cash receipts journal.

Daily postings are made to the individual customer accounts in the subsidiary accounts receivable ledger and to the general ledger accounts.

The other special columns are posted once at the end of the month as part of the summary entry.

The separate subsidiary accounts receivable ledger contains individual accounts established for each customer who buys on credit.

The sale is initially recorded in the sales journal. The debit is then posted to the customer's account in the subsidiary ledger.

When payment is received from the customer at a later date, the entry is first recorded in the cash receipts journal, and the credit is posted to the customer's account.

The summary entry from the sales journal and the cash receipts journal is posted to the accounts receivable control account in the general ledger at the end of the month.

The balance in this control account must agree with the total of the individual customers' balances from the subsidiary accounts receivable ledger. This will be evident as a result of correctly completing Computational Problems 2 and 3, Part A.

• *PURCHASES JOURNAL*

RECORDING TRANSACTIONS

We have learned that sales on credit and the subsequent cash received, regardless of source, are recorded in the sales and cash receipts journals, respectively. Whenever a special journal is used, the need for and the use made of the general journal are reduced. When the volume of transactions dealing with purchases that an organization makes on credit is great, this calls for the introduction and use of the **purchases journal.** Any kind of purchase that is made on credit is recorded in the special multicolumn purchases journal. The typical form of the purchases journal is presented on page 162.

Example: Typical Form of the Purchases Journal

Purchases Journal   Page P-1

Date 19 8–	Account Credited	PR	A/P (Cr.)	Purchases (Dr.)	General Accounts Debited		
					Account Debited	PR	Amount
Jan. 1	Smith Co. (n/30)	S	500 00	500 00			
12	Able Co. (n/30)	A	750 00		Equipment	30	750 00
17	Rand Inc. (n/60)	R	175 00		Supplies	18	175 00
28	Ace Freight Co.	A	35 00		Freight on Purchases	70	35 00
31			1460 00	500 00			960 00
			(60)	(66)			(✓)

The use of the purchases journal is very similar to that of the sales journal, except that the purchases journal is used for the purchase of *anything*, provided that the purchase is made on credit. The multicolumn purchase journal has special columns for recording recurring information. The use of the special column for purchase is obvious. In practice a special column should be set up for any account that may be used frequently. In the purchases journal illustrated, supplies are shown as part of the general accounts debited column; however, if the volume of supplies purchased on credit was significant, a special column for supplies could be included in the purchases journal.

Notice that this journal has provisions for two post-reference columns. Whenever the general accounts debit area is used, it is posted immediately to the general ledger and noted in the second post-reference column. When the purchases column is used, the posting will take place at the end of the month in summary, in a similar fashion to the summary of the sales journal.

Every purchase recorded in the purchases journal must be made on credit in order to record it to this journal. Each transaction results in the establishment of a liability known as accounts payable. In practice it is important for businesses to know specifically to whom they owe money. To keep track of this information, it is necessary to set up an additional subsidiary ledger, the **accounts payable ledger,** in which separate accounts are maintained for all the creditors of the business organization. In the general ledger the **accounts payable control account** is maintained to mirror the subsidiary ledger.

Notice that the first post-reference column is to the immediate left of the accounts payable credit column. The purpose of this post-reference column is to post the obligations of the various creditor accounts on a daily basis to the subsidiary accounts payable ledger. The workings of the accounts payable control and subsidiary ledger are very similar to those of the accounts receivable control and accounts receivable subsidiary ledger. During the month the credit entries to the various creditor accounts are posted to the subsidiary ledger and page letter designations corresponding to the first letter of the customer's last name are used to indicate that posting has taken place. It is necessary at the end of the month to ensure that whatever has been posted to the subsidiary accounts payable ledger is also reflected in the accounts payable control account in the general ledger.

THE SUMMARY ENTRY

The summary entry is made in the purchases journal on the last day of the month, as with the other special journals. Since the purchases journal is a multicolumn journal, it is first necessary to pencil-foot the money columns. The total of the debit column totals must agree with the total credit to the accounts payable column. Once this has been determined, it is appropriate to write the totals in ink and then to double underscore the columns.

The summary entry will indicate the appropriate accounts to be posted to, by the number shown under the ruled column. The total of the accounts payable column will be posted in summary to the accounts payable account in the general ledger. The debit from the purchases column will be posted in summary to the merchandise purchases account in the general ledger. The general accounts debited column will be checked off, since no posting is necessary at the end of the month. (Remember that we post the general ledger accounts debited column to the specific accounts during the month; thus no posting is necessary or appropriate at the end of the month.) A **schedule of accounts payable** is prepared from the balances in the individual creditors' accounts. The total of this schedule must agree with the balance of the accounts payable control account before a trial balance can be prepared. **Complete Computational Problem 4, Part A** (pp. 172–173).

YOU SHOULD REMEMBER

All purchases of goods and/or services on credit are recorded in the purchases journal.

Daily postings are recorded as credits to the individual creditor accounts in the accounts payable ledger, and are also made to the general ledger accounts recorded to the general accounts debited column of the purchases journal.

The end-of-month summary entry causes the total of the purchases account column to be posted as a debit to purchases account in the general ledger. The total of the accounts payable column is posted as a credit to the accounts payable control account in the general ledger.

The total of the balances in the individual creditor accounts (known as the "schedule of accounts payable") must agree with the balance in the general ledger accounts payable (control) account before a trial balance is prepared.

• *CASH PAYMENTS JOURNAL*

RECORDING TRANSACTIONS

Credit purchases, regardless of their nature or terms, eventually must be paid for. This requirement is the basis for the cash payments journal. The **cash payments journal** is used any time that there is an outlay of cash, regardless of the reason; cash payments automatically call for the use of this multicolumn special journal. The form that the cash payments journal takes will depend basically upon the needs of the organization.

Example: Typical Form of the Cash Payments Journal

Cash Payments Journal   Page CP-1

Date 19 8–	Account Debited	PR	General Accounts Dr.	Accounts Payable Dr.	Purchases Debit	Purchases Discount Cr.	Cash Cr.
Jan. 2	Purchases	✔			500 00		500 00
4	S. Allen	A		150 00			150 00
9	Jones Supply Co.	J		2000 00		40 00	1960 00
14	Rent Expense	45	200 00				200 00
19	Office Supplies	15	50 00				50 00
31			250 00	2150 00	500 00	40 00	2860 00
			(✔)	(60)	(66)	(67)	(1)

The multicolumn cash payments journal illustrated has special columns for accounts payable, purchases, purchases discounts, and cash. When recording in the last three account columns, no posting is made from these columns during the month. Since the nature of the entries to each individual column is the same, time and labor are saved in posting at the end of the month. The accounts payable column records the reduction in liabilities to individual creditor accounts. This column is posted daily to the subsidiary accounts payable ledger. Since the accounts payable account in the general ledger presents a summary of the postings to the subsidiary ledger accounts, it is necessary to post the total of the accounts payable column at the end of the month as part of the summary entry.

When there are a substantial number of cash payments dealing with a specific item such as salaries, the accountant may choose to introduce another special column, in this case for salaries expense. If this column is used, posting is made in summary at the end of the month only.

Where a special column does not exist (Jan. 14—Rent Expense), the debited account is named in the account debited column and the general accounts debited column records the amount. Since numerous different accounts are recorded in this column, posting must be made on a daily basis.

THE SUMMARY ENTRY

The summary entry for the cash payments journal is prepared in a fashion similar to that for the cash receipts journal. At the end of the month the columns are first pencil-footed. The total of the debit column totals must agree with the totals of the credit column totals. Once this has been determined, the figures are written in ink and the columns are double underscored. The accounts payable column and all special columns are then posted in total to their respective accounts in the general ledger with the appropriate posting reference numbers placed in parentheses under the amounts. A checkmark is placed under the general accounts debit column to indicate that no summary posting of that column is to be made, since the individual transactions have been posted daily.

YOU SHOULD REMEMBER

All payments of cash, regardless of the reason for the payment, are recorded in the cash payments journal.

Daily debit postings are made from the accounts payable column to the individual accounts in the subsidiary accounts payable ledger. The general accounts dr. column is also posted daily to those accounts found in the general ledger. The total of the accounts payable dr. column is posted to the accounts payable control account at the end of the month. All other special columns are posted in a similar fashion as part of the summary entry.

The separate subsidiary accounts payable ledger contains individual accounts for each creditor from whom purchases are made on credit.

The purchase is initially recorded in the purchases journal. The credit part of the entry is posted to the individual creditor account in the subsidiary accounts payable ledger.

When payment is made to the creditor at a later date, the entry is first recorded in the cash payments journal, and the debit to the creditor's account is posted to the debit column of the individual creditor's account in the accounts payable ledger.

At the end of the month the totals of the accounts payable column in both the purchases and the cash payments journal are posted to the accounts payable control account in the general ledger.

The control account mirrors the activity of the subsidiary ledger.

The schedule of accounts payable should verify the correctness of the accounts payable control account in the general ledger. If the two fail to agree, the accountant must locate the discrepancy, make the necessary corrections, and then proceed to prepare a trial balance.

The summary entries from the special journals are made so that the special columns not posted during the month are posted to the appropriate ledger accounts in the general ledger at the end of the month.

The accounts receivable and accounts payable columns in the special journals are posted daily to the subsidiary ledgers and in summary at the end of the month to the respective general ledger control accounts.

BRACKET ENTRIES

The use of subsidiary ledgers (accounts receivable ledger, accounts payable ledger) and control accounts (accounts receivable, accounts payable) in the general ledger requires that both the general ledger and the subsidiary ledger contain the same total information. The schedule of accounts receivable and accounts payable verifies the correctness of the control accounts. When the four special journals are used, the daily posting and summary entries assume that the control accounts agree with the schedules of the subsidiary ledger.

On occasion it becomes necessary to record transactions in the general journal. When these transactions involve customer or creditor accounts, unique problems result. Both the control and the subsidiary account must be posted. The use of a **bracket entry** or a **double-posting entry** solves this problem. Whenever a general journal entry requires an entry to a customer or creditor account, a bracket entry is prepared.

Example: Bracket Entry

A business received a 30-day promissory note on March 10, 198–, from R. Friend for $3,000 in payment of her oral promise.

```
198–
Mar. 10   Notes Receivable                    8      3,000
              ⎧ R. Friend           ⎫         F
              ⎩ Accounts Receivable ⎭         5               3,000
           30-day note, due 4/6.
```

Notice that the requirements of double-entry accounting have been met in that the debits are equal to the credits; however, notice also that two accounts are posted as credits. The posting of R. Friend is made to the subsidiary ledger. Since there is no special column for the customer, there is a resulting need to post the credit to the control account. This posting is also done immediately. Transactions involving sales returns as well as purchases returns are handled in a similar fashion (if the returns are the result of previous credit transactions). **Complete Computational Problem 5, Part A** (pp. 173–174).

YOU SHOULD REMEMBER

Whenever an entry involving either an accounts receivable or an accounts payable is recorded in the general journal, it must be recorded as a bracket entry, which makes possible a double posting to the control account and the individual account in the subsidiary ledger.

The bracket entry causes two accounts to be listed (thus the double posting), but only one amount to be shown.

• *OTHER SPECIAL JOURNALS*

Other special journals are introduced into the accounting system if they are required by the volume of transactions recorded or the need for a division of labor. Additional special journals are also used for analysis of data. Two special journals that may meet the criteria for use are the **purchases returns and allowances journal** and the **sales returns and allowances journal.** When these journals are used, the entries for sales returns and purchases returns are not recorded in the general journal as previously discussed, but rather in the special journal established.

The purchases returns and allowances journal may show that a large number of credit purchases are being returned by the buyer to the seller. A significant number of purchase returns indicates that there is a problem that must be rectified. The intent of a buyer in purchasing merchandise is to resell the goods and recognize a profit from doing so. Goods returned to the seller are obviously not available for resale by the purchaser. If a pattern of continued returns is established with a supplier, this situation is readily seen in the purchases returns and allowances journal. It will probably result in the reduction or total elimination of any business dealings with that particular seller (creditor).

The purchases returns and allowances journal has an account debited column in order to record the reduction in the obligation to the creditor, as well as an explanation column.

Example: Typical Form of the Purchases Returns and Allowances Journal

Purchases Returns and Allowances Journal   Page PR-1

Date		Account Debited	Explanation	PR		Amount		
19 8–								
Jan.	*3*	*R. Smith*	*Damaged Mdse.*	*S*			*7 5*	*00*
	9	*Alpine Co.*	*Wrong goods sent*	*A*			*4 5*	*00*
	31			*25/41*		*1 2 0*		*00*

Daily postings are made to the creditor accounts in the subsidiary ledger. At the end of the month, the summary entry causes a debit to be posted to the accounts payable control account in the general ledger, and a corresponding credit to be posted to the purchases returns and allowances account in the general ledger.

The need for the sales returns and allowances journal arises when there are a large number of sales returns that were originally sales to customers on credit. A large volume of transactions justifies the use of this journal, but it may also help the seller to analyze the reasons these sales returns are taking place. It is a basic assumption that the purchasers of the goods bought them in good faith with the intention of keeping them. Circumstances beyond the buyers' control caused them to request permission to return the goods to the seller. Sales returns may have resulted from incorrect goods being shipped, goods being received in damaged or soiled condition, goods being received late, and numerous other reasons. It is important for the seller to identify the reason he or she is sending a credit memorandum to the buyer and to take steps to remedy the situation. The use of the sales returns and allowances journal will highlight various problems so that corrective action may be taken.

Example: Typical Form of the Sales Returns and Allowances Journal

Sales Returns and Allowances Journal   *Page SR-1*

Date	Credit Memo #	Account Credited	Explanation	PR	Amount
19 8– Jan. 4	402	L. Breen	Soiled goods	B	6 5 00
19	403	Restin Co.	Incorrect order	R	4 3 5 00
26	404	Arnold Bros.	Soiled goods	A	1 0 00
31				35/5	5 1 0 00

Posting is made to the individual customer accounts during the month. At the end of the month, the summary entry is posted to the sales returns and allowances account in the general ledger and a credit posting is made to the accounts receivable control account in the general ledger. **Complete Computational Problem 6, Part A** (pp. 174–176).

YOU SHOULD REMEMBER

The purchases returns and allowances journal may reveal a pattern of repeated returns of credit purchases, indicating a problem with the supplier.

The sales returns and allowances journal highlights excessive returns of goods sold on credit, helping the seller to identify the problem and take corrective action.

If the sales returns and allowances journal and the purchases returns and allowances journal are not used, credit returns must be recorded in the general journal and require bracket entries.

For more practice in mastering the material in this chapter, **complete Computational Problem 7, Part A** (pp. 175–179) and **Computational Problems 1 and 2, Part B** (pp. 180–182).

KNOW THE CONCEPTS

DO YOU KNOW THE BASICS?

1. The following business transactions occurred during an accounting period. Using the five primary journals discussed, indicate in the appropriate area which journal the transaction would be recorded in.

Journal

(a) Sale of goods on account _____

(b) Sale of merchandise for cash _____

(c) Issued a credit memo to a customer _____

(d) Cash payment of a promissory note _____

(e) Sale of a service on credit _____

(f) Purchase of office furniture on credit _____

(g) Purchased merchandise for cash _____

(h) Received a credit memo from a creditor _____

(i) Adjusting entry to recognize accrued salaries _____

(j) Received a promissory note in place of an oral promise from _____
a customer

(k) Paid monthly rent _____

(l) Received a check from a customer in part payment of an oral _____
promise

(m) End-of-period adjusting entry for revenue _____

2. Test your knowledge of this chapter by classifying each of the following statements as *True* or *False*. If your answer is *False*, explain why.

(a) The use of special journals and ledgers makes it possible for several bookkeepers to work on different accounting records at the same time.

(b) If merchandise costing $500 is purchased with terms of 2/10, n/30, the amount due in 10 days is $500.

(c) The cash receipts journal is used to record the collection of cash made by the business.

(d) A sales discount represents a form of revenue to the seller.

(e) Cash refunds to customers are recorded in the sales returns and allowances journal.

(f) The purchases journal is used to record all purchases that are made on credit.

(g) Transportation costs paid on the purchase of merchandise are recorded in the merchandise purchases account.

(h) Purchases discounts represent a form of revenue to the buyer of goods.

(i) The summary entry in the sales journal is a debit to the accounts receivable account and a credit to the sales account.

(j) The accounts payable subsidiary ledger is posted to at the end of the month as part of the summary entry from the purchase and the cash payments journals.

(k) Adjusting entries at the end of the accounting period are recorded in the general journal.

(l) If a purchases returns and allowances journal is not used, any purchase returns are recorded in the general journal, assuming that the obligation has not yet been paid.

(m) A refund received from a creditor is recorded in the purchases returns and allowances journal, assuming that this journal is used by the business.

(n) The general ledger columns found in the cash receipts and the cash payments journals are not posted as part of the month-end summary entries, and checkmarks are placed under the columns.

(o) When a promissory note is sent to a creditor in exchange for an oral promise, this transaction is recorded in the cash payments journal.

TERMS FOR STUDY

accounts payable control account
accounts payable ledger
accounts receivable control account
accounts receivable ledger
bracket entry
control account

purchases returns and allowances
   journal
sales returns and allowances journal
schedule of accounts payable
schedule of accounts receivable
subsidiary journal

PRACTICAL APPLICATION

PART A. COMPUTATIONAL PROBLEMS WITH COMPLETE SOLUTIONS

1. The following business transactions took place during the month of February 198–, for the Anderson Stationery Co.:

198–

Feb. 3 Sold stationery supplies to Clearview Mfg. Co. for $680, terms: n/30.

8 Sold 10 reams of bifold computer paper to Data Word Associates for $89, terms: n/30.

17 Sold stationery supplies to HAL Corp. for $700, terms: n/30.

28 Sold 15 cases of rexo-graph paper 8½" × 11" to Clearview Mfg. Co. for $180, terms: n/30.

(a) Rule a sales journal similar to the one illustrated.
(b) Set up general ledger accounts for accounts receivable (page 5), and sales (page 40).
(c) Set up four customer accounts in the accounts receivable ledger.
(d) Journalize and post the transactions presented above.
(e) Summarize the sales journal.
(f) Prepare a schedule of accounts receivable.

2. Record the following transactions in Estelle Rafferty's sales journal and cash receipts journal for the month of October, 198–. Estelle Rafferty, the proprietor:

198–
Oct. 1 Received a check for $100 from L. Marin in partial payment of his account.

5 Sent invoice #201 to T. Ross for sale made today amounting to $100, terms: 2/10, n/30.

9 Made an additional cash investment in the business amounting to $1,500.

13 Sold goods to R. Adams for $220. Terms: n/30.

15 Received a check from T. Ross in payment of invoice dated October 5, 198–. (Note the terms of October 5 transaction.)

17 Received a check from R. Horne in payment of his note due today. The amount of the note was $450.

21 Sent an invoice to G. Crane for sale made today for $310. Terms: 2/10, n/30.

25 Received a check for $235 from T. Ross in full payment of his October 1 balance.

29 Received $350 from cash customers for miscellaneous sales of merchandise.

31 Received a check from G. Crane in payment of the invoice dated October 21.

After you have recorded the above transactions to the appropriate journals, prepare the summary entry for the sales and cash receipts journals.

3. Set up the following accounts with balances as indicated:

GENERAL LEDGER

Acc. #	Account	Balance
1	Cash	$1,100 (dr.)
5	Accounts Receivable	770 (dr.)
7	Notes Receivable	750 (dr.)
40	Estelle Rafferty, Capital	8,000 (cr.)
50	Sales	0
51	Sales Discounts	0

ACCOUNTS RECEIVABLE LEDGER

R. Adams	$210
G. Crane	180
L. Marin	145
T. Ross	235

On the basis of the solution you prepared for Computational Problem 2, post from the sales and cash receipts journal to the accounts set up. Post the summary entries, and prepare a schedule of accounts receivable to verify that the ledger agrees with the accounts receivable control account.

4. Set up a purchases journal in a form similar to the one just illustrated. Record the following journal entries to the purchases journal:

198–
Apr. 1 Purchased merchandise from the Bolden Co., amounting to $700. Terms: n/30.

5 Purchased office supplies from the Reliable Office Supply Co. for $125. Terms: n/15.

9 Bought office equipment consisting of a typewriter and table for $325. Terms: n/20 from A & B Equipment Co.

15 Purchased merchandise from the Caldwell Manufacturing Co. for $375. Terms: n/30.

After journalizing these four entries to the purchases journal, pencil-foot the journal, verify that total debits are equal to the accounts payable credit total, and rule the journal, indicating the last day of the month.

Set up general ledger "T" accounts for office supplies, office equipment, merchandise purchases, and accounts payable. Set up an accounts payable ledger account for the creditors listed in the purchases journal. Post the transactions from the purchases journal to the appropriate ledgers during the month and in summary at the end of the month.

Prepare a schedule of accounts payable to verify that the subsidiary ledger is in agreement with the accounts payable control account in the general ledger. The form of the schedule of accounts payable is similar to that of the schedule of accounts receivable illustrated on page 157.

5. Set up the following journals on appropriate accounting paper, using the forms illustrated in the text: sales journal, cash receipts journal, purchases journal, cash payments journal, and a two-column general journal.

The following transactions took place during the month of March, 198–. Record these transactions in the appropriate journals.

198–
Mar. 1 Issued a check for $150 to Landis Co. for the March rent.

3 Purchased merchandise from Harris Co. for $950. Terms: 2/10, n/30.

5 Cash sales for the week amounted to $1,000.

6 Received a credit memorandum from Harris Co. authorizing the return of $50 worth of merchandise purchased on March 3.

8 Sold merchandise to Adams Bros. for $1,200. Terms: 1/2 cash, balance in 30 days.

9 Received a check from Adams Bros. in accordance with the terms of March 8 sale.

11 Issued a $200 check to Bradleys College to pay the tuition for Mr. Reynold's son (the owner of the business).

198–

Mar. **13** Issued a check to Harris Co. to pay the invoice of March 3, less the return of March 6.

16 Merchandise sold to Stone Bros. Terms: 1/10, n/30. The amount of the invoice was $800.

17 Issued a check for $70 to Rapid Transit, Inc. for freight charges on the sale of March 16.

19 Received a 60-day, $500 promissory note from Blake Co. in settlement of its account.

20 Issued a $20 check to the Acc Stationery Co. for the purchase of office supplies.

23 Purchased $800 worth of merchandise from Young & Son. Terms: 30-day note.

24 Issued our 30-day note to Young & Son as per terms of the purchase of March 23.

25 Received a check from Stone Bros. as per terms of March 16 sale.

26 Received a check for $900 from Carson Company in payment of their 30-day promissory note due today. The note included interest of $15.

31 Paid the monthly payroll amounting to $3,450.

Summarize the journals, and indicate which columns are to be posted at the end of the month. Any column that is not to be posted at the end of the month should contain a checkmark.

6. Rule T accounts for a general ledger, an accounts receivable ledger, and an accounts payable ledger. In the general ledger the 100 series will be used for assets, the 200 series will be used for liabilities and account numbers, and 301

and 302 will be used for the proprietor's capital and drawing accounts. Account numbers 305 through 310 will be used for revenue accounts, and account numbers 311 through 330 will be used for expenses.

Rule the four special journals and the general journal discussed in this chapter.

Elizabeth Babson began a retail beauty parlor business on March 10, 198–. You are to record the following business transactions in the appropriate journals, and post to the correct ledger accounts on a daily basis. At the end of the month, summarize the journals and post the summary entries. Prepare a schedule of accounts receivable and accounts payable. If the schedules agree with the control accounts, prepare a trial balance dated March 31, 198–.

Elizabeth Babson began business on March 10 by investing the following assets in the business: Cash, $5,000; Beauty Supplies, $2,000; Equipment, $2,500. (Since the proprietor is beginning business on this date, this entry is traditionally recorded in the general journal, even though cash has been received. Record this compound entry in the general journal, recognizing the assets and the proprietor's capital. This transaction is to be posted immediately to the various ledger accounts.)

198–

Mar. 11 Sent a check for $300 to the Reliable Leasing Corp. in payment of the rent for the month of March.

12 Purchased beauty supplies from the Able Supply Co. for $260. Terms 2/10, n/30.

13 Sent a check to the Drago Insurance Co. for the premium on an insurance policy on the premises for $180.

14 Cash sale for the week amounted to $2,600.

15 Sold beauty supplies to Estelle Evans, a customer, for $200. Terms: 1/10, n/30.

16 Ms. Evans returned $50 of the beauty supplies, and a credit memorandum was issued for the return.

17 Purchased a professional hair dryer for $300 from the Consolidated Equipment Co. Terms: 3/10, 1/20, n/30.

198–

Mar. 19 Sent a check to the Able Supply Co. in payment of the invoice of March 12.

20 Received a credit memorandum from Consolidated Equipment Co. for $20. This allowance was for the repair of the dryer.

21 The proprietor withdrew $300 cash from the business for personal use.

24 Received a check from Ms. Evans for payment of the March 15 invoice less the return of March 16.

25 Cash sales from March 15 to today amounted to $5,300.

26 Sold beauty supplies on credit to Ruth Glasser for $350. Terms: 1/10, n/30.

27 Paid salaries for the 3 weeks ending today, amounting to $675.

28 Purchased store supplies from the Eveready Stationery Co. for $75 cash.

29 Sent a check to the Consolidated Equipment Co. for balance due.

30 Purchased beauty supplies from the Able Supply Co. amounting to $350. Terms: 2/10, n/30.

31 Sold beauty supplies to Estelle Evans for $600. Terms: 30-day promissory note.

31 Received promissory note from Estelle Evans as per terms of sale made today.

7. Do the following:

   (a) Set up a general journal (J5), a sales journal (S6), a purchases journal (P4), a five-column cash receipts journal (CR7), and a five-column cash payments journal (CP3) as illustrated in Chapter 6.

(b) Set up three-column general ledger accounts, allowing six lines for each account, and record the beginning balances based on the trial balance presented below:

Taft Trading Co.		
Trial Balance		
April 1, 198–		
	DEBIT	CREDIT
Cash (#101)	$12,500.00	
Accounts Receivable (#105)	6,000.00	
Supplies (#110)	375.00	
Merchandise Inventory, 1/1/8- (#115)	3,200.00	
Furniture and Fixtures (#120)	2,500.00	
Accumulated Depreciation (#121)		$ 250.00
Accounts Payable (#150)		2,750.00
Notes Payable (#155)		500.00
Alton Taft, Capital (#200)		15,000.00
Alton Taft, Drawing (#201)	3,500.00	
Sales (#210)		32,300.00
Sales Returns and Allowances (#211)	2,200.00	
Sales Discounts (#212)	325.00	
Merchandise Purchases (#215)	14,800.00	
Purchases Returns and Allowances (#216)		900.00
Purchases Discounts (#218)		130.00
Rent Expense (#220)	2,400.00	
Salaries Expense (#221)	2,775.00	
Advertising Expense (#225)	1,255.00	
	$51,830.00	$51,830.00

(c) Set up three-column accounts receivable ledger accounts recording the account title, account reference number, and explanation. Allow five lines for each customer account. Use April 1 as the date of entry for each of the following customers:

Ruth Barnes Co. (Balance due less 2% by April 3)	#105.1	$2,400.00
E. Davis & Sons (Terms: 60 day note)	#105.2	900.00
F. Hakim Co. (2% by April 8 or net April 28)	#105.3	2,000.00
Reliable Products Co. (Balance due on April 16)	#105.4	700.00

(d) Set up three-column accounts payable ledger accounts recording the account title, account reference number, and explanation. Allow five lines for each creditor account. Use April 1 as the date of entry for each of the following creditors:

Campbell Co. (n/30, due April 6)	#150.1	$1,500.00
Lang Assoc. (3% by April 12 or Net April 30)	#150.2	1,000.00
Rand Inc. (Terms: 30-day note)	#150.3	250.00

The outstanding item in notes payable, for $500, is owed to Lang Assoc. and due to be paid on April 8. Record this information in the explanation column of the general ledger account.

(e) Set up any necessary ledger accounts in the respective ledgers as needed, assigning an account page number beyond #225 regardless of the nature of the account added. Be certain that an appropriate account does not already exist on the books. Record the entries listed below to the appropriate journals, and post the portion of the entry that requires daily postings. Remember that no daily postings will be necessary from special columns except for the accounts receivable and accounts payable columns. Be certain to include the appropriate post-reference notations in both the journals and the ledger accounts.

198–
Apr. 2 Sent a check (#201) to Aronson Realty Corp. in payment of the April rent for $800.

3 Received a check from Ruth Barnes Co. in payment of the balance of April 1 less the appropriate discount taken.

5 Sold merchandise to the Reliable Products Co. for $1,300 as shown by invoice #501, terms: 2/10, n/30.

6 Sent check #202 to Campbell Co. for obligation of April 1.

7 Issued credit memorandum #065 to Reliable Products Co. for goods returned by them amounting to $150. This return reflected our invoice #501, dated April 5.

8 Sent check #203 to Lang Assoc. in payment of our note to them due today.

8 Received a check from F. Hakim Co. in payment of April 1 balance, as per our terms.

9 Received a promissory note from E. Davis & Sons as per terms of the April 1 balance in their account.

198–

Apr. 10 Cash sales for the 2 weeks ending today amounted to $4,300.

12 Sent a check (#204) to Lang Assoc. less the discount as per the terms of the April 1 balance. (Refer to accounts payable ledger.)

15 Sent a promissory note to Rand Inc. as per the terms of our April 1 obligation. (Refer to accounts payable ledger.)

16 Received a check from Reliable Products Co. in payment of its outstanding balance of April 1. (Refer to accounts receivable ledger.)

17 Purchased merchandise from Lang Assoc. for $1,250. The terms of their invoice #7654 were 3/10, n/30.

18 Received credit memo #34 from Lang Assoc. authorizing our return to them of goods valued at $140.

20 Issued check #205 to Rand Inc. for $95. This check was in payment for supplies purchased today.

23 The proprietor took merchandise out of the business valued at $300. These goods were for his personal use.

25 Received a check from Reliable Products Co. for $500 on account. (Refer to invoice #501)

27 Paid salaries amounting to $945 for the 3 weeks ending April 19. Issued check #206 for this payment.

29 Purchased goods from Campbell Co. for $800, terms: n/30. Received its invoice #A2035.

30 Recorded cash sales for the 2 weeks ending this date for $3,500.

30 The proprietor withdrew $1,250 from the business for his personal use.

   (f) Summarize the special journals and post the summary entries to the appropriate ledger accounts.

   (g) Verify the correctness of the ledger accounts in the general ledger, accounts receivable ledger, and accounts payable ledger.

   (h) Prepare a schedule of accounts receivable and a schedule of accounts payable dated April 30, 198–.

   (i) Having verified that the respective schedules are in agreement with the control accounts in the general ledger, prepare a trial balance dated April 30, 198–.

PART B. COMPUTATIONAL PROBLEMS WITH PARTIAL SOLUTIONS OR KEY ANSWERS

1. Using a sales journal and a cash receipts journal, record the following selected transactions. Summarize the special journals and indicate the postings.

198–

Feb. 1 Sold $120 merchandise to A. Vale, terms: 2/10, n/30.

2 Cash sales amounted to $325.

8 Sold merchandise to W. Quinn for $200, terms: 2/10, n/30.

11 Received a check from A. Vale in payment of our invoice dated 2/1/8–.

14 Received a check from W. Quinn for $100, on account.

16 Sold goods to A. Vale for $350, terms: 2/10, n/30.

17 Received a check from W. Quinn for the balance owed on invoice dated 2/8/8–. (Refer to 2/14 transaction.)

28 Received a check from A. Vale in payment of our invoice dated February 16, 198–.

2. Do the following:

   (a) Set up a general journal, a sales journal, and a five-column cash receipts journal as illustrated in Chapter 6.

   (b) Set up general ledger accounts based on the information that follows:

198–	Account Name and Number		Dr.	Cr.
Mar. 1	Cash	101	$2,000	
1	Accounts Receivable	110	–0–	
1	Notes Receivable	115	500	
1	A. Johnson, Capital	251		$2,500

   (c) Set up a subsidiary accounts receivable ledger to which you will post on a daily basis.

   (d) Record the following transactions in the appropriate journal, and post to the required ledger accounts. Set up additional ledger accounts as necessary.

   198–
   Mar. 3 Sold merchandise to A. Allen for $350, terms: n/10 (Inv. #1).

   4 Received a check from A. Adams in payment of his note due today.

   5 Shipped merchandise to B. Blake amounting to $520, terms: 2/10, n/30.

   6 Cash sales amounted to $700.

   7 Received part payment of $120 from B. Blake for the invoice of March 5.

   10 Sold $480 in merchandise to C. Carson, terms: ½ cash balance in 10 days.

   11 Received a check for $240 as per terms of March 10 invoice.

   12 Received a check from B. Blake for balance due on invoice of March 5. (Note credit terms given on March 5.)

198–

Mar. 13 Received a check from A. Allen in payment of March 3 invoice.

15 Sold merchandise to D. Davis for $800, terms: 15-day note.

17 Received the 15-day note from D. Davis as per sale of March 15. (Record bracket entry in general journal.)

19 Received a check from C. Carson for balance of invoice of 3/10.

23 Sold merchandise to A. Allen for $400, terms: n/10.

28 Received a check from D. Davis in payment of March 15 invoice.

29 Sold goods to C. Carson for $245, terms: 2/10, n/30.

31 Sold merchandise to B. Blake for $650, terms: 30-day note.

(e) Summarize the special journals and post the summary entries to the appropriate ledger accounts
(f) Pencil-foot the ledger accounts, and determine the balances for both the general ledger and the accounts receivable ledger.
(g) Prepare a schedule of accounts receivable dated March 31, 198–.
(h) Prepare a trial balance dated March 31, 198–.

3. Do the following:
   (a) Set up a general journal, a purchases journal, and a five-column cash payments journal, as illustrated in Chapter 6.
   (b) Set up three-column general ledger accounts, allowing four lines for each account, and record the beginning balances based on the information that follows:

198–	Account Name and Number		Dr.	Cr.
June 1	Cash	101	$5,500	
1	Supplies	104	300	
1	Equipment	110	2,500	

198–	Account Name and Number		Dr.	Cr.
June 1	Accounts Payable (Control)	150		$3,000
1	Notes Payable (R. Arlen)	151		400
1	R. S. Tandy, Capital	200		2,650
1	R. S. Tandy, Drawing	201	1,300	
1	Sales	205		6,750
1	Merchandise Purchases	210	3,200	
1	Freight on Purchases	211	–0–	
1	Discount on Purchases	212		–0–

(c) Set up three-column accounts payable ledger accounts, allowing five lines for each account, for the following creditors:

198–	Creditor Name and Page Designation		Balance
June 1	R. Arlen	A	$ 200
1	M. Blume Co.	B	1,300
1	T. Levine	L	600
1	R. Negri & Sons	N	900

(d) Record the following transactions in the appropriate journal, and post to the required ledger accounts. Set up additional ledger accounts as necessary.

198–

June 2 The proprietor, R. S. Tandy, made an additional cash investment in the business amounting to $2,500.

3 Purchased merchandise from M. Blume Co. for $500, terms: 2/10, n/30.

5 Sent our check to R. Negri & Sons for $300 on account.

7 Received a bill from the Fast Freight Co. for $25. This bill is for freight charges for the June 3 purchase and is to be paid on June 15. (Record in purchases journal.)

8 Sent a check to R. Arlen in payment of note due today that included interest of $8.

10 Purchased supplies from T. Levine for $260, terms: 1/10, n/30.

198–

June 12 Sent a check to M. Blume Co. in payment of its invoice dated June 3. (Refer to June 3 invoice.)

15 Sent a check to Fast Freight Co. for amount outstanding.

16 The proprietor, R. S. Tandy, took supplies valued at $35 home for personal use.

18 Purchased equipment from R. Arlen for $480, terms: n/30.

20 Returned a defective piece of equipment to R. Arlen. The cost of the equipment returned was $180. Received a credit memo this day authorizing the return of the purchase of June 18.

22 Purchased merchandise from R. Negri & Sons for $530, paying cash.

23 Purchased merchandise from M. Blume Co. for $800, terms: 2/10, n/30.

25 Sent a check to T. Levine in payment of the creditor's invoice of March 10.

30 Sent a check to M. Blume Co. in payment of the creditor's invoice of March 23.

(e) Summarize the special journals on June 30, and post the summary entries to the appropriate ledger accounts.

(f) Pencil-foot the ledger accounts, and determine the balance for each general ledger and subsidiary ledger account.

(g) Prepare a schedule of accounts payable dated June 30, 19–.

(h) Having verified that the schedule of accounts payable is in agreement with the balance in the accounts payable (control) account, prepare a trial balance dated June 30, 19–.

ANSWERS

KNOW THE CONCEPTS

Journal

1. (a) Sales
   (b) Cash receipts
   (c) General
   (d) Cash payments
   (e) Sales
   (f) Purchases
   (g) Cash payments
   (h) General
   (i) General
   (j) General
   (k) Cash payments
   (l) Cash receipts
   (m) General

2. (a) True.
   (b) False. If the obligation is paid in 10 days, the buyer is entitled to take a purchases discount of 2% of the purchase price. This discount amounts to $10; thus the amount to be paid in 10 days is $490 ($500 − $10).
   (c) True.
   (d) False. To the seller the sales discount is an expense. On the buyer's books the discount taken is known as a purchases discount, which to the buyer represents a form of revenue.
   (e) False. A cash refund given to a customer is recorded in the cash payments journal. If the seller had issued a credit memo, then this transaction would appropriately be placed in the sales returns and allowances journal. If no such journal was in use, then the entry for the credit memo would be recorded in the general journal.
   (f) True.
   (g) False. A separate account, entitled "Freight on Purchases" or Freight-In" or "Freight Inward," would be used to recognize this freight expense. The title of this account also indicates the direction of the transportation charges; "Freight Expense" or "Transportation Expense" would not be an appropriate account title. The merchandise purchases account is debited only for the cost of the actual merchandise purchased.
   (h) True.
   (i) True.
   (j) True.
   (k) True.
   (l) True.

(m) False. The purchases returns and allowances journal is used to record the receipt of a credit memo from the seller that authorizes the return of goods by the buyer. A refund is recorded on the purchaser's books in the cash receipts journal.

(n) True.

(o) False. This transaction is recorded in the general journal, since the transaction has no effect on either the receipt or the payment of cash.

PRACTICAL APPLICATION
PART A

1.

Sales Journal   Page S-1

Date		Account Debited	Terms	Inv. #	PR	Amount
19 8–						
Feb.	3	Clearview Mfg. Co.	(n/30)		C	6 8 0 00
	8	Data Word Associates	(n/30)		D	8 9 00
	17	HAL Corp.	(n/30)		H	7 0 0 00
	28	Clearview Mfg. Co.	(n/30)		C	1 8 0 00
	28	Dr. Accounts Receivable, Cr. Sales			5/40	1 0 4 9 00

General Ledger

Accounts Receivable   Page 5

Date		PR	Debit	Credit	Balance Debit	Balance Credit
19 8–						
Feb.	28	S-1	1 6 4 9 00		1 6 4 9 00	

Sales   Page 40

Date		PR	Debit	Credit	Balance Debit	Balance Credit
19 8–						
Feb.	28	S-1		1 6 4 9 00		1 6 4 9 00

Accounts Receivable Ledger

Clearview Mfg. Co.   Page C

Date		PR	Debit	Credit	Debit Balance
19 8–					
Feb.	3	S-1	6 8 0 00		6 8 0 00
	28	S-1	1 8 0 00		8 6 0 00

Data Word Associates   Page D

Date		PR	Debit	Credit	Debit Balance
19 8–					
Feb.	8	S-1	8 9 00		8 9 00

HAL Corp.   Page H

Date			PR	Debit	Credit	Debit Balance
19 8– Feb. 17			S-1	700 00		700 00

Anderson Stationery Co.
Schedule of Accounts Receivable
February 28, 198–

Clearview Mfg. Co.	$ 860.00
Data Word Associates	89.00
HAL Corp.	700.00
Total Accounts Receivable	$1,649.00

2.

Sales Journal

Date		Account Debited	Terms	Inv.	PR	Amount
19 8– Oct. 5		T. Ross	2/10, n/30	201		100 00
	13	R. Adams	n/30	202		220 00
	21	G. Crane	2/10, n/30	203		310 00
	31	Dr. Accounts Receivable, Cr. Sales				630 00

Cash Receipts Journal

Date 19 8–		Account Credited	PR	General Acct. Cr.	Sales Cr.	Accounts Receivable Cr.	Sales Discount Dr.	Cash Dr.
Oct.	1	L. Marin				100 00		100 00
	9	E. Rafferty, Capital		1500 00				1500 00
	15	T. Ross				100 00	2 00	98 00
	17	Notes Receivable (R. Horne)		450 00				450 00
	25	T. Ross (Oct. 1 Bal.)				235 00		235 00
	29	Sales			350 00			350 00
	31	G. Crane				310 00	6 20	303 80
	31			1950 00	350 00	745 00	8 20	3036 80

3.

Sales Journal

Date		Account Debited	Terms	Inv.	PR	Amount
19 8– Oct. 5		T. Ross	2/10, n/30	201	R	100 00
	13	R. Adams	n/30	202	A	220 00
	21	G. Crane	2/10, n/30	203	C	310 00
	31	Dr. Accounts Receivable, Cr. Sales			5/50	630 00

Cash Receipts Journal

Date 19 8-	Account Credited	PR	General Acct. Cr.	Sales Cr.	Accounts Receivable Cr.	Sales Discount Dr.	Cash Dr.
Oct. 1	L. Marin	M			1 00 00		1 00 00
9	E. Rafferty, Capital	40	15 00 00				15 00 00
15	T. Ross	R			1 10 00	2 20	1 07 80
17	Notes Receivable (R. Horne)	7	4 50 00				4 50 00
25	T. Ross (Oct. 1 Bal.)	R			2 35 00		2 35 00
29	Sales	✔		3 50 00			3 50 00
31	G. Crane	C			3 10 00	6 20	3 03 80
31			19 50 00	3 50 00	7 45 00	8 40	30 46 60
			(✔)	(50)	(5)	(51)	(1)

General Ledger:

Cash   Account #1

Date		PR	Debit	Credit	Debit Balance
19 8- Oct. 1	Balance	✔			1 1 00 00
		CR-1	30 46 60		41 46 60

Accounts Receivable   Account #5

Date		PR	Debit	Credit	Debit Balance
19 8- Oct. 1	Balance	✔			7 70 00
31		S-1	6 30 00		14 00 00
31		CR-1		7 45 00	6 55 00

Notes Receivable   Account #7

Date		PR	Debit	Credit	Debit Balance
19 8- Oct. 1	Balance	✔			7 50 00
17		CR-1		4 50 00	3 00 00

E. Rafferty, Capital   Account #40

Date		PR	Debit	Credit	Credit Balance
19 8- Oct. 1	Balance	✔			8 00 00
9		CR-1		15 00 00	95 00 00

Sales Account #50

Date			PR	Debit	Credit	Credit Balance
19 Oct.	8– 31		S-1		6 4 0 00	6 4 0 00
	31		CR-1		3 5 0 00	9 9 0 00

Sales Discounts Account #51

Date			PR	Debit	Credit	Debit Balance
19 Oct.	8– 31		CR-1	8 40		8 40

Accounts Receivable Ledger:

R. Adams Page A

Date			PR	Debit	Credit	Debit Balance
19 Oct.	8– 1	Balance	✔			2 1 0 00
	13		S-1	2 2 0 00		4 3 0 00

G. Crane Page C

Date			PR	Debit	Credit	Debit Balance
19 Oct.	8– 1	Balance	✔			1 8 0 00
	21		S-1	3 1 0 00		4 9 0 00
	31		CR-1		3 1 0 00	1 8 0 00

L. Marin Page M

Date			PR	Debit	Credit	Debit Balance
19 Oct.	8– 1	Balance	✔			1 4 5 00
	1		CR-1		1 0 0 00	4 5 00

T. Ross — Page R

Date		PR	Debit	Credit	Debit Balance
19 8– Oct. 1	Balance	✔			235 00
5		S-1	100 00		335 00
15		CR-1		100 00	235 00
25		CR-1		235 00	0

E. Rafferty
Schedule of Accounts Receivable
October 31, 198–

R. Adams	$430
G. Crane	180
L. Marin	45
Total	$655

4.

Purchases Journal — Page P-23

Date	Account Credited	PR	A/P (Cr.)	Purchases (Dr.)	General Accounts Debited Account Debited	PR	Amount
19 8– Apr. 1	Bolden Co. (n/30)	B	700 00	700 00			
5	Reliable Office Supply Co. (n/15)	R	125 00		Office Supplies	8	125 00
9	A & B Equipment Co. (n/20)	A	325 00		Office Equipment	10	325 00
15	Caldwell Manufacturing Co. (n/30)	C	375 00	375 00			
30			1525 00	1075 00			450 00
			(20)	(40)			(✔)

General Ledger:

Office Supplies — Page 8

Date		PR	Debit	Credit	Debit Balance
19 8– Apr. 1		P-23	125 00		125 00

Office Equipment — Page 10

Date		PR	Debit	Credit	Debit Balance
19 8– Apr. 5		P-23	325 00		325 00

Accounts Payable — Page 20

Date		PR	Debit	Credit	Credit Balance
19 8– Apr. 30		P-23		1525 00	1525 00

Purchases   Page 40

Date			PR	Debit	Credit	Debit Balance
19 8- Apr. 30			P-23	1 0 7 5 00		1 0 7 5 00

Accounts Payable Ledger:

Bolden Co.   Page B

Date			PR	Debit	Credit	Credit Balance
19 8- Apr. 1			P-23		7 0 0 00	7 0 0 00

Reliable Office Supply Co.   Page R

Date			PR	Debit	Credit	Credit Balance
19 8- Apr. 5			P-23		1 2 5 00	1 2 5 00

A&B Equipment Co.   Page A

Date			PR	Debit	Credit	Credit Balance
19 8- Apr. 9			P-23		3 2 5 00	3 2 5 00

Caldwell Manufacturing Co.   Page C

Date			PR	Debit	Credit	Credit Balance
19 8- Apr. 15			P-23		3 7 5 00	3 7 5 00

XXXX Company
Schedule of Accounts Payable
April 30, 198–

Bolden Co.	$ 700
Reliable Office Supply Co.	125
A & B Equipment Co.	325
Caldwell Manufacturing Co.	375
	$1,525

5.

Sales Journal

Date	Account Debited	Terms	Inv. #	PR	Amount
19 8–					
Mar. 8	Adams Bros.	1/2 cash, bal. n/30	201		1 2 0 0 00
16	Stone Bros.	1/10, n/30	202		8 0 0 00
31	Dr. Accounts Receivable, Cr. Sales			( ) / ( )	2 0 0 0 00

Purchases Journal

Date 19 8–	Account Credited	PR	A/P (Cr.)	Purchases (Dr.)	General Accounts Debited Account Debited	PR	Amount
Mar. 3	Harris Co. (2/10, n/30)		9 5 0 00	9 5 0 00			
23	Young & Son (30-day note)		8 0 0 00	8 0 0 00			
			1 7 5 0 00	1 7 5 0 00			–0–
			( )	( )			(✔)

Cash Receipts Journal

Date 198–	Account Credited	PR	General Acct. Cr.	Sales Cr.	Accounts Rec. Cr.	Sales Dis. Dr.	Cash Dr.
Mar. 5	Sales	✔		1 0 0 0 00			1 0 0 0 00
9	Adams Bros.				6 0 0 00		6 0 0 00
25	Stone Bros.				8 0 0 00	8 00	7 9 2 00
26	{ Interest Income		1 5 00				9 0 0 00
	{ Notes Receivable		8 8 5 00				
31			9 0 0 00	1 0 0 0 00	1 4 0 0 00	8 00	3 2 9 2 00
			(✔)	( )	( )	( )	( )

Cash Payments Journal

Date 198–	Account Debited	PR	General Accounts Dr.	Accounts Payable Dr.	Purchases Debit	Purchases Discount Cr.	Cash Cr.
Mar. 1	Rent Expense		1 5 0 00				1 5 0 00
11	Mr. Reynolds, Drawing		2 0 0 00				2 0 0 00
13	Harris Co.			9 0 0 00		1 8 00	8 8 2 00
17	Freight on Sales		7 0 00				7 0 00
20	Office Supplies		2 0 00				2 0 00
31	Salaries Expense		3 4 5 0 00				3 4 5 0 00
31			3 8 9 0 00	9 0 0 00	–0–	1 8 00	4 7 7 2 00
			(✔)	( )	(✔)	( )	( )

Journal

Date		Description	PR	Debit	Credit
19 8-					
Mar.	6	Harris Co./Accounts Payable		5 0 00	
		Purchases Returns & Allowances			5 0 00
		For purchase of 3/3.			
	19	Notes Receivable		5 0 0 00	
		Blake Co./Accounts Receivable			5 0 0 00
		Received 60-day note			
		from Blake.			
	24	Young & Son/Accounts Payable		8 0 0 00	
		Notes Payable			8 0 0 00
		Sent 30-day note.			

6.

Purchases Journal

Date		Account Credited	PR	A/P (Cr.)	Purchases (Dr.)	Supplies (Dr.)	General Accounts Debited Account Debited	PR	Amount
19 8-									
Mar.	12	Able Supply Co., 2/10, n/30	A	2 6 0 00		2 6 0 00			
	17	Consolidated Equip. Co.							
		3/10, 1/20, n/30	C	3 0 0 00			Equipment	102	3 0 0 00
	30	Able Supply Co., 2/10, n/30	A	3 5 0 00		3 5 0 00			
	31			9 1 0 00		6 1 0 00			3 0 0 00
				(2 0 0)	(✓)	(1 0 1)			(✓)

Sales Journal

Date		Account Debited	Inv. #	Terms	PR	Amount
19 8-						
Mar.	15	Estelle Evans	105	1/10, n/30	E	2 0 0 00
	26	Ruth Glasser	123	1/10, n/30	G	3 5 0 00
	31	Estelle Evans	167	30-day note	E	6 0 0 00
	31	Dr. Accounts Receivable, Cr. Sales			103/305	1 1 5 0 00

Cash Receipts Journal

Date 19 8-		Account Credited	PR	General Acct. Cr.	Sales Cr.	Accounts Receivable Cr.	Sales Discount Dr.	Cash Dr.
Mar.	14	Sales	✓		2 6 0 0 00			2 6 0 0 00
	24	Estelle Evans	E			1 5 0 00	1 50	1 4 8 50
	25	Sales 3/15-3/25	✓		5 3 0 0 00			5 3 0 0 00
	31			-0-	7 9 0 0 00	1 5 0 00	1 50	8 0 4 8 50
				(✓)	(3 0 5)	(1 0 3)	(3 1 6)	(1 0 0)

Cash Payments Journal

Date 19 8-	Account Debited	PR	General Accounts Dr.	Accounts Payable Dr.	Purchases Debit	Purchases Discount Cr.	Cash Cr.
Mar. 11	Rent Expense	311	300 00				300 00
13	Insurance Expense	312	180 00				180 00
19	Able Supply Co.	A		260 00		5 20	254 80
21	E. Babson, Drawing	302	300 00				300 00
27	Salaries Expense	315	675 00				675 00
28	Supplies	101	75 00				75 00
29	Consolidated Equip. Co.	C		280 00		2 80	277 20
31			1530 00	540 00	–0–	8 00	2062 00
			(✓)	(200)	(✓)	(307)	(100)

Journal

Date	Description	PR	Debit	Credit
19 8-				
Mar. 10	On March 10, Elizabeth			
	Babson began a retail			
	beauty parlor with			
	the following:			
	Cash	100	5000 00	
	Supplies	101	2000 00	
	Equipment	102	2500 00	
	E. Babson, Capital	301		9500 00
16	Sale Returns & Allowances	306	50 00	
	Estelle Evans/Accounts Receivable	E/103		50 00
	Issued Credit Memo #100.			
20	Consolidated Equipment Co./Accounts Payable	C/200	20 00	
	Equipment	102		20 00
	Received C.M. toward repair.			
31	Notes Receivable	104	600 00	
	Estelle Evans/Accounts Receivable	E/103		600 00
	Received 30-day note			
	from E. Evans.			

	Cash		100
198–		198–	
Mar. 10 13,048.50 5,000.00		Mar. 30	2,062.00
31 – 2,062.00 8,048.50			
10,986.50 13,048.50			

	Supplies		101
198–			
Mar. 10	2,000.00		
28	75.00		
31	610.00		

Equipment   102

198–				198–	
Mar. 10		2,800.00	2,500.00	Mar. 20	20.00
17		− 20.00	300.00		
		2,780.00	2,800.00		

Accounts Receivable   103

198–				198–	
Mar. 31		1,150.00	1,150.00	Mar. 16	50.00
		− 800.00		31	600.00
		350.00		31	150.00

Notes Receivable   104

198–			
Mar. 31	E. Evans, 30 days	600.00	

Accounts Payable   201

198–				198–		
Mar. 20	C.M.	20.00		Mar. 31	910.00	910.00
31		540.00			− 560.00	
		560.00			350.00	

E. Babson, Capital   301

			198–	
			Mar. 10	9,500.00

E. Babson, Drawing   302

198–		
Mar. 21	300.00	

Sales   303

			198–	
			Mar. 31	1,150.00
			31	7,900.00
				9,050.00

Sales Returns and Allowances			104
198– Mar. 16 E. Evans	50.00		

Rent Expense			311
198– Mar. 11	300.00		

Insurance Expense			312
198– Mar. 13	180.00		

Merchandise Purchases			313

Purchases Returns and Allowances			314

Salaries Expense			315
198– Mar. 27	675.00		

Sales Discount			316
198– Mar. 31	1.50		

Purchases Discount			307
		198– Mar. 31	8.00

Accounts Receivable Ledger

Estelle Evans   Page E

Date		PR	Debit	Credit	Debit Balance
19 8–					
Mar. 15	1/10, n/30	S-1	2 0 0 00		2 0 0 00
16	Credit Memo #100	J-1		5 0 00	1 5 0 00
24	Bal. Less 1% Discount	CR-1		1 5 0 00	–0–
31	30-day Note	S-1	6 0 0 00		6 0 0 00
31	Received Note	J-1		6 0 0 00	–0–

Ruth Glasser   Page G

Date			Debit	Credit	Debit Balance
19 8–					
Mar. 26	1/10, n/30	S-1	3 5 0 00		3 5 0 00

**Elizabeth Babson
Schedule of Accounts Receivable
March 31, 198–**

Ruth Glasser	$350
Total	$350

Accounts Payable Ledger

Able Supply Co.   Page A

Date		PR	Debit	Credit	Balance
19 8–					
Mar. 12	2/10, n/30	P-1		2 6 0 00	2 6 0 00
19	Less 2%	CP-1	2 6 0 00		–0–
30	2/10, n/30	P-1		3 5 0 00	3 5 0 00

Consolidated Equipment Co.   Page C

Date			Debit	Credit	Balance
19 8–					
Mar. 17	3/10, 1/20, n/30	P-1		3 0 0 00	3 0 0 00
20	C.M. Received	J-1	2 0 00		2 8 0 00
29	Less 1% Discount	CP-1	2 8 0 00		–0–

**Elizabeth Babson
Schedule of Accounts Receivable
March 31, 198–**

Able Supply Co.	$350
Total	$350

7.

Sales Journal   Page 6

Date		Inv.	Account Debited	Terms	Post. Ref.	Amount
19 Apr.	8– 5	501	Reliable Products Co.	2/10, n/30	105.4	1 3 0 0 00
Apr.	30				105 210	1 3 0 0 00

Purchases Journal   Page 4

Date 19 8–	Account Credited	Post. Ref.	A/P Cr.	Purchases Dr.	General Accounts Debited		
					Account	Post. Ref.	Amount
Apr. 17	Lang Assoc. (Inv. #7654-)	150.2	1 25 0 00	1 25 0 00			
29	Campbell Co. (Inv. #A2035)	150.1	80 0 00	80 0 00			
Apr. 30			2 05 0 00	2 05 0 00			- 0 -
			(1 50)	(2 1 5)			(√)

Cash Receipts Journal — Page 7

	Date		Credited Account	Post. Ref.	General Accounts Cr.	Sales Cr.	Accounts Receivable Cr.	Sales Discount Dr.	Cash Dr.
1	19 8– Apr.	1	Cash Balance $12,500.00	✓					
2		3	Ruth Barnes	105.1			2400.00	48.00	2352.00
3		8	F. Hakim Co.	105.3			2000.00	40.00	1960.00
4		10	Sales	✓		4300.00			4300.00
5		16	Reliable Products Co.	105.4			700.00		700.00
6		25	Reliable Products Co.	105.4			500.00		500.00
7		30	Sales	✓		3500.00			3500.00
8	Apr. 30				- 0 -	7800.00	5600.00	88.00	13312.00
9					(✓)	(210)	(105)	(212)	(101)
10									

Cash Payments Journal — Page 8

	Date 19 8–	Check No.	Debited Account	Post. Ref.	General Accounts Dr.	Accounts Payable Dr.	Purchasing Discount Cr.	Cash Cr.
1	Apr. 2	201	Rent Expense	220	800.00			800.00
2	6	202	Campbell Co.	150.1		1500.00		1500.00
3	8	203	Notes Payable (Lang Assoc.)	155	500.00			500.00
4	12	204	Lang Assoc.	150.2		1000.00	30.00	970.00
5	20	205	Supplies	110	95.00			95.00
6	27	206	Salaries Expense	221	945.00			945.00
7	30	207	Alton Taft, Drawing	201	1250.00			1250.00
8	Apr. 30	—			3590.00	2500.00	30.00	6060.00
9					(✓)	(150)	(218)	(101)
10								

Journal

	Date 19 8–		Description	Post. Ref.	Debit	Credit
1	Apr.	7	Sales Returns and Allowances	211	1 5 0 00	
2			{ Reliable Products Co. }	105.4		1 5 0 00
3			{ Accounts Receivable }	105		
4			Issued Credit Memo #065–Inv. #501			
5						
6		9	Notes Receivable	226	9 0 0 00	
7			{ E. Davis & Sons }	105.2		
8			{ Accounts Receivable }	105		9 0 0 00
9			Received 60-day note per Apr. 1 terms.			
10						
11		15	{ Rand Inc. }	150.3		
12			{ Accounts Payable }	150	2 5 0 00	
13			Notes Payable	155		2 5 0 00
14			Sent our 30-day note per Apr. 1 terms.			
15						
16		18	{ Lang Assoc. }	150.2		
17			{ Accounts Payable }	150	1 4 0 00	
18			Purchases Returns and Allowances	216		1 4 0 00
19			Received Credit Memo #34.			
20						
21		23	Alton Taft, Drawing	201	3 0 0 00	
22			Merchandise Purchases	215		3 0 0 00
23			For personal use.			
24						
25						
26						
27						

Schedule of accounts receivable total, $650; schedule of accounts payable total, $1,910; April 30, 198–, trial balance totals, $60,010

PART B

1. Sales journal total, $670; Cash receipts journal—cash column total, $988.60

2. Schedule of accounts receivable total, $1,295; March 31, 198–, trial balance totals, $6,645

3. Schedule of accounts payable total, $3,000; June 30, 198–, trial balance totals, $14,926

7
SAFEGUARDING CASH—SPECIAL CONTROLS

KEY TERMS

bank reconciliation statement A statement prepared once a month to bring about agreement between the checkbook balance and the bank balance.

check An order to the bank on which it is written to pay a specific sum of money to a designated party.

petty cash fund A small amount of money, usually $50 to $150, set aside to pay for insignificant expenditures for which a check would not be accepted or appropriate.

voucher system A method of establishing control over the making of expenditures for the payment of liabilities. All transactions that will eventually result in the payment of cash must first be recorded as liabilities, using the various books of the voucher system.

INTERNAL CONTROL

A properly designed accounting system must meet the needs of the business organization for which it is being created. Provisions must be made for the accumulation, recording, and reporting of data. Chapter 6 dealt with special journals and addressed the basic organization of the books of account in use. Once these financial records are in place, it becomes necessary to ensure that the system design provides for the following:

1. Measurement of the various phases of the business's operations.

2. Assignment of authority and responsibility.

3. Implementation of a program for the prevention of errors and fraud.

The control of an organization's operations, regardless of the size of the firm, is generally known as **internal control.** In a small organization where the owner personally supervises the employees and directs the operation of the business, the degree of internal control is not as complex as in a larger, more decentralized organization. As the number of employees and the complexity of the organization increases, however, it becomes virtually impossible for management to be involved in every phase of operations. As the firm expands, management must delegate authority and place greater reliance on the accounting systems in controlling the enterprise's operations.

Internal control must see to it that assets are safeguarded, appropriate accounting data are generated, management policies and procedures are followed, and productivity and efficiency are achieved throughout the organization.

SPECIAL CONTROLS TO SAFEGUARD CASH

The most liquid asset within any organization is cash. Because cash is easily transferable, it is the asset most susceptible to improper diversion and use by employees. Since there are numerous transactions that either directly or indirectly affect the receipt of cash and its payment, it is essential that cash be effectively safeguarded through the development and use of special controls.

Within most organizations usually no significant amounts of cash are available. Any cash received is at once or within a reasonable amount of time deposited in a bank account. Any payments made by the organization are done by check. Most businesses deposit all cash receipts in a checking account at a convenient commercial bank and make all payments by check drawn against that bank. The forms used by the depositor in working with the commercial bank are signature cards, deposit slips, checks, and bank statements.

When a checking account is first opened by a business concern, certain employees are given the responsibility of signing the checks that will be drawn on the business's checking account. The authority to sign the checks is given by the signature appearing on the **signature card.** This puts the bank on notice that the signatories on the signature card are authorized to sign the check for the concern. Usually the organization will require that the signature on the check be a two-party signature. In other words, numerous individuals may be authorized to sign the checks; however, there must at all times be two signatures on a check in order for it to be valid. The two-party check serves to reduce the possibility of misappropriation of funds, and also makes more than one individual aware of where funds are being spent.

Before an organization can write checks on an account, there must be funds within the account to cover the checks written. In order to accomplish this, a

deposit slip or **deposit ticket** must be prepared. The deposit slip, which is usually prepared in duplicate, has spaces for writing the amount of currency and coin being deposited and for listing the checks being deposited. The deposit slip has a place to write in the checking account number; or, if the deposit slip is preprinted, it already contains the account number and the name of the business organization on the face of the form.

Once the checking account has been set up and there exist funds in the account, it is possible to make cash payments by writing checks on the account. A check by definition is said to take the place of cash. The **check** is an instrument that orders the bank on which it is written to pay a specific sum of money to the party designated on the face of the check. There are three parties to a check: the bank on which the check is drawn, known as the drawee; the person to whom the check is being paid (pay to the order of), the payee; and the person who signs the check, the drawer or payor. The check or, more specifically, the check stub or duplicate copy of the check becomes the basis for the journal entry made in the cash payments journal. Although the form of the individual checks issued by different banks may vary, basically the following information is found on the typical check: the name and address of the depositor; serial numbering to facilitate the depositor's internal control; a preprinted account number; and the name of the bank on which the check is written.

The records maintained by the business organization having the checking account are usually found in the checkbook, which contains the unwritten checks and the check stubs. The bank maintains a separate record of the activity within an individual checking account, and forwards to the checking account customer a bank statement, usually on a monthly basis. The **bank statement** reflects the record that the bank maintains of activities affecting the customer's checking account for the month. Like any account that is maintained for a customer or a creditor, certain specific information is found in the bank statement. This account is treated by the bank as if the customer is actually a creditor, because the funds being safeguarded for the checking account customer, as far as the bank is concerned, represent a liability to the bank.

The bank statement contains the opening balance in the customer's account. Any increases to the account as a result of deposits are listed on the bank statement as credits. Any checks the customer has written and the bank has paid during the month are shown as reductions on the bank statement, and thus are recorded as debits to the bank statement. Any charges that the bank has made, such as monthly service charges, also appear on the bank statement and are shown as reductions from the balance in the account. When the bank has been asked to pay obligations for the customer, these payments are shown as debits to the account. When the bank has acted as a collection agent for the customer, these collections appear as credits on the bank statement.

The final line on the bank statement represents the ending balance in the statement. This balance should agree with the balance on the check stub for the same date. In actual practice this is usually not the case, as will be explained shortly.

YOU SHOULD REMEMBER

Some of the important activities of management center around the planning and controlling of cash.

Most businesses make payments by checks rather than cash.

Transactions affecting an individual checking account are recorded in the checkbook by the business organization and are shown on the bank statement by the bank.

• *BANK RECONCILIATION STATEMENT*

Two records are kept of the checking account. The records are basically maintained by the bank and the customer. The balance in a checking account can be found by referring to the balance as indicated on the last check stub or by referring to the cash balance in the general ledger plus the cash receipts, less the cash payments to date. If the bank statement is compared with the balance shown by the customer's record (regardless of the record used), the accountant will usually find that the two records are not in agreement. Bringing these records into agreement is known as a **bank reconciliation.** A bank reconciliation is the process whereby the balance in the bank's records of a checking account and the balance in the depositor's records are brought into agreement. On a monthly basis a **bank reconciliation statement** is prepared that brings the checkbook balance in the customer's checkbook into agreement with the bank's balance as found on the bank statement.

The inequality that exists between the balance per the bank statement and the balance per the checkbook is due to a number of things. When a check is written by a business, the immediate effect on the checkbook balance is to reduce the balance by the amount of the check written. The bank, however, does not reduce its record of the business's balance to the extent of the check written because at that time it has no knowledge of the check having been written. This kind of check is then known as an **outstanding check.** An outstanding check is one that has been written but has not been paid by the bank because the bank has not yet received the check. The balance per the bank statement will show a higher balance than that of the checkbook because of the outstanding checks. In this case, the customer is aware of things that the bank isn't.

In some cases it is the bank that is aware of things that the customer learns of only when the bank statement is received. The monthly bank service charge calculated by the bank is recorded on the bank statement as a debit memorandum. This charge, as well as others made by the bank, is not known to the customer until receipt of the bank statement. At that time, it is necessary for the customer to adjust the business's books to reflect the information presented on the bank statement. When the bank is authorized to act as a collection agent for the customer or to pay bills for the customer, and has done so, this information as well is not usually known by the customer until receipt of the monthly bank statement. In these situations it is necessary to adjust the checkbook balance to the extent of the information in the bank statement. Any adjustments made to the checkbook side of the bank reconciliation will not only affect the checkbook balance, *but must also result in an adjusting entry being made to the books of account.*

After the actual preparation of the bank reconciliation statement has been discussed, the adjusting entries will be illustrated.

PREPARING THE STATEMENT

The bank reconciliation statement represents a comparison between the checkbook balance and the bank statement at a specific moment in time (usually at the end of the month). The reconciliation statement will represent either the account or the report form. Regardless of the form, the headings will ask the same questions that all financial statements ask: Who, What, and When. The end result of the bank reconciliation statement is to ensure that both records are in agreement. This agreement is not merely a mathematical activity, but also represents a logical approach to what has taken place, what will take place, and how the books of account should reflect the changes.

The following illustrates the form of the bank reconciliation statement. Each item listed is explained below the presentation.

Anthony Raymond Co.
Bank Reconciliation Statement
August 1, 198–

Checkbook Balance	$3,000	Bank Balance	$4,000
Less: Bank Service		Less: Outstanding Checks	
Charge	5	Check #203 $35	
Add: Notes Receivable	905	207 65	100
Adjusted Checkbook			
Balance	$3,900	Adjusted Bank Balance	$3,900

Notice that the bottom lines of the bank reconciliation statement illustrate the equality of the balances. Both final amounts are labeled "Adjusted Balance." The reason for this statement is that changes were made to both sides and had to be recorded, thus affecting the balances on both sides. Note the changes that affected each side of the reconciliation statement.

Let's discuss the bank balance side first. The list of outstanding checks is made by comparing the checks written according to the check stubs with the checks paid according to the bank statement. Any checks not listed on the bank statement are considered to be *outstanding* and are listed on the bank side of the reconciliation statement. This is completed in this fashion because it is recognized that checks written but not yet received by the bank will be received and paid within a few days. The accountant anticipates this happening and treats the checks as if received and thus paid by the bank. Any adjustment that the bank has no knowledge of will be recorded on the bank balance side of the reconciliation statement. A *deposit in transit* that has not yet been received by the bank (as indicated by the bank statement) will be added to the bank balance side as if the deposit had been received.

The adjustments recorded on the checkbook side of the bank reconciliation statement are items that the bank usually knows about, but the customer does not until either a memorandum from the bank is received or the information appears on the bank statement. On the bank reconciliation illustrated above, it appears that the bank is charging its customer for the monthly bank service charge. The bank will automatically reduce its record of the customer's balance to the extent of the bank service charge. On the bank statement, a debit memorandum will appear in which the bank charges the customer for the service rendered. When the customer reviews the statement, the subtraction for the bank service charge is then shown on the bank reconciliation statement. If the bank is also charged with the responsibility of paying obligations for the customer, these payments are handled in the same manner. Payments by the bank are noted on the bank statement, and these payments are recorded as reductions on the checkbook side of the bank reconciliation statement. The addition of the notes receivable on the checkbook side of the illustrative bank reconciliation statement indicates that a customer has paid an obligation to Raymond Co. through the bank. The bank is acting as a collection agent. When the note was paid, the bank returned the note to the customer and credited Raymond Co.'s checking account with the value of the note collected. A credit memorandum is usually sent to the customer at the time of the settlement of the note, and this transaction will appear on the bank statement for the month. Any time that bank is called upon to act as a collecting agent for the customer and receives funds in the name of the customer, it is the bank's responsibility to credit the customer's account. The credit memorandum appears on the bank statement and is recorded as an increase on the bank reconciliation statement.

THE STEPS

The bank reconciliation statement is prepared using two documents: the bank's statement and the checkbook stubs. The bank statement contains the beginning balance, deposits made during the month, checks paid during the month, debit memoranda resulting from charges made by the bank and activities causing a reduction in the customer's balance, credit memoranda resulting from collections made by the bank for the customer, and ending bank balance. The customer's checkbook stub contains the balance in the checking account, as well as deposits and information as to the checks written.

To prepare the bank reconciliation statement, the following steps should be followed:

1. Compare the deposits found on the check stub with the deposits listed on the bank statement. Any deposits not shown on the statement are known as **deposits in transit.** These deposits in transit represent deposits made but not yet credited to the customer's account by the bank. Deposits in transit are to be added to the bank balance side of the reconciliation statement.

2. Compare the cancelled (paid) checks returned by the bank, as part of the bank statement, with the check stubs to determine which checks, if any, have been written but not yet paid by the bank. If there are any outstanding checks, they will be listed on the bank balance side of the reconciliation statement. These outstanding checks will be subtracted from the bank balance as if the checks had been paid by the bank.

3. Locate any debit and credit memoranda appearing on the bank statement. These charges and credits are recorded as adjustments to the checkbook side of the bank reconciliation statement.

4. On the basis of the above information, prepare the bank reconciliation statement.

5. Prepare the necessary adjusting entries, based on the information that has been recorded to the checkbook side of the bank reconciliation statement. Any adjustment to the checkbook side must result in the recording of an adjusting entry.

RECORDING ADJUSTING ENTRIES

When the bank reconciliation has been completed, it becomes necessary to prepare adjusting entries to correct or reconcile the cash balance. The adjusting entries will be based on the adjustments made to the checkbook balance side.

If the bank service charge as recorded on the bank statement amounted to $5, the following adjusting entry would be made:

198–
Aug. 1   Bank Service Charge Expense   5
              Cash   5
         Monthly service charge.

If the bank acted as a collection agent and collected a note in the customer's favor, charging a nominal fee, the following entry would result:

198–
Aug. 1   Cash   905
             Bank Service Charge   15
                 Notes Receivable   920
         Collection of note.

It is possible for a difference between the bank balance and the checkbook balance to result from an error in the customer's books. When such an error is discovered, its correction also requires an adjusting entry. For example, if a check was properly written for $75, but on the check stub it was recorded as $57, this transposition would result in a difference in balances of $18. The correcting entry for such an error would be as follows:

```
198–
Aug. 1   Accounts Payable/J. Jones                        18
              Cash                                                    18
         To correct checkbook error.
```

Adjusting entries are made only as a result of adjustments made to the checkbook side of the bank reconciliation statement. **Complete Computational Problems 1 and 2, Part A** (pp. 218–219).

YOU SHOULD REMEMBER

Monthly bank reconciliation statements are prepared, and the resulting adjusting entries are made by most business organizations regardless of their size (provided that they have a checking account).

Common causes of inequality between the balances on the bank statement and in the checkbook are outstanding checks and bank charges.

• *PETTY CASH FUND*

Most businesses need to have small amounts of money available for various expenditures for which writing a check would be inappropriate or impracticable. Small amounts of cash may be needed to pay for transportation charges, postage fees, supplies, or coffee, as well as other small expenditures that occur on a regular basis.

Because these small payments occur frequently and amount collectively to a considerable sum of money, it is desirable to maintain close control over the payments. This can be accomplished through the establishment of a **petty cash fund.** The purpose of the petty cash fund is to have a small amount of cash on hand with which to make some minor expenditures. The person who is in charge of this fund is generally known as the petty cashier. The petty cashier is given a check written to his or her order for between $50 and $150 to establish the petty cash fund.

The initial establishment of the fund is recorded by the following journal entry:

198–

Apr. 1   Petty Cash   100

           Cash   100

          To establish the fund.

The petty cashier then cashes the check and places the money in a petty cash box, which resembles the inside of a cash register drawer. The money is distributed by the petty cashier when requested by a signed petty cash voucher. The **petty cash voucher** is a piece of paper that states the purpose for which the funds are to be used, the date of the transaction, the voucher number, the account to be charged, the individual approving the voucher, and the fact that payment has been received. The petty cash voucher is then placed in the petty cash box. The combination of the cash in the box and the total amount of the vouchers should be equal at any time to the amount of the petty cash fund.

The petty cashier also makes use of a record called the **petty cash book** (see page 211). The purpose of the petty cash book is to keep track of the expenditures from the petty cash fund. It represents a form of cash payments journal, except that expenditures are shown not by checks but rather by petty cash vouchers.

When, during the course of a month, the amount of the disbursements from the fund begins to approach the amount of money established for the fund, it is necessary to **replenish the fund.** Replenishment of the fund is justified by the fact that expenditures were made from the fund and should be recognized. The following entry would be made in the cash payments journal to replenish the fund, based on totals obtained from the petty cash book (see page 211):

198–

Apr. 25   Transportation on Purchases   62.50

            Office Supplies   2.00

            Postage Expense   3.00

               Cash   67.50

          To replenish the petty cash fund.

This replenishment will restore the balance in the petty cash box to $100 and enable the petty cashier to continue distributing small amounts of cash. The petty cash fund is usually replenished when the balance in the fund has gotten low. However, at the end of the accounting period, the fund should be replenished so that expenses for that accounting period can be properly recognized.

The only time an entry is made to petty cash is at the time the fund is established. The replenishment recognizes the expenses incurred. If the organization feels that the amount of the petty cash fund is either too great or too small, an entry can be made adjusting the balance in the petty cash account. The basic entry, however, usually occurs only when the fund is first established. **Complete Computational Problem 3, Part A** (pp. 219–220).

Petty Cash Book

Date	Vo #	Payee	Receipts		Payments		Postage Expense		Office Supplies		Store Supplies		Transp. on Purchase		Other		Amount
19— Apr. 1	—	Check #302	100	00													
5	101	U.S. Post Office			2	00	2	00									
9	102	R & L Stationery			2	00			2	00							
11	103	Cosmo Freight			37	50							37	50			
14	104	U.S. Post Office			1	00	1	00									
24	105	Reliable Freight			25	00							25	00			
25			100	00	67	50	3	00	2	00			62	50	—		—
25		Total Payments	67	50													
25		Balance	32	50													
25	—	Check #367	67	50													
			100	00													

YOU SHOULD REMEMBER

Businesses commonly keep from $50 to $150, known as the petty cash fund, to cover small, regularly recurring expenditures.

Withdrawals are made by means of petty cash vouchers, which give such information as date, amount, purpose, and account to be charged.

Records of these expenditures are kept in the petty cash book, in which petty cash vouchers serve as evidence of withdrawals.

• *VOUCHER SYSTEM*

Just as it is important to control the expenditures of small amounts of cash through the petty cash fund, it is important to be able to control expenditures that take the form of checks. In every type of business a large number of expenditures must be made each month for goods and services. The handling of these kinds of transactions requires that the following steps be taken:

1. The expenditures must be authorized, before payment, by a purchase order or some other document that serves as evidence that the purchase was originally authorized.

2. The goods must be inspected upon receipt and verified against the specifications of the order.

3. Invoices from suppliers must be examined for correctness of prices, extensions, shipping costs, and credit terms.

4. Checks must be issued for payment with the necessary signatures and approvals.

In a very small business the sole proprietor will probably be responsible for all the steps listed above. As the size of a business increases, however, it becomes impractical for the owner of the business to be directly involved in the four steps listed. A well-designed accounting system assigns certain employees to handle each step and to guard against waste and fraud. Since the safeguarding of cash, whether it is in the form of coins and currency or of checks, is an important aspect of any business, the use of the voucher system will help to provide this needed safeguard.

The **voucher system** is a method of establishing control over the making of expenditures and the payment of liabilities. This system requires that every liability be recorded as soon as it is incurred, regardless of when it is payable, and that payment be made only when an approved voucher is prepared. The voucher is a written authorization that is prepared before every expenditure, regardless of whether the expenditure covers services, merchandise for resale, or assets for use in the business. A simple entry, such as payment of the monthly rent, will no longer involve a debit to rent expense and a corresponding credit to cash, but will now involve the establishment of a liability and then the subsequent payment. The following general journal entry illustrates the recognition and payment of the rent:

198–

Jan. 1	Rent Expense	300	
	Vouchers Payable		300
	To recognize the expense.		
1	Vouchers Payable	300	
	Cash		300
	To record the payment of the voucher.		

THE VOUCHER

A **voucher** is merely a document that contains specific information regarding the recognition and subsequent payment of an obligation. When an invoice is received as a result of purchasing a product or service, the bill is attached to the voucher. The following voucher is used by the Reliable Service Co.:

Reliable Service Co.
Chicago, Ill.

Pay to _____

Voucher No. _____
Date _____
Terms: _____

Date of Invoice _____
Invoice Number _____

Gross Amount $_____
Less: Cash Discount _____
Net Amount $_____

Approval _____
Page 1

Account Distribution

Debit	Amount
Purchases.................	_____
Supplies..................	_____
Delivery Expense..........	_____
Misc. Selling Exp.	_____
Misc. Gen'l Exp...........	_____
Credit Vouchers Payable....	_____

Voucher No. _____

Payee

_____
_____
_____

Voucher Summary
Amount _____
Adjustment _____
Discount _____
Net _____
Approved _____

Payment Summary
Date _____
Amount _____
Check No. _____
Approved _____

Page 2

The face of the voucher is completed, indicating the name and address of the creditor. A voucher number is assigned, and the date of the entry is noted along with the terms of the transaction. The date of the invoice is also recorded, as well as the gross amount of the bill. On page 2 of the voucher, the account distribution information is completed. The purchases invoice is then attached to the voucher, and both are placed in a file generally known as the **unpaid voucher file.** The unpaid voucher file is set up according to the earliest date when payment should be made in order to take advantage of the terms of the purchase.

A voucher is prepared for every transaction that will eventually require the payment of cash utilizing the checkbook. Transactions that are normally thought of as mere payments of cash, such as paying the business's monthly rent, are not treated in that manner when the voucher system is used. Each transaction must first be recorded as a credit transaction.

EFFECT OF VOUCHER SYSTEM ON BOOKS OF ORIGINAL ENTRY

The purchases journal, as we have developed it, is not used when the voucher system is in use. The purchases journal is replaced by another book of original entry known as the **voucher register,** which is used to record all transactions that result in the preparation of a voucher. Before the voucher (with invoice attached) is filed in the unpaid voucher file, the information is recorded in the voucher register. Each entry in the voucher register includes the assigned voucher number and all the information typically entered in a purchases journal. Instead of an accounts payable column appearing in the voucher register, it is usually replaced by a column called *vouchers payable.* Two additional information columns are also used to indicate the date the voucher is paid and the check number verifying the payment.

The typical form of the voucher register is shown on page 215.

The use of the voucher and voucher register also eliminates the need for the subsidiary accounts payable ledger. In place of this ledger is the unpaid voucher file. Also, a glance at the check no. and date columns in the voucher register will indicate which vouchers are outstanding. Completion of these columns indicates that the obligation has been paid. If the columns are blank, the obligation is still outstanding. The vouchers payable account replaces the accounts payable control account in the general ledger, but still shows the amount of the outstanding obligations, which the accountant needs to know to prepare the trial balance.

After entry of the voucher in the voucher register, the voucher is filed in the upaid voucher file, where it will remain until it is paid. In order to be aware of and to take advantage of discounts offered as part of the terms of a purchase, proper filing of the voucher is essential. The amount due on each voucher represents the credit balance that in a traditional system would be comparable to a creditor account in a subsidiary ledger. Since the subsidiary ledger is not used in a voucher system, it is assumed that the business will avail itself, wherever possible, of the favorable credit terms offered. In order to do so the unpaid voucher is filed according to the earliest date that payment must take place to earn the discount. Since the file is set

Voucher Register

Date	Payee	Vou-cher No.	Date Paid	Check No.	Vouchers Payable Credit	Purchases Debit	Supplies Debit	Salaries Expense Debit	Advertising Expense Debit	General Accounts		
										Debited	PR	Amount

up in a fashion similar to a calendar, the individual in charge of the file will be able to determine readily which vouchers are due for payment on any given date.

When a voucher is paid, it is removed from the unpaid voucher file and a check is usually prepared to pay the obligation. Information as to the date, check number, and payment are recorded on the voucher. If the checkbook provides for a duplicate check, this copy is usually attached to the voucher and both are then filed in the *paid voucher file,* which is organized in numerical order according to the voucher number assigned.

RECORDING VOUCHER PAYMENT

All vouchers are paid by check. The traditional accounting system utilizes the cash payments journal to record the payment. When the voucher system is used, however, the cash payments journal is replaced by a book of original entry called the **check register.** All vouchers paid by check are recorded in the check register according to the check number. Each check written is in payment of a voucher previously entered as a vouchers payable in the voucher register. The effect of each entry in the check register is to cause a debit entry to be recorded to the vouchers payable account. The only additional columns needed in the check register are columns for cash credit to indicate payment, and columns to recognize a credit entry to discount on purchases. The following check register is commonly used by businesses using a voucher system:

Check Register

Date	Payee	Voucher No.	Check No.	Vouchers Payable—Dr.	Purchases Discounts—Cr.	Cash Cr.

Notice that the check register has no provision for a post-reference column. There is no need for a post-reference column because all of the columns are special columns that require posting only once a month, at the end of the month, as part of the summary entry. Remember: the voucher system eliminates the need for a subsidiary accounts payable ledger. The check number and the date when the payment is made, as shown by the entry in the check register, are also recorded in the voucher register. Remember: the paid area (check no. and date columns) of the voucher register indicates whether the obligation has been paid.

The introduction of a voucher system eliminates the need for a purchases journal, a cash payments journal, and the subsidiary accounts payable ledger as we have used it. These account documents are replaced with the voucher register, the check register, and the paid and unpaid voucher files. All documentation, from the original purchase to the final payment, is recorded on or attached to the voucher. The use of the voucher system ensures that expenditures are properly authorized and that payments made are in legitimate fulfillment of an organization's obligations. **Complete Computational Problems 4, 5, and 6, Part A** (pp. 220–222).

YOU SHOULD REMEMBER

The voucher system is appropriate for medium- to large-sized business operations only.

Its objective is to control the incurring of liabilities and the making of expenditures.

The cash payments journal and the purchases journal are replaced by the voucher register and the check register, while the subsidiary accounts payable ledger is replaced by the unpaid and paid voucher files.

For more practice in mastering the material in this chapter, **complete Computational Problems 1, 2, and 3, Part B** (pp. 222–225).

KNOW THE CONCEPTS

DO YOU KNOW THE BASICS?

Test your knowledge of this chapter by classifying each of the following statements as *True* or *False*. If your choice is *False*, explain why.

1. Internal control of operations is equally complex in a small and in a large organization.

2. Usually two signatures are required on a business check for it to be valid.

3. Before money can be deposited in a checking account, a deposit slip must be prepared.

4. There are only two parties to a check: the person who writes it (the drawee) and the person to whom it is written (the payee).

5. When a check is written by a business, the immediate effect is to reduce both the balance shown in the checkbook and the balance on the bank's records.

6. Two documents used in preparing a bank reconciliation statement are the bank statement and the checkbook stubs.

7. The final amounts shown on both sides of the bank reconciliation statement are labeled "Adjusted Balances."

8. A common cause of inequality between the balances on the bank statement and in the checkbook is outstanding checks.

9. A petty cash fund usually contains at least $300.

10. When the voucher system is in use, the voucher register replaces the cash receipts journal.

TERMS FOR STUDY

bank reconciliation	petty cash book
bank statement	petty cash voucher
check register	replenish the fund
deposit slip	signature card
deposits in transit	unpaid voucher file
internal control	voucher
outstanding check	voucher register

PRACTICAL APPLICATION

PART A. COMPUTATIONAL PROBLEMS WITH COMPLETE SOLUTIONS

1. Prepare a bank reconciliation statement dated May 30, 198–, based on the following list of receipts and payments that were made by the Reliable Retail Store:

May Cash Receipts

Date	Receipts	Deposits
5/2	$100	$100
5/9	200	
5/9	100	300
5/16	400	400
5/23	200	200
5/30	300	300

May Cash Disbursements

Date	Check No.	Amount
5/3	101	$ 50
5/10	102	150
5/10	103	20
5/10	104	10
5/17	105	200
5/24	106	560
5/24	107	30
3/31	108	20

From the company's checkbook records:
  Cash balance (in bank) May 1, 198–: $300
  Cash balance (in bank) May 31, 198–: $560

The May 31, 198–, bank statement for the Reliable Retail Store from the First City Bank appears as follows:

Account of: Reliable Retail Store			FIRST CITY BANK	
Date 198–	Check no.	Amount	Deposits	Balance
Apr. 30				300
May 4			100	400
6	101	50		350
11	102	150	300	490
	104	10		
18			400	890
19	105	200		690
25	107	30 NSF ($10)	200	850
26	106	560		290
31		2 SC		288
May 31				288

Code Explanations: EC—Error Correction; NSF—Not Sufficient Funds (the bank charges a $10 fee for all NSF checks); Col—Collection Charge; SC—Service Charge.

After you have prepared the bank reconciliation statement for the Reliable Retail Store, prepare the necessary adjusting journal entries.

2. The following data have been accumulated for use in preparing the bank reconciliation statement for Alice Reinholt and Co. for the month of September, 198–:
   (a) Balance per depositor's records on September 30 is $4,239.35.
   (b) Balance per bank statement on September 30 is $4,581.50.
   (c) Deposits in transit total $362.80.
   (d) Checks outstanding amount to $694.10.
   (e) A check for $57 in payment of a bill was erroneously recorded on the check stub as $75.
   (f) A bank debit memo for service charges amounts to $7.15.

Prepare the bank reconciliation statement, dated September 30.

3. The Spelvin Co. established a petty cash fund of $150 on January 1, 198–. On January 24, 198–, the fund was replenished for the payments made to date as

shown by the following petty cash vouchers: Freight on Purchases, $9.50; Postage Expense, $46.00; Telephone Expense, $3.20; Repairs Expense, $31.70; Miscellaneous Expenses, $22.00. Prepare the necessary journal entries to record (a) the establishment of the fund, and (b) the replenishment of the fund on January 24, 198–.

4. The Renfield Co. uses a voucher system. Record the following business transactions in general journal form. Also indicate as an explanation the appropriate special journal that would be used for each transaction.

198–
Apr. **2**   Voucher No. 245 was prepared for the purchase of office supplies at a cost of $85 from the Buyrite Stationery Co. The terms of the transaction are 2/10, n/30.

10   Check No. 333 was issued in payment of voucher No. 245.

14   Voucher No. 246 was prepared to establish a petty cash fund amounting to $50.

15   Check No. 334 was written in payment of voucher No. 246.

16   Voucher No. 247 was prepared to replenish the petty cash fund, which contained receipts for the following: Postage, $20.00; Miscellaneous Expenses, $15.00; Delivery Expenses, $4.50.

19   Check was issued in payment of voucher No. 247.

5. Set up (a) a voucher register and (b) a check register for the Mansfield Co. Record the following transactions in the appropriate registers:

198–
Aug. **2**   Received a bill from the Best Realty Co. for the month's rent amounting to $700. (Begin with voucher No. 201.)

5   Received an invoice from Spelvin Co. for a purchase of merchandise made today amounting to $2,457. Terms: 2/10, n/30.

7   Issued check No. 435 in payment of voucher No. 201.

198–

Aug. 13 Prepared a voucher payable to the Buyrite Stationery Co. for a purchase made today of office supplies amounting to $95. Terms: 2/10, 1/15, n/30.

14 Sent a check in payment of voucher No. 202.

18 Issued voucher No. 204 for $3,769.60 in favor of L. Sprang Co. for our note. Face value of note $3720.00, interest on note $49.60.

26 Paid voucher No. 204 as per terms.

27 Prepared voucher to reimburse the petty cash fund.

The expenditures were as follows: Postage, $12.70; Transportation on Purchases, $43.10; Store Supplies, $13.80.

6. Set up (a) a petty cash book, (b) a voucher register, and (c) a check register. Record the following selected transactions, and total and rule the records at the end of the month as appropriate:

198–

Sept. 1 Purchased goods from Smith Inc. Terms: n/10, $500. Prepared voucher No. 916.

2 Issued voucher No. 917 to establish a petty cash fund amounting to $200. Issued check No. 371 in payment.

5 Received an invoice from Lantzen Co. for advertising expenses amounting to $762. Set up voucher.

7 Paid cash of $9 out of the petty cash fund for postage stamps. (Petty cash voucher No. 1.)

11 Paid voucher No. 918.

198–

Sept. 12   Received a freight bill from Hall Freight Inc. for $96 payable in 20 days. Issued a voucher.

15   Issued a check for $713 to Howard Co. in payment of voucher No. 912, which was issued last month for office supplies.

18   Paid cash from the petty cash fund for transportation on purchases amounting to $12. (Paid A.B. Freight Inc.)

19   Purchased merchandise from Bell Co., paying $45 cash from the petty cash fund.

21   Purchased goods from Texas Originals for $950. Terms: 2/10, n/30.

29   Replenished the petty cash fund.

30   Issued a check in payment of the September 21 voucher to Texas Originals.

PART B. COMPUTATIONAL PROBLEMS WITH PARTIAL SOLUTIONS OR KEY ANSWERS

1. Prepare a bank reconciliation statement for the Glenn Co., dated December 31 of the current year, based on the following information:
   (a) The cash balance at 12/31 in the checkbook was $2,782. The balance on the bank statement received on 1/03 was $2,653.60
   (b) Two checks, No. 345 for $103.50 and No. 349 for $221.30, were outstanding as of the November 30 bank statement. Check No. 349 was returned with the December canceled checks and appeared on the December bank statement.
   (c) A comparison of the checks written during December and the checks returned with the bank statement dated December 31 indicated that the following checks were outstanding: No. 387 for $68.75 and No. 392 for $84.60.
   (d) A comparison of checks paid with the corresponding entries in the cash payments journal indicated that a *transposition* had occurred in which the cash payments journal amount was recorded as $138 for check No. 379, while the correct amount paid for the check was $183.

(e) A credit memorandum for $500 appeared on the bank statement for collection of a note by the bank. The bank also included a debit memorandum for $2, which represented a collection fee on the note.

(f) A debit memorandum for $48.75 was included as a result of a check returned because of insufficient funds.

(g) A cash deposit placed in the bank's night depository on December 31 was not included on the bank statement of the same date. The deposit, however, was part of the checkbook balance as of 12/31.

After the preparation of the bank reconciliation statement, prepare the necessary general journal entries to correct the books of account.

2. Rule a petty cash book in similar fashion to the one illustrated on page 211, using the same column headings. Record the following activities in either the general journal or the petty cash book, or, where appropriate, in both places.

On November 2 of the current year a petty cash fund was established with the writing of a check for $50. Record this event in the appropriate records.

198–

Nov. 3 Paid $13.75 in express charges, preparing petty cash voucher No. 001 on the shipment of merchandise purchased.

7 Paid $9.50 foɪ minor repairs to an office typewriter, as evidenced by voucher No. 002. (Use office repair expense)

8 Paid $6 for delivery of merchandise to a customer. (Use freight on sales.)

11 Paid $5 to have the office windows washed.

15 Paid $6.50 for express charges on a shipment of merchandise purchased, as evidenced by voucher No. 005.

21 Purchased postage stamps for $5.

25 Purchased carbon paper for use in the office amounting to $2.50, as evidenced by voucher No. 007.

198–

Nov. 27 Summarized the petty cash book and prepared check No. 884 to replenish the fund.

Dec. 2 Paid $6.50 for delivery of goods to a customer.

6 Prepared petty cash voucher No. 009 in payment of $9.25 express charges on a shipment of merchandise purchased.

13 Paid $2.75 for a bottle of india ink to be used in the store.

18 Purchased postage stamps for $15.

20 Purchased various store supplies for $13.10, as evidenced by petty cash voucher No. 012.

22 Summarized the petty cash book and prepared check No. 923 to replenish the fund.

3. The Lamston Co. uses a voucher system consisting of a voucher register, a check register, and a petty cash book. Record, in general journal form, the following selected transactions for the month of June, providing an adequate explanation that includes the special register, journal, or book that normally would be used.

198–

June 3 Sent a 30-day, 10% note payable to Bally Co. for $1,600 in settlement of invoice No. 541.

5 Prepared a voucher payable to Alan Gleason to establish a petty cash fund for $75. Prepared voucher No. 245.

6 Prepared a check in payment of voucher No. 245, dated 6/5.

8 Purchased merchandise from the Myron Co. for $900. Terms: 2/15, n/30. Prepared voucher No. 246.

198–

June 11 Purchased office equipment from the Drew Office Equipment Co. for $2,400. Terms: n/30.

15 Prepared petty cash voucher No. 101 for $12.35 in payment of transportation charges on goods purchased.

17 Received a credit memo from Myron Co. for $65 as evidence of our return of merchandise purchased on June 8.

18 Paid voucher No. 246 less the return of 6/17 according to the terms of 6/8 invoice.

22 Prepared petty cash voucher No. 102 for $22.35 in payment of various office supplies obtained today.

25 Issued voucher in payment of note due today that was dated 6/3. Sent check in payment of voucher.

27 Prepared a voucher and issued a check to reimburse the petty cash fund.

ANSWERS

KNOW THE CONCEPTS

1. F   Internal control is more complex in a large organization with many employees and great diversity of operations.

2. T

3. T

4. F   The bank is also a party to the check.

5. F   The bank record is not reduced until the bank actually receives the check and pays out the face amount.

6. T

7. T

8. T

9. F   The usual amount in the petty cash fund is $50 to $150.

10. F   The voucher register replaces the purchases journal.

PRACTICAL APPLICATION
PART A

1.
Reliable Retail Store
Bank Reconciliation Statement
May 30, 198–

Checkbook Balance	$560	Bank Balance	$288
Less: Service Charge & N.S.F. Charge	12	Less: Outstanding Checks Check #103 $20	
		108 20	
		Total Outstanding Checks	40
			248
		Add: Deposits in Transit	300
Adjusted Checkbook Balance	$548	Adjusted Bank Balance	$548

2.
Alice Reinholt and Co.
Bank Reconciliation Statement
September 30, 198–

Checkbook Balance	$4239.35	Bank Balance	$4581.50
Add: Error in Check	18.00	Add: Deposits in Transit	362.80
	4257.35		4944.30
Less: Service Charge	7.15	Less: Outstanding Checks	694.10
Adjusted Checkbook Balance	$4250.20	Adjusted Bank Balance	$4250.20

3. (a) **198–**

    Jan. 1 Petty Cash   150.00

                  Cash   150.00

                  To establish the petty cash fund.

   (b)   **24** Freight on Purchases   9.50

                  Postage Expense   46.00

                  Telephone Expense   3.20

                  Repairs Expense   31.70

                  Miscellaneous Expense   22.00

                  Cash   112.40

                  To replenish the fund.

If special journals are used by the organization, both entries are recorded in the cash payments journal.

4. **198–**

  Apr. **2** Office Supplies   85.00

                  Vouchers Payable   85.00

		Debit	Credit
Apr. 2	Office Supplies	85.00	
	Vouchers Payable		85.00

Voucher #245 for Purchase from Buyrite Stationery Co. Terms: 2/10, n/30. (Voucher register)

10	Vouchers Payable	85.00	
	Cash		83.30
	Purchases Discount		1.70

Paid voucher #245 less 2% discount. (Check register)

| **14** | Petty Cash | 50.00 | |
| | Vouchers Payable | | 50.00 |

To establish fund by preparing voucher #246. (Voucher register)

| **15** | Vouchers Payable | 50.00 | |
| | Cash | | 50.00 |

Paid voucher #246 to establish fund. (Check register)

16	Postage Expense	20.00	
	Miscellaneous Expense	15.00	
	Delivery Expense	4.50	
	Vouchers Payable		39.50

Issued voucher #247 to replenish the petty cash fund. (Voucher register)

| **19** | Vouchers Payable | 39.50 | |
| | Cash | | 39.50 |

Issued check in payment of voucher #247. (Check register)

Each entry setting up a voucher is initially recorded in the voucher register. Subsequent payments are recorded in the check register. Vouchers prepared but not yet paid are filed in the unpaid voucher file according to their due dates. Once a voucher has been paid, it is refiled in the paid voucher file, which is usually organized in alphabetical order.

P. 3

Voucher Register

5.(a)

Date	Payee	PR	Voucher No.	Date Paid	Check No.	Vouchers Payable Credit	Purchases Debit	General Accounts Account	General Accounts Debit
19 8-									
Aug. 2	Best Realty Co.		201	8/7	435	700 00		Rent Expense	700 00
5	Spelvin Co.		202	8/14	436	2457 00	2457 00		
13	Buyrite Stationery Co.		203			95 00		Office Supplies	95 00
18	L. Sprang Co.		204	8/26	437	3769 60		Notes Payable	3720 00
								Interest Expense	49 60
27	Petty Cashier		205			69 60		Postage	12 70
								Transportation	43 10
								Store Supplies	13 80
31						7091 20	2457 00		4634 20

Check Register

(b)

Date	Payee	Voucher No.	Check No.	Vouchers Payable—Dr.	Purchases Discounts—Cr.	Cash Cr.
19 8-						
Aug. 7	Best Realty Co.	201	435	700 00		700 00
14	Spelvin Co.	202	436	2457 00	49 14	2407 86
26	L. Sprang Co.	204	437	3769 60		3769 60
31				6926 60	49 14	6877 46

6. (a)

Petty Cash Book

Date	Payee	Vo #	Receipts	Payments	Postage Expense	Office Supplies	Store Supplies	Purchases	Other	Amount
19 8-										
Sept. 2	Check #371	—	200 00							
7	U.S. Post Office	1		9 00	9 00					
18	A.B. Freight Inc.	2		12 00					Freight on Purchases	12 00
19	Bell Co.	3		45 00				45 00		
			200 00	66 00	9 00	-0-	-0-	45 00		12 00
	Total Payment		66 00							
	Balance		134 00							
29	Check #374	—	66 00							
			200 00							

(b)

Voucher Register

Date	Payee	Voucher No.	Explanation	Date Paid	Check No.	Vouchers Payable Credit	Purchases Debit	Office Supplies Debit	General Accounts Account	PR	Debit
19 8-											
Sept. 1	Smith Inc.	916	n/10			500 00	500 00				
2	R. Brown	917	Petty Cashier	9/2	371	200 00			Petty Cash		200 00
5	Lantzen Co.	918	—	9/11	372	762 00			Advertising Expense		762 00
12	Hall Freight Inc.	919	Freight Bill n/20			96 00			Freight on Purchases		96 00
21	Texas Originals	920	2/10, n/30	9/30	375	950 00	950 00				
29	Petty Cash	921	Replenish Fund	9/29	374	66 00	45 00		Postage Expense		9 00
									Freight on Purchases		12 00
30						2574 00	1495 00	-0-			1079 00

Check Register

(c)

Date		Payee	Voucher No.	Check No.	Vouchers Payable—Dr.	Purchases Discounts—Cr.	Cash Cr.
19	8–						
Sept.	2	R. Brown	917	371	2 0 0 00		2 0 0 00
	11	Lantzen Co.	918	372	7 6 2 00		7 6 2 00
	15	Howard Co.	912	373	7 1 3 00		7 1 3 00
	29	R. Brown	921	374	6 6 00		6 6 00
	30	Texas Originals	920	375	9 5 0 00	1 9 00	9 3 1 00
	30				2 6 9 1 00	1 9 00	2 6 7 2 00

PART B

1.

Glenn Co.
Bank Reconciliation Statement
December 31, 198–

Checkbook Balance	$2,782.00	Bank Balance	$2,653.60
Less: Error in Recording		Less: Outstanding Checks	
Check #379	45.00	Check #345 $103.50	
	2,737.00	387 68.75	
Add: Net Collection of		392 84.60	256.85
Notes Receivable	588.00		2,396.75
	3,325.00	Add: Deposit in Transit	
Less: Check Returned for		on December 31	879.50
Insufficient Funds	48.75		
Adjusted Checkbook Bal.	$3,276.25	Adjusted Bank Bal.	$3,276.25

2. November 27 replenishment, $48.25; December 22 replenishment, $46.60
3. June 27 replenishment, $34.70

8
RECEIVABLES AND PAYABLES

KEY TERMS

bad debt An expense that a business recognizes because of a customer's failure to pay an obligation usually arising as a direct result of a prior credit sale. The expense is established when it is reasonably determined that the customer will not pay.

discounting a note The process involving the sale of a promissory note to a bank or financial institution before maturity. The bank deducts from the maturity value of the note an interest charge based on the period of time the note is to be held by the bank and the rate of interest the bank charges.

promissory note An unconditional written promise to pay a stated sum of money upon demand, or at a future determinable date. It is usually prepared and signed by the debtor and given to the creditor.

SELLING GOODS AND SERVICES

Goods and services may be sold by a business organization for cash or on credit. Most organizations, if given a choice, would probably prefer to sell their products or services for cash. Because of competition and other factors, however, many businesses, out of necessity, must offer their products and/or services to customers on credit. As we learned in Chapter 6, when a sale is made to a customer on credit, the effect of the transaction is to establish an accounts receivable account on the books in the name of the customer. This account is classified as an asset. When the customer pays the obligation to the seller, the customer's account is credited and the cash account is debited as a result of the receipt of cash.

No business organization prefers to sell on credit, especially since the customer may prove to be unwilling or unable to pay his or her obligation when it becomes due. Most large businesses utilize a credit department or service to ascertain the creditworthiness of a new customer. The credit department investigates the debt-paying ability of each such customer and determines the maximum amount of credit to extend. A credit service such as Dun & Bradstreet, Inc., furnishes credit reports on prospective customers. Whether the customer is an individual or a business, some form of credit information is obtained before extending credit to the customer.

The amount of credit extended depends on a number of factors. The credit terms offered by the seller may be modified for a new customer until the debt-paying ability of the customer can be determined firsthand. A seller who normally offers credit terms of n/30 may decide to offer terms initially of only n/10 to a new customer. Many sellers who have previously sold to a buyer for cash may use such shorter terms as a means of extending credit to the customer. In smaller organizations, where competition is great, credit checks may not be made at all. A "seat of the pants" or a "gut feeling" approach may be used by these organizations.

RECOGNIZING BAD DEBTS

When sales are made without the immediate receipt of cash, a small portion of the outstanding accounts receivable may prove to be uncollectible regardless of a credit department's efforts or the credit service used. When this happens, provision must be made to match expenses and revenue by recognizing a **bad debt.** A bad debt is an *expense* recognized by a business that was caused by a customer's failure to pay an obligation arising out of a prior credit sale. The recognition of this uncollectible account receivable is handled in different ways depending on the nature of the business.

Three methods are used to recognize customer obligations that have proved to be uncollectible:

1. Direct write-off method.

2. Net sales method.

3. Aging of accounts receivable method.

YOU SHOULD REMEMBER

When a choice is available, most organizations prefer to sell their goods and services for cash rather than on credit.

When the nature of the industry dictates that credit must be extended, provision should be made for uncollectible accounts receivable.

There are basically three methods that can be utilized: (1) the direct write-off method, (2) the net sales method, and (3) the aging of accounts receivable method.

• *DIRECT WRITE-OFF METHOD*

The **direct write-off method** is used by businesses when it is possible to determine that an account will prove to be uncollectible within the same accounting period as the original sale took place. When a business sells most of its products or services for cash, the direct write-off method may be appropriate, since the amount of credit sales will be very low. Since the credit period offered by the seller is probably rather short, any uncollectible accounts can be ascertained quickly, probably within the same accounting period. Given this information, the bad debt recognition is made when the debt proves to be uncollectible.

Example: The Direct Write-off Method

On August 10, 198–, a credit sale was made to John Reston for $300; terms: n/30. On November 8, 198–, it was determined that Mr. Reston would not pay his obligation, which at that point was 2 months past due. A decision was made to write off Mr. Reston's account as uncollectible.

198–
Aug. 10 {John Reston
   Accounts Receivable}   300
    Sales   300
   Terms: n/30

Nov. 8 Bad Debt Expense   300
    {John Reston
     Accounts Receivable}   300
   To write off the uncollectible account.

The entry on August 10 represents the credit sale made to Mr. Reston. The November 8 entry recognizes that the customer will not pay his obligation. This second entry recognizes the expense and eliminates the obligation that Mr. Reston has to the seller. By writing off the account as uncollectible in the same accounting period as the original sale, the accountant is able to match cost with revenue more accurately. The effect on the debit to bad debt expense directly offsets the revenue recognized in the credit sale of August 10.

If the account proved to be uncollectible in the next accounting period, it would be written off then. However, the matching concept would not be followed. For a business where debts may not be determined as uncollectible for many months after the sale, the direct write-off method is not appropriate.

Should a customer whose debt was previously written off pay his obligation at a later date, the following reversal entry would be recorded:

198–
Nov. 25   {John Reston
           {Accounts Receivable}   300
               Bad Debts Expense   300
           To restore obligation previously written off.

     25   Cash   300
           {John Reston
           {Accounts Receivable}   300
           Payment received originally due
           on September 8, 198–.

If this reinstatement took place in the following accounting period, the bad debts expense account might temporarily have a credit balance. If this balance was not eliminated by additional write-offs in the new accounting period, the account with the credit balance would represent a form of revenue.

Although the direct write-off method is an accurate means of writing off un-collectibles, it is less desirable than other methods because of its failure to match expenses and revenue within the same accounting period. Also, it does not accrue or show the net realizable value of accounts receivable. **Complete Computational Problem 1, Part A** (p. 251).

• *NET SALES METHOD*

For the direct write-off method to be effective, the volume of credit sales should be small and the write-off should take place during the same accounting period as the original sale. Since these requirements cannot be met by most businesses, the **net sales method** is more appropriate for them. We have stated that a bad debts expense results from credit sales to customers who later fail to pay their obligations. Since the accountant's primary concern is to match costs and revenue within an accounting period, an adjusting entry is made to recognize the anticipated uncol-lectible accounts. At the end of the accounting period, the net sales method is used to estimate the amount of net sales that will become uncollectible in subsequent accounting periods. This estimate is usually expressed as a percentage of net sales. Initially a business will rely on industry statistics, which will eventually be modified based on the firm's own experience.

Example: Net Sales Method

A company decides that 1% of annual net sales of $150,000 may prove to be uncollectible. It records an adjusting entry debiting bad debts expense for $1,500 ($150,000 × .01). Since the business does not know, at that time, which debts will actually prove to be uncollectible, a credit entry is recorded in an account entitled "Allowance for Bad Debts." This account, which is classified as a contra-asset account, offsets the accounts receivable account in the general ledger. The resulting book value of the accounts receivable becomes known as the "realizable value" of the accounts receivable. This is the amount of the accounts receivable actually expected to be collected.

The adjusting entry using the net sales method to recognize the bad debts expense at the end of the accounting period would be as follows:

198–

Dec. 31	Bad Debts Expense	1,500	
	Allowance for Bad Debts		1,500
	1% of net sales.		

On the balance sheet at the end of the accounting period, the accounts receivable section appears as follows:

Accounts Receivable	$50,000	
Less: Allowance for Bad Debts	1,500	
Net Accounts Receivable		48,500

During the next accounting period, as various debts prove to be uncollectible, these accounts are written off in the following manner:

198–

Jan. 13	Allowance for Bad Debts	270	
	⎰ John Reston ⎱		
	⎱ Accounts Receivable ⎰		270
	To write off uncollectible debt.		

Note that the write-off causes a reduction in the balances in the customer's account (John Reston), the accounts receivable control account, and the allowance for bad debts account. The accounts receivable section of the balance sheet, if prepared following this entry, would appear as follows:

Accounts Receivable	$49,730	
Less: Allowance for Bad Debts	1,230	
Net Accounts Receivable		48,500

As additional customer accounts prove to be uncollectible, the same entry to write off the account will be recorded. At the end of the current accounting period, it is again necessary to prepare an adjusting entry to recognize the anticipated bad debt write-offs for the following year. If at the end of the year it is again determined that 1% of net sales is the expected rate of uncollectible debts, then an adjusting entry is once again prepared. Since it is virtually impossible to write off the exact amount of the estimate, there will be a remaining balance in the allowance for bad debts account. This balance is then changed as a result of the adjusting entry.

The net sales approach to recognizing uncollectible debt expenses and the subsequent write-off is a widely used method. It is simple to use and provides a good means for charging bad debts expense to the period in which the related sales were made.

Should a customer eventually pay all or a part of the uncollectible account previously written off, the following entries would be made:

198–
Feb. 8   { John Reston
      Accounts Receivable }   200
         Allowance for Bad Debts   200
       To restore part of uncollectible debt.

    8   Cash   200
           { John Reston
            Accounts Receivable }   200
       Part payment of previously written off A/R.

Complete Computational Problem 2, Part A (p. 251).

• AGING OF ACCOUNTS RECEIVABLE METHOD

Although the net sales method is certainly superior to the direct write-off method, it too has some limitations. If there is a credit balance in the allowance for bad debts each year before the adjusting entry is made, the balance in the account will continuously increase. No provision is usually made for this situation with the result that the bad debts expense recognized each year will tend to be overstated. To remedy this situation, another method can be used that provides a greater degree of control over the recognition of the bad debts expense, as well as providing for the proper amount to appear in the allowance for bad debts at the beginning of a new accounting period. The **aging of accounts receivable method** provides for a more realisitic presentation of the bad debts expense and the allowance for bad debts account.

The aging of accounts receivable method involves analyzing the accounts found in the accounts receivable ledger. Customer accounts are recorded in an analysis chart according to the due date of the receivables. Past-due accounts are listed according to the number of days they are past due, such as 1–30 days, 31–60 days, or 61–90 days. A percentage based on past experience is then applied to the balance not due as well as the balances past due. The amount of the estimated uncollectibles is then determined and used as a basis for the adjusting entry. The adjusting entry is the same as that for the net sales method, except that the balance in the allowance for bad debts account is considered in arriving at the adjusting entry. The recovery entry is identical for the net sales and aging of accounts methods.

Example: Aging of Accounts Receivable Method

A business determines that $2,300 will be uncollectible according to the aging of accounts receivable method. The remaining balance in the allowance for bad debts account is a credit balance of $200. Since the purpose of this method is to consider the adjusting entry made in the prior period in arriving at the current adjusting entry, the following adjusting entry will be recorded:

Dec. 31	Bad Debts Expense	2,100	
	Allowance for Bad Debts		2,100
	Using the aging method.		

Although the anticipated amount of bad debts is $2,300, the adjusting entry reflects only $2,100 because the desired balance in the allowance account is to be $2,300. This method corrects the previously overstated expense by reducing the amount via the current adjusting entry.

If the bad debts account prior to adjustment had had a debit balance of $200, the amount of the adjusting entry would be $2,500. This would give a balance in the allowance account of $2,300, the actual estimated amount to be written off. **Complete Computational Problems 3 and 4, Part A** (pp. 251–252).

YOU SHOULD REMEMBER

The method selected to recognize uncollectible accounts is determined by the amount of credit sales, the timeliness of determining the uncollectible accounts, and the degree of accuracy desired according to the concept of matching costs and revenue.

Regardless of the method selected, the effect is to recognize an expense entitled "Bad Debts Expense" and thereby adjust the income for the particular accounting period involved.

When the net sales or the aging method is used, the expense is recognized as an adjusting entry at the end of the accounting period, with subsequent write-offs being taken as the debts prove to be uncollectible.

EXTENDING CREDIT

The extension of credit to customers is an important aspect of any business's operation. When credit is given, a receivable set up on the books of the seller. As we have learned, this receivable is usually in the form of an "oral promise," known as an accounts receivable. A receivable represents a claim against an individual, a business organization, or another debtor that will eventually be settled by the receipt of cash or any other asset accepted by the creditor. When the creditworthiness or reliability of a customer is in doubt, the seller may decide to sell to the customer on credit with certain additional requirements. The seller may require the buyer to prepare a **promissory note** as evidence of the buyer's obligation to the seller.

• *PROMISSORY NOTES*

A promissory note is an unconditional written promise to pay a stated sum of money upon demand or at a future determinable date. This written promise is usually prepared by the debtor as a result of a request or requirement made by the creditor. The terms of a credit sale may read: 30-day, non-interest-bearing promissory note. Upon receipt of the invoice by the buyer, it is his or her obligation to prepare and deliver to the seller the promissory note within a reasonable time. The "maker" of the note (debtor) records the note in an account entitled "Notes Payable." If the original purchase caused a credit to be recorded to the accounts payable control account and the individual creditor's account, then the issuance of the note would represent the payment of the oral promise with a corresponding credit to the notes payable account.

Example: Promissory Note

On April 23, 198–, Reliable Equipment Co. received an invoice from the Fireside Tire Co. for $650; terms: 30-day, non-interest bearing promissory note. The following entries were recorded in general journal form:

198–

Apr. 23 Trucking Supplies   650
       { Fireside Tire Co. }
       { Accounts Payable }   650
      Terms: 30-day note.

  24 { Fireside Tire Co. }
      { Accounts Payable }   650
      Notes Payable   650
    Issued 30-day note to Fireside Tire Co.

As a result of posting to the notes payable account, the following information appears in the account:

	Notes Payable	
	Apr. 24	Fireside Tire Co. 30-day non-interest-bearing note 650

Since the notes payable account lists all the promissory notes that a company issues, it is necessary to indicate the organization or person to whom the note is payable, the terms, and, where appropriate, the due date of the note. In the above account, the explanation should have also included the due date of the note. The note begins to run as of the date of the invoice, which was April 23. The due date of the note would be May 23, which is 30 days from April 23.

While the above transactions and ledger account are made by the Reliable Equipment Co., there are also entries to be made on the books of the Fireside Tire Co. The following general journal entries would be recorded by the Fireside Tire Co.:

198–

Apr. 23	Reliable Equipment Co. ⎱ Accounts Receivable ⎰	650
	Sales	650
	30-day note	
25	Notes Receivable	650
	Reliable Equipment Co. ⎱ Accounts Receivable ⎰	650
	From Reliable Equipment Co., due on May 23, 198–.	

Note that on the books of the seller the original transaction was recorded according to the invoice date. The entry for the receipt of the note in payment of the oral promise is recorded on the day it is received. The due date of the note is shown as part of the explanation. The transaction of April 25 represents an exchange of assets. The oral promise (accounts receivable) is reduced as a result of the receipt of the written promise (notes receivable). Regardless of whether the promissory note is interest-bearing or non-interest-bearing, it is recorded at its face value in the notes receivable account. This account is handled in a fashion similar to that of the notes payable account in that the explanation must include the name of the company obligated to pay the note, as well as the due date or terms of the note.

• *INTEREST-BEARING PROMISSORY NOTES*

An **interest-bearing promissory note** is a written promise to pay a certain sum at a fixed and determinable future date, along with an additional sum known as interest. This interest is calculated based on the holding period of the note, which is usually expressed in days, and the payment of a specific, stated rate of interest, which is calculated on the face amount of the note. Interest-bearing notes in the hands of the maker are known as **notes payable.** The same interest-bearing notes in the hands of the creditor are known as **notes receivable.**

DETERMINING INTEREST

As stated above, calculation of the interest assigned to the promissory note is usually based on three factors:

1. The face value of the note, known as the *principal.*

2. The amount of time the note is in the hands of the creditor before payment is made, known as the *time*.

3. The rate of interest being charged on the note, commonly referred to as the *rate*.

The basic formula for calculating interest is:

$$\text{Principal (P)} \times \text{Rate (R)} \times \text{Time (T)} = \text{Interest (I)}$$

In using this formula certain assumptions are made. In most cases the period of time for which money is borrowed, as shown by a note, is usually less than 1 year. In fact, it is not unusual for the terms of a note to call for payment within 30, 60, 90, or 120 days. Since this is the rule rather than the exception, an assumption is made that a year consists of 360 days. This is known as a "banking year." Note the calculation of the interest, using this rule, on the following promissory note.

Example: Calculating Interest

A note for $1,000 bears a rate of interest of 6% for a period of 90 days. Using the formula P × R × T = I, find the amount of interest on the note.

$$
\begin{array}{llll}
\text{Principal} \times \text{Rate} \times \text{Time} & = \text{Interest} \\
\$1,000 \times .06 \times 90/360 & = \\
\$1,000 \times .06 \times 1/4 & = \$15
\end{array}
$$

Complete Computational Problem 5, Part A (p. 252).

SHORTCUT FOR DETERMINING INTEREST

Since we have assumed that a year consists of 360 days (banking year), and that most promissory notes will be due and payable in 30, 60, 90, or 120 days, a shortcut method is available for computing interest, known as the **60-day method of determining interest.** This 60-day method is based on the fact that the interest on an amount of money borrowed at 6% interest for a period of 60 days will *always* equal 1% of the money borrowed. Thus, an interest-bearing note for $1,000 due in 60 days and carrying a 6% rate of interest will accrue interest of $10.

The following chart will assist in the analysis and solution of the above problem:

Problem	Principal	Rate	Time
	$1,000	.06	60 days
	10		

The answer of $10 was arrived at by merely moving the decimal point two places to the left to calculate 1% of the principal. Regardless of the amount of money borrowed, if it is borrowed for 60 days at a 6% rate of interest, the cost of borrowing will always be 1% of the money borrowed.

Use of the formula initially presented as a proof results in the following:

$$
\begin{aligned}
\text{Principal} \times \text{Rate} \times \text{Time} &= \text{Interest} \\
\$1,000 \times .06 \times 60/360 &= \\
\$1,000 \times .06 \times 1/6 &= \$10
\end{aligned}
$$

Although it is obvious that this formula works for any amount borrowed at 6% for 60 days, it is not useful at today's high rates of interest for periods of time other than 60 days. The method may be modified, however, to take into consideration rates and time periods other than those used above.

Assume that the promissory note for $1,000 carried a rate of interest of 12% and was held for 60 days. The following represents the solution using the 60-day method:

$1,000	12%	60 days	(Problem line)
$10.00	6%	60 days	(Known)
+$10.00	+ 6%		
$20.00	12%	60 days	

Picture an imaginary equals sign after the principal column and before the rate column. This equals sign would indicate that whatever is done to the right side of the equation must also be done to the left side to maintain the balance. Note that on line 3, when we added 6% to the right side, we also added the value of the existing 6% to the left side of the equation, thus maintaining the equality.

Note the solution of the following problem:

$1,000	6%	90 days	(Problem line)
$10.00	6%	60 days	(Known)
+$ 5.00		+30 days	
$15.00	6%	90 days	

In this situation it was not necessary to solve for the rate, but merely for the number of days. Notice how a change on one side brings about a corresponding change on the other side. If both the rate and the time were other than the 60-day method, changes would have to be made to both. *However, only one variable can be changed at a time.*

Note the following problem and subsequent solution:

$1,000.00	12%	90 days	(Problem line)
$ 10.00	6%	60 days	(Known)
+$ 10.00	+ 6%		(Solving for rate)
$ 20.00	12%	60 days	
+$ 10.00		+ 30 days	(Solving for time)
$ 30.00	12%	90 days	

Note that borrowing 1,000 for 90 days at 12% interest will cost the borrower $30 in interest. Remember: when using the 60-day method and solving for rates or times other than 6% and 60 days, the calculations must solve for each unknown separately. **Complete Computational Problem 6, Part A** (p. 252).

RECORDING INTEREST

The interest on a note is recorded at the time the note is paid. When the note is given by the buyer to the seller, it is recorded on the books as illustrated on pages 238 and 239. Notice that the explanations indicate the terms of the notes. In both instances the notes were 30-day notes that were non-interest-bearing by virtue of the fact that no interest was included in the terms. If the notes had been interest-bearing, the explanation would have indicated that fact, perhaps by means of the following phrase: 30-day, 6% note.

The interest on a promissory note is recorded at the time the note matures.

Example: Recording the Payment of an Interest-Bearing Note

On August 1, 198–, a 60-day, 6% promissory note was issued by Able Trading Co. to Reliable Manufacturing Co. for $1,000. The following general journal entry would be recorded upon payment of the note at maturity:

198–			
Aug. 31	Notes Payable	1,000	
	Interest Expense	10	
	Cash		1,010
	Paid 6%, 60-day note to		
	Reliable Manufacturing Co.		

On the books of Reliable Manufacturing Co., the following entry would represent the receipt of the cash from Able Trading Co. in payment of its obligation:

198–			
Aug. 31	Cash	1,010	
	Notes Receivable		1,000
	Interest Income		10
	Payment of 6%, 60-day note		
	by Able Trading Co.		

Note that the interest paid on the note by Able Trading Co. represents an expense (interest expense) to the company at the time that the payment is made on the note. The interest received by the Reliable Manufacturing Co. represents income (interest income) at the time that the note receivable is paid.

If the note was payable in the next accounting period, then an adjusting entry would be recorded at the end of the accounting period to recognize the accrued interest expense on the books of Able Trading Co., and accrued interest income at the end of the accounting period would be reflected in an adjusting entry on the books of Reliable Manufacturing Co. **Complete Computational Problems 7 and 8, Part A** (pp. 252–253).

YOU SHOULD REMEMBER

A promissory note may be either interest-bearing or non-interest-bearing.

The shortcut 60-day method of determining interest is based on the fact that interest at 6% for 60 days equals 1% of the amount borrowed.

The interest on a promissory note is recognized when it is paid at maturity.

On the books of the issuer of the note, it represents a liability.

An interest-bearing note payable recognizes interest expense on the issuer's books when the note is paid.

The maturity value of the note, whether on the books of the issuer or on those of the recipient, is the face value of the note (the principal) plus the interest.

ADVANTAGES OF NOTES

If a seller of goods and/or services is given an option to sell for cash or on credit, the obvious preference is to receive cash at the time of the sale. As we have previously indicated, this choice is not usually available to the seller because of the dictates of the industry or trade. However, in selling on credit, the seller has the choice of accepting an oral or a written promise.

When a particular customer has been dealt with on an ongoing basis, an oral promise from the customer may be adequate. When, on the other hand, the seller's experience with a customer is limited, the seller may request a written promise when initially selling to the customer on credit. Should a dispute between the customer and the seller develop at a later date, the existence of a promissory note will assist the seller in having the dispute adjudicated in his or her favor. The courts will accept written evidence over oral testimony in litigation. If, when the original sale is to be consummated, the seller anticipates problems in collecting from the customer, the seller should probably not sell to the customer on credit, even with a promissory note as evidence of the transaction.

Aside from its value in litigation, the primary benefit that a promissory note has over an oral promise is its *negotiability*. This is the ability to transfer the note in exchange for cash or other assets. Negotiability is not possible with an oral promise because of its lack of substance; however, it is quite common to transfer a promissory note.

TRANSFERRING NOTES

The receipt of a promissory note from a customer enables the business to sell that note before maturity for cash rather than to hold it until the due date. In this process, known as **discounting a note,** the promissory note is sold to a bank or finance company. The note is endorsed by the seller, in a fashion similar to that for a check, and delivered to the bank. The bank deducts from the maturity value of the note (face value of the note plus interest) its discounting charges and provides the seller with the net proceeds (maturity value less discount).

When the note becomes due, the lending institution that discounted the note expects to receive the maturity value of the note from its maker. The fact that the note has been discounted and turned over to the lending institution does not eliminate the seller's involvement with the note. The endorsement of the note expedites and makes possible the negotiation of the note, but at the same time it represents a guarantee on the part of the endorser that, if the maker of the note fails to pay the bank, the seller will do so.

Although this situation does not represent an actual liability, a contingent liability has developed. A **contingent liability** is the commitment of the endorser to pay the discounter the maturity value of the note in the event that the maker of the note defaults. The discounting of the note creates the contingent liability, which continues in effect until the due date of the note. If the maker pays the appropriate amount at maturity, the contingent liability is eliminated without any action taken by the endorser. If the maker defaults, then the contingent liability becomes an actual liability. Note that the elimination of the contingent liability takes place on the due date regardless of the action or lack of action taken by the maker of the note.

The following illustrates the entries for (1) the receipt of the promissory note, (2) the discounting of the note, and (3) the entry made on the due date of the note. Amounts have been intentionally omitted so that the flow of entries could be highlighted.

198–

Apr.	1	Notes Receivable		**XXXX**
		⎰ Accounts Receivable ⎱		
		⎱ J. Jones ⎰		**XXXX**
		Received 60-day note.		

198–
May 1 Cash   xxxx
            Notes Receivable Discounted   xxxx
         Discounted note at bank.

      31 Notes Receivable Discounted   xxxx
            Notes Receivable   xxxx
         Note honored by maker

When the note is discounted on May 1, it is actually turned over to the lending institution. The contingent liability is recognized by crediting the notes receivable discounted account. Although it would be possible to credit notes receivable directly, this is not a preferred method because it is important that the contingent liability be recognized when the note is discounted.

If a balance sheet were to be prepared shortly after the transaction of May 1, the effects of this entry on the balance sheet would be as follows:

Notes Receivable   xxxx
Less: Notes Receivable Discounted   xxxx
    Net Notes Receivable   xxxx

The reader of the balance sheet is immediately made aware of the fact that a contingent liability exists.

The entry of May 31 is made regardless of whether or not the maker of the note pays the maturity value to the lending institution. This entry eliminates the contingent liability and at the same time eliminates the balance in the notes receivable account to the extent of that particular note. If the maker of the note pays the obligation to the bank, the discounter is relieved of any possible liability on the note that was discounted.

Should the maker of the note **default** on the note, an actual liability would result and the contingent liability would be eliminated. This failure to pay the obligation when it becomes due (default) on the part of the maker causes the endorser (discounter) of the note to become primarily liable. The bank or financing company will then obtain the maturity value of the note from the discounter. If the endorser of the note has an account with the lending institution, as is usually the case, the bank will subtract the maturity value of the note from the endorser's account and notify the endorser. This results in an entry reflecting payment out of the account of the endorser. The following entry is usually made:

198–
June 3   {Accounts Receivable
          { J. Jones   xxxx
            Cash   xxxx
         Dishonored note and protest fee.

The bank will return the dishonored note to the endorser, but the note, having been dishonored, is no longer recognized on the books of the endorser. In its place an accounts receivable is established consisting of the maturity value of the note and any protest fee that the bank has charged to the endorser because of the dishonored note. This total amount is charged to the customer. No expense is recognized for the protest fee since it is the obligation of the defaulting customer. The initial recourse the endorser has against the maker of the note is to request payment of the obligation in full. If the maker of the note fails to pay, the endorser takes the note and other appropriate documentation to court in order to receive relief. The endorser may also be entitled to reasonable interest on the obligation from the due date to the final settlement date of the obligation. This will usually be determined by the court as part of the adjudication.

The following problem involves the discounting of a non-interest-bearing note and its subsequent payment.

Example: Discounting a Non-Interest-Bearing Note

Albert Co. received a non-interest-bearing, 90-day note from a customer on June 1, 198–. Thirty days later the note was discounted at the Fidelity Bank. The bank held the note for 60 days and charged a 6% rate for discounting the note, which had a face value of $1,000. The following entries reflect the receipt of the note, its discounting, and subsequent payment:

198–			
June 1	Notes Receivable	1,000	
	{ Accounts Receivable		1,000
	{ A. Customer		
	90-day note from A. Customer.		
July 1	Cash	990	
	Interest Expense	10	
	Notes Receivable Discounted		1,000
	6%, 60 days at Fidelity Bank.		
Aug. 30	Notes Receivable Discounted	1,000	
	Notes Receivable		1,000
	Note honored by maker.		

Since the bank held the non-interest-bearing note for 60 days, it was entitled to interest calculated on the maturity value of the $1,000 note, which was the same as the face value because there was no interest to be earned on the note, at the discount rate of 6%. The calculation of the interest is as follows:

$$\$1,000 \times .06 \times 60/360 = \$10$$

When discounting the note, the bank subtracts the interest from the maturity value of the note to determine the net proceeds of the note. In our example the amount of cash received consisted of the maturity value of $1,000, less the bank's discount charge of $10. The credit part of the July 1 entry recognizes the contingent liability.

On August 30, the maturity date of the note, the contingent liability is eliminated. Remember that this entry is made whether or not the note is actually honored.

DISCOUNTING AN INTEREST-BEARING NOTE

The discounting of an interest-bearing promissory note is handled in the same manner as that for a non-interest bearing note, except that the maturity value of the interest-bearing note will include the interest earned on the note by the discounter at the maturity date. The bank will discount the note on the basis of the maturity value, which is the amount of money the bank will receive at the maturity date. Thus, even though the face value of the note may be $1,000, if the maturity value is $1,010 ($1,000 + $10 interest), the bank will discount the note based on the maturity value as if the discounter had borrowed $1,010 from the bank originally.

Example: Discounting an Interest-Bearing Note

Assume that a 90-day, 6% note receivable for $1,000, dated August 5, is discounted at a bank on September 4 at a rate of 8%. The following calculations will result:

Face value of note dated Aug. 5:	$1,000.00
Interest on note—6%, 90 days:	15.00
Maturity value of note on Nov. 3:	1,015.00
Discount period—Sept. 4 to Nov. 3 (60 days):	
Discount on maturity value ($1,015 × .08 × 60/360):	13.53
Net proceeds	$1,001.47

The entries recording receipt of the note and the discounting of the note would appear as follows:

198–

Aug. 5	Notes Receivable	1,000.00	
	Accounts Receivable		1,000.00
	90-day, 6% note from XXXXX.		
Sept. 4	Cash	1,001.47	
	Notes Receivable Discounted		1,000.00
	Interest Income		1.47
	Discounted at 8% for 60 days.		

If the discounter of the note had held it to maturity, the amount of interest earned on the note would have been $15. Discounting the note after 30 days caused the note to be in the hands of the bank for 60 days. The bank charged a discounting fee of 8% for the 60 days, which amounted to an interest expense to the discounter of $13.53. The excess of interest income earned ($15) over the interest expense charged by the bank ($13.53) resulted in a net interest income of $1.47 to be recorded. An alternative acceptable entry on September 4 could have been:

Sept. 4	Cash	1,001.47	
	Interest Expense	13.53	
	Notes Receivable Discounted		1,000.00
	Interest Income		15.00
	Discounted at 8% for 60 days.		

Although this second entry is acceptable, the first is preferred because it nets out the income and expense to reflect one amount. If the amount of the interest charged by the bank as a result of discounting the note had exceeded the interest income earned on the note, the first entry would have shown a debit to the interest expense account.

Whenever an interest-bearing note is discounted, the amount of the discount is always calculated on the maturity value. **Complete Computational Problems 9, 10, and 11, Part A** (pp. 253–254).

DISCOUNTING A COMPANY'S OWN NOTE

When a business wishes to borrow money from a lending institution, it may do so by issuing a promissory note payable to the bank. The bank in accepting the note will frequently discount it. Discounting a note payable results in the firm's receiving less cash than the face value of the note, to the extent of the interest charged by the bank for the privilege of borrowing the money. The discounting of the note is in actuality the process by which the bank lends money to the business.

Example: Discounting a Company's Own Note

A business issues a 90-day, non-interest-bearing promissory note payable to a bank for $2,000. The bank's discount rate is 9%. The amount of the discount is $45, and the net proceeds are $1,955. This transaction will appear on the books of the borrower as follows:

198–			
June 5	Cash	1,955	
	Interest Expense	45	
	Notes Payable		2,000
	Issued 90-day note to XXXX Bank		
	discounted at 9%.		

Notice that the note was issued and recorded at face value, which is also the maturity value. The interest expense is recorded at the time the note is issued.

When the note is paid in 90 days, the following entry will be recorded:

198–

Sept. 3	Notes Payable	2,000	
	Cash		2,000
	90-day note previously discounted.		

If the original intent of the borrower was to obtain the use of $2,000, it would be necessary to borrow a greater amount so that the net proceeds of discounting the note would amount to $2,000.

In issuing a loan, a bank may choose not to discount the note, but rather require the business to issue a 90-day, 9% note to the bank. If this was the case, the following entries for the issuance and subsequent payment would be recorded on the buyer's books:

198–

June 5	Cash	2,000	
	Notes Payable		2,000
	90-day, 9% note to XXXX Bank		
Sept. 3	Notes Payable	2,000	
	Interest Expense	45	
	Cash		2,045
	Paid note plus interest.		

Complete Computational Problem 12 and 13, Part A (p. 254).

YOU SHOULD REMEMBER

One advantage of a promissory note is that it provides written evidence of the transaction with the buyer's signature on it.

Also, the possession of a promissory note enables the seller to convert this asset to cash, before the maturity date, through the process of discounting the note.

An interest-bearing note is discounted on its maturity value (principal + interest).

When a business firm discounts its own note, it receives the face value of the note less the interest charged by the bank for lending the money.

For more practice in mastering the material in this chapter, **complete Computational Problems 1, 2, 3, 4, and 5, Part B** (pp. 254–257).

KNOW THE CONCEPTS

DO YOU KNOW THE BASICS?

For each of the following, which choice—(a), (b), or (c)—should be inserted in the blank to make a correct statement?

1. The ―――― method provides the greatest degree of accuracy over the recognition of bad debts expense. (a) direct write-off (b) net sales (c) aging of accounts receivable

2. The ―――― method is the least desirable way to recognize uncollectible accounts. (a) direct write-off (b) net sales (c) aging of accounts receivable

3. In the net sales method the expected rate of uncollectible debts is usually estimated as ――――. (a) 1% of net sales for the last accounting period (b) 1% of the gross sales for the last year (c) a percentage, based on the firm's own experience, of annual net sales

4. The issuer of a promissory note records the note in an account entitled ――――. (a) "Notes Payable" (b) "Notes Receivable" (c) "Accounts Payable"

5. The interest on $3,000 for 60 days at 6% is ――――. (a) $30 (b) $60 (c) $180

6. A person who borrows $2,000 at 12% for 120 days will pay ―――― interest. (a) $40 (b) $80 (c) $120

7. The shortcut 60-day method is based on an interest rate of ――――. (a) 5% (b) 6% (c) 10%

8. The interest on a promissory note is recorded ――――. (a) when the debt is incurred (b) when the note is paid (c) at the end of the accounting period

9. ―――― is the process whereby a note is sold for cash before it matures. (a) Transferring (b) Defaulting (c) Discounting

10. The maturity value of an interest-bearing note is ――――. (a) the face value of the note (b) the principal + interest (c) the principal + interest + a service charge imposed by the lender

TERMS FOR STUDY

aging of accounts receivable method
contingent liability
default
direct write-off method
interest-bearing promissory note

net sales method
notes payable
notes receivable
sixty- (60-) day method of
    determining interest

PRACTICAL APPLICATION

PART A. COMPUTATIONAL PROBLEMS WITH COMPLETE SOLUTIONS

1. Record the following transactions using the two-column general journal:

198–

Mar. 6 Sold goods to Standish, Inc., for $840; terms: n/30

9 Sent a credit memorandum for $60 to Standish, Inc., for returning damaged merchandise.

Apr. 14 Received a check from Standish, Inc., for $300 in part payment of the Mar. 6 invoice.

May 18 Determined that the balance Standish, Inc., owed us is uncollectible. Decided to write off the account.

26 Received a check from Standish Inc., for $100. This represented partial restoration of the account previously written off.

2. The Ruth Allen Co. had these account balances at the end of the calendar year: accounts receivable, $541,300; allowance for bad debts, $10,912. Make entries in general journal form for the following transactions for the new year:
   (a) Sales made on credit amounted to $5,456,575.
   (b) Cash sales made during the year amounted to $121,214.
   (c) Collections of accounts during the year were as follows: actual cash collected, $5,381,642; sales discounts allowed, $130,004.
   (d) Wrote off uncollectible accounts amounting to $9,280.
   (e) Collected $2,340 for an account that had previously been written off.
   (f) Made the adjusting entry to recognize bad debts based on 1% of net credit sales for the year.

3. A company prepared an aging schedule of accounts receivable for the end of the year. The estimated adjusting entry for the uncollectible receivables amounted to $9,150. At the end of the year, before the adjusting entry, the allowance for bad debts had a credit balance of $350. Make the necessary adjusting entry at the end of the year.

4. The aging of accounts receivable estimate determines that write-offs for the coming year will amount to $2,445. The allowance for bad debts account,

before the adjusting entry, shows a debit balance of $185. Record the adjusting entry under the aging of accounts receivable method.

5. Determine the interest on the following notes, using the formula illustrated on page 240:

	Face Amount	Number of Days	Interest Rate
(a)	$3,000	360	8%
(b)	2,600	60	9%
(c)	1,000	90	10%
(d)	5,000	45	6%
(e)	4,000	30	12%

6. Using the 60-day method, determine the interest charges on the following notes:

	Face Amount	Rate of Interest	Time
(a)	$600	6%	60 days
(b)	600	9%	60 days
(c)	600	6%	90 days
(d)	600	9%	90 days
(e)	600	3%	60 days
(f)	600	6%	30 days
(g)	600	3%	30 days
(h)	600	9%	30 days
(i)	600	3%	90 days

7. A business organization issues a 60-day, 9% promissory note for $10,000 to a creditor in payment of an obligation. Present in general journal form entries to (a) record the issuance of the note, and (b) record the payment of the note, including appropriate interest.

8. A promissory note dated December 1, 198–, bearing interest at a rate of 12% and due in 90 days, is sent to a creditor. The face value of the note is $900.

(a) Determine the due date of the note.
(b) Determine the total interest income that will be earned on the note.
(c) Assuming that the note is held for 30 days in the old accounting period (December 1–31), find the interest that would be earned on the note for that period (accrued interest income).
(d) Prepare the general journal entry for the receipt of the note.
(e) Record the adjusting entry on December 31, and any necessary reversal entries.

    (f) Record the entry for the receipt of the payment of the note by the customer.

    (g) Record entries 4, 5, and 6 on the books of the customer who issued the note.

9. On March 10, 198–, Arthur Cromwell received from a customer a 120-day, non-interest-bearing note for $1,500 from the Black Co. The note was discounted at the Jackson National Bank on April 24, 198–. The Jackson National Bank charged Cromwell 6% for discounting the note. Answer the following questions, based on the above information:

    (a) What is the due date of the note?

    (b) What is the maturity value of the note?

    (c) How many days did Cromwell hold the note?

    (d) How many days did the bank hold the note?

    (e) What interest is the bank entitled to on the note?

    (f) What entry will Cromwell record for the receipt of the note?

    (g) What entry will Cromwell record for the discounting of the note?

    (h) What entry will Cromwell record on the due date of the note?

    (i) What entry will result if the note is dishonored on the due date by the maker, assuming a protest fee of $15?

10. Arthur Henderson holds a 90-day, 7% note for $1,200 dated April 18 that was received from a client on account. On May 27, the note is discounted to the Town Bank at a rate of 8%. Answer the following questions relating to the above information:

    (a) What is the maturity value of the note?

    (b) How long did Hendersen hold the note?

    (c) How long did Town Bank hold the note?

    (d) What is the amount of the discount on the note?

    (e) What is the amount of the net proceeds as a result of discounting the note?

    (f) What is the general journal entry to be made on May 27 when the note is discounted?

11. White Co. received the notes listed below during the last quarter of its calendar year:

	Date	Face Amount	Terms	Interest Rate	Date Discounted	Discount Rate
(1)	Oct. 8	$3,600	30 days	—	Oct. 18	9%
(2)	Sept. 22	$8,000	60 days	6%	Oct. 1	7%
(3)	Nov. 15	$3,000	90 days	7%	Nov. 20	8%
(4)	Nov. 17	$900	30 days	8%	Dec. 7	7%
(5)	Dec. 1	$2,000	60 days	6%	—	—

Find:

(a) The due date of each note.
(b) The amount of the interest due at maturity for each note.
(c) The maturity value of each note.
(d) The discount period (where applicable).
(e) The net proceeds of each discounted note.
(f) The interest expense or income on the individual notes.
(g) The general journal entries for the discounting of notes (1)–(4).
(h) The adjusting entry necessary on December 31, the end of the accounting period, if note (5) is to be held until maturity.

12. Roberts Co. issues a 30-day, non-interest-bearing note for $15,000 to the First National Trust Co., which the bank discounts at 6%. Record the necessary entries in general journal form to (a) issue the note and (b) pay the note at maturity. Assume that the note was written on January 3.

13. You are given a choice by your bank as to the nature of the loan you are negotiating. You may (1) issue a $5,000, non-interesting-bearing note that the bank will discount at a rate of 12%, or (2) issue a $5,000 note bearing interest at a rate of 12% that will be accepted at face value.

(a) Determine the amount of interest expense for each option.
(b) Determine the amount of the net proceeds for each option.
(c) Indicate which option is more favorable to you and why.

PART B. COMPUTATIONAL PROBLEMS
WITH PARTIAL SOLUTIONS OR KEY ANSWERS

1. The following ledger accounts and balances appear on the books of the MH Sales Co.:

General Ledger Accounts and Balances (selective)

Accounts Receivable (control)	$ 20,400
Sales	106,500
Bad Debts Expense	320

Accounts Receivable Ledger

A. Burns	$3,100
H. Conroy	8,400
R. Daly	4,800
K. Evans	1,200
R. Falkner	3,000

The MH Sales Co. is owned and operated by Marion Hoffman. Set up ledger accounts for the accounts listed above, showing the normal balances as of the beginning of the current calendar year. The following selected transactions are to be recorded in general journal form with postings to take place where appropriate. No additional ledger accounts are to be established.

As the accountant for the firm you have chosen to use the direct write-off method of accounting for bad debts.

198–
Feb. 3 Received a part payment from H. Conroy amounting to $4,600.

23 Determined that the amount owed us by K. Evans is uncollectible. We have written off the account balance.

Mar. 8 Received a check from A. Burns for $2,900. He claims that the balance owed should be eliminated as a result of defective goods that his company received but was never given credit for.

Apr. 10 Received a check from K. Evans for $800 as part payment of the balance owed us, which we had previously written off.

23 Wrote off as uncollectible the balance owed us by A. Burns.

2. On January 1 of the current year, the ledger of K. Lane shows the allowance for bad debts account with a credit balance of $2,750. This company uses the net sales method of accounting for bad debts. During the current year the following transactions affecting bad debts and uncollectible accounts occurred. Record these transactions in general journal form, set up an allowance for bad debts account, and post specifically to this account only.

198–
Mar. 2 Received word that Lennox Co., a customer, had been declared bankrupt, owing K. Lane $2,614.

May 14 Received a check from H. Patterson, whose account had been written off in the preceding year, for the amount of $265.

July 3 Determined that the account of T. Minor, a deceased customer, who owed $2,460, was collectible only to the extent of 60% thereof. We wrote off the uncollectible part of the receivable.

Sept. 9 Received $783 from Lennox Co. as final settlement of its indebtedness to use. (Refer to transaction of Mar. 2.)

Dec. 31 Recorded the adjusting entry to recognize bad debts by taking 1.5% of the balance in net sales ($205,600).

3. A partial trial balance of J. Leader on December 31, 198A contains the following balances:

	DEBITS	CREDITS
Accounts Receivable	$56,300.00	
Allowance for Bad Debts		$ 1,346.00
Sales		563,200.00
Sales Returns and Allowances	14,200.00	

On December 31, 198A, a provision for bad debts based on the aging of accounts receivable method was set up equal to ½ of 1% of the net sales.

During 198B (the next year), the following accounts were written off:

January 31	F. Partner	$1,740.00
August 11	G. Henry	1,530.00

The 198B net sales amounted to $520,000. The amount to be recognized as the allowance for bad debts at the end of the year should be equal to ¾ of 1% of net sales. Accounts receivable on December 31, 198B amounted to $48,000.

During 198C (the third year) the following accounts were written off:

February 26	S. Grant	$2,160.00
November 13	R. Patritte	1,890.00

On December 3, 198C, a check was received from S. Grant in the sum of $100 as a first and final payment resulting from the liquidation of the business.

For the year ended December 31, 198C, net sales amounted to $540,000. The amount to be added to the allowance for bad debts account at the end of the year should be equal to ¾ of 1% of the net sales. On December 31, 198C, accounts receivable amounted to $49,000.

(a) Prepare adjusting entries for each of the foregoing years. Make all other entries, in general journal form, that affect the bad debts expense and the allowance for bad debts accounts.

(b) Show how the allowance for bad debts account would appear during the period covered by the problem, using the T-account or Boston ledger form.

4. A. C. Creditor holds a 90-day, 9% note for $6,000, dated September 16, that was received from a customer as payment of an obligation. Ten days from the date of the note, it is discounted at A. C. Creditor's bank, which charged a discount rate of 12%. On the basis of this information, answer the following questions:

(a) What is the maturity value of the note?

(b) How many days are there in the discount period?

(c) If A. C. Creditor held the note until maturity, what would be the amount of interest income earned?

(d) What is the cost to A. C. Creditor for discounting the note on September 26?

(e) What are the net proceeds to A. C. Creditor for discounting the note?

(f) What is the general journal entry to record the discounting of the note by A. C. Creditor?

(g) What is the general journal entry when the discounted note matures?

(h) Assuming that the matured note is dishonored by the maker, what general journal will be recorded as a result?

5. Record the following transactions in general journal form:

198–

Mar. 1 Received a 60-day, 7% note for $9,000, dated today, from Glick Co.

31 Discounted Glick Co.'s note at our bank; charged a discount rate of 10%.

Apr. 30 The note is dishonored. The bank took the amount owed on the note out of our account, plus a protest fee of $5.

Jun 29 Received the amount due on the note from Glick Co., plus the protest fee and interest at 6% from the date the note was dishonored.

ANSWERS

KNOW THE CONCEPTS

1. c	4. a	7. b	9. c
2. a	5. a	8. b	10. b
3. c	6. b		

PRACTICAL APPLICATION

PART A

1. 198–

Mar. 6	Standish Inc./Accounts Receivable	840	
	Sales		840
	Terms: n/30.		

9	Sales Returns and Allowances	60	
	Standish Inc./Accounts Receivable		60
	Credit memo for damaged merchandise.		

Apr. 14	Cash	300	
	Standish Inc./Accounts Receivable		300
	Part payment		

May 18	Bad Debts Expense	480	
	Standish Inc./Accounts Receivable		480
	Write-off of uncollectible account.		

26	Standish Inc./Accounts Receivable	100	
	Bad Debts Expense		100
	To restore part of account previously written off.		

26	Cash	100	
	Standish Inc./Accounts Receivable		100
	Part payment received of account previously written off.		

2. (a) Accounts Receivable   5,456,575
         Sales   5,456,575
    Total credit sales for the year.

(b) Cash   121,214
         Sales   121,214
    Total cash sales for the year.

(c) Cash   5,381,642
    Sales Discount   130,004
         Accounts Receivable   5,511,646
    Total collections for the year.

(d) Allowance for Bad Debts   9,280
         Accounts Receivable   9,280
    Wrote off uncollectibles.

(e) Accounts Receivable   2,340
         Allowance for Bad Debts   2,340
    To restore an account previously written off.
    Cash   2,340
         Accounts Receivable   2,340
    Collection from an account previously written off

(f) Bad Debts Expense   54,565.75
        Allowance for Bad Debts   54,565.75
     Adjusting entry based on 1% of net credit sales.

Allowance for Bad Debts

(d)	9,280.00	Bal.		10,912.00
		(e)	3,972.00	2,340.00
		(f)	58,537.75	54,565.75
				67,817.75

3. 198–
    Dec. 31   Bad Debts Expense   8,800
                        Allowance for Bad Debts   8,800
                  Adjusting entry to recognize uncollectible
                  account expense for the year.
                  ($9,150 estimated uncollectibles − $350 credit
                  balance in allowance account = $8,800 bad
                  debt expense to be recognized.)

4. 198–
    Dec. 31   Bad Debts Expense   2,630
                        Allowance for Bad Debts   2,630
                  Adjusting entry to recognize uncollectible
                  account expense for the year.
                  *($2,445 estimated uncollectibles + $185
                  debit balance in allowance account − $2,630
                  bad debt expense to be recognized.)

*Under the aging of accounts receivable method, the remaining balance in the allowance account is considered in preparing the year-end adjusting entry. Thus, if the allowance account has a credit balance at the end of the year, the adjusting entry subtracts that balance from the anticipated bad debts to arrive at the appropriate year-end adjusting entry. If the allowance account has a debit balance, this balance is added to the anticipated bad debts to arrive at the appropriate year-end adjusting entry.

5.   Interest
    (a) $240   ($3,000 × 8% × 1)
    (b)   39   ($2,600 × 9% × 60/360)
    (c)   25   ($1,000 × 10% × 90/360)
    (d) 37.50 ($5,000 × 6% × 45/360)
    (e)   40   ($4,000 × 12% × 30/360)

6.   Interest

(a)	$ 6	(f)	3
(b)	9	(g)	1.50
(c)	9	(h)	4.50
(d)	13.50	(i)	4.50
(e)	3		

7. (a)   Accounts Payable   10,000
               Notes Payable   10,000
             Issued 60-day, 9% note this day.

     (b)   Notes Payable   10,000
             Interest Expense   150
                Cash   10,150
             Paid interest-bearing note today.

8. (a)   The due date of the note is 90 days from the date the note was issued. In this case it was issued on December 1. The due date is March 1 of the following year.

     (b)   The total interest income on the note is $27.

     (c)   The interest income that has accrued by December 31 is $9.

     (d)   **198–**

Dec. 1	Notes Receivable	900	
	Accounts Receivable		900
	For 12%, 90-day note received.		

     (e)   **198–**

Dec. 31	Interest Receivable	9	
	Interest Income		9
	Accrued interest on note.		

          198–

Jan. 1	Interest Income	9	
	Interest Receivable		9
	Reversal entry.		

     (f)   **198–**

Mar. 1	Cash	927	
	Interest Income		27
	Notes Receivable		900
	Received maturity value of note.		

     (g)   **198–**

Dec. 1	Accounts Payable	900	
	Notes Payable		900
	Issued 90-day, 12% note.		
31	Interest Expense	9	
	Interest Payable		9
	To recognize accrued interest on note.		

198–
Jan. 1 Interest Payable   9
             Interest Expense   9
             Reversal entry.
198–
Mar. 1 Notes Payable   900
             Interest Expense   27
             Cash   927
             Paid note plus interest.

9. (a) The due date of the note is July 8.
   (b) The maturity value of the non-interest-bearing note is $1,500.
   (c) 45 days.
   (d) 75 days.
   (e) $1,500 × 6% × 75/360 = $18.75.
   (f) **198–**
       Mar. 10 Notes Receivable   1,500.00
                     Accounts Receivable   1,500.00
                     Received 120-day,
                     non-interest-bearing note.
   (g) **198–**
       Apr. 24 Cash   1,481.25
                     Interest Expense   18.75
                     Notes Receivable Discounted   1,500.00
                     Discounted at 6%.   for 75 days
   (h) **198–**
       July 8   Notes Receivable Discounted   1,500.00
                     Notes Receivable   1,500.00
                     Discounted note is payable today.
   (i) **198–**
       July 8   Accounts Receivable   1,515.00
                     Cash   1,515.00
                     For dishonored note
                     plus protest fee.

10. (a) The maturity value of the note is $1,221.
    (b) Henderson held the note for 40 days.
    (c) Town Bank held the note for 50 days.
    (d) The amount of the discount on the note is $13.57, calculated as follows:
        Maturity Value of Note = $1,200 × 7% × 90 days = 21
        Principal + Interest = Maturity Value = $1,221
        Maturity Value of Note × Time   × Discount Rate = Discount
                    $1,221 × 50 days × 8%   = $13.57
    (e) Maturity Value of Note − Discount = Net Proceeds
                    $1,221 − $13.57   = $1,207.43

(f) **198–**
May 27 Cash   1,207.43
            Interest Income   7.43
            Notes Receivable Discounted   1,200.00
        Discounted 90-day 7% note at a
        discount rate of 8% for 50 days at
        Town Bank.

11.

	(a) Due Date	(b) Interest Due at Maturity	(c) Maturity Value	(d) Discount Period	(e) Net Proceeds	(f) Interest Expense (Interest Income)
(1)	Nov. 7	–0–	$3,600.00	20 days	$3,582.00	$18.00
(2)	Nov. 21	$80.00	8,080.00	51 days	7,999.87	.13
(3)	Feb. 13	52.50	3,052.50	85 days	2,994.84	5.16
(4)	Dec. 17	6.00	906.00	10 days	904.24	(4.24)
(5)	Jan. 30	20.00	2,020.00	–	–	(20.00)

(g) Entries for Discounting Notes (1)–(4):
    (1)   Cash   3,582.00
          Interest Expense   18.00
             Notes Receivable Discounted   3,600.00
    (2)   Cash   7,999.87
          Interest Expense   .13
             Notes Receivable Discounted   8,000.00
    (3)   Cash   2,994.84
          Interest Expense   5.16
             Notes Receivable Discounted   3,000.00
    (4)   Cash   904.24
            Interest Income   4.24
            Notes Receivable Discounted   900.00

(h) Adjusting Entry:
    198–
    Dec. 31 Interest Receivable   10.00
               Interest Income   10.00
        To recognize accrued interest income.

12. (a) **198–**
    Jan. 3 Cash   14,925.00
          Interest Expense   75.00
            Notes Payable   15,000.00
        Discounted our note at First
        National Trust Co. at 6%.

(b) **198–**
    Feb. 2   Notes Payable   15,000.00
                  Cash   15,000.00
                  Paid discounted note due today.

13. (a) The interest expenses under the two options are identical.
    (b) The net proceeds cannot readily be determined since the holding period was not given. However, let us assume a holding period by the bank of 60 days. Under option (1), the net proceeds are $4,900 ($5,000 × 12% × 60/360). The net proceeds under option (2) are $5,000.
    (c) Option (2) is more favorable since under this option the amount of money available is $5,000, rather than $4,900 if the note is discounted. Most lending institutions will opt to give customers a loan based on discounting the obligation. Thus, if you wanted to borrow $5,000 and the bank required you to discount the loan, you would actually have to borrow a sum greater than $5,000 to obtain net proceeds of $5,000. In this case you would have to borrow approximately $5,110 in order to obtain net proceeds of $5,000.

PART B
1. **198–**
    Feb. **3**   Cash   4,600.00
                  H. Conroy/Accounts Receivable   4,600.00
                  Receive partial payment from
                  H. Conroy.

        23   Bad Debts Expense   1,200.00
                  K. Evans/Accounts Receivable   1,200.00
                  To write-off uncollectible account.

    Mar. **8**   Cash   2,900.00
                  A. Burns/Accounts Receivable   2,900.00
                  Part payment of obligation of A. Burns.

    Apr. **10**   K. Evans/Accounts Receivable   800.00
                  Bad Debts Expense   800.00
                  To restore part of account
                  previously written off.

        10   Cash   800.00
                  K. Evans/Accounts Receivable   800.00
                  Part payment of obligation previously
                  written off.

198–

Apr. 23 Bad Debt Expense   200.00
                        A. Burns/Accounts Receivable   200.00
                  To write off uncollectible account.

2. December 31 adjusting entry, $3,084

3. 198A adjusting amount, $1,399; 198B adjusting amount, $4,425; 198C adjusting amount, $4,100

4. Maturity value, $6,135; net proceeds, $5,971.40

5. Net proceeds as of March 31, $9,029.13

9
LONG-LIFE AND INTANGIBLE ASSETS

LONG-LIFE ASSETS

We have previously defined an asset as anything owned that has money value. Assets were further classified in terms of their useful life. An asset that can readily be expected to be consumed or converted to cash within a year or less is considered to be a **current asset**. Any asset that has a useful life of more than 1 year is usually considered to be a **long-life asset**. Other terms used to describe a long-life asset include **fixed asset** and **property, plant, and equipment**.

• *USING LONG-LIFE ASSETS*

Long-life assets are acquired through purchase for use in the operation of the business and are not usually intended for resale. Assets included in this category are equipment, tools, furniture, machinery, automotive equipment, buildings, and land. In order for the above-mentioned items to be classified as plant assets, they must be used in the business, though not necessarily continuously, and must have a minimum useful life of at least 1 year.

The function of long-life assets is to assist in the generation of revenue, which is the primary activity of most business organizations. A fixed asset such as a delivery truck enables a firm to transport goods that have been sold to the organization's various customers. Thus, this long-life asset is an integral part of the consummation of the sale. Without this fixed asset the firm would have to incur the expense of hiring a delivery service to complete the transaction. The cost of hiring a delivery service is an obvious expense, but the use of the firm's delivery truck is also an expense, although is not so apparent, that must be recognized over the assigned useful life of the truck.

• DETERMINING PLANT AND EQUIPMENT COSTS

The cost of plant and equipment includes all expenditures necessary to acquire and place the asset in use by the organization. Costs include the purchase price of the asset, plus any applicable sales taxes, the cost of transporting the equipment to its place of use, the installation costs, and any other incidental costs necessary to make the asset operational for the organization. The justification for including all the costs indicated, rather than recording some as expenses, is that every one of these costs is an integral part of making the asset usable by the organization. The benefits derived from the cost assigned will be recognized over the useful life of the asset. The **cost principle**, discussed in Chapter 1, states that every asset is set up on the books at its actual cost. This cost includes any specific or incidental costs necessary to place the asset in use by the firm. This principle is an integral part of the concept of matching costs and revenue.

Example: The Cost Principle

A business wishes to acquire a machine that has a list price of $5,000. The seller offers a trade discount of 20%. There is a delivery charge of $175, and applicable sales taxes on the net purchase price amounting to 8%. Also, in order to make the machine operational, a special cement pad must be constructed at a cost of $500. The installation charge amounts to $250. The following represents the determination of the total cost of the machine as it will appear on the buyer's books should the organization decide to acquire the asset:

List Price of Machine	$5,000
Less: Trade Discount (20%)	(1,000)
Net Purchase Price	4,000
Add: Sales Tax (8%)	320
Delivery Charge	175
Cement Pad	500
Installation Charge	250
Total Cost of Machine	$5,245

On the books of the buyer, the machine will be set up at a total cost of $5,245. Any subsequent costs, such as repairs, would be treated as expenses. This asset will remain on the books at the value assigned, unless the asset is sold or there is a subsequent **capital expenditure**. A capital expenditure is a material expenditure that usually increases the useful life of a fixed asset and is charged to the fixed asset. For example, replacement of a roof on a building is a capital expenditure that increases the cost of the building on the books and also may increase the building's useful life. A repair to the roof, however, is considered an expense that does not increase the cost of the asset. This expense is commonly known as a revenue expenditure. **Complete Computational Problem 1, Part A** (p. 286).

YOU SHOULD REMEMBER

A long-life asset is an asset, such as buildings, land, or equipment, that has a useful life of more than 1 year.

The cost principle requires that all long-life assets be set up on the books at their actual costs and that the cost remain on the books until such time as the asset is sold, discarded, or adjusted as a result of a capital expenditure.

• *ALLOCATING PLANT AND EQUIPMENT COSTS*

A short-life (current) asset such as supplies is adjusted annually to reflect the fact that it has been used up. This conversion from an asset to an expense is accomplished by recording an adjusting entry. At the end of the accounting period, an inventory is taken of the actual supplies that are on hand. The difference between the book value of the supplies and the inventory tells the accountant the value of the supplies used up, and becomes the basis for the adjusting entry.

Plant and equipment cannot be treated in the same fashion because there is no apparent change in the value of the asset that can be readily measured. However, the approximate useful life of a plant asset can be determined. This useful life, expressed in years or usage, becomes the basis for assigning a cost or expense for the asset periodically. The term used to describe the recognition of an annual expense for a plant asset is **depreciation**.

Depreciation is the recognition of a loss in value of a plant asset due to wear and tear over time. Thus, the recognition of depreciation causes a portion of the asset value to be converted to an expense in the same way that the asset supplies was converted. In recognizing this annual expense, the accountant must still follow the dictates of the cost principle. The value assigned to the fixed asset on the books must remain the same unless the asset is sold or changed as a result of a capital improvement.

• *DEPRECIATION*

The entry to record depreciation is an adjusting entry and is usually recorded at least once a year. Some organizations may choose to record depreciation monthly, quarterly, or semiannually. Regardless of when it is recorded, it still represents an adjusting entry similar to the conversion of the asset supplies to an expense. It is necessary to retain the original balance in the account for a plant asset; therefore, the adjusting entry first recognizes the expense by debiting an account entitled "Depreciation Expense." The corresponding credit is made, not directly to the asset account, but rather to an account that is classified as a **contra-asset**.

A contra-asset, as pointed out in Chapter 4, is a negative account that will always represent a credit entry offsetting a specific plant asset. If the plant asset being depreciated is equipment, the contra-asset account will be entitled "Accumulated Depreciation—Equipment." If we were to recognize annual depreciation of the asset equipment amounting to $500, the following adjusting entry would be recorded in the general journal at the end of the first year:

198–

Dec. 31	Depreciation Expense—Equipment	500	
	Accumulated Depreciation—Equipment		500
	To recognize annual depreciation.		

The depreciation expense account is handled in the same manner as any other expense. Shortly after the adjusting entry is recorded and posted at the end of the accounting period, it is closed to income summary and becomes a part of the income statement that is prepared.

The credit entry is to accumulated depreciation—equipment is a contra-asset account and as such will not be closed but rather appear as a subtraction from the asset account on the balance sheet of the business when it is prepared. The asset and related contra-asset will appear on the balance sheet of the business as follows:

Equipment	$12,400	
Less Accumulated Depreciation	500	
		$11,900

At the end of the second full year another adjusting entry to recognize depreciation is recorded. The asset and related contra-asset will appear on the balance sheet after the second year as follows:

Equipment	$12,400	
Less Accumulated Depreciation	1,000	
		$11,400

Depreciation may result from one of two major causes. One is **physical deterioration** due to the plant asset being used. Some assets are depreciated based on the somewhat arbitrary useful lives (in years) assigned to them, and other assets are depreciated based on their capacity to complete a number of specific functions. For example, a machine may be depreciated on the basis of its ability to stamp out a specified number of items; the machine's output is used to determine the depreciation expense. Another cause of depreciation is **obsolescence**, that is, the process of becoming obsolete or out of date. A mainframe computer designed a mere 2 years ago may be considered obsolete today, even though it is operational, because a more sophisticated computer has been developed. Obsolescence may also occur when a plant asset cannot meet the needs of a rapidly growing business. Inadequacy of a plant asset may necessitate replacement with a larger unit, even though the original asset is in good physical condition and is not obsolete.

YOU SHOULD REMEMBER

Depreciation is the loss in value of a plant asset over time due to wear and tear or obsolescence.

Depreciation is recorded, usually at least once a year, as an adjusting entry.

Expense is recognized by debiting an account called "Depreciation Expense."

The corresponding credit is made to a contra-asset account entitled "Accumulated Depreciation."

CALCULATING DEPRECIATION

The method used to calculate depreciation will vary depending on a number of factors. An asset that is used infrequently would probably be depreciated based on actual usage, rather than on useful life. Another asset that is in continuous use may be appropriately depreciated based on useful life. The depreciation of another asset may be accelerated because of rapid changes in the value of the asset or other factors, such as anticipated repair costs.

A business organization utilizes as many methods of recognizing depreciation as are suitable for the assets being depreciated. The four methods most commonly used to recognize depreciation are **straight-line, units of production, double-declining balance,** and **sum of the years' digits**.

THE STRAIGHT-LINE METHOD

The straight-line method is the simplest and most widely used method of recognizing depreciation. This method provides for the annual recognition of depreciation in equal amounts over the useful life of the asset. If the asset being depreciated is expected to lose value in a uniform manner year after year, then this method will probably be appropriate.

The amount of the asset that is subject to depreciation is known as the **depreciable value**. The depreciable value is determined by subtracting from the total cost of the asset the salvage or scrap or **residual value** of the asset. This residual value, which is usually an estimate, represents the value of the asset after it has been fully depreciated and also the minimum amount that can be obtained for the asset when it is no longer of use to its owner. If a plant asset has a total cost of $10,000 and a residual value of $500, then the depreciable value would be determined as follows:

$$\text{Cost} - \text{Residual value} = \text{Depreciable value}$$
$$\$10,000 - \$500 \qquad = \$9,500$$

The useful life, usually expressed in years, is divided into the depreciable value to determine the annual depreciation expense to be recognized.

$$\frac{\text{Cost} - \text{Residual value}}{\text{Useful life (in years)}} = \text{Annual depreciation expense}$$

If the above asset with a depreciable value of $9,500 had a useful life of 10 years, then the annual depreciation would be calculated as follows:

$$\frac{\$9,500}{10 \text{ years}} = \$950 \text{ (Annual depreciation)}$$

The annual depreciation can also be expressed as a rate. The first step is to develop a fraction with 1 as the numerator and the number of years of useful life as the denominator. Thus, in the above situation, a useful life of 10 years would be expressed as the fraction $\frac{1}{10}$, which converted to a percentage would represent annual depreciation of 10% under the straight-line method.

This calculation would take the depreciable value ($9,500) and multiply it by the straight-line rate of 10%.

$$\$9,500 \times .10 = \$950$$

Complete Computational Problem 2, Part A (p. 286).

RECORDING DEPRECIATION

In the preceding illustration, the adjusting entry for the first full year's depreciation would be recorded as follows:

198–
Dec. 31   Depreciation Expense—Equipment   950
                Accumulated Depreciation—Equipment   950
          To recognize first year's depreciation.

As a result of this entry being posted to the ledger accounts, the accounts would appear as follows:

Equipment

198X	
Jan. 1 10,000	

Accumulated Depreciation—Equipment

	198X
	Dec. 31 950

After the second year's depreciation expense was recognized, the equipment account would remain as illustrated above; however, the accumulated depreciation—equipment account would appear as follows:

Accumulated Depreciation—Equipment

	198X
	Dec. 31 (After 1st Year) 950
	198Y
	Dec. 31 (After 2nd Year) 950

Notice that the accumulated depreciation account has increased from $950 at the end of the first year's depreciation recognition to $1,900 after the recognition of the second year's depreciation. The balance sheet after the second year would show the asset equipment as follows:

Equipment $10,000
Less: Accumulated Depreciation   1,900
                                                                  $8,100

The resulting balance of $8,100 for the equipment represents its **book value**. The book value is the original cost of the asset as established on the books, less the accumulated depreciation. The book value for this asset at the end of the third year would be $7,150 ($10,000 − $950 − $950 − $950 = $7,150).

If the asset was to be fully depreciated over its useful life of 10 years, the resulting book value would be its scrap value of $500 ($10,000 − $9,500 = $500). Remember that book value represents the original cost ($10,000), less accumulated depreciation ($9,500).

The depreciation expense account would be closed to income summary at the end of each accounting period. **Complete Computational Problem 3, Part A** (p. 287).

THE UNITS OF PRODUCTION METHOD

The units of production method allocates the cost of a plant asset to the various accounting periods on the basis of the actual output by the asset. Thus, the useful life of the asset may be unlimited in terms of time, but limited as to the number of items that can be produced using the asset. In this method, as in the straight-line method, the portion of the cost of the asset subject to depreciation is known as the depreciable value. By dividing the depreciable value by the estimated productive capacity, the accountant can ascertain the depreciation expense to be charged against each unit produced by the machine.

$$\frac{\text{Depreciable value}}{\text{Productive capacity}} = \text{Per-Unit depreciation}$$

If the number of units produced for the accounting period is then multiplied by the per-unit depreciation, the total adjusting entry for depreciation expense can be determined.

A lathe acquired at a total cost of $20,750, with a salvage value of $750, is to be depreciated using the units of production method. The estimated productive capacity of the lathe is 40,000 hours. The per-hour depreciation is determined as follows:

$$\frac{\$20,750 \text{ (cost)} - \$750 \text{ (salavage value)}}{40,000 \text{ hours (productive capacity)}} = \$0.50 \text{ (per-hour depreciation)}$$

If the lathe was used for 1,500 hours during an accounting period, the number of hours multiplied by the $0.50 rate of depreciation would mean a depreciation expense of $750 for the year.

When the amount of usage of a plant asset varies greatly from year to year, the units of production method is more appropriate than the striaght-line method. Certainly costs are more appropriately charged against revenue for the specific accounting period, as dictated by the matching of costs and revenue principle. **Complete Computational Problem 4, Part A** (p. 287).

ACCELERATED DEPRECIATION

Accelerated depreciation is the recognition of greater amounts of depreciation in the early years of use of the plant asset and reduced amounts in later years. Accelerated depreciation is automatically recognized with the units of production method, since this method recognizes that use may be greater in the early years of the asset. Some assets may not be appropriately depreciated using the units of production or the straight-line method, however, if a greater amount of depreciation should be recognized in the early years.

An automobile used in business might normally be depreciated using the straight-line method, and yet this method may not adequately reflect the use made of the automobile. If the productivity of the automobile is greater in its earlier years of use, a form of accelerated depreciation should be used. For many plant assets, maintenance and repair costs increase the longer the asset is kept in service. An automobile may not be subject to repair charges within the first 2 or 3 years of its use, but it can be expected to incur greater repair costs as the years progress. When accelerated depreciation in the earlier years, and lower depreciation in the later years, are recognized, the maintenance and repair costs tend to equalize the overall cost recognition for the asset being depreciated. This philosophy is consistent with the basic accounting concept of matching costs and revenue.

THE DOUBLE-DECLINING BALANCE METHOD

This method is appropriate when the asset subject to depreciation contributes to the production of earnings to a greater extent in its early years of use than in its later life. This method modifies the straight-line method in that depreciation is taken at "double" the straight-line rate. Thus, an asset with a useful life of 10 years is depreciated under the straight-line method at a rate of 10% per year. With the double-declining balance method the same asset is depreciated at a rate of 20% per year on the remaining balance or book value of the asset. When this method is used, the residual value is not a part of the calculation. The formula used to calculate first-year depreciation under this method is:

Cost × Double-declining balance rate = First-year depreciation

---

The plant asset costing $10,000, with a useful life of 10 years and a salvage value of $500, would be depreciated under the double-declining balance method as follows:

$$\$10,000 \times .20 = \$2,000.$$

Note that the salvage value is ignored in this calculation. The depreciation recognition in subsequent years is based on the book value of the asset multiplied by the double-declining balance rate.

The depreciation of the above asset over its useful life would be calculated as follows:

Equipment Cost—$10,000; Salvage Value—$500 (ignored)
Useful Life—10 years; Straight-Line Rate 10% (1/10)
Double-Declining Balance Rate—20% (2/10)

Year	Computation (Book Value × Rate)	Depreciation Expense	Accumulated Depreciation	Book Value
1	$10,000.00 × 20%	$2,000.00	$2,000.00	$8,000.00
2	8,000.00 × 20%	1,600.00	3,600.00	6,400.00
3	6,400.00 × 20%	1,280.00	4,880.00	5,120.00
4	5,120.00 × 20%	1,024.00	5,904.00	4,096.00
5	4,096.00 × 20%	819.20	6,723.20	3,276.80
6	3,276.80 × 20%	655.36	7,378.56	2,621.44
7	2,621.44 × 20%	524.29	7,902.85	2,097.15
8	2,097.15 × 20%	419.43	8,322.28	1,677.72
9	1,677.72 × 20%	335.54	8,657.82	1,342.18
10	1,342.18 × 20%	268.44	8,926.26	1,073.74

The last amount shown in the book-value column following the calculation of the tenth year's depreciation represents the salvage value of the asset, based on this method of calculating depreciation. Note that this book value represents the salvage value to be assigned under the double-declining balance method. Comparison of this accelerated depreciation method with the straight-line method will graphically show the difference in the amount of depreciation recognized each year.

Following the determination of the first full year's depreciation, the calculations for the second and subsequent years are based on the book value (cost − accumulated depreciation) multiplied by the double-declining balance rate (straight-line rate × 2).

If the above asset had not been acquired at the beginning of the accounting period, which is usually the case, the amount of depreciation to be recognized would be a fraction of the year, based on the portion of the year the asset was used. Let us assume that the above asset was acquired on April 2 of the same year. The first year's depreciation would be calculated based on the asset's being used from April 2 through December 31, a period of 9 months. The first year's double-declining balance depreciation for the 9 months would be calculated as follows:

$$\$10,000 \times 20\% \times 9/12 = \$1,500$$

The book value of the asset after the above adjusting entry would be $8,500.

This amount would be used to calculate the second full year's depreciation as follows:

$$\$8,500 \times 20\% = \$1,700$$

The book value of the asset after the second year's adjusting entry would be $6,800. This amount would be used to calculate the third full year's depreciation as follows:

$$\$6,800 \times 20\% = \$1,360$$

Regardless of when the asset is acquired, the amount of depreciation to be recognized for the first year is based on the amount of time the asset is in service for that year. The first year's depreciation is usually not calculated for periods of time less than ½ month. Thus, an asset acquired on May 10 will probably be depreciated from May 15 through December 31 for the calendar year (7½ months). The fraction used in this case would be $^{15}\!/_{24}$, which would be reduced to $^{5}\!/_{8}$. Some businesses will depreciate the asset only on the basis of a full month; thus, an asset acquired on Feburary 10 would be depreciated from February 1. An asset acquired on February 17 would be depreciated from March 1. **Complete Computational Problems 5 and 6, Part A (p. 287).**

THE SUM OF THE YEARS' DIGITS METHOD

Comparison of the straight-line method with the double-declining balance method shows a substantial difference in the amount of depreciation recognized, especially during the early years of depreciation. An accelerated form of calculating depreciation may be desirable that provides a depreciation expense greater than under the straight-line method, but not as severe as with the double-declining method. An appropriate compromise can be accomplished using the sum of the years' digits (SYD) method.

The SYD method produces a depreciation expense in a form similar to, but not as extreme as, the double-declining balance method. The yearly depreciation declines steadily over the estimated useful life of the asset because a successively smaller fraction is applied each year to the original cost of the asset less the estimated salvage value. The fraction used to determine the SYD depreciation expense is determined by finding the sum of the years' digits. For example, if an asset has a useful life of 5 years, the sum of the years' digits would be $5 + 4 + 3 + 2 + 1 = 15$. The number 15 becomes the value assigned to the denominator of the fraction to be used. The numerator of the fraction will change each year over the useful life of the asset. Since the earlier years should be charged greater depreciation under this accelerated approach, the first year's numerator will be the highest year (5), the second year's numerator will be the next highest year (4), and so forth. The first year's fraction will be 5/15, the second year's fraction will be 4/15, the third year's fraction will be 3/15, and so forth. Each year's depreciation is obtained by multiplying the appropriate fraction by the original cost, *less the residual value.* The plant asset discussed above would be depreciated using the SYD method as follows:

Year	Cost Less Residual Value × Rate	Depreciation for Year	Accumulated Depreciation	Book Value at Year End
1	$9,500.00 × 10/55	$1,727.27	$1,727.27	$8,272.73
2	9,500.00 × 9/55	1,554.55	3,281.82	6,718.18
3	9,500.00 × 8/55	1,381.82	4,663.64	5,336.36
4	9,500.00 × 7/55	1,209.09	5,872.73	4,127.27
5	9,500.00 × 6/55	1,036.37	6,909.10	3,090.90
6	9,500.00 × 5/55	863.64	7,772.74	2,227.26
7	9,500.00 × 4/55	690.91	8,463.65	1,536.35
8	9,500.00 × 3/55	518.18	8,981.83	1,018.17
9	9,500.00 × 2/55	345.45	9,327.28	672.72
10	9,500.00 × 1/55	172.72	9,500.00	500.00

After the asset has been fully depreciated, the remaining book value of the asset is its residual value. In order to obtain the denominator of the fraction for the SYD method it was necessary to add the sum of the digits (10 + 9 + 8 · · · + 1). The denominator can more easily be determined by using the following formula, where S = sum of the digits, and N = number of years of estimated useful life:

$$S = \frac{N(N + 1)}{2}$$

$$S = \frac{10(10 + 1)}{2} = 55$$

Each year's depreciation expense is 1/55 less than the preceding year's, multiplied by the original cost less the salvage value. The above illustration again assumes that the asset was acquired at the beginning of the accounting period and will be depreciated for the entire first year. In practice, assets are acquired when needed, and the first year's depreciation must reflect the period of time for which the asset was used. If the above plant asset had been acquired on April 5, then the first year's depreciation expense would be calculated as follows:

$$\$9,500 \times 10/55 \times 9/12 = \$1,295.45$$

The ⁹⁄₁₂ represents the fraction of the first year for which the asset was used. The calculation for the second *full* year's depreciation would be as follows:

$$\$9,500 \times 10/55 \times 3/12 = \quad \$431.82$$
$$\$9,500 \times 9/55 \times 9/12 = \quad \underline{1,165.91}$$
$$\$1,597.73$$

Calculation of subsequent years' depreciation using the SYD method would follow the form illustrated for the second year. Remember that the asset will be fully depreciated after 10 years, which in this case means that 3 months' depreciation will be recognized at the beginning of the eleventh year. The calculation for the last 3 months (first 3 months of the eleventh year) would be:

$$\$9,500 \times 1/55 \times 3/12 = \$43.18$$

Complete Computational Problems 7, 8, and 9, Part A (pp. 287–288).

YOU SHOULD REMEMBER

The methods used to recognize depreciation are (1) straight-line; (2) units of production; (3) double-declining balance; and (4) sum of the years' digits.
The equation for method (1) is

$$\frac{\text{Cost} - \text{Residual value}}{\text{Useful life (in years)}} - \text{Annual depreciation expense}$$

The equation for method (2) is

$$\frac{\text{Depreciable value}}{\text{Productive capacity}} = \text{Per-Unit depreciation}$$

The third and fourth methods are considered to be accelerated forms of calculating depreciation that recognize greater depreciation in the earlier years of the asset's use.

DISPOSAL OF PLANT ASSETS

Plant assets may be disposed of at any time. They may be disposed of because of obsolescence, sale, or deterioration before, at, or after becoming fully depreciated. The details as to the entries for disposal will vary, but in all cases it is necessary to remove the book value of the asset from the accounts. The two accounts always affected are the asset account and the accumulated depreciation (contra-asset) account. The mere fact that an asset has been fully depreciated does not mean that it should be removed from the books. Many assets that have been fully depreciated and have zero book values are still in use and retained on the books until they are actually disposed of.

An asset that has been fully depreciated, has no residual value, and is of no further service to the business is discarded. When this occurs, the following entry is made to record the disposal:

```
198–
Nov. 26   Accumulated Depreciation—Equipment         10,000
              Equipment                                         10,000
          To write off equipment discarded.
```

If this asset had been fully depreciated but still had a book value of $500 representing its residual value, and it was sold for its residual value, the following entry would be recorded:

```
198–
Nov. 26   Cash                                          500
          Accumulated Depreciation—Equipment          9,500
              Equipment                                         10,000
```

When an asset is sold before being fully depreciated, an adjusting entry is recorded at the time of sale to reflect the depreciation for the current accounting period up to the date of sale. Following the adjusting entry, an entry recording the disposal is made. The following illustration shows the recognition of depreciation to the date of sale and the disposal of the asset where the proceeds of the sale are less than the remaining book value of the asset:

```
198–
Jun 27   Depreciation Expense—Equipment                475
             Accumulated Depreciation—Equipment                 475
         To record depreciation to the date of sale.

    27   Cash                                            900
         Accumulated Depreciation—Equipment           9,025
         Loss on Disposal of Equipment                   75
             Equipment                                         10,000
         To write off equipment sold.
```

If the asset had been sold for $1,000, the following entry for its sale would be recorded:

198–

Jun 27	Cash	1,000	
	Accumulated Depreciation—Equipment	9,025	
	Gain on Sale of Equipment		25
	Equipment		10,000
	To write off equipment sold.		

Whenever an asset is sold or otherwise disposed of and the cash received is in excess of the asset's book value, the resulting difference is recorded as a gain. When the cash received is less than the book value of the asset, the resulting difference is recorded as a loss. Both gains and losses on the disposal of plant assets are nonoperating items and are reported on the income statement in the respective nonoperating sections. **Complete Computational Problem 10, Part A (p. 288).**

TRADE-IN OF PLANT ASSETS

Certain assets, when no longer of use to the organization, may be traded for similar or different assets. The treatment of a trade-in depends on whether the asset given up is different from or similar to the asset acquired.

When the asset being traded is *different* from the one being acquired, there is a recognition of the gain or loss as a result of the transaction. The **trade-in allowance** is the amount of credit the seller is willing to extend to the buyer for the asset being traded in. To determine whether a gain or loss is recognized, the book value of the old asset is compared with the trade-in allowance given by the seller for this asset.

The following facts will be used to illustrate the entries required to record the trade-in of different assets: (1) new asset cost—$9,400; (2) trade-in allowance on old asset—$1,675; and (3) book value of old asset after adjusting depreciation to the date of sale—$1,500 (original cost, $6,000).

A comparison of the trade-in allowance ($1,675) with the book value of the old asset ($1,500) indicates that the seller is giving the buyer an allowance of $175 in excess of the book value for the old asset. This excess represents the gain on the trade-in that is recognized by the buyer. The following general journal entry represents the trade-in:

198–

Aug. 6	Furniture	9,400	
	Accumulated Depreciation—Furniture	4,500	
	Cash		7,725
	Equipment		6,000
	Gain on Trade-In of Equipment		175
	To record the trade-in of equipment for furniture.		

Had the asset furniture been purchased outright without a trade-in, the cost of the furniture would have been $9,400 in cash. The amount of cash paid in this case is $7,725. This was determined by taking the cost of the asset ($9,400) less the trade-in allowance given by the seller ($1,675).

Whenever one asset is traded in for another asset that is *different* in nature, the gain or loss resulting from the trade-in must be recognized. If the trade-in allowance is less than the book value of the asset given up, then the difference is a loss that is recorded in an account entitled "Loss on Trade-In of Plant Asset."

When one plant asset is traded in for a *similar* asset, the gain on the trade-in is *not* recognized. This method, referred to as the **income tax method,** permits a *postponement* of the recognition of gain that is spread out over the useful life of the similar asset acquired. If the asset acquired in the above illustration had been similar to the one given, the gain of $175 would have reduced the cost of the new asset acquired. The new asset would have been recorded on the books at $9,225 rather than $9,400 as illustrated.

The income tax method also postpones the recognition of a loss on trade-in. Such a postponement causes the cost of the new asset acquired to be increased to the extent of the loss. If a loss in trade-in of $200 occurred, then the new asset would be set up on the books at $9,600, rather than at the purchase price of $9,400.

The Accounting Principles Board differs in its interpretation of a loss resulting from a trade-in of similar assets. Generally accepted accounting principles require that significant losses on trade-ins be recognized rather than deferred. **Complete Computational Problem 11, Part A** (p. 288).

YOU SHOULD REMEMBER

Long-life assets are maintained on the books until such time as they are converted through sale, trade-in, or obsolescence.

Any cash received in excess of the book value of the asset is reported as a gain, and any amount received that is less than the book value of the asset is recognized as a loss.

When like assets are traded in or exchanged, recognition of any gain or loss is postponed.

Generally accepted accounting principles, unlike the income tax method, recognize the loss in trade-in of similar assets.

• *DEPLETION*

Not all long-life assets are subject to depreciation. The land on which the depreciable asset building stands is not subject to depreciation. The reason for this should be obvious: the land does not lose its value, even though the building does.

Other assets, because of their nature, may not be subject to depreciation, but may still lose value, as has to be recognized. For example, a business may own land that it uses for purposes other than the placement of a building. Land may be used for farming or for the extraction of metal ores and other minerals. The business may not even actually own the land, but may merely lease the right to use the land for a period of years.

The cost of the lease or the cost of the land owned can be converted to an expense based on the fact that the use made of the land may cause its value to decrease. An oil company may estimate that there are 20,000 barrels of crude oil beneath the land it leases. If the leasehold on the land calls for a total payment of $20,000, then, for every barrel of oil extracted from the land, a cost of $1 can be assigned to the cost of the oil.

This form of depreciation that applies to land use is known as **depletion.** Depletion is the pro-rata allocation of the cost of land (through direct ownership or by lease) to the units of natural resources removed from the land.

CALCULATING DEPLETION

The calculation of depletion is very similar to the units-of-production form of depreciation previously discussed. Since depletion represents the assignment of a cost to that which is extracted from land, two factors must be known: (1) the cost of the land (ownership or lease costs), and (2) the number of units expected to be extracted from the land.

Once these two factors are known, it is then possible to assign the depletion expense for a particular accounting period based on the rate of extraction from the land.

Assume that a company leases the right to extract coal from a mine estimated to contain 2 million tons of coal. The cost of the lease is $1 million. The depletion charge per unit extracted is calculated by dividing the anticipated number of total units to be extracted (2 million tons) into the cost of the lease ($1 million). Each ton of coal extracted would carry an assigned cost of $.50. The adjusting entry to recognize the depletion based on extraction of 250,000 tons would be as follows:

```
198–
Dec. 31   Depletion Expense                        125,000
              Accumulated Depletion—Coal
          To record extraction of 250,000 tons.                  125,000
```

Notice that the entry for depletion is very similar to the entry for depreciation. In this case an accumulated depletion account is used in place of the accumulated depreciation. The book value of the lease or the land owned is the cost of the investment (land or lease), less the accumulated depletion.

When the land is leased for a specific period of time and the amount of minerals that will be extracted cannot be readily determined, a straight-line approach similar to straight-line depreciation is used. Naturally, no residual value is recognized since at the end of the lease the land reverts back to the owner. **Complete Computational Problem 12, Part A (p. 288).**

YOU SHOULD REMEMBER
Depletion is the loss in value of land resulting from the extraction of metal ores or other minerals.   Depletion converts the cost of the land or the cost of the lease on the land to an expense based on what is being taken from the land.

INTANGIBLE ASSETS

We learned in Chapter 1 that an **intangible asset** is something that cannot readily be seen or touched; it has no physical substance. Examples of intangible assets include leaseholds, copyrights, franchises, licenses, trademarks, and goodwill. In order for these items to qualify as assets, they must be owned (or the rights of use must be owned) and they must have a money value.

A **leasehold** is the right of a tenant to use and occupy real property under a lease. A **copyright** is the exclusive right, applied for to the federal government and granted to an individual or organization, to use and control a literary or artistic work. This right currently extends for 50 years beyond the life of the creator. A **franchise** and a **license (patent)** are rights given by a company or governmental unit to conduct a certain type of business in a specific area. These rights are purchased. A **trademark** is a symbol or design used to distinguish a firm's product or service. Trademarks are issued by the United States Patent Office. The golden arches of McDonald's restaurants are an example of a trademark. **Goodwill** is usually said to represent the reputation and managerial skill of a business. It represents the excess earnings of a particular business organization over the normal rate of return of other businesses in the same industry. Goodwill is usually recognized by the buyer of a business as the excess paid for the business above the value of the tangible assets acquired.

• *AMORTIZATION*

Unlike depreciation and depletion, which can be readily measured, the expense of intangible assets is determined in a somewhat arbitrary fashion. The systematic write-off of the cost of an intangible asset over the period of its economic life is known as **amortization.** The entry to record amortization of an intangible asset is a debit to amortization expense and a credit directly to the intangible asset account. The period of time for which a particular intangible asset is to be written off depends on the asset but should never exceed 40 years. Goodwill should not be written off for a period of less than 60 months, and usually not more than 40 years. A copyright, as stated above, is granted for 50 years beyond the life of its creator; however, this period may be impractical from the standpoint of recognizing amortization. If the specific work covered by the copyright is expected to have a useful life of 25 years, then this would be an appropriate period over which to recognize amortization.

Other intangible assets may also be subject to amortization, such as organizational costs and research and development costs. Determining the useful life of these assets is usually left to the discretion of the accountant. A general guide is that they should not be amortized over less than 5 years, unless it can be substantiated that their benefits will be for a lesser period of time. The fact that a useful life has been assigned to an intangible asset does not mean that it cannot be adjusted at a later date. If the holder of a franchise that has a useful life of 10 years finds that the benefits of the franchise will not extend beyond the eighth year, an adjustment in amortization would be appropriate.

When an intangible asset is deemed worthless, it should immediately be written off as a nonrecurring loss.

Example: Amortizing an Intangible Asset

A business is purchased for $300,000. The assets of the business totaled $265,000, and the balance represents goodwill. The buyer expects the goodwill to be of value for a period of 7 years. The following entries represent the purchase and first full year's amortization of goodwill·

198–			
Jan. 10	Assets (various)	265,000	
	Goodwill	35,000	
	Cash		300,000
	For purchase of business.		
Dec. 31	Amortization Expense—Goodwill	5,000	
	Goodwill		5,000
	To write off annual goodwill.		

YOU SHOULD REMEMBER

Amortization is the conversion of the cost of an intangible asset to an expense because of the asset being used up.

The period of time used to take this write-off depends on the period of time benefitted by the intangible asset.

CAPITAL IMPROVEMENTS

We have seen that a plant asset when acquired is set up at its actual cost, which includes any costs necessary to get the asset operational within the organization. Subsequent maintenance and repair costs are treated as current expenses and do not directly affect the accounting for the plant asset. As the asset is used on a continuous basis, however, there may come a time when major repairs or improvements are needed to keep the asset operational. When this situation arises, there may be a need for a **capital improvement.**

Capital improvements are costs that add to the utility of a plant asset for more than one accounting period. Overhauling the engine of a delivery truck is an example of a capital improvement. Although the cost of the expenditure is relevant, the primary consideration in designating this work as a capital improvement or expenditure is that, without the overhaul, the continued use of the asset may be impossible. Since this work is necessary and will probably extend the useful life of the asset, the expense is **capitalized,** meaning that the cost of the overhaul is added to the original cost of the asset.

Example: Recording a Capital Expenditure

Original Cost of Truck	$10,500
Salvage Value	500
Depreciation Method—Straight-Line	
Useful Life—10 Years	
Accumulated Depreciation	7,000
Capital Expenditure after Seventh Year	2,400

Entry to record capital expenditure:

198–
Jan. 4 Delivery Truck ... 2,400
     Cash ... 2,400
    To record capital expenditure
    and increase useful life by 1 year.

Dec. 31 Depreciation Expense—Delivery Truck ... 1,350
     Accumulated Depreciation ... 1,350
    To recognize adjusted annual depreciation $\left(\dfrac{5,400}{4 \text{ YEARS}} \right)$.

Note that the annual depreciation recognized has changed. This change resulted because of the capital expenditure, which increased the original cost of the truck. The following calculations resulted in the new depreciation recognition, as well as the extension of the useful life of the delivery truck:

Original Cost of Delivery Truck	$10,500
Salvage Value	500
Depreciable Value (10 years)	10,000
Accumulated Depreciation (after 7 years)	7,000
Book Value (after 7 years)	3,000
Capital Expenditure	2,400
New Book Value (extending life by 1 year)	5,400
New Annual Depreciation Rate ($5,400/4 years of useful life)	1,350

In this example both the useful life and the depreciation to be recognized have changed. If the useful life of the truck had not been affected, then only the depreciation expense recognized would have been increased over the remaining 3 years to the extent of $800 per year. **Complete Computational Problems 13 and 14, Part A** (pp. 288–289).

YOU SHOULD REMEMBER

A capital improvement causes the value of an asset to be increased by the extent of the improvement.

This will affect the remaining depreciation to be recognized, regardless of whether or not the useful life of the asset is extended.

For more practice in mastering the material in this chapter, **complete Computational Problems 1, 2, 3, 4, 5, and 6, Part B** (pp. 289–290).

KNOW THE CONCEPTS

DO YOU KNOW THE BASICS?

Test your knowledge of this chapter by classifying each of the following as *True* or *False·*

1. A leasehold is an example of a long-life asset.

2. Depreciation expense is usually recorded at least once a year.

3. The units of production method is the simplest and most widely used method of recognizing depreciation.

4. Two methods of recognizing accelerated depreciation are the straight-line and the double-declining balance method.

5. To determine depreciation expense the SYD method uses a fraction in which the numerator is the sum of the digits that represent the years over which the asset will have a useful life.

6. The gain or loss on the trade-in of an asset for a similar asset, according to the income tax method, is not recognized at the time of the trade.

7. The form of depreciation that applies to land use is known as depletion.

8. Amortization is the conversion of the cost of an intangible asset to an expense.

9. Research and development costs represent an intangible asset.

10. Repair of a generator is a capital expenditure.

TERMS FOR STUDY

accelerated depreciation	income tax method
book value	leasehold
capital expenditure	license
capital improvement	obsolescence
contra-asset account	patent
copyright	physical deterioration
cost principle	property, plant, and equipment
current asset	residual value
depreciable value	straight-line method
double-declining balance method	sum of the years' digits method
franchise	trade-in allowance
goodwill	units of production

PRACTICAL APPLICATION

PART A. COMPUTATIONAL PROBLEMS WITH COMPLETE SOLUTIONS

1. A building with an assessed value of $70,000 for property tax purposes is offered for sale at $95,000. The building is acquired by a business firm for $32,000 cash and the balance in the form of a 2-year non-interest-bearing note. The real estate brokerage fee is 5% of the selling price. Legal fees for the contract and closing are $2,500. Determine the cost of the building to be recorded on the books of the purchaser.

2. An asset is acquired at the beginning of the accounting period at a total cost of $7,850. It is expected to have a useful life of 5 years and a scrap value of $350.

   Determine:
   (a) The annual rate of depreciation using the straight-line method.
   (b) The depreciable value of the asset.
   (c) The amount of annual depreciation expense to be recognized.
   (d) The total depreciation recognized after the third year.
   (e) The net asset value after recognizing 3 years of depreciation.

3. A mimeograph machine acquired for use in the office on July 1 of the current year cost $3,250. It has a useful life of 8 years and an estimated salvage value of $50. Using the straight-line method, answer the following questions:
   (a) What is the annual rate of depreciation?
   (b) What is the depreciable value of the asset?
   (c) What is the amount of annual depreciation to be recognized?
   (d) What is the amount of depreciation to be recognized for the first year? (July 1–December 31)
   (e) What is the adjusting entry to be recorded for depreciation at the end of the first calendar year?
   (f) What is the balance in the accumulated depreciation account at the end of the second year after the appropriate adjusting entry?
   (g) When the asset has been fully depreciated, what will its book value be?

4. A van is acquired by the Acme Delivery Service at a cost of $15,600. The expected salvage value is $600, and the useful life as expressed in mileage is estimated to be 150,000 miles. Using the units of production method answer the following questions:
   (a) What is the depreciable value of the van?
   (b) What is the rate of depreciation per mile?
   (c) What is the adjusting entry for the first year's depreciation if the van is driven 23,200 miles?
   (d) What is the balance in the accumulated depreciation account after the van has been driven for 65,400 miles?
   (e) What is the book value of the van, given the information in question (d)?

5. On January 6 of the current year, the Halpern Service Co. acquired a plant asset at a cost of $5,000. The asset is expected to have a useful life of 5 years and a scrap value of $450. Using the double-declining balance method, determine the depreciation to be recognized on the asset over its useful life. Prepare a table similar to the one illustrated on page 274.

6. On July 1 of the current fiscal year ending December 31, Balley and Co. acquired a plant asset at a total cost of $70,000. The asset has an expected useful life of 4 years, and no salvage value is anticipated. Using the double-declining balance method, determine the depreciation over its useful life. Prepare a table similar to the one illustrated on page 274. Be careful to recognize the first fiscal year's depreciation only from July through December. Also, the last year's depreciation recognition will be only from January through June.

7. Using the information provided in Problem 5, determine the depreciation expense in tabular form, using the SYD method.

8. Referring to Problem 6, determine the depreciation expense in tabular form, using the SYD method.

9. A factory is acquired on January 3 at a cost of $325,000 and has an estimated

useful life of 25 years. Assuming that it has no residual value, determine the depreciation for each of the first 2 years by (a) the straight line method, (b) the double-declining balance method, and (c) the SYD method.

10. A depreciable plant asset was sold for $22,000. At the end of the previous accounting period, the balance in the accumulated depreciation account was $90,000, and the original cost of the asset was $115,000. The adjusting entry on the date of sale (October 22) is $5,000. Record the adjusting entry to recognize depreciation on the date of sale, and record the sale of the plant asset.

11. A computer was purchased on January 1 for $75,000 cash. The useful life was estimated to be 6 years, with a salvage value of $10,000. The SYD method of depreciation was used. Four and one-half years later, on July 1, the computer was traded in on another computer. The following information is available: (a) cost of new computer—$100,000, and (b) trade-in allowance on the old computer—$20,000.

   The company is on a calendar-year basis. Prepare the adjusting entries needed on July 1 to record the trade-in.

12. Timber rights on a tract of land were purchased for $60,000. The amount of timber to be harvested is estimated at 600,000 board feet. During the current year, 45,000 feet of timber were cut. Record the entry to recognize the depletion expense for the fiscal year.

13. A factory with an original cost of $450,000 and an expected useful life of 30 years has been depreciated using the straight-line method for 20 years (no scrap value). The roof of the building is replaced at a cost of $45,000 after the twentieth year, and the new roof is expected to extend the useful life of the structure by 5 years. Determine:

   (a) The annual depreciation recognized per year before the capital improvement.
   (b) The accumulated depreciation over the 20 years.
   (c) The entry to record the capital improvement.
   (d) The book value of the building before the capital improvement.
   (e) The book value of the building after the capital improvement.
   (f) The depreciation expense to be recognized annually as a result of the capital improvement. (Life extended 5 years.)

14. Record the following selected transactions:

   (a) Goodwill in the amount of $75,000 was purchased on January 9 of the current calendar year. At the end of the accounting period it was decided to amortize this intangible asset over the minimum period suggested. Record the January 9 and December 31 transactions.
   (b) Timber rights on a tract of land were leased for $90,000. It is estimated that the harvest of lumber will result in 600,000 board feet. Record the entry to recognize that 76,000 board feet of timber were cut this year.

(c) A patent acquired at a cost of $280,000 is determined to have an estimated useful life of 10 years. Record the entry to recognize the amortization of the patent this year, which happens to be the third year that the patent is in use.

PART B. COMPUTATIONAL PROBLEMS
WITH PARTIAL SOLUTIONS OR KEY ANSWERS

1. A plant asset acquired at a total cost of $37,500 has an estimated scrap value of $2,500 and an anticipated useful life of 7 years. Determine:
   (a) The annual rate (expressed as a percentage or fraction) of depreciation using the straight-line method.
   (b) The annual depreciation using the straight-line method.
   (c) The first year's straight-line depreciation, assuming that the asset was acquired 3 months into the current accounting period.
   (d) Continuing with assumption 3, the value of the accumulated depreciation account after the second year's depreciation is recognized.
   (e) The residual value for the plant asset after the asset has been depreciated for 7 years.

2. An electrically powered compressor with an original cost of $100,000 and an estimated scrap value of $10,000 is expected to have a useful operating life of 120,000 hours. During the current accounting period, the compressor is operated for 9,300 hours. Determine the depreciation to be recognized for the year. What would be the per-hour rate of depreciation to be recognized, using the units of production method?

3. Refer to the information presented in Exercise 1, and again determine the five items assuming that the asset is being depreciated using the double-declining balance method of recognizing depreciation.

4. Refer to the information presented in Exercise 1, and again determine the five items assuming that the asset is being depreciated using the sum of the years' digits method.

5. A delivery truck which cost $28,800 has an estimated useful life of 7 years and an estimated residual value of $800. The depreciation method used is straight-line.
   (a) Record the necessary general journal entries based on the following assumptions:
      (1) The delivery truck is sold for cash of $18,000 at the end of the second full year of use.
      (2) The delivery truck is sold for cash of $13,500 after 3½ years use. (Record the necessary adjusting entry for the half year before the sale of the plant asset.)
      (3) The delivery truck is sold for cash of $8,350 after 5 years of use.
   (b) What was the book value of the delivery truck at the time of sale in each of the above situations?

6. A plant asset with a book value of $30,000 was traded in on a similar plant asset with a list price of $300,000. The trade-in allowance for the old plant asset was $45,000.

 (a) Answer the following questions:
    (1) How much cash must be paid for the new plant asset?
    (2) What is the value of the new plant asset on the books?
 (b) Answer questions (1) and (2) assuming the same facts as previously stated, except that the asset acquired for $300,000 was not similar to the plant asset traded-in.

ANSWERS

KNOW THE CONCEPTS

1. False	4. False	7. True	9. True
2. True	5. False	8. True	10. False
3. False	6. True		

PRACTICAL APPLICATION
PART A

1.
Purchase Price	$95,000
Real Estate Broker's Fee	4,750
Legal Fees	2,500
Total Cost of Building	$102,250

2. (a) Since the useful life of the asset is 5 years, each year's depreciation recognized under the straight-line method will be 1/5 of the total depreciation, or 20%.
 (b) Subtracting the scrap value of the asset from its total cost gives the depreciable value of the asset. Thus, the depreciable value would be calculated as follows: $7,850 − $350 = $7,500.
 (c) Depreciable value × Straight-line rate = Annual depreciation ($7,500 × 20% = $1,500).
 (d) Annual depreciation × 3 years = Total depreciation for the period ($1,500 × 3 = $4,500).
 (e)
Total Asset Value	$7,850
Less 3 Years' Depreciation	4,500
Net Asset Value	3,350

3. (a) The annual depreciation rate is 1/8 or 12.5%.
 (b) The depreciable value is $3,200.
 (c) Annual depreciation recognized is $3,200 × 12.5% = $400.
 (d) Depreciation for 6 months of the first year is $200.

(e) **198–**

Dec. 31 Depreciation Expense   200
                    Accumulated Depreciation   200
                    For 6 months' depreciation.

(f) $600 ($200 first year + $400 second year).

(g) The book value of a fully depreciated asset under the straight-line method is equal to its scrap value, which in this case is $50.

4. (a) The depreciable value is $15,600 − $600 = $15,000.

(b) $15,000/150,000 miles = $.10 per mile.

(c) **198–**

Dec. 31 Depreciation Expense   2,320
                    Accumulated Depreciation   2,320
                    (23,200 miles × $.10)

(d) A credit balance of $6,540.

(e) If it is assumed that the total mileage driven was 65,400 miles, the book value of the asset would be:

Original Cost	$15,600
Less Accumulated Depreciation	6,540
Book Value	$ 9,060

5. Original cost of asset: $5,000
   Scrap value: $450
   Useful life: 5 years
   Method used: double-declining balance
   DDBM rate = Straight-line rate × 2 (20% × 2 = 40%)

Year	Computation (BV × Rate)	Depreciation Expense	Accumulated Depreciation	Book Value
1	$5,000 × 40%	$2,000.00	$2,000.00	$3,000.00
2	3,000 × 40%	1,200.00	3,200.00	1,800.00
3	1,800 × 40%	720.00	3,920.00	1,080.00
4	1,080 × 40%	432.00	4,352.00	648.00
5	648 × 40%	259.20	4,611.20	338.80

Remember: scrap value is ignored when using the double-declining balance method of calculating depreciation. The remaining book value of $338.80 represents the scrap value of this particular asset.

6. Original cost of asset: $70,000
   Scrap value: 0
   Useful life: 4 years
   Method used: double-declining balance.
   DDBM rate = Straight-line rate × 2 (25% × 2 = 50%)

Year	Computation (BV × Rate)	Depreciation Expense	Accumulated Depreciation	Book Value
1	$70,000 × 50% × 1/2 (6 mo.)	$17,500.00	$17,500.00	$52,500.00
2	52,500 × 50%	26,250.00	43,750.00	26,250.00
3	26,250 × 50%	13,125.00	56,875.00	13,125.00
4	13,125 × 50%	6,562.50	63,437.50	6,562.50
5	6,562.50 × 50% × 1/2 (6 mo.)	1,640.63	65,078.13	4,921.87

Note that in this problem the asset was acquired 6 months into the year. Thus, the first year's depreciation was calculated for only half a year. The fifth year's depreciation calculation is for the 6-month period from January through June, which is the last 6 months' depreciation on the asset.

7. Original cost of asset: $5,000
   Scrap value: $450
   Useful life: 5 years
   Method used: sum of the years' digits

Year	Cost Less Residual Value × Rate	Depreciation for Year	Accumulated Depreciation	Book Value End of Year
1	$4,550 × 5/15	$1,516.67	$1,516.67	$3,483.33
2	4,550 × 4/15	1,213.33	2,730.00	2,270.00
3	4,550 × 3/15	910.00	3,640.00	1,360.00
4	4,550 × 2/15	606.67	4,246.67	753.33
5	4,550 × 1/15	303.33	4,550.00	450.00

8. Original cost of asset: $70,000 (asset acquired on July 1)
   Scrap value: 0
   Useful life: 4 years
   Method used: sum of the years' digits

Year	Cost Less Residual Value × Rate	Depreciation for Year	Accumulated Depreciation	Book Value
1	$70,000 × 4/10 × 1/2 (6 mo.)	$14,000.00	$14,000.00	$56,000.00
2	70,000 × 4/10 × 1/2 + 70,000 × 3/10 × 1/2	24,500.00	38,500.00	31,500.00
3	70,000 × 3/10 × 1/2 + 70,000 × 2/10 × 1/2	17,500.00	56,000.00	14,000.00
4	70,000 × 2/10 × 1/2 + 70,000 × 1/10 × 1/2	10,500.00	66,500.00	3,500.00
5	70,000 × 1/10 × 1/2 (final 6 mo. depreciation)	3,500.00	70,000.00	–0–

Since the asset was acquired on July 1, after the first 6 months' depreciation is taken each subsequent year's depreciation consists of the second half of the first year's and the first half of the second year's depreciation calculation. The fifth year's depreciation is the last half of the fourth year's depreciation. In this problem, there was no scrap value so that the book value at the end of the 4 years' depreciation is zero.

9. Original cost of asset: $325,000
   Scrap value: 0
   Useful life: 25 years
   Methods used: a. Straight-line method
                  b. Double-declining balance method
                  c. Sum of the years' digits method

   (a) Annual straight-line depreciation is $325,000/25 years = $13,000. With this method each of the 2 years' depreciation would amount to $13,000.
   (b) The straight-line rate is 4% (1/25) per year. The double-declining balance rate would then be 8% each year on the book value of the asset.
       1st year's depreciation = $325,000 × 8% = $26,000.
       2nd year's depreciation = $299,000 × 8% = $23,920.
   (c) The sum of the years' digits fraction is determined as follows:
       S = N × (N + 1)/2 (325 = 25 × (25 + 1)/2).
       1st year's depreciation = $325,000 × 25/325 = $25,000.
       2nd year's depreciation = $325,000 × 24/325 = $24,000.

10. **198–**

Oct.	**22**	Depreciation Expense	5,000.00	
		Accumulated Depreciation		5,000.00
		To recognize depreciation to the date		
		on disposal of the asset.		
	22	Cash	22,000.00	
		Accumulated Depreciation	95,000.00	
		Depreciable Asset		115,000.00
		Gain on Sale of Asset		2,000.00
		Sale of depreciable asset		

11. **198–**

July	**1**	Depreciation Expense	3,095.24	
		Accumulated Depreciation		3,095.24
		To recognize 6 months' depreciation.		

1 Computer (New)	96,190.48	
Accumulated Depreciation	58,809.52	
Computer (old)		75,000.00
Cash		80,000.00
To record trade-in of like assets.		

Trade-in Allowance:		$20,000.00
Original Cost	$75,000.00	
Accumulated Depreciation	58,809.52	
Book Value of Old Asset:		16,190.48
Gain on Trade-in to Be Postponed:		$ 3,809.52
Assigning Cost of New Asset on the Books:		
Original Cost	$100,000.00	
Less: Gain to be Postponed	3,809.52	
Value Assigned to New Asset on the Books:		$96,190.48

12. Depletion is based on the relationship between the units to be taken from the land and the cost of the rights to use the land. Thus, $60,000/600,000 board feet will give us an amount per board foot of $.10. If 45,000 feet of timber were cut, the depletion recognized would be calculated as follows: 45,000 feet × $.10 = $4,500.

198–
Dec. 31   Depletion Expense   4,500
          Accumulated Depletion   4,500

13. (a) Annual straight-line depreciation $450,000/30 = $15,000.
    (b) Annual depreciation × 20 years = $15,000 × 20 = $300,000.
    (c) **198–**
       Jan. 1   Building   45,000
               Cash   45,000
               To recognize capital improvement that
               will extend the useful life by 5 years.
    (d) Original cost ($450,000) − Accumulated depreciation ($300,000) = Book value ($150,000).
    (e) $150,000 + Capital improvement $45,000 = $195,000.
    (f) $195,000/15 years = $13,000 annual depreciation after the capital improvement. The old life remaining was 10 years; the capital improvement extended the life by 5 years.

14. (a) **198–**

Jan.	**9**	Goodwill	75,000.00	
		Cash		75,000.00

To recognize the purchase of goodwill.

Dec. 31		Amortization Expense— Goodwill	15,000.00	
		Goodwill		15,000.00

To write off goodwill for the first year.

(b)	**31**	Depletion Expense	11,400.00	
		Accumulated Depletion— Timber		11,400.00

76,000 board feet × .15 for the year.

(c)	**31**	Amortization Expense—Patent	28,000.00	
		Patent		28,000.00

To recognize annual amortization based on a write-off totaling 10 years.

PART B

1. Annual depreciation rate, 1/7 or 14.3%

2. Year's depreciation, $6,975

3. Annual depreciation rate, 2/7 or 28.6% of book value without considering scrap value

4. Annual depreciation rates, 7/28; 6/28; 5/28; 4/28; 3/28; 2/28; 1/28

5. (1) Book value, $20,800; (2) book value, $14,800; (3) book value, $8,800

6. Cash paid for new asset, $255,000

10
INVENTORIES

WHAT IS MERCHANDISE INVENTORY?

In Chapter 5 you were introduced to a trading form of business organization in which the primary function of the business was the sale of a product. At the end of the accounting period for this form of business it was necessary to determine the value of the ending merchandise inventory. Expressing the value of the inventory on the balance sheet and the income statement was illustrated, with particular emphasis on the procedures used to determine the cost of goods available for sale and the cost of goods sold. **Merchandise inventory** was defined as the cost of the goods on hand as of the date the inventory was taken. We have previously illustrated the taking of the inventory at the end of the accounting period. The valuation of the inventory taken is based on its cost. Keep in mind that merchandise inventory represents only the assets that were acquired exclusively for the purpose of resale in the normal course of business. The purpose of taking of an inventory of supplies, on the other hand, is to convert an asset on the books to an expense to the extent these supplies had been used up.

• *INVENTORIES AND THE TRADING BUSINESS*

A multistep income statement for a trading business highlights the fact that between 40% and 60% of revenue from sales is accounted for as the cost of goods sold.

Cost of goods sold = Cost of goods available for sale
(beginning merchandise inventory
+ net purchases) − Ending
merchandise inventory

In a wholesale or retail trading business, merchandise held for resale in the normal course of business is one of the largest assets owned by the organization. For this reason it is vital that accurate up-to-date records be maintained when goods are acquired and inventories taken.

Merchandise inventory is listed on the balance sheet under the current asset section, which usually follows cash and accounts receivable. Because of the relatively large value of merchandise inventory and its appearance on both the balance sheet and the income statement, an error in calculating inventory can have a significant effect on the recognition of income and the financial position for the accounting period. Also, since the ending merchandise inventory for one accounting period becomes the beginning merchandise inventory for the next period, an erroneous merchandise inventory figure will effect future accounting periods, as well as the current one.

• *ERRORS IN VALUING MERCHANDISE INVENTORIES*

The following income statement for the Classic Fabric Co. illustrates the effects of stating the ending merchandise inventory incorrectly:

Classic Fabric Co.
Income Statement
For the Year Ended December 31, 198–

	Correct Ending Inventory		Overstated Inventory		Understated Inventory
Sales		$500,000		$500,000	$500,000
Cost of Goods Sold					
Merchandise Inv. 1/1	$150,000		$150,000		$150,000
Net Purchases	300,000		300,000		300,000
Cost of Goods					
Available for Sale	450,000		450,000		450,000
Less: Merchandise					
Inventory 12/31	150,000		180,000		120,000
Cost of Goods Sold		300,000		270,000	330,000
Gross Profit on Sales		200,000		230,000	170,000
Operating Expenses		150,000		150,000	150,000
Net Income		$ 50,000		$ 80,000	$ 20,000

First, note the differences reported for net income between the correctly and incorrectly stated inventory columns on the income statement. The overstatement of the ending merchandise inventory causes an understatement of the cost of goods sold to the extent of the error ($30,000) in the ending inventory. This causes the gross profit on sales to be overstated to the extent of the error in ending inventory. Not only are the gross and net income affected, but the error will also affect the value assigned to current assets on the balance sheet. Remember that the ending merchandise inventory is set up on the books at the end of the accounting period and will be shown as a current asset; thus an overstatement of the ending inventory will cause a corresponding overstatement of the merchandise inventory on the balance sheet at the end of the accounting period. The overstatement of net income will cause an overstatement of the proprietor's permanent capital, since profits not taken out of the business are transferred to the proprietor's capital account. Since the merchandise inventory account in the next accounting period is overstated, the determination of profit for that year will be in error. If it is assumed that the second year's ending inventory is properly stated, the overstatement of the beginning inventory for the second year will probably result in an overstatement of the cost of goods sold at the end of the second year.

If the ending merchandise inventory is understated, there will be a corresponding overstatement of the cost of goods sold, which will result in an understatement of the gross profits and net income for the year. Since the ending inventory becomes the beginning inventory for the next accounting period, the balance sheet will show the current asset merchandise inventory to be understated. In the preceding example the net income at the end of the accounting period is understated by $30,000, and this will cause an understatement of the proprietor's capital account on the balance sheet. In the second year of operations, the understatement of merchandise inventory will result in an understatement of the cost of goods sold, thus inflating net income at the end of the second year.

The effects on net income, current assets, and proprietor's capital of incorrectly determining the ending merchandise inventory can be summarized as follows:

An *overstatement* of ending merchandise inventory causes:

1. Understatement of cost of goods sold.

2. Overstatement of net income.

3. Overstatement of current assets.

4. Overstatement of proprietor's capital.

An *understatement* of ending merchandise inventory causes:

1. Overstatement of cost of goods sold.

2. Understatement of net income.

3. Understatement of current assets.

4. Understatement of proprietor's capital.

Remember that an incorrectly stated ending inventory not only affects the current accounting period, but will also have an adverse effect on the next accounting period in regard to the statement of current assets, proprietor's capital, and the determination of net income.

YOU SHOULD REMEMBER

The stock in trade of a retail business is its inventory.

Between 40% and 60% of the revenues received by a retail business go to cover the cost of the goods sold.

Thus, the maintenance of records relating to inventories is a most important aspect of the accounting function.

An inadvertent overstatement of the ending merchandise inventory will cause an understatement of the cost of goods sold, an overstatement of gross profit, and an overstatement of the value assigned to the current assets and proprietor's capital on the balance sheet.

If the ending inventory is understated, the opposite errors will result.

• TYPES OF INVENTORY SYSTEMS

THE PERIODIC SYSTEM

Basically, two inventory systems are used in accounting: the periodic and the perpetual inventory systems. So far we have discussed only the former. When the **periodic inventory system** is used, only the income from sales is recorded when sales are made. No entries are made in either the merchandise inventory or the purchases account to recognize the cost of the particular items sold. Periodically (at least once a year, usually at the end of the accounting period), a physical inventory is taken to determine the cost of the ending inventory. A comparison between the cost of goods available for sale (beginning merchandise inventory + net purchases) and the ending merchandise inventory enables the accountant to determine the cost of goods sold.

Most businesses use the periodic inventory system, especially if the goods sold consist of large quantities of diverse, low-valued products. With the advent of high technology and the sharp decline in computer costs, this system may be modified somewhat by many trading organizations.

THE PERPETUAL INVENTORY SYSTEM

With the **perpetual inventory system**, accounting records that continuously disclose the amount of inventory are maintained. A separate subsidiary ledger contains a separate account for each type of inventory item. Increases in a particular inventory item are debited directly to the specific account, and corresponding decreases due to sales or returns are credited directly to the specific account. Thus, the balance in the individual subsidiary ledger account at any moment in time represents the actual amount of that particular product on hand. Since this method is time-consuming and expensive to maintain, it is used primarily by organizations that sell relatively small numbers of items with high unit costs, such as automobile dealerships. While a perpetual inventory system may be used for the sale of automobiles, the parts department of the dealership may use a periodic inventory system.

To use the perpetual inventory system, the actual costs of the goods assigned to the various accounts in the subsidiary inventory ledger must be known. While the periodic system segregates cost and revenue items related to merchandise purchased into specific accounts, such as purchases returns and allowances, purchases discounts, and freight on purchases, this is not done under the perpetual system. The cost assigned to each of the various inventory accounts under the perpetual system is composed of the purchase price and all other costs incurred in acquiring the merchandise, less savings from discounts and any subsequent authorized purchase returns. The most significant difference in using the perpetual system is the activity that takes place in the merchandise inventory account, which replaces the merchandise purchases account used in the periodic system.

The following general journal entries are typical entries relating to the acquisition and subsequent sale of goods, using a perpetual inventory system:

198–

Feb. 3	Merchandise Inventory	5,000	
	Accounts Payable		5,000
	1000 units at $5 per unit		
10	Cash	2,700	
	Sales		2,700
	300 units at $9 per unit		
10	Cost of Goods Sold	1,500	
	Merchandise Inventory		1,500
	300 units at $5 = $1,500		
14	Merchandise Inventory	3,060	
	Cash		3,060
	600 units at $5.10 per unit		
17	Cash	7,200	
	Sales		7,200
	800 units at $9 per unit		
17	Cost of Goods Sold	4,010	
	Merchandise Inventory		4,010

700 units at $5.00 per unit = $3,500
100 units at $5.10   =   510
                      $4,010

The entry of February 3 records the purchase of merchandise on credit. This entry and others that follow would normally be recorded to special journals; however, for ease of analysis they are recorded here in simple two-column general journal form. Unlike the periodic system, which uses the merchandise purchases account, the perpetual system records purchases of merchandise directly in the inventory account. Each type of good acquired is posted to a specific subsidiary ledger account that contains an explanation similar to that of the journal entry.

The actual subsidiary ledger account is also known as a **stock record card**. The purpose of the stock record card is to list specific information pertaining to the goods acquired and subsequently sold.

Note that the stock record card contains the date of the transaction and the number of units, unit cost, and total cost of goods received and issued, as well as a running balance. The posting of the February 3 entry to the stock record card records the receipt of goods and then extends the information to the balance column. As of February 3, the balance in this inventory account consisted of 1,000 units at a per-unit cost of $5, for a total cost value of $5,000.

Example: Typical Form of the Subsidiary Ledger, Stock Record Card

Item Stock # -432A				Description: Hand Tool					
Location: Bin 5E				Basis—FIFO					
	Received			Issued			Balance		
Date	Units	Unit Cost	Total Cost	Units	Unit Cost	Total Cost	Unit	Unit Cost	Total Cost
198-Feb.3	1,000	5.00	5,000				1,000	5.00	5,000
10				300	5.00	1,500	700	5.00	3,500
14	600	5.10	3,060				700	5.00	3,500
							600	5.10	3,060
									6,560
17				700	5.00	3,500			
				100	5.10	510	500	5.10	2,550

The first general journal entry (p. 301) for February 10 initially records the sale of the product as it would be recorded regardless of the inventory system in use. The second entry for the tenth, however, represents the recognition of the cost assigned to the product being sold. Because the accountant can specifically identify the cost of the goods being sold, this entry charges the cost to a new account entitled "Cost of Goods Sold." This account is used when the perpetual inventory system is employed by a trading organization.

The cost of goods sold account is classified as an expense that will offset net sales in order to determine the gross profit on sales. Gross profit on sales can thus be determined at any moment in time by simply comparing the net sales with the cost of goods sold account. The explanation to the entry indicates how the value was assigned to the transaction. Referring to the stock record card, note the entry and the extension to the balance column. As of February 10, the balance in this particular inventory account consists of 700 units at a unit cost of $5, for a total cost of $3,500.

The February 14 entry records the additional acquisition of 600 units at a unit cost of $5.10. The stock record card records the receipt as well as the extension. Notice that the extension utilizes three lines. This is necessary because different unit costs are assigned to the goods in the inventory at this date. The first balance represents the February 10 balance still on hand as of February 14. The second line represents the additional inventory acquired at a per-unit cost of $5.10. The total value of the inventory as of February 14 (which is shown on the third line) amounts to $6,560.

The first entry on February 17 records the cash sale of 800 units at the selling price of $9 per unit. The second entry for that date represents the assignment of the cost of the goods sold in a similar fashion to the second entry of the tenth. The explanation for this entry differs from the one for February 10 in that the sale of the 800 units is taken from two separate inventory costs. This inventory method assumes that units will be sold in the order in which they were acquired; thus, the earliest cost is charged against the earliest sale. If you refer to the stock record card for the balance on February 14, you will notice that two separate inventory balances are listed: first, 700 units at $5.00, and then 600 units at $5.10. The earliest acquisition has a remaining balance of 700 units, which is first charged against the 800 units sold. Since these units now have been exhausted, the accountant will take the remaining 100 units out of the 600 units remaining at a cost of $5.10 per unit. Note the entry on the stock record card for the issuance of February 17. The authorization for charging the cost against the units sold is obtained from the expression "FIFO," which appears after "Basis—" and means "first-in, first-out."

Five-hundred units remained after this transaction at a per-unit cost of $5.10. If we wished at this time to determined our gross profit on sales, we would subtract the cost of goods sold ($5,510) from our net sales ($9,900) to arrive at the gross profit on sales ($4,390).

YOU SHOULD REMEMBER

Inventory systems used by trading businesses may be on either a periodic basis (usually taken once a year) or a perpetual basis (usually taken almost daily). The choice of system depends on the kinds of products sold and the specific information needed.

The use of a perpetual inventory system creates an account entitled "Cost of Goods Sold," which is charged with the cost of the goods sold in each transaction, thereby reducing the amount of the merchandise inventory account.

A merchandise purchases account is not maintained with a perpetual system, being replaced by a merchandise inventory account, which is used to record all goods acquired for resale in the normal course of business.

On the stock record card, used as part of a subsidiary inventory ledger, changes are posted as a result of goods being purchased, returned, and sold.

DETERMINING THE COST OF INVENTORIES

A major aspect of financial reporting is the determination of the cost of the ending merchandise inventory. Whether the periodic or the perpetual inventory system is used, it is necessary to use a specific method for the assignment of costs to the ending inventory, as well as to the goods sold account. Since goods are usually purchased at different costs during the accounting period, the assignment of costs can become a rather complex procedure.

The beginning point used in determining the value of the ending inventory and the cost assigned to the goods sold is the **cost-flow assumption**. This procedure permits the consistent recognition of costs assigned to the ending inventory, as well as the goods sold account. There are three cost-flow assumptions generally used: FIFO (first in, first out); LIFO (last in, first out); and the **weighted average**. Each method will generate a different outcome and is used according to an organization's needs.

• *THE FIFO METHOD*

The basis for the assignment of inventory costs on the stock record card illustrated on page 302 was FIFO. This method dictates that the oldest cost assigned to the inventory is charged against the cost of goods sold first. In other words, the cost assigned to the first goods in, is charged to the first sales made. Obviously, there must be a sufficient number of units at the earliest price in the inventory to absorb the units first sold. If this is not the case, then part of the subsequent purchases will be used to meet the deficiency.

Example: The FIFO Method

Referring to the stock record card, we see that the units sold on February 10 were taken from the inventory of February 3, However, the units sold on February 17 were first taken from the earliest remaining inventory of 700 units, with the balance of 100 units coming from the goods acquired later. If the unit costs of the merchandise acquired on February 3 and 14 had been the same, there would have been no need to differentiate between them. The cost assigned to the cost of goods sold through February 17 would be $5,510. The value assigned to the ending inventory under the FIFO basis would be $2,550 as of February 17. Notice that the per-unit cost assigned to the ending inventory represents the most recent unit cost of $5.10.

Although business organizations are free to choose among a number of inventory methods, many adopt FIFO simply because there is a tendency to dispose of goods in the order of their acquisition. While this method is not as accurate as one that would specifically identify the item being sold, it is a close approximation. During a period of rising costs, this method will cause the value of the ending inventory to be high, thereby more closely approximating the current replacement cost of the goods and assigning a realistic cost to the inventory. **Complete Computational Problem 1, Part A** (pp. 311–312).

• *THE LIFO METHOD*

The LIFO method of assigning costs to inventory assumes that the most recent cost of merchandise acquired should be charged against the most recent sales. Thus, the assignment of a cost to the ending inventory represents the cost of all earlier purchases, without regard to the order in which the goods are actually sold, since we can assume that the goods are all the same and readily interchangeable.

The justification for using this method is that, as goods are sold, more goods must be acquired to replenish the stock in inventory. The cost assigned to current sales should closely reflect the cost of replacing such goods sold. The concept of matching costs and revenue applies as well, under the theory that the current cost of merchandise should be matched against the current sales price. As the cost of purchasing merchandise increases, there is a tendency for this additional cost to be passed along to the consumer in the form of a higher selling price for the product.

Example: The LIFO Method

Item Stock # -432A Location: Bin 5E							Description: Hand Tool Basis—LIFO		
	Received			Issued			Balance		
Date	Units	Unit Cost	Total Cost	Units	Unit Cost	Total Cost	Units	Unit Cost	Total Cost
198- Feb 3	1,000	5.00	5,000				1,000	5.00	5,000
10				300	5.00	1,500	700	5.00	3,500
14	600	5.10	3,060				700	5.00	3,500
							600	5.10	3,060
									6,560
17				600	5.10	3,060			
				200	5.00	1,000	500	5.00	2,500

The information on this stock record card is the same as on the previous card, except that the basis (LIFO) and the resulting cost flow assumptions as indicated in the body of the card are different. The general journal entries will also be the same as those previously illustrated, except for the amount assigned to the cost of goods sold on February 17. Note that for the entry of February 17 on the stock record card, the first units to be transferred to cost of goods sold were the last units acquired (600 units at $5.10). Once the most recent acquisition has been exhausted, the balance is obtained from the earlier inventory purchase. The final balance in the ending inventory under LIFO is $2,500, as compared with $2,550 under the FIFO method. Should additional goods be received before the next sale, the newest goods would be charged against that sale. **Complete Computational Problem 2, Part A** (p. 312).

• *THE WEIGHTED AVERAGE METHOD*

The **weighted average** method determines the cost to be assigned to the ending inventory and the cost of goods sold by determining an average unit cost for all the goods available for sale during the accounting period. The total cost of the goods available for sale is divided by the number of units available for sale. This provides an average cost per unit, which is then multiplied by the number of units remaining in the ending merchandise inventory. The resulting figure is the total cost of the ending inventory.

This method is primarily used when the trading concern uses a periodic inventory system. It permits the taking of a physical inventory in terms of available units only, rather than specifically identifying the cost of each physical unit being counted.

Example: The Weighted Average Method

Cost of goods available for sale:	$45,000
Number of units available for sale:	3,000
Average unit cost:	= $ 15

Ending merchandise inventory (250 units × $15) = $ 3,750

$$\text{Average unit cost} = \frac{\text{Cost of Goods Available for Sale}}{\text{Number of Units Available for Sale}}$$

$$\text{Ending merchandise inventory} = \begin{array}{l}\text{Number of units} \\ \text{in the ending inventory} \\ \times \text{ Average unit cost}\end{array}$$

Since this method does not take into consideration the cost of the goods purchased at any specific time during the accounting period, as does LIFO or FIFO, it may not enable the accountant to match costs and revenue appropriately. This deficiency is offset, however, by its ease in calculation and other cost-saving benefits derived from its use. **Complete Computational Problem 3, Part A (p. 312).**

YOU SHOULD REMEMBER

The costs to be assigned to the cost of goods sold account and the ending inventory are based on either the FIFO, LIFO, or weighted average method.

In accounting periods where costs remain relatively constant, the FIFO method is probably the most appropriate.

If it is important that replacement costs relate as closely as possible to the cost of the goods sold, the LIFO method is better.

The weighted average method is a third option, even though it does not necessarily bring about the matching of costs and revenue. Its simplicity may have a cost-saving effect.

• *RECOGNIZING SIGNIFICANT CHANGES IN INVENTORY VALUE*

The dollar value assigned to inventory, as well as other assets, is based on the actual cost of obtaining the inventory. Circumstances may cause this value assigned to differ significantly from the replacement cost of the inventory. For example, if handheld calculators were originally purchased by a firm for $10 each, but the same calculators can now be purchased for $4 each, this decline represents a significant and perhaps permanent change in the replacement cost of the asset. Or, if this same asset became obsolete before it could be sold, that would also cause a significant change in the value of the asset.

In either case a permanent decline in the value of the asset must be recognized. Since it would be virtually impossible to sell the asset at what would be considered its normal selling price of perhaps $20, it is necessary to recognize and adjust for the loss in value so that the asset can at least be sold at a competitive price. The loss incurred by reason of obsolescence or a decline in the price level may appropriately be recognized as a loss in the current accounting period by reducing its cost to a level that approximates the replacement cost of the asset. This concept is known as the **lower of cost or market rule.** This rule permits the recognition of a permanent reduction in the value of inventory due to physical deterioration of the asset, a permanent price decline in terms of the replacement cost, or obsolescence. Under the lower of cost or market rule, merchandise inventory is revalued at cost or current replacement cost (market), whichever is lower.

The entry to recognize this permanent reduction in value when the market value is less than the cost converts this difference to an expense:

198–

Dec. 31	Loss from Inventory Decline	2,150	
	Merchandise Inventory		2,150
	To recognize permanent decline.		

The effect of recognizing this loss in value of the inventory as an expense is to reduce the income recognized for the period. When the perpetual inventory system

---

YOU SHOULD REMEMBER

When it is ascertained that there has been a permanent reduction in the market value of the inventory, the lower of cost or market rule can be applied in assigning a value to the ending inventory.

If the market price for the inventory is less than its cost, the reduction in merchandise inventory causes a corresponding recognition of an expense.

is used, the expense may also be charged directly to the cost of goods sold account, with the same effect.

Should the replacement cost (market price) of this inventory increase in the next or subsequent accounting periods, an increase in the firm's profits would result from the higher selling price, as compared to the reduced inventory value assigned.

ESTIMATING INVENTORY VALUE

Two methods are widely used to estimate inventory: (1) the **gross profit method** and (2) the **retail method.**

• *THE GROSS PROFIT METHOD*

The periodic inventory system requires that a physical inventory be taken at least once a year, usually at the end of the accounting period. For financial accounting purposes, inventory information may be needed more frequently. Because of the cost involved in taking physical inventories, the gross profit method can provide a viable alternative. This method is used to estimate the cost of goods sold and the ending inventory for an accounting period or for interim statement purposes.

The gross profit method utilizes information that is available from past accounting periods and applies it to the current period. The following formula is used:

$$\frac{\text{Cost of goods sold for past period}}{\text{Net sales for past period}} = \frac{\text{Ratio of cost of goods sold}}{\text{to net sales}}$$

$$\frac{\$75,000}{\$100,000} = 0.75 \text{ or } 75\%$$

Example: Gross Profit Method

This calculation determines that 75% of past period net sales actually represented the cost of goods sold. This percentage is then applied to the current net sales figure. If net sales for the current year amounted to $120,000, then, by using the gross profit method, the cost of goods sold for the current period would be $90,000 ($120,000 × 75%). If we were then to subtract the cost of goods sold ($90,000) from the cost of goods available for sale, we would have the value of the ending merchandise inventory for the current accounting period.

Using this formula, we can also determine the gross profit percentage of net sales. If we know that net sales is equal to 100%, and we subtract the cost of goods sold percentage determined above (75%), the resulting percentage of 25% represents our gross profit percentage. Thus, for every dollar of sales, $.25 would be the company's gross profit. In the above illustration, the gross profit would be $30,000 ($120,000 × 25%).

The use of the gross profit method is usually based on the actual rate for the preceding year, adjusted for any known or anticipated changes during the current year. When interim statements are needed, this method is an invaluable tool for determining the value of the ending inventory, cost of goods sold, and gross profits on sales. **Complete Computational Problem 4, Part A** (p. 312).

• *THE RETAIL METHOD*

The second method frequently used to estimate the ending merchandise inventory is the retail method, which is widely used by retail businesses that use the periodic inventory system. Unlike the gross profits method, which relies on data obtained from prior accounting periods, the **retail method** uses a ratio based on actual information currently available to the business. The total cost of the goods available for sale is divided by the total selling price of all the goods. The resulting ratio is the average cost of goods sold to be applied to each dollar of sales. The ratio is computed as follows:

$$\frac{\text{Total cost of goods available for sale}}{\text{Total selling price of all goods available for sale}}$$
$$= \text{Ratio (or percentage) of cost of goods sold to net sales}$$

Example: Retail Method

The following information is available to the accountant:

	Cost	Retail
Merchandise Inventory, Jan. 1	$ 20,000	$ 40,000
Net Purchases for the Year	230,000	410,000
Total Cost of Goods Available, at Cost and Retail	250,000	450,000
Retail Method Ratio: $250,000/$450,000 = 55.6%		
Net Sales for the Year		420,000
Merchandise Inventory, 12/31 at Retail		30,000
Estimated Merchandise Inventory, 12/31 at Cost		
($30,000 × 55.6% =)		16,680

It is important to recognize that each item sold did not cost the retailer 55.6% of net sales and that the actual gross profits did not amount to 44.4% of net sales. It is assumed that using the *average* of all sales will amount to the above percentages. When the markups on different products in the inventory vary substantially, it is advisable to develop separate ratios for each of the various items.

The retail method does not eliminate the need to take a physical inventory at the end of the year; however, it does provide valuable information, especially for interim statement purposes. Many retailers prepare interim statements on a monthly basis for analytical purposes. In addition to assisting in the frequent determinations of income, the retail method provides a business with the value of the inventory at retail as well as at cost, and acts as a means of disclosing the extent of inventory shortages. **Complete Computational Problem 5, Part A** (p. 312).

YOU SHOULD REMEMBER

The gross profit method and the retail method are used to estimate the value of the ending merchandise inventory.

The gross profit method uses information from past years to approximate the value of the current ending inventory.

The retail method compares the total cost of the goods available at both cost and retail to ascertain the average percentage of cost to selling price. This percentage is then applied to the ending physical inventory for the current year to assign a cost to the inventory.

For more practice in mastering the material in this chapter, **complete Computational Problems 6 and 7, Part A** (p. 313), and **Computational Problems 1, 2, 3, and 4, Part B** (pp. 313–314).

KNOW THE CONCEPTS

DO YOU KNOW THE BASICS?

Test your knowledge of this chapter by matching each item in the left-hand column below with the most appropriate item in the right-hand column:

1. Gross profit method

2. Lower of cost or market rule

3. Merchandise inventory account

4. Periodic inventory system

5. Perpetual inventory system

(a) Used to list specific information concerning goods acquired and subsequently sold

(b) Used to estimate the value of the ending merchandise inventory based on average percentage of cost to selling price

(c) Used to estimate the value of the ending merchandise inventory based on information from past years

(d) Used to recognize a permanent reduction in the value of inventory

(e) Used especially when the goods sold consist of small quantities of items with high unit costs

6. Retail method

(f) Used especially when the goods sold consist of large quantities of diverse products

7. Stock record card

(g) Used in the perpetual inventory system to recognize the primary cost component of items sold at retail (selling price)

8. Weighted average method

(h) Used in the perpetual inventory system to record all goods acquired for resale in the normal course of events

9. Cost of goods sold account

(i) Used to assign a value to the ending inventory when a perpetual or periodic inventory system is used

10. FIFO

(j) Used to take a physical inventory in terms of available units only

TERMS FOR STUDY

FIFO

LIFO

lower of cost or market rule

periodic inventory method

perpetual inventory method

stock record card

weighted average method

PRACTICAL APPLICATION

PART A. COMPUTATIONAL PROBLEMS WITH FULL ANSWERS

1. The following transactions relating to the purchase and subsequent sale of merchandise took place during the month of May for the current year.

198–

May 3 Acquired 500 units of goods at $10.00 per unit.

5 Purchased 300 units of goods at $10.20 per unit.

9 Sold 150 units.

10 Sold 400 units.

15 Purchased 200 units of goods at $10.10 per unit.

24 Sold 300 units.

(a) Rule a stock record card similar to the one illustrated on page 302. Record the above transactions on the card, determining the appropriate balances after each transaction.

(b) Prepare general journal entries for the above transactions. Assume that the unit selling price of the items sold was $20 in each case. Further assume that the sales were cash sales and the purchases were paid for in cash.

2. Referring to Problem 1, complete that problem using the LIFO method of determining the cost of the merchandise inventory.

3. The following information was obtained from the Able Trading Co. during the current accounting period:

Purchases—500 units at $6.50, 240 units at $5.90, 370 units at $6.10, and 320 units at $6.00.

Ending merchandise inventory physical count—290 units.

Determine:

(a) The average cost per unit.

(b) The cost assigned to the ending inventory.

(c) The cost of goods sold.

4. The owner of the D&L Trading Co. wants to know the value of the company's ending inventory as of April 30, which is the end of the fourth month of the accounting period. The following information is available about the current year's operations to date:

Beginning Merchandise Inventory	$22,500
Net Purchases to Date	15,750
Net Sales to Date	30,000

During the preceding year, the actual net sales amounted to $100,000 and the actual cost of goods sold amounted to $65,000. Use the gross profit method to determine:

(a) The gross profit rate.

(b) The value of the ending inventory.

(c) The cost of goods sold to date.

(d) The gross profit on sales to date.

5. On the basis of the following information, determine the cost of the ending inventory using the retail method:

	Cost	Retail
Merchandise Inventory, January 1	$ 90,000	$160,000
Net Purchases (January 1–June 30)	350,000	640,000
Net Sales (January 1–June 30)		730,000

6. The following purchases and subsequent sales of merchandise took place during the month of September of the current year.

198–
Sept. **1** Purchased 20 units at a cost per unit of $40 each.

5 Sold 8 units at a price of $60 each.

7 Purchased 20 units at a cost per unit of $45 each.

15 Sold 22 units at a price of $60 each.

28 Sold 5 units at a price of $60 each.

(a) Prepare a stock record card similar to that illustrated on page 302. Record the above transactions to the card, determining the correct balances after each transaction.
(b) Prepare general journal entries for the above transactions. Assume that all the purchases and sales were made on a cash basis and that the method of valuing inventory is FIFO.

7. From the information presented in Problem 6, prepare a stock record card and complete all the activities above, using the LIFO method of valuing inventory.

PART B. COMPUTATIONAL PROBLEMS WITH PARTIAL SOLUTIONS OR KEY ANSWERS

1. Using the information presented in Exercise 6 of Part A, prepare a stock record card and complete all the activities called for, using the weighted average method of valuing inventory.

2. A local electronics store has in inventory the items listed below. You are called upon to value the inventory of merchandise based on the lower of cost or market rule. Assume that the rule is applied to individual items in the inventory.

		Unit Price	
Item	Quantity	Cost (FIFO)	Market
Television monitors	115	$192	$196
Phonographs	72	96	114
Video tape recorders	96	360	336
Walkman-type radios	112	87	63

The costs of the various items appear in the merchandise inventory account in the general ledger. Make the necessary entry to adjust the inventory to reflect the lower of cost or market rule.

3. On February 24 of the current year an early spring flood destroyed the inventory of the Bradley Soap Co. Up until that date the following information was available from the accounting records:

Sales (1/1–2/24)	$80,000
Merchandise Inventory (1/1)	23,000
Net Purchases	50,000
Scrap Value of Inventory	5,000

Analysis of the previous year's financial statements indicated that net sales had amounted to $860,000 and that the cost of goods sold for the same period was $473,000.

From the above information, using the gross profit method of valuing inventory, determine the amount of the loss due to the flood.

4. The financial records of the Avery dry goods store indicate the following information for the fiscal year ending April 30:

Inventory	$25,000	Purchases (at cost)	$175,000
Purchase Returns	5,000	Purchases Discount	3,000
Transportation on Purchases	6,000	Sales (fiscal year)	215,000
Inventory (5/1)		Selling Price of	
at selling price	31,250	Net Purchases	213,000

Using the retail method, calculate the value of the ending inventory at cost, at the end of the fiscal year.

ANSWERS

KNOW THE CONCEPTS

1. c	4. f	7. a	9. g
2. d	5. e	8. j	10. i
3. h	6. b		

PRACTICAL APPLICATION
PART A
1. (a)

				Basis—FIFO						
		Received			Issued			Balance		
Date	Units	Unit Cost	Total Cost	Units	Unit Cost	Total Cost	Units	Unit Cost	Total Cost
198–										
May 3	500	10.00	5,000.00				500	10.00	5,000.00
5	300	10.20	3,060.00				500 300	10.00 10.20	5,000.00 3,060.00
9				150	10.00	1,500.00	350 300	10.00 10.20	3,500.00 3,060.00
10				350 50	10.00 10.20	3,500.00 510.00	250	10.20	2,550.00
15	200	10.10	2,020.00				250 200	10.20 10.10	2,550.00 2,020.00
24				250 50	10.20 10.10	2,550.00 505.00	150	10.10	1,515.00

(b) **198–**

May 3 Merchandise Inventory 5,000
    Cash 5,000
    Acquired 500 units at $10.00
    per unit.

5 Merchandise Inventory 3,060
    Cash 3,060
    Bought 300 units at $10.20
    per unit.

9 Cash 3,000
    Sales 3,000
    150 units at $20 per unit.
    Cost of Goods Sold 1,500
    Merchandise Inventory 1,500
    150 units at $10 = $1,500.

10 Cash 8,000
    Sales 8,000
    Sold 400 units at $20 per unit.
    Cost of Goods Sold 4,010
    Merchandise Inventory 4,010
    350 units at $10   = $3,500.
    50 units at $10.20 =   510.
                        $4,010.

198–

May 15	Merchandise Inventory	2,020	
	Cash		2,020
	Bought 200 units at $10.10 per unit.		

24	Cash	6,000	
	Sales		6,000
	Sold 300 units at $20 each.		

| 24 | Cost of Goods Sold | 3,055 | |
| | Merchandise Inventory | | 3,055 |

250 units at $10.20 = $2,550.
50 units at $10.10 =   505.
$3,055

2. (a)

Location				Basis—LIFO					
	Received			Issued			Balance		
Date	Units	Unit Cost	Total Cost	Units	Unit Cost	Total Cost	Units	Unit Cost	Total Cost
198–									
May 3	500	10.00	5,000.00				500	10.00	5,000.00
5	300	10.20	3,060.00				500	10.00	5,000.00
							300	10.20	3,060.00
9				150	10.20	1,530.00	500	10.00	5,000.00
							150	10.20	1,530.00
10				150	10.20	1,530.00			
				250	10.00	2,500.00	250	10.00	2,500.00
15	200	10.10	2,020.00				250	10.00	2,500.00
							200	10.10	2,020.00
24				200	10.10	2,020.00			
				100	10.00	1,000.00	150	10.00	1,500.00

(b) **198–**

May 3	Merchandise Inventory	5,000	
	Cash		5,000
	Bought 500 units at $10.00 per unit.		

5	Merchandise Inventory	3,060	
	Cash		3,060
	Bought 300 units at $10.20 per unit.		

198–
May 9 Cash   3,000
     Sales   3,000
   Sold 150 units at $20 each.
   Cost of Goods Sold   1,530
     Merchandise Inventory   1,530
   150 units at $10.20 = $1,530.

10 Cash   8,000
     Sales   8,000
   Sold 400 units at $20 each.
   Cost of Goods Sold   4,030
     Merchandise Inventory   4,030
   150 units at $10.20 = $1,530.
   250 units at $10.00 = 2,500.
                        $4,030.

15 Merchandise Inventory   2,020
     Cash   2,020
   Purchased 200 units at $10.10
   per unit.

24 Cash   6,000
     Sales   6,000
   Sold 300 units at $20 per unit.
   Cost of Goods Sold   3,020
     Merchandise Inventory   3,020
   200 units at $10.10 = $2,020.
   100 units at $10.00 = 1,000.
                        $3,020.

3. (a)   500 units at $6.50 = $3,250.
      240 units at $5.90 =   1,416.
      370 units at $6.10 =   2,257.
       320 units at $6.00 =   1,920.
      1,430   8,843
     Average cost per unit:
     $8,843/1,430 = $6.18.
   (b) $6.18 × 290 = $1,792.20.
   (c) Cost of goods available for sale: $8,843.00
      Ending merchandise inventory: 1,792.20
      Cost of goods sold: $7,050.80

4. Gross profit method: Cost of goods sold/Net sales = $65,000/$100,000 = 65% (Last Year).

   (a) 100% − 65% = 35% (gross profit rate).

   (b)

Beginning inventory:	$22,500
Net purchases:	15,750
Cost of goods available:	$38,250
− Cost of goods sold:	19,500 ($30,000 × 65% = $19,500)
Ending inventory value:	$18,750

   (c) Cost of goods sold = $30,000 × 65% = $19,500.

   (d) Gross profit on sales = $30,000 × 35% = $10,500.

5. Retail method: Total cost available/Total retail available = $440,000/$800,000 = 55%.

Total cost of goods available for sale:	$440,000
Cost of goods sold ($730,000 × 55%):	−401,500
Ending inventory at cost:	$ 38,500

6. (a)

Item Stock # Location							Basis—FIFO			
		Received			Issued			Balance		
Date	Units	Unit Cost	Total Cost	Units	Unit Cost	Total Cost	Units	Unit Cost	Total Cost
198–										
Sept. 1	20	$110	$800.				20	$40	$800
5				8	$40	$320	12	40	480
7	20	45.	900.				12 20	40 45	480 900
15				12 10	40 45	480 450	10	45	450
28				5	45	225	5	45	225

(b) **198–**

Sept.	**1**	Merchandise Inventory	800	
		Cash		800
	5	Cash	480	
		Sales		480
		Cost of Goods Sold	320	
		Merchandise Inventory		320
	7	Merchandise Inventory	900	
		Cash		900

198–

Sept. 15 Cash   1320

      Sales   1320

  Cost of Goods Sold   930

      Merchandise Inventory   930

  12 units at $40 = $480.

  10 units at $45 = <u> 450.</u>

              930

28 Cash   300

      Sales   300

  Cost of Goods Sold   225

      Merchandise Inventory   225

  5 units at $45 = $225.

7. (a)

Item Stock # Location					Basis—LIFO					
		Received			Issued			Balance		
Date	Units	Unit Cost	Total Cost	Units	Unit Cost	Total Cost	Units	Unit Cost	Total Cost
198–										
Sept. 1	20	$40	$800				20	$40	$800
5				8	$40	$320	12	45	480
7	20	45	900				12 20	40 45	480 900
15				20 2	45 40	900 80	10	40	400
28				5	40	200	5	40	200

(b)   Entries of Sept. 1, 5, and 7 are same for Exercise 6.

198–

Sept. 15 Cash   1320

      Sales   1320

  Cost of Goods Sold   980

      Merchandise Inventory   980

  20 units at $45. = $900.

  2 units at $40. = <u>$ 80.</u>

             $980.

28 Cash   300

      Sales   300

  Cost of Goods Sold   200

      Merchandise units at Inventory   200

  5 units at $40. = $200.

PART B

1. September 28 inventory balance (LIFO), 5 units at $40 = $200

2. Inventory value, $68,304

3. Loss, $29,000 less $5,000 scrap value

4. Inventory value, $23,850

11
PAYROLL

KEY TERMS

cumulative employee earnings record A record maintained to accumulate the weekly earnings of each employee. The record is summarized quarterly and makes it possible to determine each employee's cumulative earnings at any given point in time.

employee's withholding allowance certificate A form filled out by an employee when he or she begins work for a company. This form, also known as a "W-4," asks for the number of withholding exemptions the employee wishes to take. The payroll department uses this information to determine how much income tax to withhold from the employee's salary.

payroll A list of all employees and their respective salaries for a given period.

wage and tax statement A document, also known as a "W-2 Form," indicating an employee's total earnings during the calendar year and also the total taxes withheld from his or her salary. It is prepared by the employer at the end of every calendar year and sent to the employee shortly thereafter for use in the preparation of his or her personal income tax return.

WHAT IS PAYROLL?

One of the largest expenses that most businesses incur on a regular, ongoing basis is payroll. **Payroll** represents the compensation that is regularly paid to the employees of a business organization. Labor costs and the related payroll taxes represent a large and constantly increasing portion of the total cost of operating most business organizations. Based on the dollar expenditures and the governmental regulations relating to payroll, the latter is one of the most important accounting activities. Although the worker tends to think in terms of his or her payroll check at the end of the particular payroll period, there is more to payroll than just take-home pay.

All employees of a business organization receive compensation for the activities they perform within the organization. The compensation is known as salary, wages, or other more descriptive terms, such as commissions or piecework earnings. The payroll system in use must be designed to perform the intricate computations required by the various governmental authorities, process the payroll data quickly, and assure the payment of the correct amount to each employee. The system should also provide for safeguards against payments to nonexistent employees or other misappropriations of funds.

PAYROLL DEDUCTIONS

The amount earned by an employee, whether paid on an hourly, weekly, semi-monthly, monthly, piecework, or commission basis, is the employee's **gross pay**. Gross pay is the total earnings of the employee for the particular payroll period. The amount of money the employee actually takes home is known as **take-home pay** or **net pay**. Net pay is arrived at by subtracting certain *deductions* from the gross pay. **Deductions** consist of various taxes that the employer is required to withhold from the employee's pay on a regular basis that coincides with the payroll period in use.

Form **W-4** (Rev. January 1982)	Department of the Treasury—Internal Revenue Service **Employee's Withholding Allowance Certificate**	OMB No. 1545–0010 Expires 4–30–83

1 Type or print your full name
ANNETTE RIVERS

2 Your social security number
071 – 39 – 4005

Home address (number and street or rural route)
463 MAIN ST.

City or town, State, and ZIP code
ANYTOWN, NEW YORK, 11797

3 Marital Status
☐ Single ☒ Married
☐ Married, but withhold at higher Single rate
Note: If married, but legally separated, or spouse is a nonresident alien, check the Single box.

4 Total number of allowances you are claiming (from line F of the worksheet on page 2) **3**

5 Additional amount, if any, you want deducted from each pay . . . . $

6 I claim exemption from withholding because (see instructions and check boxes below that apply):

  a ☐ Last year I did not owe any Federal income tax and had a right to a full refund of ALL income tax withheld, AND

  b ☐ This year I do not expect to owe any Federal income tax and expect to have a right to a full refund of ALL income tax withheld. If both a and b apply, enter "EXEMPT" here . . . . ▶

  c If you entered "EXEMPT" on line 6b, are you a full-time student? . . . . ☐ Yes ☐ No

Under the penalties of perjury, I certify that I am entitled to the number of withholding allowances claimed on this certificate, or if claiming exemption from withholding, that I am entitled to claim the exempt status.

Employee's signature ▶ annette Rivers   Date ▶ 2/18 , 19 8⁻

7 Employer's name and address (including ZIP code) (FOR EMPLOYER'S USE ONLY)
REYNOLDS TRADING CO.
4287 BROADWAY
ANYTOWN , NEW YORK 11797

8 Office code

9 Employer identification number

---------- Detach along this line----------

In order for the employer to withhold taxes from the employee's paycheck, there are certain things the employer must know about the employee. This needed information is obtained through the employee's preparation of a W-4 Form, the **employee's withholding allowance certificate** (see above), which is available from the Internal Revenue Service (IRS). This certificate asks for the employee's full name, social security number, home address, marital status, and the number of dependents that the person is claiming. The form is then signed and dated by the employee and used by the employer to determine the amounts of the various deductions to be taken from the employee's gross pay.

The typical deductions made by the employer from the employee's gross pay include:

1. Social Security Tax (FICA).

2. Federal Income Taxes Withheld.

3. State and Local Income Taxes Withheld (where applicable).

4. State Disability Insurance (where applicable).

5. Other Voluntary Deductions.

YOU SHOULD REMEMBER

The maintenance of payroll records within an organization is one of the most important financial activities of the firm.

Not only is payroll a substantial expense for the business, but also the federal, state, and local governmental taxing authorities make the firm a collecting agent for the various taxes withheld from the employee's salary, as well as the taxes that are the obligation of the employer.

The net pay, or takehome pay, that the employee receives is calculated by taking the employee's gross pay (wages earned) and deducting from it FICA tax, federal withholding tax, state and city withholding taxes (if applicable), disability benefits tax, and any voluntary deductions.

• *SOCIAL SECURITY TAX*

The Social Security tax is the result of the Federal Insurance Contributions Act (FICA). This act provides for monthly pension benefits to be paid to retirees, for survivor benefits, and for disability benefits. The Social Security tax is levied on all employees, the funds received going to support the above-mentioned programs. Except in the case of self-employed persons, the employer is required to match the employee's contribution, which is treated as an expense (FICA tax expense) by the employer.

This tax is known as a **nonprogressive tax** because every individual has withheld from his or her salary the same percentage, regardless of the amount of the earnings for the pay period. The tax rate for 1985 in 7.05% of the gross pay of the employee. There is a ceiling on the amount of gross pay subject to this tax.

For 1985 the employee is taxed on the first $39,600 earned during the calendar year. Thus, once an individual has earned gross pay to this ceiling, the employer no longer withholds the FICA tax from the employee's salary. Obviously, a person who earns only $20,000 during the calendar year will have Social Security withheld only up to that amount of earnings.

Example: The FICA Tax

The following employees would have the Social Security tax withheld as indicated based on a rate of 7.05%, not having reached the ceiling for withholding:

Employee	Gross Pay	FICA Tax
A. Adams	$345.00	$24.32
B. Brown	100.00	7.05
C. Campbell	250.00	17.63
D. Davis	630.00	44.42

As an employee's earnings approach the ceiling, the accountant must calculate the Social Security tax so as not to withhold the tax on income in excess of the ceiling.

Example: The FICA Tax

For a ceiling of $39,600, the following represents the withholding tax for E. Eddy, based on current pay period earnings as compared with the cumulative earnings to date:

	Gross Pay	FICA Tax
E. Eddy (cumulative earnings $39,500)	$450.00	$7.05

Note that the FICA tax was withheld for only $100, which is the remaining amount of earnings necessary to reach the ceiling of $39,600.

As noted above, the employer is required to withhold Social Security taxes from the employee's salary and also to match the amount withheld, which is an expense to the employer. These funds are usually deposited at a federal depository (commercial bank) on a monthly or even more frequent basis, depending on the amount of money being withheld.

In order to finance the Social Security system adequately, legislation has been enacted, practically yearly, increasing the rate of the tax and/or the amount of earnings subject to the tax. **Complete Computational Problem 1, Part A** (p. 341).

YOU SHOULD REMEMBER

The FICA tax is a nonprogressive tax deducted from the employee's salary at a rate of 7.05% on cumulative yearly earnings up to $39,600 (1985).

The employer is responsible for remitting the FICA tax to the appropriate depository.

In addition, the employer must match the FICA tax withheld from the employee; this represents an expense to the employer.

• *FEDERAL INCOME TAX*

The federal income tax is a pay-as-you-go tax. The amount withheld from the employee's salary every pay period is not actually a tax, but rather is income withheld in anticipation of the federal income tax. All employees (individuals) are considered to be calendar-year taxpayers, that is, calculation of their federal income taxes is based on earnings from January 1 through December 31 of any calendar year. By the following April 15, each taxpayer is required to prepare and submit an income tax return covering the preceding calendar year. The tax liability of the individual is determined on the basis of the income tax return, and the funds withheld by the employer are matched against the tax liability. If the amount withheld during the year is in excess of the actual tax liability, the taxpayer is entitled to a *refund*. If the tax liability is greater than the total federal income tax withheld, the taxpayer owes the balance, known as *balance due*, which must accompany the income tax return.

The calculation of the payroll period federal income tax withheld is based on three factors: (1) earnings for the pay period, (2) marital status, and (3) number of allowances claimed by the taxpayer.

Since the federal income tax is a **progressive tax,** the more money the taxpayer earns, the greater will be the percentage of his or her income paid in taxes. A single individual is considered to have lower expenses than a married person and thus has a somewhat greater amount withheld. The more dependents a taxpayer claims as allowances, the lower the amount withheld from the gross pay and the lower the eventual tax liability.

Partial withholding tax tables provided by the federal government are shown on pages 327 and 328 for (1) single individuals and (2) married persons. Note that in each case the amounts withheld depend on gross pay and number of allowances claimed. The employer refers to the W-4 Form to determine the marital status and the number of allowances claimed by the employee.

Note that, in either of the two tables reproduced, as the amount of earnings increases, the amount of withholding taxes increases within the same withholding allowance column. For example, an individual who is single and earns $55 per week, claiming one withholding allowance, will have $1.10 withheld from his or her wages. If that same individual earned $65 a week, $2.30 would be withheld; earnings of $80 result in withholding $4.20.

As either table is read horizontally, the amount of withholding taxes decreases as a direct result of the increase in the number of withholding allowances claimed. A married individual earning $150 a week will have $13.10 withheld if "0" allowances are claimed. The same earnings with "3" allowances claimed will result in $6.10 withhheld.

Recall that marital status also affects the amount of withholding taxes. A single individual earning $150 and claiming "3" withholding allowances will have $9.00 withheld, as compared to $6.10 for his or her married counterpart.

The employer is required to safeguard the federal incomes taxes withheld from an employee's gross earnings by turning the funds over to a federal depository, usually on a monthly basis, along with any Social Security taxes withheld and the employer's matching payments. **Complete Computational Problem 2, Part A** (pp. 341–342).

• STATE AND LOCAL TAXES

A business may also be liable for state and local income taxes depending on where it is located. For a business located in the city of New York, there are both New York State and New York City income taxes. The rules for withholding taxes for these taxing authorities are similar to those of the federal government. These taxing authorities also publish withholding tax tables, which the employer uses to determine the amount of taxes to be withheld. These taxes are then turned over to the appropriate taxing authority, usually on a monthly basis.

Some government entities also levy taxes called nonresident taxes against employees who work within the taxing authority, but reside outside of its jurisdiction. These taxes too are withheld by the employer and turned over to the taxing authority on a monthly basis.

The tables on pages 329 and 330 illustrate the income tax rates of the state of New York and the city of New York. Notice that these taxing authorities are concerned only with the individual's gross pay and allowances; they do not distinguish between single and married individuals. **Complete Computational Problem 3, Part A** (p. 342).

• DISABILITY INSURANCE TAXES

Many states also have **state disability insurance** programs which require each employee to contribute a nominal sum each week to fund the program. An amount such as $0.30 per week is taken from the employee's gross pay to fund this program. Employees who become temporarily disabled then receive compensation from the state during their periods of disability. In some industries this cost is

SINGLE Persons—WEEKLY Payroll Period

And the wages are—		And the number of withholding allowances claimed is—										
At least	But less than	0	1	2	3	4	5	6	7	8	9	10
		The amount of income tax to be withheld shall be—										
$0	$27	$0	$0	$0	$0	$0	$0	$0	$0	$0	$0	$0
27	28	.10	0	0	0	0	0	0	0	0	0	0
28	29	.20	0	0	0	0	0	0	0	0	0	0
29	30	.30	0	0	0	0	0	0	0	0	0	0
30	31	.40	0	0	0	0	0	0	0	0	0	0
31	32	.50	0	0	0	0	0	0	0	0	0	0
32	33	.70	0	0	0	0	0	0	0	0	0	0
33	34	.80	0	0	0	0	0	0	0	0	0	0
34	35	.90	0	0	0	0	0	0	0	0	0	0
35	36	1.00	0	0	0	0	0	0	0	0	0	0
36	37	1.10	0	0	0	0	0	0	0	0	0	0
37	38	1.30	0	0	0	0	0	0	0	0	0	0
38	39	1.40	0	0	0	0	0	0	0	0	0	0
39	40	1.50	0	0	0	0	0	0	0	0	0	0
40	41	1.60	0	0	0	0	0	0	0	0	0	0
41	42	1.70	0	0	0	0	0	0	0	0	0	0
42	43	1.90	0	0	0	0	0	0	0	0	0	0
43	44	2.00	0	0	0	0	0	0	0	0	0	0
44	45	2.10	0	0	0	0	0	0	0	0	0	0
45	46	2.20	0	0	0	0	0	0	0	0	0	0
46	47	2.30	0	0	0	0	0	0	0	0	0	0
47	48	2.50	.20	0	0	0	0	0	0	0	0	0
48	49	2.60	.30	0	0	0	0	0	0	0	0	0
49	50	2.70	.40	0	0	0	0	0	0	0	0	0
50	51	2.80	.50	0	0	0	0	0	0	0	0	0
51	52	2.90	.60	0	0	0	0	0	0	0	0	0
52	53	3.10	.80	0	0	0	0	0	0	0	0	0
53	54	3.20	.90	0	0	0	0	0	0	0	0	0
54	55	3.30	1.00	0	0	0	0	0	0	0	0	0
55	56	3.40	1.10	0	0	0	0	0	0	0	0	0
56	57	3.50	1.20	0	0	0	0	0	0	0	0	0
57	58	3.70	1.40	0	0	0	0	0	0	0	0	0
58	59	3.80	1.50	0	0	0	0	0	0	0	0	0
59	60	3.90	1.60	0	0	0	0	0	0	0	0	0
60	62	4.10	1.80	0	0	0	0	0	0	0	0	0
62	64	4.30	2.00	0	0	0	0	0	0	0	0	0
64	66	4.60	2.30	0	0	0	0	0	0	0	0	0
66	68	4.80	2.50	.20	0	0	0	0	0	0	0	0
68	70	5.00	2.70	.40	0	0	0	0	0	0	0	0
70	72	5.30	3.00	.70	0	0	0	0	0	0	0	0
72	74	5.50	3.20	.90	0	0	0	0	0	0	0	0
74	76	5.80	3.50	1.20	0	0	0	0	0	0	0	0
76	78	6.00	3.70	1.40	0	0	0	0	0	0	0	0
78	80	6.30	3.90	1.60	0	0	0	0	0	0	0	0
80	82	6.60	4.20	1.90	0	0	0	0	0	0	0	0
82	84	6.90	4.40	2.10	0	0	0	0	0	0	0	0
84	86	7.20	4.70	2.40	0	0	0	0	0	0	0	0
86	88	7.50	4.90	2.60	.30	0	0	0	0	0	0	0
88	90	7.80	5.10	2.80	.50	0	0	0	0	0	0	0
90	92	8.10	5.40	3.10	.80	0	0	0	0	0	0	0
92	94	8.40	5.60	3.30	1.00	0	0	0	0	0	0	0
94	96	8.70	5.90	3.60	1.20	0	0	0	0	0	0	0
96	98	9.00	6.10	3.80	1.50	0	0	0	0	0	0	0
98	100	9.30	6.40	4.00	1.70	0	0	0	0	0	0	0
100	105	9.80	6.90	4.50	2.10	0	0	0	0	0	0	0
105	110	10.50	7.60	5.10	2.70	.40	0	0	0	0	0	0
110	115	11.30	8.40	5.70	3.30	1.00	0	0	0	0	0	0
115	120	12.00	9.10	6.30	3.90	1.60	0	0	0	0	0	0
120	125	12.80	9.90	7.00	4.50	2.20	0	0	0	0	0	0
125	130	13.50	10.60	7.80	5.10	2.80	.50	0	0	0	0	0
130	135	14.30	11.40	8.50	5.70	3.40	1.10	0	0	0	0	0
135	140	15.00	12.10	9.30	6.40	4.00	1.70	0	0	0	0	0
140	145	15.80	12.90	10.00	7.10	4.60	2.30	0	0	0	0	0
145	150	16.50	13.60	10.80	7.90	5.20	2.90	.60	0	0	0	0
150	160	17.70	14.80	11.90	9.00	6.10	3.80	1.50	0	0	0	0
160	170	19.20	16.30	13.40	10.50	7.60	5.00	2.70	.40	0	0	0
170	180	20.70	17.80	14.90	12.00	9.10	6.20	3.90	1.60	0	0	0
180	190	22.20	19.30	16.40	13.50	10.60	7.70	5.10	2.80	.50	0	0
190	200	24.10	20.80	17.90	15.00	12.10	9.20	6.30	4.00	1.70	0	0
200	210	26.00	22.40	19.40	16.50	13.60	10.70	7.80	5.20	2.90	.60	0

MARRIED Persons—WEEKLY Payroll Period

And the wages are—		And the number of withholding allowances claimed is—										
At least	But less than	0	1	2	3	4	5	6	7	8	9	10
		The amount of income tax to be withheld shall be—										
$0	$47	$0	$0	$0	$0	$0	$0	$0	$0	$0	$0	$0
47	48	.20	0	0	0	0	0	0	0	0	0	0
48	49	.30	0	0	0	0	0	0	0	0	0	0
49	50	.40	0	0	0	0	0	0	0	0	0	0
50	51	.50	0	0	0	0	0	0	0	0	0	0
51	52	.60	0	0	0	0	0	0	0	0	0	0
52	53	.80	0	0	0	0	0	0	0	0	0	0
53	54	.90	0	0	0	0	0	0	0	0	0	0
54	55	1.00	0	0	0	0	0	0	0	0	0	0
55	56	1.10	0	0	0	0	0	0	0	0	0	0
56	57	1.20	0	0	0	0	0	0	0	0	0	0
57	58	1.40	0	0	0	0	0	0	0	0	0	0
58	59	1.50	0	0	0	0	0	0	0	0	0	0
59	60	1.60	0	0	0	0	0	0	0	0	0	0
60	62	1.80	0	0	0	0	0	0	0	0	0	0
62	64	2.00	0	0	0	0	0	0	0	0	0	0
64	66	2.30	0	0	0	0	0	0	0	0	0	0
66	68	2.50	.20	0	0	0	0	0	0	0	0	0
68	70	2.70	.40	0	0	0	0	0	0	0	0	0
70	72	3.00	.70	0	0	0	0	0	0	0	0	0
72	74	3.20	.90	0	0	0	0	0	0	0	0	0
74	76	3.50	1.20	0	0	0	0	0	0	0	0	0
76	78	3.70	1.40	0	0	0	0	0	0	0	0	0
78	80	3.90	1.60	0	0	0	0	0	0	0	0	0
80	82	4.20	1.90	0	0	0	0	0	0	0	0	0
82	84	4.40	2.10	0	0	0	0	0	0	0	0	0
84	86	4.70	2.40	0	0	0	0	0	0	0	0	0
86	88	4.90	2.60	.30	0	0	0	0	0	0	0	0
88	90	5.10	2.80	.50	0	0	0	0	0	0	0	0
90	92	5.40	3.10	.80	0	0	0	0	0	0	0	0
92	94	5.60	3.30	1.00	0	0	0	0	0	0	0	0
94	96	5.90	3.60	1.20	0	0	0	0	0	0	0	0
96	98	6.10	3.80	1.50	0	0	0	0	0	0	0	0
98	100	6.30	4.00	1.70	0	0	0	0	0	0	0	0
100	105	6.80	4.50	2.10	0	0	0	0	0	0	0	0
105	110	7.40	5.10	2.70	.40	0	0	0	0	0	0	0
110	115	8.00	5.70	3.30	1.00	0	0	0	0	0	0	0
115	120	8.60	6.30	3.90	1.60	0	0	0	0	0	0	0
120	125	9.20	6.90	4.50	2.20	0	0	0	0	0	0	0
125	130	9.80	7.50	5.10	2.80	.50	0	0	0	0	0	0
130	135	10.40	8.10	5.70	3.40	1.10	0	0	0	0	0	0
135	140	11.00	8.70	6.30	4.00	1.70	0	0	0	0	0	0
140	145	11.60	9.30	6.90	4.60	2.30	0	0	0	0	0	0
145	150	12.20	9.90	7.50	5.20	2.90	.60	0	0	0	0	0
150	160	13.10	10.80	8.40	6.10	3.80	1.50	0	0	0	0	0
160	170	14.30	12.00	9.60	7.30	5.00	2.70	.40	0	0	0	0
170	180	15.50	13.20	10.80	8.50	6.20	3.90	1.60	0	0	0	0
180	190	16.70	14.40	12.00	9.70	7.40	5.10	2.80	.50	0	0	0
190	200	18.40	15.60	13.20	10.90	8.60	6.30	4.00	1.70	0	0	0
200	210	20.10	16.80	14.40	12.10	9.80	7.50	5.20	2.90	.60	0	0
210	220	21.80	18.50	15.60	13.30	11.00	8.70	6.40	4.10	1.80	0	0
220	230	23.50	20.20	16.90	14.50	12.20	9.90	7.60	5.30	3.00	.70	0
230	240	25.20	21.90	18.60	15.70	13.40	11.10	8.80	6.50	4.20	1.90	0
240	250	26.90	23.60	20.30	17.10	14.60	12.30	10.00	7.70	5.40	3.10	.80
250	260	28.60	25.30	22.00	18.80	15.80	13.50	11.20	8.90	6.60	4.30	2.00
260	270	30.30	27.00	23.70	20.50	17.20	14.70	12.40	10.10	7.80	5.50	3.20
270	280	32.00	28.70	25.40	22.20	18.90	15.90	13.60	11.30	9.00	6.70	4.40
280	290	33.70	30.40	27.10	23.90	20.60	17.30	14.80	12.50	10.20	7.90	5.60
290	300	35.40	32.10	28.80	25.60	22.30	19.00	16.00	13.70	11.40	9.10	6.80
300	310	37.10	33.80	30.50	27.30	24.00	20.70	17.50	14.90	12.60	10.30	8.00
310	320	38.80	35.50	32.20	29.00	25.70	22.40	19.20	16.10	13.80	11.50	9.20
320	330	40.50	37.20	33.90	30.70	27.40	24.10	20.90	17.60	15.00	12.70	10.40
330	340	42.20	38.90	35.60	32.40	29.10	25.80	22.60	19.30	16.20	13.90	11.60
340	350	43.90	40.60	37.30	34.10	30.80	27.50	24.30	21.00	17.70	15.10	12.80
350	360	45.60	42.30	39.00	35.80	32.50	29.20	26.00	22.70	19.40	16.30	14.00
360	370	47.30	44.00	40.70	37.50	34.20	30.90	27.70	24.40	21.10	17.90	15.20
370	380	49.30	45.70	42.40	39.20	35.90	32.60	29.40	26.10	22.80	19.60	16.40
380	390	51.50	47.40	44.10	40.90	37.60	34.30	31.10	27.80	24.50	21.30	18.00
390	400	53.70	49.50	45.80	42.60	39.30	36.00	32.80	29.50	26.20	23.00	19.70
400	410	55.90	51.70	47.50	44.30	41.00	37.70	34.50	31.20	27.90	24.70	21.40

NY STATE – WEEKLY PAYROLL PERIOD

TABLE I

WAGES At Least	But Less Than	0	1	2	3	4	5
		TAX TO BE WITHHELD					
$0	$17	$.00					
17	18	.10					
18	19	.10					
19	20	.10					
20	21	.10					
21	22	.10					
22	23	.20					
23	24	.20					
24	25	.20					
25	26	.20					
26	27	.20					
27	28	.30					
28	29	.30					
29	30	.30					
30	31	.30					
31	32	.30					
32	33	.40	$.10				
33	34	.40	.10				
34	35	.40	.10				
35	36	.40	.10				
36	37	.50	.10				
37	38	.50	.20				
38	39	.50	.20				
39	40	.60	.20				
40	41	.60	.20				
41	42	.60	.20				
42	43	.70	.30				
43	44	.70	.30				
44	45	.70	.30				
45	46	.70	.30				
46	47	.80	.30				
47	48	.80	.40				
48	49	.80	.40	$.10			
49	50	.90	.40	.10			
50	51	.90	.40	.10			
51	52	.90	.50	.10			
52	53	1.00	.50	.10			
53	54	1.00	.50	.20			
54	55	1.00	.50	.20			
55	56	1.00	.60	.20			
56	57	1.10	.60	.20			
57	58	1.10	.60	.20			
58	59	1.10	.70	.30			
59	60	1.20	.70	.30			
60	62	1.20	.70	.30			
62	64	1.30	.80	.40			
64	66	1.30	.90	.40	$.10		
66	68	1.40	.90	.50	.10		
68	70	1.40	1.00	.50	.20		
70	72	1.50	1.00	.60	.20		
72	74	1.60	1.10	.60	.20		
74	76	1.70	1.20	.70	.30		
76	78	1.70	1.20	.80	.30		
78	80	1.80	1.30	.80	.40	$.10	
80	82	1.90	1.30	.90	.40	.10	
82	84	2.00	1.40	.90	.50	.10	
84	86	2.10	1.50	1.00	.50	.20	
86	88	2.10	1.50	1.10	.60	.20	
88	90	2.20	1.60	1.10	.70	.30	
90	92	2.30	1.70	1.20	.70	.30	

WAGES At Least	But Less Than	0	1	2	3	4	5	6	7	8	9	10 or more
		TAX TO BE WITHHELD										
$92	$94	$2.40	$1.80	$1.20	$.80	$.30						
94	96	2.50	1.80	1.30	.80	.40	$.10					
96	98	2.50	1.90	1.40	.90	.40	.10					
98	100	2.60	2.00	1.40	1.00	.50	.20					
100	105	2.80	2.10	1.50	1.10	.60	.20					
105	110	3.00	2.30	1.70	1.20	.80	.30					
110	115	3.20	2.50	1.90	1.40	.90	.40	$.10				
115	120	3.40	2.70	2.10	1.50	1.10	.60	.20				
120	125	3.70	2.90	2.30	1.70	1.20	.70	.30				
125	130	3.90	3.20	2.50	1.90	1.40	.90	.40	$.10			
130	135	4.20	3.40	2.70	2.10	1.50	1.00	.60	.20			
135	140	4.40	3.70	2.90	2.30	1.70	1.20	.70	.30			
140	145	4.70	3.90	3.10	2.50	1.90	1.30	.90	.40	$.10		
145	150	4.90	4.20	3.40	2.70	2.10	1.50	1.00	.60	.20		
150	160	5.40	4.50	3.80	3.00	2.40	1.80	1.30	.80	.40		
160	170	6.00	5.00	4.30	3.50	2.80	2.20	1.60	1.10	.60	$.20	
170	180	6.50	5.60	4.70	3.90	3.20	2.50	1.90	1.40	.90	.40	$.10
180	190	7.00	6.10	5.20	4.40	3.60	2.90	2.30	1.60	1.20	.70	.30
190	200	7.50	6.60	5.70	4.80	4.00	3.20	2.60	2.00	1.40	.90	.50
200	210	8.10	7.10	6.20	5.20	4.40	3.70	2.90	2.30	1.70	1.20	.70
210	220	8.70	7.60	6.60	5.70	4.80	4.10	3.30	2.60	2.00	1.40	1.00
220	230	9.30	8.20	7.10	6.20	5.30	4.50	3.70	3.00	2.40	1.70	1.20
230	240	9.90	8.80	7.70	6.70	5.80	4.90	4.10	3.40	2.70	2.10	1.50
240	250	10.50	9.40	8.30	7.20	6.30	5.40	4.50	3.80	3.00	2.40	1.80
250	260	11.20	9.90	8.90	7.80	6.80	5.90	5.00	4.20	3.40	2.70	2.10
260	270	11.80	10.60	9.40	8.40	7.30	6.40	5.40	4.60	3.80	3.10	2.50
270	280	12.50	11.30	10.00	8.90	7.90	6.90	5.90	5.00	4.30	3.50	2.80
280	290	13.20	12.00	10.70	9.60	8.50	7.40	6.50	5.50	4.70	3.90	3.10
290	300	14.10	12.80	11.50	10.30	9.20	8.10	7.10	6.10	5.20	4.40	3.60
300	310	15.00	13.60	12.30	11.10	9.90	8.80	7.70	6.70	5.80	4.90	4.10
310	320	15.90	14.50	13.10	11.90	10.70	9.50	8.40	7.40	6.40	5.50	4.60
320	330	16.80	15.40	14.00	12.70	11.50	10.20	9.10	8.10	7.00	6.10	5.20
330	340	17.80	16.30	14.90	13.50	12.30	11.00	9.80	8.80	7.70	6.70	5.80
340	350	18.80	17.30	15.80	14.40	13.10	11.80	10.60	9.50	8.40	7.30	6.40
350	360	19.80	18.30	16.80	15.30	14.00	12.60	11.40	10.20	9.10	8.00	7.00
360	370	20.80	19.30	17.80	16.20	14.90	13.50	12.20	11.00	9.80	8.70	7.60
370	380	21.80	20.30	18.80	17.20	15.80	14.40	13.00	11.80	10.50	9.40	8.30
380	390	22.80	21.30	19.80	18.20	16.70	15.30	13.90	12.60	11.30	10.10	9.00
390	400	23.80	22.30	20.80	19.20	17.70	16.20	14.80	13.40	12.10	10.90	9.70
400	410	24.80	23.30	21.80	20.20	18.70	17.10	15.70	14.30	12.90	11.70	10.50
410	420	25.80	24.30	22.80	21.20	19.70	18.10	16.60	15.20	13.80	12.50	11.30
420	430	26.80	25.30	23.80	22.20	20.70	19.10	17.60	16.10	14.70	13.30	12.10
430	440	27.80	26.30	24.80	23.20	21.70	20.10	18.60	17.10	15.60	14.20	12.90
440	450	28.80	27.30	25.80	24.20	22.70	21.10	19.60	18.10	16.50	15.10	13.80
450	460	29.80	28.30	26.80	25.20	23.70	22.10	20.60	19.10	17.50	16.00	14.70
460	470	30.80	29.30	27.80	26.20	24.70	23.10	21.60	20.10	18.50	17.00	15.60
470	480	31.80	30.30	28.80	27.20	25.70	24.10	22.60	21.10	19.50	18.00	16.50
480	490	32.80	31.30	29.80	28.20	26.70	25.10	23.60	22.10	20.50	19.00	17.40
490	500	33.80	32.30	30.80	29.20	27.70	26.10	24.60	23.10	21.50	20.00	18.40
500	510	34.80	33.30	31.80	30.20	28.70	27.10	25.60	24.10	22.50	21.00	19.40
510	520	35.80	34.30	32.80	31.20	29.70	28.10	26.60	25.10	23.50	22.00	20.40
520	530	36.80	35.30	33.80	32.20	30.70	29.10	27.60	26.10	24.50	23.00	21.40
530	540	37.80	36.30	34.80	33.20	31.70	30.10	28.60	27.10	25.50	24.00	22.40
540	550	38.80	37.30	35.80	34.20	32.70	31.10	29.60	28.10	26.50	25.00	23.40
550	560	39.80	38.30	36.80	35.20	33.70	32.10	30.60	29.10	27.50	26.00	24.40
560	570	40.80	39.30	37.80	36.20	34.70	33.10	31.60	30.10	28.50	27.00	25.40
570	580	41.80	40.30	38.80	37.20	35.70	34.10	32.60	31.10	29.50	28.00	26.40
580	590	42.80	41.30	39.80	38.20	36.70	35.10	33.60	32.10	30.50	29.00	27.40
590	600	43.80	42.30	40.80	39.20	37.70	36.10	34.60	33.10	31.50	30.00	28.40
$600 & over		10 percent of the excess over $600 plus —										
		44.30	42.80	41.30	39.70	38.20	36.60	35.10	33.60	32.00	30.50	28.90

CITY OF NY — RESIDENT TAX

Weekly Payroll Period

TABLE I

At Least	But Less Than	0	1	2	3	4	5
		TAX TO BE WITHHELD					
$0	$17	$.00					
17	18	.05					
18	19	.05					
19	20	.05					
20	21	.05					
21	22	.05					
22	23	.05					
23	24	.10					
24	25	.10					
25	26	.10					
26	27	.10					
27	28	.10					
28	29	.15					
29	30	.15					
30	31	.15					
31	32	.15					
32	33	.15					
33	34	.15	.05				
34	35	.20	.05				
35	36	.20	.05				
36	37	.20	.05				
37	38	.25	.05				
38	39	.25	.10				
39	40	.25	.10				
40	41	.25	.10				
41	42	.30	.10				
42	43	.30	.10				
43	44	.30	.10				
44	45	.30	.15				
45	46	.35	.15				
46	47	.35	.15				
47	48	.35	.15				
48	49	.40	.15	.05			
49	50	.40	.20	.05			
50	51	.40	.20	.05			
51	52	.40	.20	.05			
52	53	.45	.20	.05			
53	54	.45	.25	.05			
54	55	.45	.25	.10			
55	56	.50	.25	.10			
56	57	.50	.30	.10			
57	58	.50	.30	.10			
58	59	.50	.30	.10			
59	60	.55	.30	.15			
60	62	.55	.35	.15			
62	64	.60	.35	.15			
64	66	.60	.40	.20	.05		
66	68	.65	.40	.20	.05		
68	70	.65	.45	.25	.10		
70	72	.70	.50	.25	.10		
72	74	.75	.50	.30	.10		
74	76	.75	.55	.30	.15		
76	78	.80	.55	.35	.15		
78	80	.85	.60	.40	.15	.05	
80	82	.85	.60	.40	.20	.05	
82	84	.90	.65	.45	.20	.05	
84	86	.95	.70	.45	.25	.10	
86	88	1.00	.70	.50	.25	.10	
88	90	1.00	.75	.50	.30	.10	
90	92	1.05	.75	.55	.35	.15	
92	94	1.10	.80	.55	.35	.15	

At Least	But Less Than	0	1	2	3	4	5	6	7	8	9	10 or more
		TAX TO BE WITHHELD										
$94	$96	$1.10	$.85	$.60	$.40	$.15	$.05					
96	98	1.15	.90	.65	.40	.20	.05					
98	100	1.20	.90	.65	.45	.25	.05					
100	105	1.25	1.00	.70	.50	.30	.10					
105	110	1.35	1.05	.80	.55	.35	.15					
110	115	1.45	1.15	.90	.65	.40	.20	.05				
115	120	1.55	1.25	.95	.70	.50	.25	.10				
120	125	1.65	1.35	1.05	.80	.55	.35	.15				
125	130	1.75	1.45	1.15	.90	.65	.40	.20	.05			
130	135	1.85	1.55	1.25	.95	.70	.50	.25	.10			
135	140	1.95	1.65	1.35	1.05	.80	.55	.35	.15			
140	145	2.05	1.75	1.45	1.15	.85	.60	.40	.20	.05		
145	150	2.15	1.85	1.55	1.25	.95	.70	.45	.25	.10		
150	160	2.30	2.00	1.70	1.35	1.10	.80	.60	.35	.15		
160	170	2.55	2.20	1.90	1.55	1.30	1.00	.70	.50	.30	.10	
170	180	2.75	2.40	2.05	1.75	1.45	1.15	.90	.65	.40	.20	.05
180	190	2.95	2.60	2.25	1.90	1.60	1.30	1.05	.75	.55	.30	.15
190	200	3.15	2.80	2.40	2.10	1.80	1.45	1.20	.90	.65	.45	.20
200	210	3.35	2.95	2.60	2.25	1.95	1.65	1.35	1.05	.80	.55	.35
210	220	3.55	3.15	2.80	2.45	2.10	1.80	1.50	1.20	.95	.65	.45
220	230	3.75	3.40	3.00	2.65	2.30	1.95	1.65	1.35	1.10	.80	.55
230	240	3.95	3.60	3.20	2.85	2.50	2.15	1.80	1.50	1.25	.95	.70
240	250	4.20	3.80	3.40	3.00	2.65	2.30	2.00	1.70	1.40	1.10	.80
250	260	4.40	4.00	3.60	3.25	2.85	2.50	2.15	1.85	1.55	1.25	.95
260	270	4.65	4.20	3.80	3.45	3.05	2.70	2.35	2.00	1.70	1.40	1.10
270	280	4.85	4.45	4.05	3.65	3.25	2.90	2.55	2.20	1.85	1.55	1.25
280	290	5.10	4.70	4.25	3.85	3.50	3.10	2.75	2.40	2.05	1.75	1.45
290	300	5.65	5.20	4.75	4.30	3.90	3.50	3.10	2.75	2.35	2.05	1.70
300	310	5.95	5.50	5.05	4.60	4.20	3.80	3.35	3.00	2.60	2.25	1.90
310	320	6.25	5.80	5.35	4.90	4.45	4.05	3.65	3.25	2.85	2.50	2.15
320	330	6.60	6.10	5.65	5.15	4.75	4.30	3.90	3.50	3.10	2.70	2.35
330	340	6.90	6.40	5.95	5.45	5.00	4.60	4.15	3.75	3.35	2.95	2.60
340	350	7.25	6.75	6.25	5.80	5.30	4.85	4.45	4.00	3.60	3.20	2.85
350	360	7.55	7.05	6.55	6.10	5.60	5.15	4.70	4.30	3.90	3.45	3.10
360	370	7.90	7.40	6.90	6.40	5.90	5.45	5.00	4.55	4.15	3.75	3.35
370	380	8.25	7.70	7.20	6.70	6.20	5.75	5.30	4.85	4.40	4.00	3.60
380	390	9.00	8.45	7.90	7.35	6.85	6.35	5.85	5.35	4.90	4.45	4.05
390	400	9.35	8.80	8.25	7.70	7.20	6.65	6.15	5.70	5.20	4.75	4.30
400	410	9.75	9.15	8.60	8.05	7.50	7.00	6.50	6.00	5.50	5.05	4.60
410	420	10.10	9.50	8.95	8.40	7.85	7.35	6.80	6.30	5.85	5.35	4.90
420	430	10.50	9.90	9.35	8.75	8.20	7.70	7.15	6.65	6.15	5.65	5.20
430	440	10.90	10.30	9.70	9.15	8.55	8.00	7.50	6.95	6.45	6.00	5.50
440	450	11.30	10.65	10.10	9.50	8.95	8.40	7.85	7.30	6.80	6.30	5.80
450	460	11.70	11.05	10.45	9.90	9.30	8.75	8.20	7.65	7.15	6.60	6.15
460	470	12.15	11.50	10.85	10.25	9.65	9.10	8.55	8.00	7.45	6.95	6.45
470	480	12.55	11.90	11.25	10.65	10.05	9.45	8.90	8.35	7.80	7.30	6.75
480	490	13.00	12.30	11.70	11.05	10.45	9.85	9.25	8.70	8.15	7.65	7.10
490	500	13.40	12.75	12.10	11.45	10.80	10.25	9.65	9.10	8.50	7.95	7.45
500	510	13.85	13.20	12.50	11.85	11.25	10.60	10.00	9.45	8.90	8.30	7.80
510	520	14.30	13.65	12.95	12.30	11.65	11.00	10.40	9.80	9.25	8.70	8.15
520	530	14.80	14.05	13.40	12.70	12.05	11.40	10.80	10.20	9.60	9.05	8.50
530	540	15.25	14.50	13.85	13.15	12.50	11.85	11.20	10.60	10.00	9.40	8.85
540	550	15.70	15.00	14.25	13.60	12.90	12.25	11.60	10.95	10.40	9.80	9.20
550	560	16.20	15.45	14.75	14.05	13.35	12.70	12.05	11.40	10.75	10.15	9.60
560	570	16.65	15.95	15.20	14.50	13.80	13.10	12.45	11.80	11.15	10.55	9.95
570	580	17.15	16.40	15.70	14.95	14.25	13.55	12.90	12.25	11.60	10.95	10.35
580	590	17.60	16.90	16.15	15.45	14.70	14.00	13.30	12.65	12.00	11.35	10.75
590	600	18.10	17.35	16.65	15.90	15.20	14.45	13.75	13.10	12.45	11.80	11.15
$600 & over		4.73 percent of the excess over $600 plus —										
		18.35	17.60	16.85	16.15	15.40	14.70	14.00	13.30	12.65	12.00	11.35

absorbed by the employer, usually as a result of a collective bargaining agreement. Regardless of who actually pays for this program, the money collected is usually turned over to the state on a quarterly basis.

The New York State disability insurance program deducts a weekly payment equal to 0.5% of an employee's gross earnings up to maximum earnings of $120. Thus, if an employee earns $120 or more in any given week, the total disability insurance withheld from his or her salary will be $0.60. An employee earning $80 per week will have $0.40 withheld for disability insurance.

• *VOLUNTARY DEDUCTIONS*

The deductions discussed above are compulsory and must be made by the employer. If the employer fails to do so, the company can be held liable for the various deductions.

In addition to these compulsory deductions, many **voluntary deductions** may be taken from the employee's salary if authorized by the employee. These voluntary deductions include union dues, insurance premiums, payroll savings plans, charitable contributions, and supplementary pension plans. These deductions are withheld as a service by the employer to the employee. The employer is responsible for turning each of these withheld funds over to the appropriate agency.

YOU SHOULD REMEMBER

In addition to the FICA tax, the federal income tax is also withheld from the employee's pay. Since this a progressive tax, the more money earned the larger is the amount owed.

Depending on location, employers may also be required to withhold state and/or local income taxes and disability insurance taxes.

In addition to the compulsory deductions, certain voluntary deductions, such as union dues and insurance premiums, may be withheld if the employee authorizes the employer to do so.

THE PAYROLL REGISTER

We will assume that the payroll period we are working with is a week, but the same procedures are followed regardless of the payroll period used by the firm. A **payroll register (book)** is used to record the total employees who worked during a given payroll period. This book contains the employees' names and lists their total earnings and the various deductions that have been taken from their gross pay, arriving at their net pay. At this point we will be concerned, not with how the individual employee's gross pay was determined, but rather how the individual deductions, and thus the net pay, were arrived at.

The completed payroll register on page 333 illustrates the solutions to Computational Problems 2 and 3 on pages 341 and 342. In addition to the Social Security tax, the New York State disability tax and other deductions are included in the register. Note that the register has special columns for the various mandatory deductions as well as an "Other Deductions" section for the items we have called voluntary deductions. Columns are provided for total deductions and net pay as well. The register is summarized as illustrated and is double underscored once it has been determined that the sum of the individual deductions agrees with the total for the total deductions column, and that the total deductions subtracted from the total gross pay column agrees with the sum of the net pay column.

The summary of the payroll register becomes the basis for the entry required in the cash payments journal for the payment of the weekly wages. An expanded form of the cash payments journal would probably be used. This journal contains special columns for the various liability accounts, as well as a column to record the salaries expense. The general journal form of this payroll entry is as follows:

1985			
Apr. 5	Salaries Expense	1,277.80	
	FICA Taxes Payable		90.08
	FWT Payable		115.10
	NYSWT Payable		46.60
	NYCWT Payable		19.30
	NYS Disability Ben. Payable		3.00
	Union Dues Payable		12.00
	Pension Payable		40.00
	U.S. Bonds Payable		12.50
	Payroll Payable		939.22
	To record the payroll for the week ending April 5, 1985.		

Notice that the entry recognized a credit to an account entitled "Payroll Payable." The follow-up entry would be the payment of the liability, which would cause a debit to payroll payable for $939.84 and a corresponding credit to cash. **Complete Computational Problem 4, Part A** (p. 342).

THE EMPLOYEE EARNINGS RECORD

In addition to the payroll register, an individual **cumulative employee earnings record** is maintained for each employee. This record is usually summarized on a quarterly basis. It permits the employer to determine the cumulative earnings of

Example: Completed Payroll Register

Adams Stationery Co.
Payroll Register—Week Ending April 5, 1985

Name	S & E	Gross Pay	FICA Tax	Federal Withholding Tax	N.Y.S. Withholding Tax	N.Y.C. Withholding Tax	N.Y.S. Dis. Ben. Tax	Other Deductions Item	Other Deductions Amount	Total Deductions	Net Pay
Brown, G	S.1	146 50	10 33	13 60	4 20	1 85	60	Union Dues	12 00	42 58	103 92
Albert, L	M.2	234 80	16 55	18 60	7 70	3 20	60		—	46 65	188 15
Talley, R	M.3	400 —	28 20	44 30	20 20	8 05	60	Pension	40 00	141 35	253 65
Russo, S	S.2	196 50	13 85	17 90	5 70	2 40	60		—	40 45	156 05
Santini, M	M.5	300 —	21 15	20 70	8 80	3 80	60	U.S. Bonds	12 50	67 55	232 45
		1277 80	90 08	115 10	46 60	19 30	3 00		64 50	338 58	939 22

an employee for Social Security tax ceiling purposes and also maintains data required by the various taxing authorities at the end of the calendar year.

The form of the cumulative earnings record is similar to the payroll register in that the column headings are basically the same. (See the cumulative earnings record on page 335.) Instead of listing the earnings of various employees, only the earnings of a single employee appear on the individual cumulative earnings record, along with the date the wages were earned. The heading of the record includes the employee's name, address, Social Security number, rate of pay if hourly employee, date service began, and the marital status and number of exemptions claimed as they appear on the W-4 Form. At the end of the calendar year, the quarterly summary entries are combined to provide the total employee earnings, deductions, and net pay. Another use that is made of the cumulative earnings record by the employer will be discussed shortly.

YOU SHOULD REMEMBER

Payroll records maintained by the employer include the payroll register, which lists the wages paid to all employees for each payroll period and provides for the calculation of gross pay, a listing of the various deductions, and the determination of net pay.

The information from the payroll register is transferred to the individual cumulative earnings record maintained for each employee and used to calculate the maximum FICA tax to be withheld and the unemployment compensation taxes, and to complete the employee's annual wage and tax statement at the end of the calendar year.

PAYROLL AND GOVERNMENT REGULATIONS

We have learned that the employer is required to turn over to the various governmental taxing authorities the monies collected, usually on a monthly basis. In addition, there is a responsibility to match some taxes, such as the Social Security tax. Using the payroll record illustrated and the general journal just presented, the accountant would make the following entry at the end of the month, or a few days into the next month, to turn over the taxes withheld to the proper agency.

For simplicity, let us assume that the only payroll period for the month of April was the one illustrated for April 5, 1985. By the tenth day of the next month, the entry on page 336 would be recorded to send the federal withholding tax and the Social Security taxes to the federal depository.

EMPLOYEE'S RECORD

Year _____

Name _____
Address _____
Soc. Sec. No. _____
Status (M, S) _____ Exemptions _____
Phone _____ Date Employed _____ Date Released _____

YEARLY SUMMARY BY QUARTERS

Qtr.	Total Earnings	FICA	FWT	SWT	CWT	Other Deductions	Total Deductions	Net Payment
1								
2								
3								
4								
TOTALS								

FIRST QUARTER

Payroll Period	Total Earnings	FICA	FWT	SWT	CWT	Other Deductions	Total Deductions	Net Pay
TOTAL								

SECOND QUARTER

Payroll Period	Total Earnings	FICA	FWT	SWT	CWT	Other Deductions	Total Deductions	Net Pay
TOTAL								

THIRD QUARTER

Payroll Period	Total Earnings	FICA	FWT	SWT	CWT	Other Deductions	Total Deductions	Net Pay
TOTAL								

FOURTH QUARTER

Payroll Period	Total Earnings	FICA	FWT	SWT	CWT	Other Deductions	Total Deductions	Net Pay
TOTAL								

```
1985
May 10   FICA Tax Expense                        90.08
         FICA Taxes Payable                       90.08
         FWT Payable                             115.10
             Cash                                             295.26
         To recognize FICA tax expense and send tax
         obligation to the federal depository.
```

The entry to send the required monthly New York State and New York City withholding taxes to the state would be made so that the payment would be received by the fifteenth day of the next month.

```
1985
May 15   NYSWT Payable                            46.60
         NYCWT Payable                            19.30
             Cash                                              65.90
         To remit monthly withholding taxes to
         New York State.
```

The New York State disability benefits tax is usually remitted on a quarterly basis by the end of the following month. The entry would cause a debit to the liability account and a corresponding credit to cash. If by agreement with a union this tax is an expense of the employer, the entry would represent a debit to an expense account such as New York State disability benefits expense, and a credit to cash when payment is remitted. In the latter case, no liability column would be established in the payroll register, since the tax is an expense of the employer and is not to be withheld from the employee's salary. **Complete Computational Problem 5, Part A** (p. 342).

• *UNEMPLOYMENT COMPENSATION TAXES*

Unlike the matching Social Security tax previously discussed, some taxes are not the responsibility of the employee. Thus, **unemployment compensation taxes** are levied upon employers by the federal and state governments. This tax provides temporary relief to employees who become unemployed, usually as a result of economic factors beyond their control. The 1985 level of earnings subject to this unemployment tax is $7,000. In other words, the first $7,000 of earnings is subject to this tax by the federal government, at a rate of 3.5% for the calendar year 1985. Generally, the employer is able to take a 2.7% credit for the amount of unemployment taxes turned over to the state government. Thus, if the state unemployment tax rate is 2.7% or greater, this amount can be taken as a credit and the actual rate to the federal government becomes 0.8%.

The state unemployment tax rate varies, depending on the **experience rating** of the employer. This experience rating is determined by the turnover of employees within the organization. The experience rating, as established by the state, is then multiplied by the first $7,000 in earnings to determine the employer's tax liability for each employee. Both federal unemployment and state unemployment compensation taxes are calculated quarterly, with payments remitted the month following the quarter. Since both taxes are the obligation of the employer, the entry for the payment recognizes expenses such as federal unemployment tax expense and state unemployment tax expense.

The cumulative earnings record previously discussed is used to determine when the first $7,000 subject to these unemployment taxes has been earned. Assuming that the majority of workers are employed from the beginning of the calendar year, the greater unemployment expense will be recognized in the first and second quarters of the calendar year. **Complete Computational Problem 6, Part A** (p. 342).

YOU SHOULD REMEMBER

The employer is required to turn over to the various governmental taxing authorities, on a regular basis, the monies withheld for the FICA tax, the federal income tax, and (where applicable) state and local income taxes and the disability benefits tax.

Unemployment compensation taxes levied on the employer by the federal and state governments represent expenses that are paid on a quarterly basis.

• *CALCULATING EMPLOYEE EARNINGS*

Earnings received by an employee are usually dependent on the nature of the work performed and the job description. An individual whose pay is based on the completion of a specific task is said to be paid on a **piecework basis.** This individual will receive remuneration at a specific dollar amount times the number of tasks completed. For example, if the person is given a piecework rate of $0.30 per unit completed, and completes 765 units, the earnings will be $229.50.

Other employees may be paid on a **commission basis,** in which a certain predetermined percentage is given to the employee for the sale of a product or a service. Thus, if a vacation package costs the customer $3,500 and the agent who sold it is entitled to a commission rate of 7%, the agent will earn $245.

Individuals may be employed for an annual salary that for payment purposes is broken down into weekly, semimonthly, or monthly payments. A combination of salary and commission earnings is also common in many kinds of selling occupations. All forms of employee earnings are subject to the various deductions previously mentioned.

The vast majority of employees are paid for their services on an hourly basis, that is, the employee is paid a specific amount of money for each hour worked. Specific laws govern the number of hours that this kind of employee can work, as well as the added compensation that must be paid for excessive hours worked. The amount of money received per hour is known as the hourly rate. An hourly employee's gross pay is determined by multiplying the hours worked in a given week by the hourly rate. An employee who has worked 36 hours in a week and is paid at an hourly rate of $3.65 would earn gross pay for the week of $131.40.

Individuals who work directly for a business organization are generally considered to be employees of that firm. On the other hand, an **independent contractor** is an individual or a business that is not directly employed by the firm, but is used only to perform specific activities. Examples of independent contractors are public accountants, lawyers, and maintenance contractors. Usually the various deductions discussed above are not made from the fee paid to the independent contractor.

OVERTIME EARNINGS

A normal 5-day workweek usually consists of 40 hours. In industries that call for a 6-day workweek, the usual number of hours worked is 48. Government regulations require that additional compensation known as **overtime** be paid for any hours worked in excess of the employee's normal workweek. Overtime is calculated at 1½ times the regular rate of pay for each hour worked beyond the normal workweek.

We will assume that a normal workweek consists of 5 days and a total of 40 hours. Thus any hours worked beyond 40 hours will be calculated at the **overtime rate,** that is, the hourly amount of money that will be paid for each hour worked beyond 40 hours in a 5-day workweek. **Overtime earnings** represent the remuneration received for the overtime hours worked.

Example: Calculation of Earnings

An employee worked a total of 43 hours in a given workweek and is paid an hourly rate of $4.00. The following calculations represent the determination of the regular earnings, overtime earnings, and the resulting gross pay:

$$\begin{array}{ll} \text{40 hours} \times \$4.00 & = \$160 \\ \text{3 overtime hours} \times (1\frac{1}{2} \times \$4) = & \underline{18} \\ \text{Gross Pay} & \$178 \end{array}$$

The first 40 hours worked were calculated based on the hourly rate of $4.00. The overtime rate was calculated by multiplying 1½ times the regular rate of pay to arrive at an overtime rate of $6. This overtime rate multiplied by the overtime hours results in overtime earnings of $18.

Overtime is calculated based on the hours worked beyond the normal 40-hour workweek. An individual who normally works a 35-hour workweek but in a given week works a total of 37 hours is not automatically entitled to overtime earnings under the minimum requirements established by the Department of Labor. However, this does not prevent the payment of overtime in such a situation. In some cases payment at a rate twice the regular hourly rate for overtime can be made by union contract or merely by employer-employee agreement. Thus, individuals who are required to work on a holiday may be entitled to double time for that day, even though the total number of hours worked for the week do not call for this payment. **Complete Computational Problems 7 and 8, Part A** (p. 343).

YOU SHOULD REMEMBER

There are several criteria for determining gross pay.

Employees may be paid on a number of bases—piecework, commission, annual salary paid at various intervals, actual hours worked, or a combination of these methods.

Labor laws require that hourly employees be compensated at an overtime rate of 1½ times the regular hourly rate for each hour worked beyond 40 hours in a 5-day workweek.

Union contracts may establish overtime at higher rates and for specific days worked, regardless of the total number of hours an employee works (holiday and weekend overtime compensation).

• *THE W-2 FORM*

The employer prepares the payroll register reflecting the payroll periods of the organization. We have learned that this information is transferred to the cumulative earnings record maintained for each employee. This second record is used in determining the maximum earnings subject to the Social Security tax and unemployment insurance tax.

At the end of the calendar year, the totals from the individual earnings report are used for the preparation of the **Form W-2 wage and tax statement.** This statement is prepared at the beginning of the following calendar year and must be given to the employee by January 31. The employer must also submit this form to the Social Security Administration by the end of February. The purpose of the W-2 Form is to provide the employee with information as to his or her total earnings for the year. This document will be used to prepare, and must be included with, the income tax return that the employee must send to the government by April 15 after the close of the calendar year covering the return.

The heading of the wage and tax statement contains the employer's name, address, and federal identification number. Each form indicates the employee's name, address, and Social Security number, which the employer obtains from the W-4 Form or other payroll records maintained on the employee. The federal income tax withheld for the calendar year is listed on the form, along with the total wages earned, total FICA wages (to the maximum wages earned subject to FICA Tax), FICA withholding tax, state withholding taxes, and local withholding taxes, if applicable. The original copy of the form is sent to the Social Security Administration; a duplicate is sent to the state taxing authority, and the remaining three duplicates go to the employee.

YOU SHOULD REMEMBER

By January 31 the employer must provide the employee with a W-2 Form wage and tax statement, showing his or her total earnings for the year.

This form, which the employer sends also to the Social Security Administration, must accompany the employee's income tax return.

For more practice in mastering the material in this chapter, **complete Computational Problems 1 and 2, Part B** (pp. 343–344).

KNOW THE CONCEPTS

DO YOU KNOW THE BASICS?

Classify each of the following as (a) an involuntary deduction or (b) a voluntary deduction:

1. Charitable contributions

2. Federal income tax

3. Disability insurance tax

4. FICA tax

5. Payroll savings plan

Classify each of the following as (a) paid entirely by the employee, (b) paid entirely by the employer, or (c) paid jointly by the employer and the employee:

6. FICA tax

7. Federal income tax

8. Unemployment compensation tax

Choose the item—(a) or (b)—that should be inserted in the blank in each of the following to make a correct statement:

9. Overtime is calculated at ___ times the regular rate of pay for each hour worked beyond the normal workweek, (a) 1½ (b) 2

10. Another name for the employee's withholding allowance certificate is the ___ . (a) W-2 Form (b) W-4 Form

TERMS FOR STUDY

commission basis	overtime earnings
deductions	overtime rate
experience rating	payroll register
FICA	piecework basis
gross pay	progressive tax
independent contractor	state disability insurance
net pay	take-home pay
nonprogressive tax	unemployment compensation taxes
overtime	voluntary deductions

PRACTICAL APPLICATION

PART A. COMPUTATIONAL PROBLEMS WITH COMPLETE SOLUTIONS

1. The following wages were earned for the week ending November 8, 1985. Next to the total wages appears the cumulative wages to date, excluding the current week. Determine for each employee the amount of the Social Security tax to be withheld from his or her earnings for the week, using the percentage rate and the ceiling for 1985.

Employee	Wages	Cumulative Earnings	FICA Tax
A. Albert	$356.25	$29,385.60	_____
B. Black	568.40	34,320.80	_____
C. Carter	298.00	13,356.90	_____
D. Delphine	704.80	39,926.90	_____
E. Edwards	621.50	39,420.00	_____

2. The following employees had weekly earnings as indicated. In addition, the status (S = single, M = married) and number of allowances claimed on the W-4 Form appear in parentheses immediately after the employee's name. For each employee determine the amount of federal income tax to be withheld.

Employee	Gross Pay	Federal Withholding Tax
G. Brown (S,1)	$146.50	_____
L. Albert (M,2)	234.80	_____
R. Talley (M,3)	400.00	_____
S. Russo (S,2)	196.50	_____
M. Santini (M,5)	300.00	_____

3. From the employee information obtained from Problem 2, determine the New York State and New York City withholding taxes to be taken out of each employee's gross pay.

4. Prepare a payroll register similar to the one illustrated on page 333. Complete the register for the week ending August 16, 1985, from the following information. Use the various tax tables provided in this chapter.

Albert Gibbs (M,5)	$385.40
Jerry Hand (M,4)	348.75
Jim King (M,4)	296.00
Steven Feld (S,2)	185.00
Harold Finney (S,1)	147.50

After completing the payroll register, make a general journal entry to record the payment of the payroll for the week ending August 16, 1985.

5. Referring to Problem 4, prepare the necessary general journal entries to remit the appropriate taxes to the various taxing authorities at the end of the month.

6. The following employees had cumulative earnings for the first quarter of 1985 as shown on their individual cumulative earnings reports. The state experience rating for their employer for unemployment insurance purposes is 4.2%. Determine the federal and state unemployment taxes that must be remitted to the respective taxing authorities at the end of the quarter.

Employee	Cumulative Earnings	FU Tax	SU Tax
A. Taylor	$5,465.00		
S. Steiner	7,543.00		
A. Rothstein	3,565.40		
J. Shapiro	9,400.00		
S. Bailey	6,550.90		

7. Calculate the gross pay for the following employees based on the hours worked and their hourly rates. Distinguish between regular and overtime earnings.

Employee	Total Hours	Hourly Rate	Regular Earnings	Overtime Earnings	Gross Pay
Albert (S,2)	42	$3.35			
Baker (M,4)	39	4.10			
Cox (S,3)	45	4.20			
Daley (S,1)	47	3.50			
Evans (M,2)	41	5.15			
Fall (M,5)	44	4.80			

8. On the basis of the gross pay determined for the employees in Problem 7, prepare a payroll register. After completing the register, record in general journal form the entries needed to pay the payroll and remit the various taxes to the taxing authorities. Use the appropriate tax tables presented in this chapter.

PART B. COMPUTATIONAL PROBLEMS WITH PARTIAL SOLUTIONS OR KEY ANSWERS

1. Ruth Ederly is a part-time employee of the A&B Dress Co. Ruth resides at 1224 Clearmont Avenue, Brooklyn, NY 11299. She is married and claims three exemptions. She first began her employment on August 24, 1967. For the first quarter of 1984 Ruth earned the following weekly amounts:

Payroll Period Week Ending	Gross Earnings	Payroll Period Week Ending	Gross Earnings
January 4	$180.00	January 11	$300.00
January 18	265.75	January 25	245.50
February 1	297.00	February 8	262.00
February 15	205.00	February 22	306.50
March 1	253.00	March 8	275.00
March 15	285.45	March 22	307.40
March 29	284.35		

Using the individual employee earnings record illustrated in this chapter and the various withholding tax tables, complete Ruth Ederly's employee earnings record for the first quarter of 1984. Be certain to summarize and verify the first quarter.

2. The payroll summary of the Exeter Sales Corp. for the first quarter of the current calendar year showed the following salaries paid:

T. Nelson	$3,985
U. Lauder	4,498
V. Rubler	7,389
J. Santiago	7,150
A. Spelvin	5,600

The payroll summary of the Exeter Sales Corp. for the second quarter of the current calendar year showed the following salaries paid:

T. Nelson	$4,254
U. Lauder	4,765
B. Owen	6,210
V. Rubler	6,890
J. Santiago	2,345
A. Spelvin	4,280

Record the following transactions in general journal form:

198–

Apr. 3 Recorded the FICA tax (employer's share) for the first quarter of the current year.

15 Sent a check to NYS Unemployment Insurance based on our experience rating of 3.3%.

16 Sent a check to the Internal Revenue Service for the federal unemployment insurance for the first quarter of the calendar year. (Remember to take the NYS unemployment taxes credit.)

July 4 Recorded the FICA tax (employer's share) for the second quarter of the current year.

14 Sent a check to NYS Unemployment Insurance based on our experience rating of 3.3%.

14 Sent a check to the Internal Revenue Service for the federal unemployment insurance for the second quarter of the calendar year. (Remember to take the NYS unemployment taxes credit.)

ANSWERS

KNOW THE CONCEPTS

1. **b**	2. **a**	3. **a**	4. **a**	5. **b**
6. **c**	7. **a**	8. **b**	9. **a**	10. **b**

PRACTICAL APPLICATION
PART A

1. The income ceiling on Social Security withholding taxes for 1985 is $39,600, with a rate of 7.05%.

   A. Albert $25.12
   B. Black $40.07
   C. Carter $21.01
   D. Delphine   –0–
   E. Edwards $12.69 (on $180 only)

2. G. Brown (S, 1) $13.60
   L. Albert (M, 2) $18.60
   R. Talley (M, 3) $44.30
   S. Russo (S, 2) $17.90
   M. Santini (M, 5) $20.70

3.

Employee	NYS Withholding Taxes	NYC Withholding Taxes
Brown	$4.20	$1.85
Albert	$7.70	$3.20
Talley	$20.20	$8.05
Russo	$5.70	$2.40
Santini	$8.80	$3.80

4.

Payroll Register—Week Ending August 16, 1985

Name	S & E	Gross Pay	FICA Tax	Federal Withholding Tax	N.Y.S. Withholding Tax	N.Y.C. Withholding Tax	N.Y.S. Dis. Ben. Tax	Total Deductions	Net Pay
A. Gibbs	M, 5	385 40	27 17	34 30	15 30	6 35		83 12	302 28
J. Handshaf	M, 4	348 75	24 59	30 80	13 10	5 30		73 79	274 96
J. King	M, 4	296 00	20 87	22 30	9 20	3 90		56 27	239 73
S. Feldman	S, 2	185 00	13 04	16 40	5 20	2 25		36 89	148 11
H. Finney	S, 1	147 50	10 40	13 60	4 20	1 85		30 05	117 45
		1362 65	96 07	117 40	47 00	19 65	–0–	280 12	1082 53

1985

Aug. 16 Salary Expense   1,362.65

   FICA Taxes Payable   95.39

   FWT Payable   117.40

   NYSWT Payable   47.00

   NYCWT Payable   19.65

   Cash   1,083.21

   Payroll for week ending 8/17.

5. 1985

Sept. 6 FWT Payable   117.40

   FICA Payable   95.39

   FICA Tax Expense   95.39

   Cash   308.18

   To remit payroll taxes to
   federal depository.

   6 NYSWT Payable   47.00

   NYCWT Payable   19.65

   Cash   66.65

   To remit payroll taxes to state.

6.

Employee	Federal Unemployment	State Unemployment
A. Taylor	$43.72	$229.53
S. Steiner	56.00	294.00
A. Rothstein	28.52	149.75
J. Shapiro	56.00	294.00
S. Bailey	52.41	275.14

7., 8.

Payroll Register—Week Ending _____

Name	S & E	Total Hours Reg.	O.T.	Hourly Rate	Earnings Regular	Overtime	Total	FICA Tax	Fed. With. Tax	N.Y. State With. Tax	N.Y. City With. Tax	Total Ded.	Net Pay
Albert	S, 2	40	2	3 35	134 00	10 05	144 05	10 16	10 00	3 10	1 45	24 71	119 34
Baker	M, 4	39	00	4 10	159 90	-0-	159 90	11 27	3 80	2 40	1 10	18 57	141 33
Cox	S, 3	40	5	4 20	168 00	31 50	199 50	14 06	15 00	4 80	2 10	35 96	163 54
Daley	S, 1	40	7	3 50	140 00	36 75	176 75	12 46	17 80	5 60	2 40	38 26	138 49
Evans	M, 2	40	1	5 15	206 00	7 73	213 73	15 07	15 60	6 60	2 80	40 07	173 66
Fall	M, 5	40	4	4 80	192 00	28 80	220 80	15 57	9 90	4 50	1 95	31 92	188 88
					999 90	114 83	1114 73	78 59	72 10	27 00	11 80	189 49	925 24

1.

YEARLY SUMMARY BY QUARTERS

Qtr.	Total Earnings	FICA	FWT	SWT	CWT	Other Deductions	Total Deductions	Net Payment
1	3466 95	244 43	276 20	113 10	46 75		680 48	2786 47
2								
3								
4								
TOTALS								

FIRST QUARTER

Payroll Period	Total Earnings	(7.05%) FICA	FWT	SWT	CWT	Other Deductions	Total Deductions	Net Pay
1/4	180 00	12 69	9 70	4 40	1 90		28 69	151 31
1/11	300 00	21 15	27 30	11 10	4 60		64 15	235 85
1/18	265 75	18 74	20 50	8 40	3 45		51 09	214 66
1/25	245 50	17 31	17 10	7 20	3 00		44 61	200 89
2/1	297 00	20 94	25 60	10 30	4 30		61 14	235 86
2/8	262 00	18 47	20 50	8 40	3 45		50 82	211 18
2/15	205 00	14 45	12 10	5 20	2 25		34 -	171 -
2/22	306 50	21 61	27 30	11 10	4 60		64 61	241 89
3/1	253 00	17 84	18 80	7 80	3 25		47 69	205 31
3/8	275 00	19 39	22 20	8 90	3 65		54 14	220 86
3/15	285 45	20 12	23 90	9 60	3 85		57 47	227 98
3/22	307 40	21 67	27 30	11 10	4 60		64 67	242 73
3/29	284 35	20 05	23 90	9 60	3 85		57 40	226 95
TOTAL	3466 95	244 43	276 20	113 10	46 75		680 48	2786 47

Year **1985**

EMPLOYEE'S RECORD

Name **Ruth Ederly**

Address **1224 Clearmont Ave, Bklyn, NY 11221**

Soc. Sec. No. _____

Status (M, S) **M**   Exemptions **3**

Phone _____ Date Employed **8/24/67** Date Released _____

THIRD QUARTER

Payroll Period	Total Earnings	FICA	FWT	SWT	CWT	Other Deductions	Total Deductions	Net Pay
TOTAL								

2. April 15, $926.74; July 14, $433.19

12

FINANCIAL STATEMENTS FOR PARTNERSHIP AND CORPORATE FORMS OF BUSINESS ORGANIZATIONS

KEY TERMS

common stock A class of stock that usually sells for a considerably lower price than other classes of stock. It has voting rights and the right to share in the distribution of income by the corporation in the form of dividends.

corporation An artificial being, invisible, intangible, and existing only on contemplation of the law. It is a legal entity separate from its owners.

dividends A corporation's distribution of income to the stockholders of the corporation. The form of the dividend may be either cash or additional shares of stock.

partnership An organization of two or more individuals that agree to join forces for the common purpose of earning a profit within a business environment.

preferred stock A class of stock that has certain guaranteed rights, such as a percentage dividend, the receipt of dividends before distribution to other classes of stock, or preference in the event of a liquidation. The purchase price of preferred stock is usually considerably higher than that of common stock.

> **stockholders' equity** The ownership of the assets of a corporation as evidenced by transferable shares of stock. On the balance sheet, the stockholders' equity section consists of the stock sold by the corporation and the retained earnings (income retained by the corporation).

FORMS OF BUSINESS ORGANIZATIONS

Up to this point, we have presented numerous accounting concepts and principles using the form of business organization known as the **sole proprietorship.** Concentrating on this form of business organization gave continuity to the information presented. However, although the most prevalent form of ownership in the United States is the sole proprietorship, other forms of business organizations such as **partnerships** and **corporations** play important roles in business. The primary distinction between these forms of business organizations lies in the area of owner's equity.

After a brief treatment of the characteristics of the partnership, the financial statements for this type of business organization will be discussed and illustrated. A similar presentation for the corporation will follow.

THE PARTNERSHIP

• *CHARACTERISTICS OF THE PARTNERSHIP*

The basic accounting procedures for a partnership are very similar to those for a sole proprietorship. Some distinctions should be recognized, however, because they are unique to the partnership form of business.

The special characteristics of a partnership are as follows:

1. Formation requirements.

2. Agency relationship.

3. Co-ownership of assets.

4. Limited life.

5. Unlimited liability.

6. Participation in profits and losses.

7. Articles of partnership.

FORMATION REQUIREMENTS

A partnership's formation requirements are satisfied when two or more parties agree to join forces for the common purpose of earning a profit within a business environment. The parties simply agree to enter into a partnership. If, at a later date, the partners should decide not to continue the relationship, they can just as easily terminate the association.

AGENCY RELATIONSHIP

All parties dealing with a partner have the right to assume that the individual partner is acting within the scope of his or her normal authority. Thus each partner acts as an agent for the partnership.

CO-OWNERSHIP OF ASSETS

Assets once contributed by the individual partners become the property of the partnership. The rights of individual partners extend only to the dollar values of their investments in the partnership.

LIMITED LIFE

Dissolution is said to occur as a result of any change in the composition of a partnership, and **liquidation** takes place if the partnership is terminated. The limited life of a partnership is a result of any change to the partnership composition.

The procedures for winding up (liquidating) the partnership are as follows:

1. The assets are sold.

2. Any gains or losses resulting from the sale of the assets are reflected in the respective capital accounts according to the profit and loss sharing ratio.

3. Liabilities owed to creditors are paid.

4. The remaining cash is distributed to the partners according to their respective capital balances.

UNLIMITED LIABILITY

As in a sole proprietorship, the liability of the partnership is unlimited. Each partner is jointly and severally responsible for the liabilities of the partnership. If one or more partners fail to pay their share of the partnership's debts, these debts become the exclusive responsibility of the solvent partner(s).

PARTICIPATION IN PROFITS AND LOSSES

Profits and losses are determined according to the profit- and loss-sharing ratio. This ratio is assumed to be equal unless there is written agreement as to the distribution.

ARTICLES OF PARTNERSHIP

The rights and responsibilities of each partner in the partnership should be in written form to eliminate any disputes that may arise from an oral agreement. Such a written agreement is a contract and is referred to as the **articles of partnership.** Although there is no legal or governmental requirement for a written form as evidence of a partnership, the existence of such a document will serve to outline the obligations of the partners, their specific duties, and the effect on the partnership of such occurrences as the death of a partner. Other provisions that should be included in the articles are the amount of investment by each partner, the limitations on the withdrawal of funds, the policy with regard to the admission or withdrawal of partners, and any other contingencies that can be anticipated at the time that the articles are prepared. The articles should be amended from time to time to recognize changes in the operation of the organization.

YOU SHOULD REMEMBER

The form of business organization in which two or more persons operate as co-owners for profit is a partnership.

While the partnership agreement may be written or oral, a written document, known as the articles of partnership, is preferred.

The formation of a partnership requires the contribution of assets to the business by the various partners.

The value assigned to the assets contributed is based on negotiation among the partners.

The assets become the property of the partnership, and each contributing partner has a claim based on the value of the capital balance, and not against the specific assets contributed.

A capital deficiency by one partner has to be absorbed by the remaining partners based on the profit- and loss-sharing ratio of the remaining solvent partners.

• ADVANTAGES AND DISADVANTAGES OF THE PARTNERSHIP

The advantages of this form of business organization are as follows:

1. More investment capital is available through the formation of the partnership.

2. The various skills of the partners are available to the organization.

3. The partnership is more easily formed than a corporate form of business.

However, there are also disadvantages:

1. The partnership has limited life.

2. The partners have unlimited liability for the debts of the partnership.

3. There is limited ability to raise capital.

• *THE PARTNERSHIP CAPITAL AND DRAWING ACCOUNTS*

THE CAPITAL ACCOUNT

As with a sole proprietorship, each partner's investment in the partnership is shown by a specific *capital account* in the name of the individual partner. Through initial investment, or the subsequent admission of a new partner, each investment made by an individual partner is credited to his or her respective capital account. Unlike a sole proprietorship in which there is only one capital account, in a partnership there are as many capital accounts as there are partners. **Complete Computational Problem 1, Part A** (p. 370).

THE DRAWING ACCOUNT

The drawing account was previously defined as a temporary capital account utilized by an owner for the purpose of withdrawing cash and other assets from the business in anticipation of profit. Just as each partner in a partnership has an individual capital account, so he or she has a separate *drawing account*. The individual drawing accounts record the partners' withdrawals of cash and other assets from the business for personal use. Partners, unlike employees, are not entitled to salaries, thus the drawing account acts as a quasi-salary account until the actual income of the partnership is determined and distributed to the individual partners.

Example: Capital Account, Drawing Account, and Distribution of Income

The three partners in the partnership of Christian, Rath, and Zimmer share in the profits in the following ratio: 2:2:3. Their respective capital balances are $20,000, $20,000, and $40,000. Each is entitled to interest on her capital balance equal to 5%, and their respective salary allowances are $10,000, $6,000, and $6,000. The net income earned by the partnership amounts to $30,000. During the year each partner withdrew from the business the following amounts: $13,000, $5,500, and $9,500, respectively. First, we determine the total earnings that each partner is entitled to:

Christian: Salary Allowance =	$10,000	
Interest on Capital Balance =	1,000	$11,000
Rath: Salary Allowance =	$6,000	
Interest on Capital Balance =	1,000	7,000
Zimmer: Salary Allowance =	$6,000	
Interest on Capital Balance =	2,000	8,000
Total before distribution according to profit- and loss-sharing ratio		$26,000

Note that, although the partnership had a total net income of $30,000 for the accounting period, $26,000 represented interest on capital balances and salary allowances to which the partners were entitled regardless of the amount of income or loss earned by the partnership. The remaining $4,000 is distributed according to the profit- and loss-sharing ratio as indicated below.

Net Income	$30,000
Prior Distribution per Articles	(26,000)
Distribution According to P & L Sharing Ratio	$ 4,000

Christian: $2/7 \times \$4,000 = \$1,142.86$
Rath: $2/7 \times \$4,000 = 1,142.86$
Zimmer: $3/7 \times \$4,000 = 1,714.28$

Total Profit Earned by Each Partner	Partner Drawing
Christian: $11,000 + $1,142.86 = $12,142.86	$13,000
Rath: $ 7,000 + $1,142.86 = $ 8,142.86	5,500
Zimmer: $ 8,000 + $1,714.28 = $ 9,714.28	9,500

The entries to transfer the income earned to the respective partners' capital accounts are as follows:

198–			
Dec. 31	Income Summary	30,000.00	
	Christian, Capital		12,142.86
	Rath, Capital		8,142.86
	Zimmer, Capital		9,714.28
	To transfer profit to capital.		

The entries to close the respective drawing accounts to capital are as follows:

198–			
Dec. 31	Christian, Capital	13,000.00	
	Rath, Capital	5,500.00	
	Zimmer, Capital	9,500.00	
	Christian, Drawing		13,000.00
	Rath, Drawing		5,500.00
	Zimmer, Drawing		9,500.00
	To close drawing to capital.		

As a result of closing the drawing accounts and the income summary accounts to capital, the following new capital balances appear for each partner:

Christian, Capital	$19,142.86
Rath, Capital	22,642.86
Zimmer, Capital	40,214.28

Since Christian's drawing exceeded her share of income, the net result was a reduction in the capital balance from $20,000 to $19,142.86. In the cases of Rath and Zimmer, their respective incomes exceeded their withdrawals, so that their new capital balances reflected the increases in capital.

YOU SHOULD REMEMBER

Each partner, in addition to having a capital account, is provided with a drawing account that is handled similarly to that of the sole proprietor.

During the accounting period, cash and other assets taken by the individual partners are charged (debited) to their drawing accounts.

At the end of the year, when the partners' shares of the profits are determined, their respective capital accounts are credited (debited in the case of a loss distribution), and the individual drawing accounts are closed to their capital accounts.

If the total drawing exceeds a partner's share of the partnership's profits, the resulting difference causes a decrease in that partner's capital balance.

An excess of income over drawing causes an increase in the partner's capital balance.

• *FINANCIAL STATEMENTS OF A PARTNERSHIP*

The three financial statements discussed in Chapter 2 apply not only to a sole proprietorship form of business organization, but to a partnership as well.

The *income statement* for a partnership is prepared in the same manner as shown for a sole proprietorship in Chapters 2 and 5 and will not be illustrated here.

Although the *statement of capital* is also similar for a partnership, the accountant must show changes in capital for each partner. The following statement of capital represents the example just illustrated:

	Christian	Rath	Zimmer
Christian, Rath, and Zimmer			
Statement of Capital			
For the Year Ended December 31, 198–			
Partnership Capital, January 1, 198–	$20,000.00	$20,000.00	$40,000.00
Net Income for the Year	12,142.86	8,142.86	9,714.28
Less: Partner's Drawing	13,000.00	5,500.00	9,500.00
Net Increase (Decrease) in Capital	(857.14)	2,642.86	214.28
Partnership Capital, December 31, 198–	$19,142.86	$22,642.86	$40,214.28

The partnership does not file an income tax return, but files merely an information return that indicates the share of profits distributed to each partner. As in a sole proprietorship, the profits of the partnership are the incomes of the individual partners, which are subject to income tax whether or not the total income was withdrawn from the business.

The *balance sheet* for a partnership contains the capital balance for each partner as determined on the statement of capital. The partnership balance sheet is identical to those previously illustrated for the sole proprietorship except for the inclusion of the individual partners' capital balances. The partnership balance sheet for Christian, Rath, and Zimmer follows:

Christian, Rath, and Zimmer
Balance Sheet
December 31, 198–

Assets			**Liabilities and Capital**		
Cash		$31.000.00	Accounts Payable		$15,000.00
Accounts Receivable		13,250.00	Christian, Capital	$19,142.86	
Delivery Equipment	$42,000.00		Rath, Capital	22,642.86	
Less: Accum. Depr.	18,750.00	21,250.00	Zimmer, Capital	40.214.28	
Plant Equipment	$35,000.00		Total Capital		81,999.00
Less: Accum. Depr.	3,501.00	31,499.00	Total Liabilities		
Total Assets		$96,999.00	and Capital		$96,999.00

Complete Computational Problem 2, Part A (p. 371).

YOU SHOULD REMEMBER

The income statement for a partnership is prepared in the same way as that for a sole proprietorship.

The statement of capital must show changes in capital for each partner.

The balance sheet shows the capital balance for each partner.

For more practice in mastering the material in this chapter, **complete Computational Problems 1, 2, and 3, Part B** (pp. 374–375).

THE CORPORATION

In Chapters 1–11 financial accounting was presented primarily from the view of a sole proprietorship. In the preceding pages of this chapter we have seen how a partnership form of business organization differs from a sole proprietorship, the difference involving the area of capital recognition and distribution of earnings. A third form of business organization is the corporation.

• *CHARACTERISTICS OF THE CORPORATION*

A **corporation** has been defined as "an artificial being, invisible, intangible, and existing only in contemplation of the law." Prior discussions have referred to the fact that certain forms of "personal service" businesses are prohibited from adopting the corporate form of organization and thus must organize as either sole proprietorships or partnerships. The reason for this prohibition relates to the fact that limitations are placed on the liability of the owners of a corporation. This aspect will be discussed in greater detail shortly.

A corporation is a legal entity separate from its owners. A sole proprietorship and a partnership are relatively unstable. A partnership has a limited life because of the dissolution that results from the death or retirement of a partner or a change in the composition of the partnership. A sole proprietorship can also be looked upon as having a limited life since the death of the proprietor may result in dissolution and liquidation, especially if certain specific skills are not available to the proprietor's heirs.

With the exception of "personal service" businesses, practically any form of business may choose to organize as a corporation. Corporations may be classified as **profit corporations** or **not-for-profit corporations**. A profit corporation engages in business activities and depends on profitable operations in order to continue in existence. A not-for-profit corporation includes charitable, governmental, philanthropic, educational, and recreational organizations that depend on contributions from their members or on gifts or grants from public and private sources.

Profit corporations may be further classified as public corporations or close corporations. A **public corporation** is a profit corporation whose ownership is widely distributed among the public, such as the General Motors Corporation. A **close corporation** is a profit corporation in which the stock is held by relatively few individuals, such as the immediate family of the individual or group of individuals who organized and operate the corporation.

Corporations may consist of service businesses, retail businesses, manufacturing businesses, and wholesale businesses. With the exceptions noted above, practically any type of business may organize as a corporation. Regardless of the nature or purpose of the corporations, they are created by charter, in accordance with state statutes.

The primary difference in accounting for a corporation involves the capital of the organization. The capital section on the balance sheet of a corporation is known as **stockholders' equity**. Stockholders' equity represents the ownership of the assets of the corporation as shown by transferable shares of stock. The owners of the corporation are called **stockholders** or **shareholders**. A corporation is said to have an **unlimited life** because ownership in the corporation is in the form of shares of stock, which are easily transferable; thus, the death of a stockholder has no effect on the continuance of the organization.

Although the stockholders are the owners of the corporation, they have no direct duties or responsibilities in the running of the organization. This activity is the responsibility of a **board of directors** elected to their positions by the stockholders. The directors then select a president and other corporate officers to carry on active management of the business.

• ADVANTAGES AND DISADVANTAGES OF THE CORPORATION

The advantages of this form of business organization include:

1. Virtually unlimited ability to raise necessary capital.

2. A separate legal existence that permits the acquisition and disposal of assets in the corporate name.

3. Limited liability for the stockholders to the extent of their investments in the organization.

4. Negotiability of stock.

5. Unlimited life that is not affected by changes in corporate ownership.

6. A professional management staff separate from the owners.

The disadvantages of this form of business organization include:

1. The cost and difficulty of organizing the corporation.

2. Governmental regulation of the creation of the corporation, issuance of stock, and operations of the organization.

3. The separation of ownership and control of the firm.

4. The higher rate of taxation on the corporation.

YOU SHOULD REMEMBER

A corporation is an artificial being existing only in contemplation of the law.

The formation of a corporation requires the incorporators to file articles of incorporation which stipulate the nature of the business and the number and kinds of shares of stock to be sold.

At the top of the organizational structure are the stockholders, who elect the board of directors to oversee the operations of the organization.

The board, in turn, appoints a president and other executive officers, who are responsible for the day-to-day operations.

• *CORPORATE CAPITAL*

The primary source of corporate capital is the issuance of stock. The **incorporators** subscribe to shares of stock in the corporation. The **articles of incorporation** state the classes and the quantities of stock to be sold by the corporation. Sufficient stock is sold to permit the business to operate. The shares of stock that the corporation is permitted to sell at the time of its incorporation and at future dates are known as **authorized stock**. This is the maximum quantity of stock, of various classes, that the charter permits to be sold.

Successful operation of the business should generate profits. The profits, or income remaining, after the payment of corporate income taxes, may be retained in the business as an additional source of capital. A corporation will pay **dividends** (distribution of corporate profits to stockholders) out of after-tax dollars. These dividends will reduce the amount of earnings retained in the business. However, since a corporation is not obligated to pay dividends, all of the after-tax earnings may be retained by the business as a source of capital.

STOCKHOLDERS' EQUITY

As stated above, the capital section of the balance sheet is known as the stockholders' equity. In regard to this section, the balance sheet of the corporation is quite different from that of the sole proprietorship or partnership. All income not taken out of the other forms of businesses, by the owners, is transferred to the respective owners' capital accounts. In a corporation, a distinction is made between the investment made by the stockholders and the income retained by the corporation.

The following stockholders' equity section of a corporate balance sheet illustrates the difference:

Stockholders' Equity

Capital Stock
Common Stock	$180,000	
Retained Earnings	40,000	
Total Stockholders' Equity		$220,000

The *capital stock* section represents the investment made by the shareholders as a result of purchasing stock. The *retained earnings* section represents the income, after corporate income tax, that was retained in the business. This retained earnings balance will increase each year that the corporation earns a profit and retains it in the business. If the corporation sustains a loss, a reduction in the balance of the retained earnings account will result. The stockholders' equity section illustrated is in its simplest form. The capital stock section would have to be expanded if various classes of stock were sold (see the next section) or if other factors relating to the price stockholders pay for the stocks were considered.

• TYPES OF STOCK

The articles of incorporation stipulate the quantity and kind of capital stock that will be sold by the firm. There are two principal kinds of stock that may be issued: (1) common stock and (2) preferred stock.

When more than one class of stock is issued, one kind is usually called **common stock**. Common stock gives the stockholders the rights to vote for the directors of the corporation, to maintain their percentages of ownership in the corporation, known as **preemptive rights**, and to share in dividends; also, in the event of liquidation they may share in the distribution of corporate assets. The term "common" refers to the fact that the stock traditionally is sold at a price that can be afforded by practically all investors, at least when it is first issued by the corporation.

Issued stock refers to stock that is sold by the corporation and is in the hands of the shareholders. When common stock is traded on the open market, the price of the stock will vary based on supply and demand and other factors, such as the successful operation of the corporation. Common stock, as well as other classes of stock, is usually assigned an arbitrary money value known as **par value**. This par value is printed on the stock certificate, but does not necessarily represent the price for which the stock was sold by the corporation, which may be higher or lower than the par value. Stock may also be issued without par, in which case it is known as "no-par" stock. Some states require that no-par stock be assigned a **stated value** by the board of directors. The effect of this action is to cause a stated value stock to be similar to a par value stock in its treatment.

The second class of stock that a corporation may issue is generally known as **preferred stock**. The purchase price of preferred stock is usually higher than that of common stock. Preferred stock also has a par or stated value assigned to it. The difference in cost between common stock and preferred stock can be seen in their par values. A corporation may assign an arbitrary par value to its common stock of $10 per share, and a $50 par value to its preferred stock. Although purchasers will not necessarily pay the par value in either case, this example indicates the substantial difference in the anticipated selling prices of the two types of stock. A corporation may offer different categories of preferred stock based on the benefits that each class provides to stockholders.

SPECIAL FEATURES OF PREFERRED STOCK

The term "preferred" indicates that there are certain advantages to owning this class of stock that justify the higher price. The following characteristics of preferred stock should be noted when deciding which class of stock to invest in:

1. Dividends are stated as a percentage on the face of the preferred stock cer tificate and are distributed to all classes of preferred stock before distribution to common stock. If the certificate indicates **cumulative preferred stock** the corporation is obligated to pay dividends to preferred stockholders for past years before distribution to common stockholders. If in past years a corporation has been unable to pay dividends, or has merely decided not to, then the arrearage for those past years, as well as current dividends, must be paid to the preferred stockholder before the current year's dividends can be paid on common stock. If the certificate indicates **noncumulative preferred stock** then any dividends not paid at the end of a given year are lost. In a year in which dividends are paid there still exist preference rights for the preferred stock. Cumulative rights will obviously cause this form of preferred stock to be more costly to the investor than noncumulative stock. Many corporations refrain from offering noncumulative stock because of the disadvantage in th' possible loss of dividends.

2. **Preferred stock** may also have a provision for participation in the dividend distribution beyond the stated dividend percentage on the certificate. **Participating preferred stock** participates dollar-for-dollar with the common stock in any dividend paid in excess of the stated rate on the preferred stock. Generally, when there are adequate funds to pay both preferred and common dividends, the common dividend is paid at the same rate as preferred. Any additional distribution is shared by the common and preferred stockholders based on a ratio of the number of shares of each class of stock.

Example: Distribution of Dividends to Preferred and Common Stock

A corporation with both preferred stock and common stock declares a dividend amounting to $70,000. The preferred stock is participating and is entitled to an 8%

dividend based on its par value of $100. There are 2,000 shares of preferred stock, and 5,000 shares of common stock, eligible for dividends. The distribution of dividends would be as follows:

	Preferred Dividend	Common Dividend	Total Dividend
Preferred (2,000 × $8)	$16,000	—	$16,000
Common (5,000 × $8)	—	$40,000	40,000
Pro-rata Distribution			
(7,000)	4,000	10,000	14,000
Total	$20,000	$50,000	$70,000
Dividends per Share	$10	$10	

The initial dividend obligation to participating preferred stock was 8% of $100 par or $8 per share. This accounted for the initial total dividend on preferred stock of $16,000. The common stock then receives a comparable distribution totaling $40,000. The balance of the dividend distribution amounted to $14,000. Total eligible preferred and common stock amounted to 7,000 shares (2,000 + 5,000). The 7,000 shares were divided into the remaining amount to be distributed ($14,000) to obtain the second distribution, amounting to $2 per share. Each class of stock then receives $2 per share times the eligible number of shares. Preferred receives $4,000 ($2 × 2,000), and common receives $10,000 ($2 × 5,000).

If, in this example, the total dividend declared had amounted to only $20,000, preferred would have received $16,000 in dividends with the balance, amounting to $4,000, going to common stock. The preferred stock, even though preferred participating, would not participate in this case because common has not received its pro-rata share of the dividend, and so there was inadequate cash remaining for preferred and common to share. If preferred stock is nonparticipating, then no additional dividend is paid to the preferred stockholders.

3. Most preferred stock has what is known as a **callable provision.** At the option of the issuing corporation, the preferred stock may be bought back by the corporation at the stated price, usually above the original purchase price. The callable provision will be stated on the stock certificate. A corporation (usually when organizing) issues callable preferred stock, in addition to other classes of stock in order to be able eventually to buy the stock back when profits are adequate to do so. The callable provision is exercised at the discretion of the corporation.

4. In the event of liquidation of the corporation, the preferred stockholders are entitled to receive a distribution of the assets of the corporation after the settlement of all outstanding obligations to creditors. The preferred stockholder "stands" behind the creditors, but in front of the common stockholder

in the distribution upon liquidation. Preferred stockholders are entitled to payment in full of the par value of their stock, or even a higher stated liquidation value, before any payment is made to common stockholders. Also, if the stock is cumulative preferred, any arrearage must also be paid before payment to the common stockholders.

5. A provision less commonly found in a preferred stock indenture is a **conversion clause,** which permits the preferred stockholder to convert this stock into common stock. This provision makes the stock more attractive to future investors. The stock certificate indicates the conversion ratio. Should the company prosper and the value of the common stock increase, the holder of preferred stock may exercise this conversion privilege and benefit from the increased value of the company's common stock. **Complete Computational Problem 3, Part A** (p. 371).

A final characteristic of preferred stock should be mentioned: preferred stock, regardless of its class, lacks voting rights. The advantage to the corporation in issuing preferred stock is that capital can be raised without granting preferred stockholders control of the corporation through the election of the board of directors. Common stock is the only class of stock with voting rights.

YOU SHOULD REMEMBER

Corporate stockholders have certain rights unique to this form of business organization: voting rights, preemptive rights, the right to receive a distribution of earnings of the corporation in the form of dividends, and the right to receive a pro-rata share of the assets in the event of liquidation.

There are generally two classes of stock that a corporation may issue: common stock and preferred stock.

The arbitrary par value assigned to preferred stock is usually considerably higher because of certain features of the stock.

Although preferred stock does not have voting rights, it may be participating and cumulative with regard to dividends. Also, the stock certificate indicates the dividend obligation of the corporation on its face.

In the event of corporate liquidation, the preferred stockholders are entitled to any dividend in arrears, and to a return of their investments before common stockholders are paid.

Of the two classes of stock, common stock has a considerably greater number of shares authorized because its lower par value makes it affordable to more investors.

• RECORDING STOCK TRANSACTIONS

As stated previously, the articles of incorporation set the number and classes of stock that a corporation may sell. The number of shares of stock that the charter permits to be sold constitute the authorized shares. When all or part of the authorized shares are sold, these shares are said to be issued. The shares remaining in the hands of the stockholders are known as the **outstanding stock.**

From time to time a corporation may, in addition to selling shares, go into the open market and buy back its own previously issued shares. Such shares become known as **treasury stock.** The difference between the number of shares issued and the number outstanding represents treasury stock. When a corporation buys back its own stock, the stock loses certain rights that the traditional stockholder enjoys. Treasury stock does not share in dividend distributions and, if the stock is common, voting rights are lost as well.

Entries on the corporate books are made only when the following kinds of stock transactions take place:

1. Corporate sale of authorized stock.

2. Corporate purchase of its own stock in the open market.

3. Corporate sale of treasury stock.

CORPORATE SALE OF AUTHORIZED STOCK

When a corporation sells its authorized stock, this stock, regardless of its class, may be sold at par (stated value), above par, or below par value. Stock is sold at par when the selling price is identical with the par value.

Example

A corporation is authorized to sell 10,000 shares of $10 par common stock. It issues 1,500 shares at par. The following entry illustrates this sale:

```
198–
May 4   Cash                               15,000
            Common Stock                               15,000
        Sold 1,500 shares at par.
```

Even though the par or stated value of stock is an arbitrary value, new issues of stock would probably sell for these values. The price at which stock is sold is influenced by many factors, including financial conditions, potential earning power, the availability of money in the economy for investment purposes, and the general business and economic conditions. A successful corporation wishing to raise additional capital for expansion purposes may find it easier to sell additional authorized shares at a **premium.** When shares are sold at a premium, the amount of cash generated from the sale is in excess of the par or stated value of the stock. When this situation occurs, the following entry is recorded:

```
198–
May 16   Cash                                        115,000
             Preferred Stock (8%)                              100,000
             Premium on Preferred Stock                         15,000
         Sold 2,000 $50 par 8% preferred stock at a
         premium.
```

The excess over the par value of $15,000 would be shown on the balance sheet as an account called "Additional Paid-in Capital." The additional paid-in capital section of a balance sheet represents the excess proceeds of a stock issue over the par value of the stock.

A number of factors influence whether the stock is sold at, above, or below par. If the demand for the stock is not great, the corporation may be forced to offer the stock for sale at a price lower than par. When this occurs the stock is said to be sold at a **discount.** In other words, when the issued price is less than the par value of the stock, it is sold at a discount. The entry to recognize this is as follows:

```
198–
May 10   Cash                                         90,000
         Discount on Preferred Stock                  10,000
             Preferred Stock (6%)                              100,000
         Issued 1,000 shares of 6% preferred
         stock at a discount.
```

The amount of cash generated from the sale of the shares of preferred stock is $10,000 less than the par value of the stock; thus, a discount is recognized. On the capital section of the balance sheet, the preferred stock will be shown at par value ($100,000) and the discount on preferred stock will be a reduction in additional paid-in capital.

The stockholders' equity section of the balance sheet would appear as follows:

Stockholders' Equity

Capital Stock:
    Preferred 8% stock, $50 par value,
    5,000 shares authorized, and
    2,000 shares issued and outstanding $100,000

    Preferred 6% stock, $100 par value,
    4,000 shares authorized, and
    1,000 shares issued and outstanding   100,000

Common stock, $10 par value,
10,000 shares authorized, and
1,500 shares issued and outstanding   15,000 $215,000

Stockholders' Equity

Additional Paid-in Capital:
    Premium on 8% preferred stock   15,000
    Discount on 6% preferred stock   (10,000)
        Total additional paid-in capital   5,000
    Total Capital Stock   220,000
    Retained Earnings   45,000
    Total Stockholders' Equity $265,000

Note that the discount on preferred stock is shown as a reduction in the additional paid-in-capital section of the balance sheet, while the premium on the 8% preferred stock is shown as an addition. Subsequent sales of the various classes of stock will result in changes to this additional paid-in-capital account.

Also note that the discount on preferred stock may be shown as a reduction from shares sold at par to arrive at the book value of this class of stock. The premium received on the 8% preferred stock may be shown as an addition to arrive at the paid-in capital. Subsequent sales of the various classes of stock will result in changes to the premium and discount accounts. When this approach is used, the capital stock section is known as "Paid-in Capital," and the book value of each class of stock is readily seen.

Stockholders' Equity

Paid-in Capital:

Preferred 8% stock, $50 par
(5,000 shares authorized, 2,000 shares issued) $100,000
Premium on preferred stock: 15,000 $115,000
Preferred 6% stock, $100 par
(4,000 shares authorized, 1,000 shares issued) $100,000
Less discount on preferred stock   10,000   90,000
Common stock, $10 par (10,000 shares
authorized, 1,500 shares issued)   15,000
    Total Paid-in Capital $220,000
    Retained Earnings   45,000
    Total Stockholders' Equity $265,000

Complete Computational Problem 4, Part A (p. 371).

CORPORATE PURCHASE OF ITS OWN STOCK

From time to time a corporation may go into the open market and purchase its own stock, which then is known as treasury stock. Treasury stock must have been originally issued by the corporation, purchased and paid for, subsequently reacquired by the corporation, and not canceled or reissued. Treasury stock is not entitled to participate in dividend distributions, nor does it have voting rights. Since treasury stock is not an asset in the usual sense, it is treated as a subtraction from the stockholders' equity section of the balance sheet. The entry to record the purchase of treasury stock would be as follows:

198–			
Jun. 10	Treasury Stock	7,500	
	Cash		7,500
	Purchased 500 shares of common stock ($10 par).		

The price paid for the treasury stock is entered on the books regardless of the par value. No gain or loss is recognized when the stock is purchased.

SALE OF TREASURY STOCK

If 200 shares of treasury stock were subsequently sold, the difference between the selling price and the purchase price would be shown in an account for loss or gain from the sale of treasury stock. The balance in this account would represent either an increase or a decrease in the paid-in capital section of the stockholders' equity section of the balance sheet. The following entry illustrates the sale of the 200 shares of treasury stock:

198–			
Sept. 5	Cash	3,400	
	Loss or Gain from Sale of Treasury Stock		400
	Treasury Stock		3,000
	Sold 200 shares of treasury stock.		

Each share of treasury stock had an assigned cost of $15. The stock was sold at $17 per share; thus, a total gain of $400 was recognized from its sale.

Corporations are not in the business of dealing or speculating in their own stock. In this case the stock might have initially been repurchased for distribution to employees as part of a profit-sharing plan or some other arrangement. Remember that the benefits available to other stockholders are not available to holders of treasury stock.

Occasionally, a corporation may purchase assets and pay for them through the issuance of stock. When this sale of stock takes place, the assets are set up on the books at their cash value. If the value of the stock given is greater than the assets acquired, a discount is recorded. The same procedure is followed in recognizing a premium. The assets acquired simply take the place of the cash that would have otherwise been received as a result of a traditional sale of stock. **Complete Computational Problems 5, 6, 7, and 8, Part A** (pp 372–373).

YOU SHOULD REMEMBER

The number of shares of a particular class of stock that may be sold is said to be "authorized," and the stock that is actually sold is said to be "issued."

Treasury stock acquired by the corporation is reduced from the stock originally issued.

The net stock remaining in the hands of the stockholders is said to be "outstanding."

Regardless of the class of stock sold, any funds received from the sale in excess of the par or stated value are recognized as a premium and recorded as an addition to the paid-in capital section of the balance sheet.

If the stock is sold for less than the par or stated value, the deficiency is recorded as a discount, which is a reduction in paid-in capital.

• *FINANCIAL STATEMENTS FOR A CORPORATION*

All forms of business organizations prepare financial statements at least once a year. These statements are required by the various governments (federal, state, and city) for income tax purposes. Business firms, as well as other interested parties, utilize the information provided by these statements.

The *income statement* for a corporation is identical to that of a sole proprietorship and a partnership.

Since the ownership of a corporation is in the form of shares of stock, no statement of capital is prepared, as previously illustrated. Income earned by a corporation and dividends paid are reflected in an account entitled "Retained Earnings." It becomes necessary therefore for a corporation to prepare a *retained earnings statement*, which shows the changes in retained earnings from the beginning of the accounting period to the end of the accounting period. The following statement of retained earnings is based in part on the example on page 360.

Typical Corporation
Statement of Retained Earnings
For the Year Ended December 31, 198–

Retained Earnings, January 1, 198–		$135,000
Net Income for 198–	$93,500	
Less: Dividends Paid for 198–	70,000	
Net Increase in Retained Earnings		23,500
Retained Earnings, December 31, 198–		$158,500

The *balance sheet* for a corporation contains a stockholders' equity section rather than a capital section, as do the balance sheets for a sole proprietorship and a partnership. This section consists of basically two subdivisions, "Capital Stock" and "Retained Earnings." The following represents an expanded corporate balance sheet.

Illustrative Corporation
Balance Sheet
December 31, 198–

Assets		
Cash		$70,000
Accounts Receivable		35,000
Merchandise Inventory		50,000
Equipment	$120,000	
Less: Accum.		
Depreciation	15,000	105,000
Intangible Assets		10,000
Total Assets		$270,000
Liabilities		
Accounts Payable	$12,000	
Notes Payable	38,000	
Total Liabilities		$50,000
Stockholders' Equity		
Common Stock	$180,000	
Retained Earnings	40,000	
Total Stockholders' Equity		220,000
Total Liabilities and		$270,000
Stockholders' Equity		

A more detailed stockholders' equity section of the balance sheet could also be included on the corporate balance sheet as illustrated on page 364 or 365.

In order for the corporate accountant to be able to prepare the balance sheet, the statement of retained earnings must first be prepared to obtain the end-of-year retained earnings balance. The preparation of the retained earnings statement relies on information as to net income or loss from the income statement. **Complete Computational Problems 9 and 10, Part A (p. 373).**

YOU SHOULD REMEMBER

The accounting records maintained for a corporate form of business organization are primarily the same as those for a sole proprietorship and a partnership, except for the capital accounts.

The accountant must maintain accurate, detailed records as to the various classes of stock, each stockholder's number of shares, the total shares issued, reacquired treasury stock, and any other factors affecting the stockholders' equity section of the balance sheet.

KNOW THE CONCEPTS

DO YOU KNOW THE BASICS?

Test your knowledge of this chapter by selecting the word or phrase—(a), (b), or (c)—that will make each of the following a complete, correct statement.

1. One disadvantage of the partnership form of business organization is (a) limited life (b) limited liability (c) separation of ownership and control

2. Of the three financial statements used in business, the one that is the same for a partnership as for a sole proprietorship is the (a) income statement (b) statement of capital (c) balance sheet

3. The corporate form of organization cannot be adopted by certain forms of (a) charitable organizations (b) retail businesses (c) "personal service" businesses

4. The primary difference in the accounting for a corporation, as opposed to a sole proprietorship or a partnership, lies in the area of (a) income (b) capital (c) liabilities

5. Two advantages of the corporate form of organization are practically unlimited ability to raise capital and (a) lack of governmental regulation of activities (b) unlimited life (c) lower rate of taxation on corporations

6. The class of stock that has voting rights is (a) common stock (b) preferred stock (c) treasury stock

7. If a corporation is liquidated, after creditors are paid, a return on investment is made first to the holders of (a) common stock (b) preferred stock (c) treasury stock

8. The number of shares of a particular class of stock that a corporation may offer for sale is known as (a) authorized stock (b) issued stock (c) outstanding stock

9. When the issued price of stock is less than the par value, the stock is said to be sold at a (a) conversion (b) discount (c) premium

10. The income earned by a corporation and the dividends paid are shown in an account entitled (a) "Common Stock" (b) "Retained Earnings" (c) "Stockholders' Equity"

TERMS FOR STUDY

articles of incorporation	not-for-profit corporation
articles of partnership	outstanding stock
authorized stock	par value
board of directors	participating preferred stock
callable stock provision	preemptive rights
close corporation	premium
common stock	profit corporation
conversion clause	public corporation
cumulative preferred stock	shareholder
discount	sole proprietorship
dissolution	stated value
incorporators	stockholder
issued stock	treasury stock
liquidation	unlimited life
noncumulative preferred stock	

PRACTICAL APPLICATION

PART A. COMPUTATIONAL PROBLEMS WITH COMPLETE SOLUTIONS

1. Cain and Abel entered into a partnership. The agreement called for Cain to contribute the following assets: Cash, $2,000; accounts receivable having a balance in Cain's books of $5,500; and an allowance for bad debts of $750. The partnership agreement called for recognition of accounts receivable for $5,200 and a new allowance account with a credit balance of $1,600. Record the general journal entry necessary for the admission of Cain into the partnership.

2. The capital balances of Tinker and Chance are $32,500 and $50,000, respectively, at the beginning of the accounting period. During the year Tinker invests an additional $5,000, and the partners withdraw $9,500 and $15,200, respectively. The profit and loss sharing ratio is 3 : 2 (no provision for interest on capital or salary allowance). The income earned by the partnership amounts to $30,000.

   (a) Record in general journal form these entries:

   (1) For the additional investment by Tinker.
   (2) For the distribution of the net income to the partners.
   (3) For the closing of the respective drawing accounts.

   (b) Prepare a partnership statement of capital, similar to the statement illustrated on page 355.

3. The Albert Corporation has two classes of stock: 10,000 shares of common stock, with a par value of $50, and 1,000 shares of cumulative 8% preferred stock, with a par value of $100. The board of directors has voted to distribute the following dividends during the next 5 years: year 1, $6,000; year 2, $3,500; year 3, $12,000; year 4, $30,000; year 5, $36,000.

For each of these years, calculate the dividend distribution that the preferred stockholders and the common stockholders are entitled to. Use a chart similar to the one illustrated on page 361 for each year's distribution. Remember that the preferred stock is only cumulative.

4. On April 3 of the current year, the Alice Walden Co. was organized. The corporate charter authorized the sale of 20,000 shares of cumulative preferred 8% stock, $100 par, and 50,000 shares of $10 par common stock. Record the following transactions in general journal form:

198–
Apr. 5 Sold 3,000 shares of common stock at par for cash.

   10 Sold 2,000 shares of preferred stock at $105 per share for cash.

Aug. 4 Sold 5,000 shares of preferred stock at $99 per share for cash.

Oct. 6 Sold 2,500 shares of common stock at $12 per share for cash.

5. Record the following transactions in general journal form:

198–
Jan. 23   Issued 3,000 shares of common stock, par value $50, for $52 per share.

29   Sold 5,000 shares of $100 par cumulative preferred stock for $95 per share.

30   Purchased land, building, and equipment from L. Tweed. The appraised values were:

Land	$300,000
Building	125,000
Equipment	25,000

Issued 7,200 shares of common stock (with a market value of $52 per share) for the assets. Signed a 12%, 10-year note for the balance.

Remember that recognition of a premium or a discount is based on the market value of the stock as compared to its par value

6. A newly formed corporation issued 10,000 shares of its common stock on August 10 of the current year for cash of $80,000 and for building and equipment with a fair market value of $40,000 and $20,000, respectively. Record the issuance of the stock in general journal form, assuming the following conditions:

(a) The stock had a par value of $10 per share.
(b) The stock had a par value of $15 per share.
(c) The stock had a stated value of $12 per share.

7. The Dismal Recreation Corporation's articles of incorporation authorizes the company to issue 500,000 shares of $5 par value common stock and 100,000 shares of $100 par value, 6% cumulative preferred stock. The company completed the following transactions on the dates indicated:

198–
Apr. 3   Sold 10,000 shares of common stock, receiving cash amounting to $60,000.

12   Issued 100,000 shares of its common stock for land which had a fair market value of $510,000.

16   Issued 1,000 shares of common stock for accounting and legal services amounting to $5,500 as organizational costs.

May 4 Sold 4,000 shares of preferred stock, receiving cash amounting to $375,000.

Record the above business transactions in general journal form, providing an adequate explanation for each transaction.

8. A corporation has the following classes of stock outstanding:
   (a) Preferred stock—$50 par value, 4% cumulative, participating, 10,000 shares authorized, issued, and outstanding.
   (b) Common stock—$5 par value, 150,000 shares authorized, issued, and outstanding.
   (c) The corporation paid dividends in each of 4 years as follows:

   Year 1—$15,000
   Year 2— 15,000
   Year 3— 47,000
   Year 4— 65,000

Determine the dividend distribution to each class of stock for each year. Use a form similar to that illustrated above.

9. The Lance Corporation was organized by three incorporators on August 12 of the current year. Its authorized capital stock was 50,000 shares of $10 par value each. Each organizer of the corporation purchased 1,000 shares at par, for cash. The stock was issued immediately. On August 24, the corporation also issued 100 shares to N. Stiff for services rendered in connection with organizing the corporation. On August 30, the corporation sold 150 shares to M. Nitch for $11 per share, cash.

Record the entries necessary for the above information. Prepare a balance sheet, dated August 31, 198–, for the corporation.

10. Randolph Corporation reports the following results of transactions affecting net income and retained earnings for its second fiscal year of operations ending March 31:

Retained earnings, April 1, 198–	$ 35,800
Income before income tax	122,100
Income tax	41,600
Cash dividends declared	25,000

Prepare a retained earnings statement for the fiscal year ended March 31.

PART B. COMPUTATIONAL PROBLEMS WITH PARTIAL SOLUTIONS OR KEY ANSWERS

1. The partnership of Barbara, Donald, and Lester is formed on June 1 of the current year. The articles of partnership call for each partner to contribute assets with an assigned value based on the market value of the assets at the date of contribution. Record the necessary general journal entries for the admission of the three partners based on their contributions:

Barbara

Cash		$5,000
Equipment	$45,000	
Accumulated Depreciation	18,000	
Book Value		27,000
(Market Value = $24,500)		
Land		30,000
(Market Value = $45,000)		
Accounts Payable		13,000

Donald

Cash		$10,000
Accounts Receivable	$22,000	
Allowance for Bad Debts	1,500	20,500
(Partners increased allowance by $1,500)		

Lester

Cash		$12,000
Office Supplies		8,500
(Market Value = $7,900)		
Net Accounts Receivable		32,000
(Partnership agreed to accept $30,500)		
Notes Payable		4,300

2. The trial balance of Samuel Simms on April 1 of the current year was as follows:

Samuel Simms
Trial Balance
April 1, 198–

	DEBIT	CREDIT
Cash	9,650.00	
Accounts Receivable	14,000.00	
Prepaid Insurance	780.00	
Merchandise Inventory	14,470.00	
Equipment	7,800.00	
Accumulated Depreciation—Equipment		2,340.00
Accounts Payable		13,660.00
Accrued Expenses Payable		1,380.00
Taxes Payable		1,320.00
Samuel Simms, Capital		28,000.00
	$46,700.00	$46,700.00

Samuel Simms and Louise Robbins agree to form an equal partnership on April 1. Robbins is to contribute a building worth $60,000 and land worth $10,000, both of which are subject to a mortgage of $40,000. As of April 1, the prepaid taxes on the building were $465 and the accrued interest on the mortgage was $375.

The partnership is to take over all of Simms's assets and liabilities. Simms is also to invest such an amount of cash as will make the capital accounts of the partners equal.

Using a general journal form, prepare all necessary entries to open the books of the partnership and to record the initial investments of the respective partners.

3. On January 1, 198–, the capital accounts of Albert and Brown, a partnership, were $18,230 and $21,410, respectively During the 6 months ended June 30, 198–, the business earned a net income of $18,240, and Albert and Brown withdrew $8,000 and $10,000, respectively. Assuming that the articles of partnership failed to specify how profit and losses are to be distributed, prepare a capital statement for the partnership for the 6 months ended June 30, 198–.

ANSWERS

KNOW THE CONCEPTS

1. **a**	4. **b**	/. **b**	9. **b**
2. **a**	5. **b**	8. **a**	10. **b**
3. **c**	6. **a**		

PRACTICAL APPLICATION

PART A

1. Cash   2,000
   Accounts Receivable   5,200
      Allowance for Bad Debts   1,600
      Cain, Capital   5,600
   To record contributions of Cain.

2. (a) (1) Cash   5,000
        Tinker, Capital   5,000
      For additional investment by partner.
   (2) Income Summary   30,000
        Tinker, Capital   18,000
        Chance, Capital   12,000
      To distribute partnership profit according to their respective profit-and-loss sharing ratio of 3 : 2.

(3) Tinker, Capital   9,500
     Chance, Capital   15,200
            Tinker, Drawing   9,500
            Chance, Drawing   15,200
     To close respective drawing accounts to the
     individual capital accounts.

(b) The new balances in the partnership capital accounts are calculated as
     follows:

	Tinker	Chance
Beginning Capital Balances:	$32,500	$50,000
Additional Investment:	5,000	—
	37,500	50,000
Net Income Distribution:	18,000	12,000
Less: Drawing	(9,500)	(15,200)
Net Change in Capital:	8,500	(3,200)
Ending Capital Balances:	$46,000	$46,800

3. Year	Preferred Dividend	Common Dividend	Total Dividend
1			
Preferred	$ 6,000	–0–	$ 6,000
(Arrears owed to preferred stockholders amount to $2,000.)			
2			
Preferred	$ 3,500	–0–	$ 3,500
(Arrears owed to preferred stockholders amount to $6,500.)			
3			
Preferred	$12,000	–0–	$12,000
(Arrears owed to preferred stockholders amount to $2,500.)			
4			
Preferred	$10,500	—	$10,500
Common		$19,500	$19,500
Total			$30,000
5			
Preferred	$ 8,000	—	$ 8,000
Common	—	$28,000	28,000
Total			$36,000

4. **198–**
   Apr. 5 Cash   30,000
                Common Stock   30,000

Apr. 5 Cash	30,000	
Common Stock		30,000
10 Cash	210,000	
Premium on Preferred Stock		10,000
Preferred Stock		200,000
Aug. 4 Cash	495,000	
Discount on Preferred Stock	5,000	
Preferred Stock		500,000
Oct. 6 Cash	30,000	
Premium on Common Stock		5,000
Common Stock		25,000

5. **198–**

Jan. 23 Cash	156,000	
Premium on Common Stock		6,000
Common Stock		150,000
29 Cash	475,000	
Discount on Preferred Stock	25,000	
Preferred Stock		500,000
30 Land	300,000	
Building	125,000	
Equipment	25,000	
Premium on Common Stock		14,400
Common Stock		360,000
Notes Payable		75,600

6. (a) **Aug. 10**

Cash	80,000	
Building	40,000	
Equipment	20,000	
Premium on Common Stock		40,000
Common Stock		100,000

   (b) **Aug. 10**

Cash	80,000	
Building	40,000	

	Equipment	20,000	
	Discount on Common Stock	10,000	
	Common Stock		150,000
(c) **Aug. 10**	Cash	80,000	
	Building	40,000	
	Equipment	20,000	
	Common Stock		120,000

7. **198–**

Apr. 3 Cash   60,000

            Premium on Common Stock   10,000

            Common Stock   50,000

            Sold 10,000 shares of common.

12 Land   510,000

            Premium on Common Stock   10,000

            Common Stock   500,000

            Issued 100,000 shares of common.

16 Organizational Costs   5,500

            Premium on Common Stock   500

            Common Stock   5,000

            Issued 1,000 shares of common.

May 4 Cash   375,000

            Discount on Preferred Stock   25,000

                Preferred Stock   400,000

            Sold 4,000 shares of preferred at a discount.

8.

Year	Preferred Dividend	Common Dividend	Total Dividend
1			
Preferred	$15,000	–0–	$15,000

(Arrears owed to preferred stockholders amount to $5,000.)

2			
Preferred	$15,000	–0–	$15,000

(Arrears owed to preferred stockholders amount to $10,000.)

3			
Preferred	$30,000	—	$30,000
Common	—	$17,000	17,000
Total			$47,000

4			
Preferred	$20,000	—	$20,000
Common	—	$30,000	30,000
Additional Distribution	6,000	9,000	15,000
Totals	$26,000	$39,000	$65,000

After the holders of preferred and common stocks have received their initial dividend distributions, the distribution of the balance of $15,000 is based on each class of stock's ratio. Thus, the ratio is $500,000 : $750,000 or 2 : 3. (2/5 × $15,000 = $6,000 and 3/5 × $15,000 = $9,000.)

Note that in years 1 and 2 no dividend distribution was made to the common stockholders. In year 3, the distribution to common stockholders was limited to $17,000 because the arrearage owed to preferred stockholders from years 1 and 2 nad to be made up first. The high dividend distribution in year 4 enabled both the preferred and the common stockholders to share in the extra distribution of $15,000 according to their total capital ratios. If the preferred stock had been nonpartici-pating, the entire sum in excess of the obligation to the preferred stockholders ($20,000) would have been distributed to the common stockholders and would have amounted to $45,000. Both the issuing corporation and the future investor must take the preference rights of the preferred stockholder into consideration because of their obvious effect on the distribution of dividends.

9. **198–**

Aug. 12	Cash		30,000.00	
	Common Stock			30,000.00
	Incorporators purchase 3,000 shares at $10 par.			
24	Organizational Costs		1,000 00	
	Common Stock			¹,000.00
	Issuance of 100 shares at par to N. Stiff in payment for services rendered in organizing the corp.			
30	Cash		1,650.00	
	Premium on Common Stock			150.00
	Common Stock			1,500.00
	Sold 150 shares at $11 each to M. Nitch			

Lance Corporation
Balance Sheet
August 31, 198–

Assets		Equities	
Cash	$31,650.00	Stockholders' Equity	
Organizational Costs	1,000.00	Common Stock	$32,500.00
		Premium on C/S	150.00
Total Assets	$32,650.00	Total Equities	$32,650.00

10.

Randolph Corporation
Statement of Retained Earnings
For the Year Ended March 31, 198–

Retained Earnings, April 1, 198–		$35,800.00
Net Income	$80,500.00	
Less: Dividends	25,000.00	
Net Increase in Retained Earnings		55,500.00
Retained Earnings, March 31, 198–		$91,300.00

PART B

1. Barbara: capital $61,500; Donald: capital, $29,000: Lester: capital, $46,100
2. Simms: additional cash contribution, $2,090; Robbins: capital, $30,090
3. June 30, 198–, capital balances: $19,350, $20,530

APPENDIX

ACCOUNTING AND THE MICROCOMPUTER

A mere 20 years ago, the term *automation* generated fear and trepidation in the hearts of many workers. Today *automation* has been replaced by the term *high technology*. Although the same apprehensive feelings are not being generated by this latest term, a certain distrust of the unknown continues to exist. Those who have not experienced the microcomputer through game programs, word processing, or business applications are somewhat skeptical as to the advantages of this new technology.

In the mid-1970s, with the introduction of the inexpensive small electronic calculator, a new world emerged in which everyone had ready access to a hand-held calculator. The slide rule, a prerequisite in most science classes, became obsolete thanks to the hand-held calculator. The accountant of today has turned in his/her desk adding machine and replaced it with a modern calculator. Although most of today's state-of-the-art calculators can perform numerous functions, the requirements of the accountant are much more conservative. Fortunately, the basic functions performed by the traditional adding machine are available on today's calculator. Two important features are the percentage key and the ability to print as well as display information. Some calculators also provide the user with the ability to generate the information found on amortization and present value tables. While this information is helpful, it is not critical to the accountant's needs.

In the accounting profession, the microcomputer will shortly be as common a tool on the accountant's desk as the printing calculator is today. As smaller businesses introduce mini- and microcomputers into the recordkeeping aspects of their operations, the need to know how to use the computer becomes more critical to the accountant.

Today's microcomputer has been described by many as merely a "glorified adding machine." To a certain extent, this statement is accurate. On the other hand, the power, speed, and convenience in use of the microcomputer are indisputable. It is almost as if the microcomputer was created primarily for the accountant.

The key to the computer is not the hardware, but rather the software (program) that causes the computer to function. Software that is readily available to the accounting profession includes the electronic worksheet, data base, word processor, and graphics. Each software package has a specific application that represents a powerful tool not only for the accountant but also for other groups of professionals in the business community.

ELECTRONIC SPREADSHEET

Problems that are commonly solved using a calculator, a pencil, and a sheet of paper can be solved more quickly using the personal computer and the electronic spreadsheet program. The preparation of financial statements, comparative financial statements, sales projections, income taxes, financial ratios, cost estimates, and other business and personal calculations can now be accomplished utilizing the memory and display capabilities of the personal computer. The computer's screen represents the window that shows a portion of the electronic worksheet. The spreadsheet is organized as a grid of rows and columns. The intersections of the rows and columns define thousands of entry positions. Each position (commonly known as a cell) can represent either a label (description) or a value (formula). The combinations of labels and values within the spreadsheet are used to design various charts, tables, and records.

DATA BASE

Use of the data base eliminates the everyday task of recording and filing information by means of the traditional manual filing system consisting of file folders and a filing cabinet. Data are stored on magnetic disks after being entered using the computer's screen and keyboard. Once information is sorted on disks, the data can be retrieved and viewed, updated, deleted, sorted, or used to create reports. The information stored on disks is set up in a file designed by the operator to meet his/her particular need. Information for report purposes can be retrieved from the file in alphabetic or numerical order.

WORD PROCESSOR

The word processor program enables the user to enter, edit, format, print, store, and retrieve text. The tremendous power of this program is seen in the user's ability to prepare text, without the need to retype the document, and to store, organize, search, and manipulate data. Documents can be prepared and revised in a highly efficient manner. Previously stored documents may be revised and updated as required, without the need to retype. The only prerequisite needed for word processing is a knowledge of basic keyboarding skills.

GRAPHICS

The saying "A picture is worth a thousand words" is appropriate in this instance A graphics program is used to convert numerical data into either a chart or a graph Charts and graphs can be used for forecasting sales and for preparing businesses presentations in which relationships are graphically shown, such as using a pie chart to highlight the relationship between total sales, cost of goods sold, gross profit, and net profit. Charts and graphs are created from numeric data stored on the magnetic disk. The creation of the numeric data file becomes the vehicle for the preparation of various charts and graphs that can be displayed on the computer's screen and then printed.

The software programs described above, although typically purcnased and used independently of one another, can be acquired as an integrated package. The constant refinement and revision being made to this software now permit the transfer of data from one software program to another. The accountant using the electronic spreadsheet has the ability to use this information to create a graphic presentation of the data. The data may also be incorporated into a wordprocessed annual report. Information related to data bases may also be incorporated into the annual report in both text and graphic form.

The software industry has also developed pure accounting application software. This software eliminates the repetitive nature of many accounting and bookkeeping functions. General ledger programs are available that automatically post general journal entries to the appropriate ledger accounts. The need for preparing a trial balance, income statement, statement of capital, and balance sheet is eliminated because the computer program will automatically prepare these reports. Do not be misled, however, by all these technological capabilities. The computer does not eliminate the need for the bookkeeper or accountant, nor does it obviate the necessity for a sound accounting education. The operator of the accounting application program must be thoroughly trained in bookkeeping and accounting in order to make successful use of the power of the program.

Other, more sophisticated integrated accounting programs are also available and are used in business. These programs include the general ledger, accounts receivable, accounts payable, and payroll system. Since these programs are integrated, the entire financial records of a business can be maintained on the computer.

The era of high technology has arrived. It is up to the reader to become familiar with the computers and software programs that the profession will require nim/her to use.

GLOSSARY

accelerated depreciation The recognition of greater amounts of depreciation in the early years of use for a fixed plant asset and of reduced amounts in the later years.

account An individual record of specific items that a business owns (assets) and owes (liabilities), as well as a recognition of ownership (capital).

accounting The art of organizing, maintaining, recording, and analyzing financial activities.

accounting equation The relationship between the assets, liabilities, and capital of a business organization. The equation states: Assets = Liabilities + Capital.

accounting period The period of time, no more than 1 year, covered by the three financial statements.

account payable A current liability for which an oral promise to pay, made to the creditor, serves as evidence.

account receivable A current asset for which an oral promise to pay, made by the customer, serves as evidence.

accounts payable control account A general ledger account that mirrors the value of the subsidiary accounts payable ledger. The purpose of this control account is to provide a balance that is equal to the sum of the balances in the subsidiary ledger accounts.

accounts payable ledger A subsidiary ledger that contains various creditor accounts. All credit transactions from the purchases journal and the cash payments journal, as well as certain transactions from the general journal, are posted daily to the various creditor accounts in the accounts payable ledger.

accounts receivable control account A general ledger account that mirrors the value of subsidiary accounts receivable ledger. The purpose of this control account is to provide a balance that is equal to the sum of the balances in the individual subsidiary ledger accounts.

accounts receivable ledger A subsidiary ledger that contains individual customer accounts. All transactions involving customers are posted daily from either the sale or the cash receipts journal and under certain circumstances from the general journal to the individual customer accounts in the accounts receivable ledger.

accrual An accumulation of assets or expenses or revenue items, as well as liabilities, whose value has been incurred but for which no cash has yet been transferred.

accrual basis An accounting system that recognizes the receipt of cash when it is earned rather than when it is actually received, and records an expense when it is actually incurred rather than when the cash is disbursed. When a sale of a product or a service is made on credit, this transaction is recognized as revenue even though the cash is not received until later. Most businesses are on the accrual basis.

accrued revenue Revenue that has been earned but not yet received. This concept allows the company to match revenue earned in the same accounting period in which the associated costs were incurred.

adjusting entries Journal entries recorded in order to reflect properly the appropriate balances in the various ledger accounts for a specific accounting period. The entries are usually prepared at the end of the accounting period but may be prepared at any time that the accountant considers appropriate.

agency relationship A relationship in which a person is authorized by a principal to make contracts with a third party on the principal's behalf. The agent is a principal's representative; therefore, any contracts entered into by the agent are binding upon the principal.

aging of accounts receivable method A method used to record adjusting entries at the end of the year to recognize and provide for the write-off of uncollectible accounts. Comparison of this method with the direct-write-off and the net sales methods shows that the aging method is by far the most accurate.

amortization The systematic write-off of the cost of an intangible asset over its economic life.

articles of incorporation The charter under which a corporation conducts business in the particular state in which it is incorporated, as well as in other states.

articles of partnership A contract prepared by individuals or entities before the beginning of a partnership. Information as to the sharing of profits and losses, as well as other aspects of the partnership, should be included in the partnership agreement.

asset Anything that is owned and has money value.

authorized stock The shares of stock that the articles of incorporation permit a corporation to sell.

bad debt An expense that a business recognizes as a result of a customer's failure to pay an obligation usually arising as a direct result of a prior credit sale. The expense is established when it has been reasonably determined that the customer will not pay the obligation.

balance The value or worth, expressed in monetary terms, of a specific ledger account. An individual account may be said to have a debit balance, a credit balance, or no (zero) balance.

balance sheet A financial statement that shows the financial position of a business at a particular moment in time—a detailed presentation of the assets, liabilities, and owner's equity. Actually, it is a detailed accounting equation, in which the total value of the assets is equal to the total liabilities plus proprietor's capital.

bank reconciliation The process by which an account's balance as shown on the bank's records is brought into agreement with the balance shown on the depositor's records.

bank reconciliation statement A statement prepared once a month to bring about agreement between the checkbook balance and the bank balance.

bank statement A record that is sent by the bank, usually on a monthly basis, to indicate the bank's record of the activities, including deposits, paid checks, various bank charges, collections made by the bank to the customer's account, and payments authorized from the customer's account, within an individual checking account.

board of directors The elected officials of a corporation who oversee the operations of the firm and appoint the various officers who actually run the corporation. The board is elected by the stockholders of the corporation. Usually only the common stockholders have voting rights.

book value The original cost of a fixed asset, less the accumulated depreciation.

Boston ledger A three-column ledger account. The money columns include a debit column, a credit column, and a balance column. The advantage of this form of ledger account is that a running balance may be maintained in the account after each transaction has been recorded in it.

bracket entry An entry recorded in a two-column general journal that represents the need to post to a subsidiary ledger account as well as to the corresponding control account in the general ledger.

business entity concept The accounting principal that says a business is separate and apart from the individual who owns (or the individuals who own) it. The asset of the owner(s) should not be combined with the assets of the business

business transaction Any business activity that affects what a business owns or owes, as well as the ownership of the business.

callable provision A provision that enables the issuing corporation to buy back its stock at a stated price, which is usually above the original purchase price. The callable provision is at the option of the corporation, but is stated on the stock certificate.

capital The ownership of the assets of a business by the proprietor(s).

capital expenditure A material expenditure, for an asset that will be used for more than 1 year, that increases the value or useful life of that fixed asset

capital improvement An expenditure (cost) made to a fixed asset in order to increase the useful life of the asset over several accounting periods. Examples include the installation of a new motor in an old truck and the addition of a room to a building.

cash An asset consisting of coins, bills, money orders, checks, certificates of deposit, or treasury bills.

cash basis An accounting system that recognizes the revenue when the cash is received, and the expense when the cash is disbursed. It does not match the expense with the related revenue produced during the same accounting period. This system is used mainly by individuals for income tax purposes.

cash discount A reduction in price offered by a seller to a buyer as an incentive to pay the obligation to the seller before the buyer is actually required to do so.

cash payments journal A journal that records all transactions involving the payment of cash regardless of the reason.

cash receipts journal A journal that records all transactions involving the receipt of cash regardless of the source.

charter The articles of incorporation as approved by a particular state.

chart of accounts The table of contents of a ledger—a listing of the account pages and account titles in the ledger. It is traditionally set up in the order of the accounting equation, that is, assets followed by liabilities, permanent capital, and temporary capital accounts.

check An order to the bank on which it is written to pay a specific sum of money to a designated party.

check register A register replacing the cash payments journal when the voucher system is in use. It serves the same function as the cash payments journal, except that the account in this register is debited to vouchers payable.

close corporation A profit corporation that is owned by a few individuals such as the immediate members of a family.

closing entries Journal entries usually prepared at the end of the accounting period to eliminate the balances in the temporary capital account and to transfer these balances to the income summary account and eventually to the permanent capital account.

closing the ledger The process by which the temporary capital accounts are eliminated. The closing process involves sending the balances from the respective temporary capital accounts to an account entitled "Income Summary."

commission basis A form of employee compensation, usually calculated as a percentage of the value of an item sold by the employee.

common stock A class of stock that usually sells for a considerably lower price than other classes of stock. It has voting rights and the right to share in the distribution of income by the corporation in the form of dividends.

compound entry A journal entry in which two or more accounts are debited or credited as part of the transaction. If the compound entry contains two debits and one credit, the total value assigned to the debits must agree with the value of the credit entry, as required by double-entry accounting.

contingent liability A liability that will be incurred only if a particular event takes place. The endorser of a discounted note is committed to pay the discounter the maturity value of the note in the event the maker defaults on the note, in which case the contingent liability becomes an actual liability.

contra-account Any account that offsets a related account to reflect the proper amount on the financial statements. An example of a contra-account is the sales returns and allowances account, which offsets the sales account.

contra-asset account An account that has a credit balance and reduces an asset account to reflect the proper amount on the balance sheet. The accumulated depreciation account and the allowance for bad debts account are examples of contra-asset accounts.

control account An account that presents a summary of a group of accounts found in a subsidiary ledger. The accounts receivable and the accounts payable accounts in the general ledger are examples of control accounts.

conversion clause A provision on a stock certificate that allows a stockholder to convert the stock owned to another class of stock.

copyright The exclusive right granted by the federal government to authors, artists, and composers to publish and market their intellectual work. This right expires 50 years after the death of the originator.

corporation An artificial being, invisible, intangible, and existing only in contemplation of the law. It is a legal entity separate from its owners.

cost-flow assumption The beginning point used to determine the value of the ending inventory and the cost assigned to the goods sold.

cost principle The cost assigned to an asset, including the purchase price, transportation charges, installation charges, and any other costs associated with placing the asset into use by the organization.

credit The right side of a ledger account. It represents a position or location within a specific account.

credit balance The balance that results when the total credit amount exceeds the total debit amount.

credit memorandum A document granting permission for the buyer to return goods to the seller. The effect of the credit memorandum is to reduce the obligation of the buyer by crediting the account receivable. If the goods were paid for before their return, the buyer receives a refund.

creditors Individuals or companies that are owed obligations by others. A creditor is normally known as an accounts payable if the evidence for the obligation is an oral promise.

cumulative employee earnings record A record maintained to accumulate the weekly earnings of each employee. The record is summarized quarterly and makes it possible to determine each employee's cumulative earnings at any given point in time.

cumulative preferred stock A class of stock that conveys to the holder the right to receive dividend distributions owed from prior years, as well as from the current year, before any distribution is made to other classes of stock.

current asset An asset that can reasonably be expected to be used up or converted into cash or sold within 1 year or less.

current liability A debt that is payable within 1 year or the current accounting period, whichever is longer.

debit The left side of a ledger account. It represents a position or location within a specific account.

debit balance The balance that results when the total debit amount exceeds the total credit amount.

deductions Taxes that the employer is required to withhold from an employee's pay on a regular basis.

default To fail to meet an obligation when it comes due.

deferral Postponement of the recognition of either an expense or a revenue item.

depletion The pro-rata allocation of the cost of land (through direct ownership or lease) to the units of natural resources removed from the land.

deposits in transit Deposits that have been sent but not yet received by the bank.

deposit slip A form prepared in order to place money into a checking account. The resulting balance after the deposit is made is then used to pay checks that are issued on that account.

deposit ticket See **deposit slip**.

depreciable value The original cost of a fixed asset, less the residual value of the asset. Depreciable value represents the total cost of the asset that is subject to depreciation.

depreciation The systematic and rational allocation of the cost of an asset over its useful life.

direct write-off method A method of not recognizing the expense of an uncollectible account (bad debt) until it can be determined that the debtor will not pay. This method does not necessarily match the expense associated with the uncollectible account in the same period as the revenue was earned.

discount (1) A reduction in price offered by a seller to a buyer. (2) A term describing the sale of stock at a price lower than par.

discounting notes The process involving the sale of a promissory note to a bank or financial institution before maturity. The bank deducts from the maturity value of the note an interest charge based on the period of time the note is to be held by the bank and the rate of interest the bank charges.

dissolution The result of any charges in the composition of a partnership, necessitating the preparation of new articles of partnership so that the business may be reorganized and continue in operation.

dividends A corporation's distribution of income to the stockholders of the corporation. The form of the dividend may be either cash or additional shares of stock.

double-declining balance method An accelerated method of depreciation that uses a rate twice as high as the straight-line method. The rate is applied to the remaining balance (book value) of the asset every year.

double-entry accounting A method of accounting in which, for every debit entry, there must be a corresponding credit entry of the same amount. Every business transaction *must* be represented by at least two changes.

double-posting entry See **bracket entry**.

double taxation The taxing of corporate dividends twice—once in the form of corporate income tax and once as income tax paid by the stockholders receiving the dividends.

drawing account A temporary capital account, set up in the name of the sole proprietor or a partner, from which he or she can withdraw money or other assets in anticipation of profit.

employee's withholding allowance certificate A form filled out by an employee when he or she begins work for a company. This form, also known as a "W-4," asks for the number of withholding allowances the employee wishes to take. The payroll department uses this information to determine how much income tax to withhold from the employee's salary.

exchange of assets A business transaction in which one asset is acquired by giving up another asset.

expenses The costs of doing business, that is, the costs that must be incurred in order for an organization to generate revenue. A retail store must incur the expense of renting the store in order to operate the business.

experience rating The unemployment compensation tax rate assigned to an employer by the state, based on how stable a work force the employer has maintained.

FICA The Federal Insurance Contributions Act, which established the Social Security system. The FICA, or Social Security tax, is one of a number of deductions taken from an employee's salary.

FIFO First in, first out. In this method of assigning costs to an inventory of merchandise, the first goods received are charged against the earliest sales of the merchandise.

fixed asset An asset that has an expected useful life of 1 year or more. Fixed assets are also referred to as "plant assets" or "property, plant and equipment."

footing The process of adding a column of numbers. Since this activity is usually done in pencil, it is commonly called "pencil-footing."

form W-2 See **wage and tax statement**.

form W-4 See **employee's withholding allowance certificate**.

four-column ledger account A form of ledger, most commonly used in organizations that utilize accounting posting machines, that provides four money columns: a debit column, a credit column, a debit-balance column, and a credit balance column. The advantage is that a running balance may be maintained in the account after each transaction has been recorded in it.

franchise A right or privilege to sell or distribute a product in accordance with special conditions.

freight-on purchases An expense related to the cost of acquiring goods for resale; also frequently referred to as "freight-in" or "freight-inward." Any transportation charge related to the cost of acquiring goods to be resold is charged to this account.

goodwill The dollar value assigned to a business's managerial skills and reputation. It is usually recognized at the time the business is sold.

gross pay The earnings of an employee before any required taxes have been deducted.

gross profit method A method of estimating the cost of goods sold and the ending inventory for an accounting period based on the relationship between a prior year's gross profit and net sales. A percentage is determined for this relationship and is used for the current year's calculation.

gross sales The balance in the sales ledger account before any consideration is made for possible sales returns, which are recorded to a separate account.

hourly employee basis A form of employee compensation under which an employee is paid a specific rate of pay for each hour worked.

income statement A financial statement that presents revenue and expenses and the net income or loss for a specific period of time.

income summary See **net earnings summary**.

income tax method A method whereby, when a plant asset is traded in for a similar asset, recognition of the gain or loss on the trade is spread out over the useful life of the new asset acquired.

incorporators The individuals who bring about the formation of the corporation and are major stockholders.

independent contractor An individual or business not directly employed by a firm, but used to perform specific activities for the firm, usually on an irregular basis.

intangible asset An asset that cannot readily be seen or touched. Examples include copyrights, franchises, patents, and trademarks. Intangible assets have no physical substance, but are of value to the owners of the organization.

interest-bearing promissory note A note that has a specific rate of interest indicated on its face. When the note matures, its maturity value is its face value plus the interest earned.

interim (financial) statement A statement prepared for any period of time less than a complete accounting period (1 year).

internal control Control of an organization's operations, through procedures designed to safeguard its assets, generate appropriate accounting data, and ensure efficient productivity.

investments Assets that are not used in the operation of a business, and are not expected to be converted into cash within 1 year.

issued stock The authorized shares sold by the corporation to the stockholders.

journal A book of original or first entry. The basic two-column journal provides for entering business transactions in dated order. All parts of every transaction are recorded, and provision is made for an adequate explanation.

leasehold Real estate held by a tenant as a result of a lease.

ledger A book of secondary or final entry, containing individual accounts. The term "ledger account" refers to an individual account in the ledger. A ledger may be a bound book, a looseleaf-type book, or a computer printout.

liabilities Amounts due creditors and other interested parties; also, the ownership of the assets of an organization by its creditors. The ownership extends to the creditors' right to collect what is due them before any distribution to the owners of the business.

license A right, usually purchased, to market or use a particular process or product.

LIFO Last in, first out. In this method of assigning costs to goods sold, the most recent costs are charged against the most recent sales of the merchandise.

limited life A term that usually refers to an asset which is expected to have a useful life of less than 1 year.

liquidation The winding up of an organization, involving the conversion of all assets to cash, payment of creditors, and return of investment to the owners of the organization.

long-term liability an obligation that is not expected to mature and become payable within 1 year. A mortgage note payable is an example of this type of liability.

long-life asset See **fixed asset**.

lower of cost or market rule A rule requiring the recognition of a permanent reduction in the value of inventory due to physical deterioration of an asset, a permanent price decline in terms of the replacement cost, or obsolescence. Inventory is valued at its actual cost or the current replacement cost (market price), whichever is lower.

matching principle See **principle of matching costs and revenue.**

maturity value The principal and the interest that the note will have earned on the due date of the note.

merchandise inventory The goods on hand at the end of an accounting period. The value of the inventory is determined by taking a physical inventory of goods previously purchased but not sold during the current accounting period. The ending inventory becomes the beginning merchandise inventory at the beginning of the new accounting period. During the new accounting period no adjustments are made to this account on the books.

merchandise purchases The goods that a trading business purchases for the purpose of resale. During the year this account is treated as an asset. However, its location on the chart of accounts indicates that it is actually an expense, the assumption being that since the goods were bought for resale they represent expenses. Goods that were actually sold become part of the calculation of cost of goods sold, which is an expense category.

monetary principle An assumption made by the accounting profession that the dollar is a stable unit of value in measuring economic transactions

money value The value, expressed in monetary terms, of an item within the accounting environment. All assets, liabilities, and capital are expressed in monetary terms.

negotiability of stock The ability to transfer ownership of a corporation through the sale of stock.

net earnings summary A temporary capital account used to close out all other temporary capital accounts at the end of the accounting period.

net pay The actual amount of money an employee takes home after deductions have been made from his or her gross pay.

net proceeds The amount of money the endorser of a discounted note receives from the discounter when the note is discounted.

net sales The results of subtracting sales returns and allowances and sales discounts from the sales account. These sales represent the actual sales that remained sold.

net sales method A method used to estimate, usually as a percentage, the amount of credit sales that will become uncollectible in subsequent accounting periods.

noncumulative preferred stock A class of preferred stock that does not participate in dividends that were not paid in previous years

nonprogressive tax A tax that is *not* based on the amount of money that an individual earns.

notes payable Written promises, in the hands of the makers, that serve as evidence of debts.

notes receivable Written promises, in the hands of the creditors, that serve as evidence of debts.

not-for-profit corporation A corporation organized for altruistic purposes—usually for charitable or research activities—that merely uses the corporate form of organization in doing business. Such organizations are not usually subject to corporate income tax.

obsolescence The condition whereby an asset is no longer useful to an organization because of technological improvement or business reorganization of the process for which the asset was previously used.

organizational costs The legal, accounting, and any additional fees that must be paid before a business is incorporated.

organizational structure The chain of command as established by management. The various authorities and responsibilities are usually specified on an organizational chart.

outstanding check An item on a bank reconciliation statement that represents a check issued to the payee, but not yet paid by the bank and therefore not shown on the bank statement.

outstanding stock The shares of stock that have been issued and remain in the hands of the stockholders.

overtime Compensation calculated at 1½ times an employee's hourly rate of pay for each hour worked beyond a normal 5-day, 40-hour workweek.

overtime earnings earnings based on the number of hours worked beyond the normal workweek and on the overtime rate. See also **overtime rate**.

overtime rate A rate paid for services over the "normal" workweek of 40 hours The rate is determined by agreement between the employer and either the employee or his or her union. The minimum rate is calculated at 1½ times the regular rate of pay.

ownership The right to dispose of property as well as to determine its use.

participating preferred stock A class of stock that participates in any additional dividend paid after the other classes of stock have received dividends comparable to the one originally paid to the preferred stockholder.

partnership An organization of two or more individual entities that agree to join forces for the common purpose of earning a profit within a business environment.

par value An arbitrary money value assigned to a share of stock. It does not necessarily have any relationship to the actual worth of the stock.

patent An exclusive right, given by the federal government, to an individual or a group to market or use a particular process or invention. See also **license**.

payroll A list of all employees and their respective salaries for a given period.

payroll register A record of the total hours employees worked during a given payroll period. This book contains employees' names, total earnings, and the various deductions that were taken from gross pay to arrive at net pay for all employees on the register.

periodic inventory method The taking of a physical count of the merchandise on hand at the end of an accounting period.

permanent capital The owner's equity in a business organization that is not expected to change other than as a result of an increase or a decrease in the owner's investment in the business.

permanent investment An investment designated by management or the proprietor to remain with the company until the dissolution of the company.

perpetual inventory system The continuous taking of a physical count of the goods available for sale. This system is usually used only by concerns that sell high-ticket, low-volume goods.

petty cash book A book maintained to record the outlay of cash from the petty cash fund.

petty cash fund A small amount of money, usually $50 to $150, set aside to pay for insignificant expenditures for which a check would not be accepted or appropriate.

petty cash voucher A document prepared as evidence of the outlay of a small sum of money and signed by the person receiving the money from the petty cashier.

physical deterioration The wearing out of a plant asset due to use.

piecework basis A form of compensation based on employee productivity. An employee is paid a predetermined fee for each operation completed or unit of work done in the manufacturing process.

post-closing trial balance A trial balance prepared after closing the ledger. Temporary capital accounts, having no balances after the closing entries have been posted, will not be found in the post-closing trial balance.

posting The process of transferring debits and credits from the journal to the appropriate ledger account.

post reference column A column in a ledger account used to indicate the source of an entry; conversely, a column in a journal indicating the ledger account to which an entry was posted.

preemptive rights A stockholder's right to maintain the same percentage of ownership in the stock of a corporation when additional shares of stock are issued

preferred stock A class of stock that has certain guaranteed rights, such as a percentage dividend, the receipt of dividends before distribution to other classes of stock, or preference in the event of liquidation. The purchase price of preferred stock is usually considerably higher than that of common stock.

premium Excess cash above the par or stated value of stock realized from the sale of shares.

prepaid expense An asset account—an item that normally is considered to be an expense but, because it is paid in advance, is classified as an asset. When the value of the asset has been used up, an adjusting entry will convert this prepaid expense (asset) to an actual expense.

principle of matching costs and revenue An accounting concept whereby revenue is recognized when earned, regardless of when received, and expense is recognized when incurred, regardless of when paid. This is accomplished using the accrual basis of accounting.

profit and loss sharing A plan outlined in the partnership agreement for distributing profits and losses among members. If the partnership agreement is silent as to the method of distribution, the law will interpret this to mean that each partner shares equally in the profits and losses of the company.

profit corporation A corporation organized for the purpose of generating profits.

profit The excess revenue after expenses.

progressive tax A tax that is based on the amount of money that an individual earns.

promissory note An unconditional written promise to pay a stated sum of money upon demand, or at a future determinable date. It is usually prepared and signed by the debtor and given to the creditor.

property, plant, and equipment Assets that have a useful life of more than 1 year and are used in the continuing operations of the organization.

public corporation A profit corporation whose stock is widely distributed among many owners.

purchases discount A reduction in price taken by a buyer as a result of a discount being offered by a seller. On the books of the buyer, this discount represents a decrease of cost.

purchases journal A journal that records all purchases on credit.

purchases returns and allowances A contra or negative account that offsets the merchandise purchases account. When goods previously purchased are returned, the entry for the return causes a credit to be recorded in this contra-account.

purchases returns and allowances journal A journal used by the seller of goods to acknowledge the receipt of a credit memorandum from the seller authorizing the return of goods and the reduction or elimination of the buyer's obligation to the seller.

reference column See **post reference column**.

replenish the fund To replace in a petty cash fund the amounts withdrawn from it. The process involves the preparation of a check and the recognition of the expenses that caused the fund to become depleted.

residual value The value of a fixed asset after it has been fully depreciated. It is an estimate of what the asset will be sold for when it is no longer usable.

retail method A method of estimating the cost of goods sold and the ending inventory, using a ratio of the total cost of goods available for sale to the total selling price of all the goods. This ratio is then applied to each dollar of sales to determine the cost of goods sold and the gross profit.

revenue The receipt, from sales of a product or service, of assets such as cash or accounts receivable that will eventually have an effect on the owner's equity.

reversing entries Entries recorded at the very beginning of the new accounting period, each representing the exact opposite of the adjusting entry recorded at the end of the previous accounting period. A reversing entry is necessary any time an adjusting entry sets up an account that will not be closed at the end of the accounting period and that does not normally carry a balance on the books during the year.

salary allowance A fee paid to a partner of a company for services rendered, as provided in the terms of the partnership agreement, before any other distribution of the profits or losses to the other partners in the company.

sales discount A reduction of sales price offered by a seller to a buyer. The difference between the amount owed by the customer and the amount of cash received is known as the sales discount.

sales journal A journal that records all sales of goods and services on credit.

sales returns and allowances A contra-revenue account that specifically offsets the sales account. Any time goods previously sold are returned to the seller, the return is recorded as a debit to the sales returns and allowances account.

sales returns and allowances journal A journal used by the seller of goods to record the issuance of a credit memorandum, which serves as evidence of the return of merchandise to the seller, giving the buyer credit for the return.

salvage value See **residual value**.

schedule of accounts payable A listing of the balances in the subsidiary accounts payable ledger. The total of this schedule must agree with the balance in the control account in the general ledger.

schedule of accounts receivable A listing of the balances in the subsidiary accounts receivable ledger. The total of this schedule must agree with the balance in the control account in the general ledger.

scrap value See **residual value**.

separate legal existence The legal existence of a company which entitles it to own assets, incur debts, or enter into contracts.

shareholder See **stockholder**.

signature card A card required to open a checking account and listing the signatures of the authorized signers of an organization's checks.

sixty-day (60-day) method of determining interest A method of calculating interest based on the fact that interest at 6% for 60 days equals 1% of the amount borrowed.

sole proprietorship A business formed by one individual.

special journal A book of original entry in which all transactions of a similar nature, such as credit sales or credit purchases, are recorded.

state disability insurance A fund established by the state to pay for benefits to individuals who become disabled. The money for this fund is provided by employees through a payroll deduction unless by union agreement the cost of this insurance is to be paid by the employer.

stated value An arbitrary value assigned to no-par stock.

statement of capital A financial statement that shows any change in the value of the ownership in a business over a period of time. The change in capital is due to income or loss and withdrawals by the owner over a period of time.

stockholder The owner of stock in a corporation.

stockholders' equity The ownership of the assets of a corporation as shown by transferable shares of stock. On the balance sheet, the stockholders' equity section consists of the stock sold by the corporation and the retained earnings (income retained by the corporation).

stock record card A ledger account that is used to keep track of merchandise received and issued. It also contains information as to the unit cost of goods received and issued.

straight-line method The most common method used by companies to reflect the deterioration of assets. The total cost of the asset, less any residual value, is divided by the useful life of the asset to determine the annual depreciation cost. The name given to the method reflects the fact that the same depreciation is recognized each year for a given plant asset.

subsidiary ledger A detailed record of individual customer or creditor accounts which, when totaled, equal the control account in the general ledger. A subsidiary ledger can be set up for any group of accounts for which detailed information is needed but does not have to be shown in the general ledger other than in the form of a control account.

sum of the years' digits method An accelerated method of recognizing depreciation. The rate used is a fraction that has as its numerator the remaining life of the asset and as its denominator the sum of all the years of useful life.

take-home pay The net salary earned by an employee after all payroll deductions have been made.

temporary capital Capital accounts that will be eliminated at the end of the accounting period. Examples include revenue, expenses, and proprietor's drawing accounts.

temporary investment Money or other assets that are lent by the proprietor and are expected to be returned to him or her by the business.

terms The means or method of payment of an obligation. Terms are established by the seller and are included on the invoice.

trade-in allowance A reduction in the purchase price of a new plant asset in exchange for the asset being replaced.

trademark A symbol, name, or other device designating the origin or ownership of a unique product. A trademark is legally reserved for exclusive use by the owner.

treasury stock Shares of stock of a corporation that have been purchased on the open market by the corporation. These shares do not have voting rights or dividend rights while in the hands of the corporation.

trial balance A record prepared at any moment in time to prove the accuracy of the ledger. If the totals of the debit and credit balances in the individual ledger accounts agree, the ledger is said to be in balance.

unearned revenue An advance payment for services that have not yet been performed. Unearned revenue represents a liability or obligation of the company receiving the payment for a service not yet rendered.

unemployment compensation taxes Taxes levied against employers by federal and state governments to provide for compensation to unemployed workers.

units of production method A depreciation method based on use rather than time. The following formula is used:

$$\frac{\text{Cost} - \text{Salvage value}}{\text{Estimated total number of units to be produced}} = \text{Depreciation per unit of measure}$$

The resulting rate is then multiplied by the number of units produced each year in order to determine the annual depreciation expense.

unlimited liability A characteristic of a sole proprietorship or partnership that allows creditors to settle their debts by claiming the personal property of the owner(s) of the organization when business assets are inadequate to settle the obligation.

unlimited life A term reflecting the fact that shares of stock in a corporation are transferable, so that the death of a stockholder has no effect on the continued existence of the corporation.

unpaid voucher file A file containing unpaid vouchers that is organized according to the due dates of the vouchers.

unrecorded expenses Expenses incurred but not recorded. Usually these expenses will be recorded when paid. To adhere to the concept of matching costs and revenue, it is necessary to record the unrecorded expenses as an adjusting entry at the end of the accounting period.

unrecorded revenue Payment due for services that have been rendered but not yet billed. By the end of the accounting period an adjusting entry should be made to recognize this revenue, even though it has not actually been received in the form of cash, thus converting unrecorded revenue to recorded revenue.

voluntary deductions Noncompulsory deductions, such as union dues and charitable contributions, that the employee authorizes the employer to deduct.

voucher A document that contains specific information dealing with the recognition and subsequent payment of an obligation.

voucher register A register taking the place of the purchases journal when the voucher system is used by an organization. All prepared vouchers are recorded in the voucher register, and subsequent payments are listed in the register for information purposes.

voucher system A method of establishing control over the making of expenditures related to the payment of liabilities. All transactions that will eventually result in the payment of cash must first be recorded as liabilities using the various books of the voucher system.

wage and tax statement A document, also known as a "W-2" form, indicating an employee's total earnings during the calendar year and also the total taxes withheld. It is prepared by the employer at the end of every calendar year and sent to the employee shortly thereafter for use in the preparation of his or her personal income tax return.

weighted average method A method of assigning a cost to the ending inventory and to goods sold by determining an average unit cost for all the goods available for sale during the accounting period.

worksheet An expanded trial balance. The purpose of the worksheet is to enable the accountant to prepare easily the adjusting entries as well as various financial statements, including the income statement, statement of capital, and balance sheet.

INDEX

More selected BARRON'S titles:

DICTIONARY OF FINANCE AND INVESTMENT TERMS
John Downes and Jordan Goodman
Defines and explains over 2500 Wall Street terms for professionals, business students, and average investors.
Paperback $8.95, Canada $12.95/ISBN 2522-9, 495 pages
"This is an invaluable fog-cutter for investors."
—*William S. Rukeyser, Managing Editor, FORTUNE Magazine*

DICTIONARY OF REAL ESTATE TERMS
Jack P. Friedman, Jack C. Harris, and Bruce Lindeman
Defines over 1200 terms, with examples and illustrations. A key reference for everyone in real estate. Comprehensive and current.
Paperback $8.95, Canada $12.95/ISBN 3898-3, 224 pages

REAL ESTATE HANDBOOK
Jack P. Friedman, Jack C. Harris, and Bruce Lindeman
A dictionary/reference for everyone in real estate. Defines over 1500 legal, financial, and architectural terms.
Cloth $19.95, Canada $28.95/ISBN 5758-9, 700 pages

HOW TO PREPARE FOR REAL ESTATE LICENSING EXAMINATIONS-SALESPERSON AND BROKER, 3rd EDITION
Jack P. Friedman and Bruce Lindeman
Reviews current exam topics and features updated model exams and supplemental exams, all with explained answers.
Paperback, $9.95, Canada $13.95/ISBN 2996-8, 340 pages

BARRON'S FINANCE AND INVESTMENT HANDBOOK
John Downes and Jordan Goodman
This hard-working handbook of essential information defines more than 2500 key terms, and explores 30 basic investment opportunities. The investment information reflects new Federal Tax Act provisions effective in 1987.
Cloth $21.95, Canada $31.95/ISBN 5729-5, 864 pages
"...an excellent investment guide...almost any serious investor will want this book."—*Christian Science Monitor*

BARRON'S FINANCIAL TABLES FOR BETTER MONEY MANAGEMENT
Stephen S. Solomon, Dr. Clifford Marshall, and Martin Pepper
Pocket-sized handbooks of interest and investment rates tables that can be used easily by average investors and mortgage holders.
Volume 1: Savings and Loans
Paperback $5.50, Canada $7.95/ISBN 2745-0, 272 pages
Volume 2: Real Estate Loans
Paperback $5.50, Canada $7.95/ISBN 2744-2, 336 pages
Volume 3: Mortgage Payments
Paperback $5.50, Canada $7.95/ISBN 2728-0, 304 pages
Volume 4: Stocks and Bonds
Paperback $5.50, Canada $7.95/ISBN 2727-2, 256 pages
Volume 5: Comprehensive Annuities
Paperback $5.50, Canada $7.95/ISBN 2726-4, 160 pages
Volume 6: Canadian Mortgage Payments
Paperback $5.50, Canada $8.95/ISBN 3939-4, 336 pages

All prices are in U.S. and Canadian dollars and subject to change without notice. At your bookseller, or order direct adding 10% postage (minimum charge $1.50), N.Y. residents add sales tax.

Barron's Educational Series, Inc.
250 Wireless Boulevard, Hauppauge, NY 11788
Call toll-free: 1-800-645-3476, in NY 1-800-257-5729
In Canada: Georgetown Book Warehouse
34 Armstrong Ave., Georgetown, Ontario L7G 4R9